Cable and Harness Design

Autodesk®
Inventor® 2021

October 2020

Published by:

ASCENT Center for Technical Knowledge
630 Peter Jefferson Parkway, Suite 175
Charlottesville, VA 22911
866-527-2368
www.ascented.com

Contents

Introduction

The *Autodesk® Inventor® 2021: Cable and Harness Design* learning guide is designed for use in Authorized Training Center (ATC) locations, corporate training settings, and other classroom settings. Although this courseware is designed for instructor-led courses, you can also use it for self-paced learning.

This introduction covers the following topics:

- Course Objectives
- Prerequisites
- Using This Learning Guide
- Downloading and Installing the Exercise Files
- Setting Up the Project File
- Feedback
- Free Autodesk Software for Students and Educators

This learning guide is complementary to the software documentation. For detailed explanations of features and functionality, refer to the Help in the software.

Course Objectives

After completing this course, you will be able to:

- Describe the functionality of Cable and Harness and the basic workflow to add and document cable and harness designs.
- Wire a harness assembly by adding or importing wires and cables, adding ribbon cables, adding route segments, and routing wires and cables through the segments.
- Refine a cable and harness design by editing the wires, cables, routes, or cable ribbons; by adding and editing splices; or by adding and editing virtual parts.
- Communicate your cable and harness to others by creating and annotating 2D drawings and exporting the design data.
- Create and manage the library file and configuration files.
- Create, author, and publish electrical parts and connectors to a custom Content Center library.

Prerequisites

This learning guide is designed for experienced users of the Autodesk Inventor software. The following is recommended:

- Users should have completed the *Autodesk® Inventor® 2021: Introduction to Solid Modeling* learning guide, or have an equivalent understanding of the Autodesk Inventor user interface and working environments.
- Knowledge of part modeling, assembly modeling, and drawing view creation and annotation is recommended.

Using This Learning Guide

The lessons are independent of each other. However, it is recommended that you complete these lessons in the order that they are presented unless you are familiar with the concepts and functionality described in those lessons.

Each chapter contains:

- **Lessons** - Usually two or more lessons in each chapter.
- **Exercises** - Practical, real-world examples for you to practice using the functionality you have just learned. Each exercise contains step-by-step procedures and graphics to help you complete the exercise successfully.

Downloading and Installing the Exercise Files

The Exercise Files page in this learning guide contains a link and instructions on how to download and install all of the data needed to complete the exercises.

Setting Up the Project File

Most engineers work on several projects at a time, and each project might consist of a number of files. You can use Autodesk Inventor projects to organize related files and maintain links between files. This guide has a project file that stores the paths to all the files that are related to the exercises. When you open a file, Autodesk Inventor uses the paths in the current project file to locate other required files. To work on a different project, you make a new project active in the Project Editor. Follow the instructions below to locate the Cable and Harness Design project file for this courseware and make it active.

1. Start the Autodesk Inventor software.

2. In the *Get Started* tab, in the Launch panel, click **Projects**.

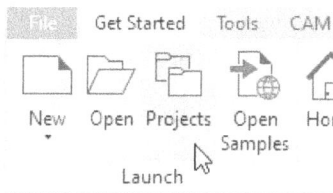

3. At the bottom of the Projects dialog box, click Browse.

   Browse to *C:\Autodesk Inventor 2021 Cable and Harness Design Exercise Files\.*

   Click *Cable and Harness Design.ipj.*

   Click Open.

4. Click Done to close the Projects dialog box.

Feedback

We always welcome feedback on the learning guides. After completing this course, if you have suggestions for improvements or want to report an error in the learning guide or with the class files, please send your comments to *feedback@ASCENTed.com.*

Students and Educators Can Access Free Autodesk Software and Resources

Autodesk challenges you to get started with free educational licenses for professional software and creativity apps used by millions of architects, engineers, designers, and hobbyists today. Bring Autodesk software into your classroom, studio, or workshop to learn, teach, and explore real-world design challenges the way professionals do.

Note: Free products are subject to the terms and conditions of the end-user license and services agreement that accompanies the software. The software is for personal use for education purposes and is not intended for classroom or lab use.

Get started today - register at the Autodesk Education Community and download one of the many Autodesk software applications available.

Visit www.autodesk.com/joinedu/

Exercise Files

To download the exercise files for this learning guide, use the following steps:

1. Type the URL *exactly as shown below* into the address bar of your Internet browser, to access the Course File Download page.

   Note: If you are using the ebook, you do not have to type the URL. Instead, you can access the page simply by clicking the URL below.

   ## https://www.ascented.com/getfile/id/brassavola

   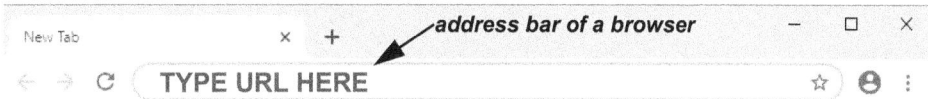

2. On the Course File Download page, click the **DOWNLOAD NOW** button, as shown below, to download the .ZIP file that contains the exercise files.

3. Once the download is complete, unzip the file and extract its contents.
   The recommended exercise files folder location is:
   C:\Autodesk Inventor 2021 Cable and Harness Design Exercise Files

   Note: It is recommended that you do not change the location of the exercise files folder. Doing so may cause errors when completing the exercises.

Getting Started Creating Cable and Harness Designs

In this chapter, you learn about the Autodesk® Inventor® Cable and Harness functionality and the basic workflow to create and document a design.

Objective

After completing this chapter, you will be able to:

- Describe the process for creating a complete cable and harness design, create a harness assembly in an assembly design, and insert electrical parts.

Lesson: Creating Cable and Harness Designs

This lesson describes the process for creating a complete cable and harness design, how to create a harness assembly, and how and where to insert electrical parts.

When you are designing a machine or consumer product, your design very often includes an electrical system requirement. Creating the cable and harness runs in your designs helps you ensure that all of the electrical components fit into the design. Creating the cable and harness content is also useful for calculating the lengths of wire and cable required to traverse a specific route and for avoiding bends with too small of a radius.

The following figure is a picture of the inside of a battery charger. To design and manufacture this product, several sheet metal parts need to be designed and documented. Within the sheet metal case, the actual workings of the charger need to be wired to ensure correct clearance and determine the required wire lengths. For this product, the wiring consists of individual wires run from one connector to another. The alternating current is carried into the case through a cable, and the direct current to the battery is carried through another cable.

Objectives

After completing this lesson, you will be able to:

- Describe the functionality and benefits of Cable and Harness.
- Explain the process to create and document a cable and harness design.
- Create a harness assembly in an assembly design.
- Access and configure the Harness Settings.
- Insert electrical parts into your design that may or may not originate from the Content Center.
- Modify the properties of an electrical part occurrence, including its reference designator.

About Cable and Harness

When you create electro-mechanical designs, you benefit from including the electrical wires and cables in the 3D virtual model to ensure everything fits in the design. You also benefit downstream by having cable and harness information included in reports and drawing documentation. To achieve these benefits while creating and visualizing cable and harness paths, you need to first understand the full functionality and benefits of cable and harness design in the Autodesk Inventor software.

The following images show real wires and cables that are used within different products and machines. Adding this content as 3D design data within your virtual prototypes helps ensure that your design can be manufactured and that it meets its requirements for use.

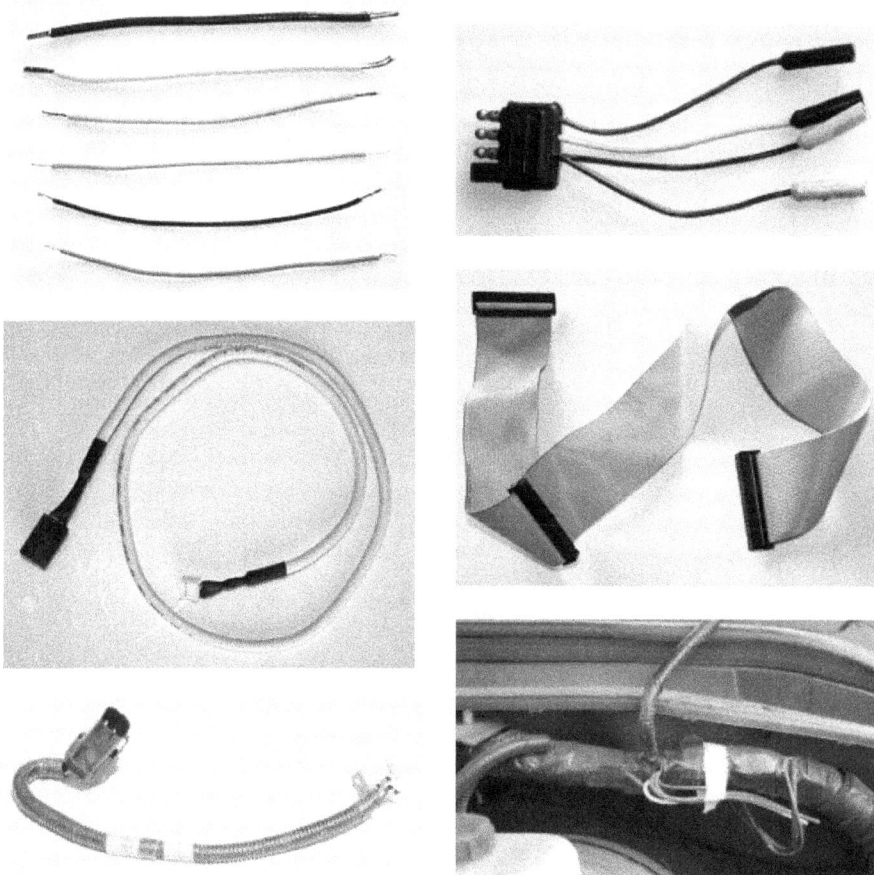

Definition of Cable and Harness

A cable and harness is typically thought of as a bundle of multiple cables or wires. In an electrical design, the number and type of components are dictated by the design. The types of components can be individual wires, cables consisting of multiple wires shielded in a single component, or a group of wires and cables bundled into a harness. The start location for wires and cables is specified by the pin locations on an electrical connector part.

The cable and harness design functionality assists you in designing and documenting the wires, cables, and harnesses that are required in a product or machine. Cable and harness functionality includes being able to:

- Define custom electrical connectors.
- Add wires and cables between connectors in a design.
- Import large wire lists from the AutoCAD® Electrical software or third-party schematic design applications.
- Manually route critical wires or have the Autodesk Inventor software automatically determine the optimal route based on the route segments you have created.
- Create the corresponding documentation for the cables or harnesses in the form of nailboards and other drawing views.
- Generate reports of the cable and harness data.

To control and specify the information and display characteristics of cable and harness geometry, you can set the properties globally for the harness assembly, or you can set the properties individually for each wire, connector pin, and so on. The property settings can include how lengths are calculated, setting minimum bend radiuses, specifying wire ID, setting pin information, displaying as a centerline or as rendered, and setting how the wire information displays in a nailboard drawing.

Example of a Cable and Harness Design

The types and quantity of connectors, wires, cables, and harnesses vary from design to design. The design shown in the following figure contains wires bundled into harnesses and a wire cable.

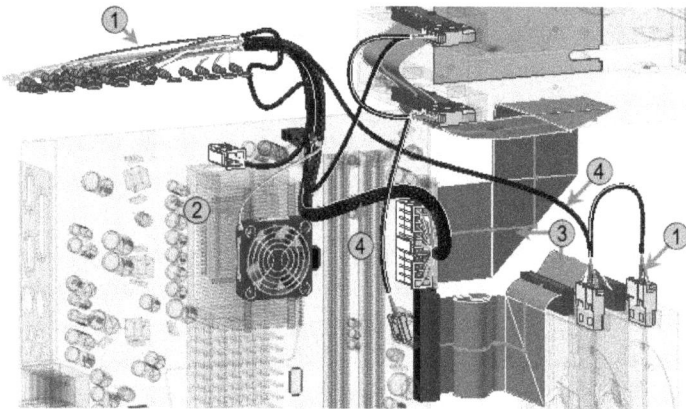

1. Individual wire

2. Cable

3. Ribbon cable

4. Wire harness

Creating a Cable and Harness Design

When you create a cable and harness design, you are presented with a new set of tools and options for creating content and controlling its display. The content you create is automatically created and structured in a slightly different way from standard part and assembly modeling. By understanding these unique characteristics and areas in cable and harness design, it becomes easier to create and edit cable and harness designs. By having an overall understanding of the process, it is easier to understand the importance of a specific tool or procedure for creating or editing a cable and harness design.

In the following figure, a section of the assembly is shown before and after the creation of the required cable and harness design content.

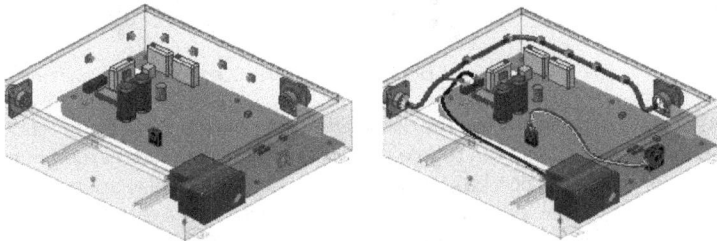

Access Cable and Harness Tools

When you install the software, additional tools, panels, and shortcut menu options are available for design creation and editing. In the Environments tab, in the Begin panel, the Cable and Harness tool is included so that you can create new harness assemblies within the overall assembly design. When a harness assembly is active for editing, the Cable & Harness ribbon tab displays with all the tools required to create and edit the cable and harness assembly. When you are editing a part file, an additional panel is available for selection. You switch to the Harness Part Features panel to create the part as an electrical connector. You manually switch between the available panel bars in the active environment to complete other modeling tasks.

In the following figures, the Cable & Harness tab in the ribbon is shown on the left. This ribbon tab automatically displays when a harness assembly is active for editing. The Harness panel for part modeling is shown on the right. You manually switch to this panel bar when you are editing a part file and you want to add or edit connector content or properties.

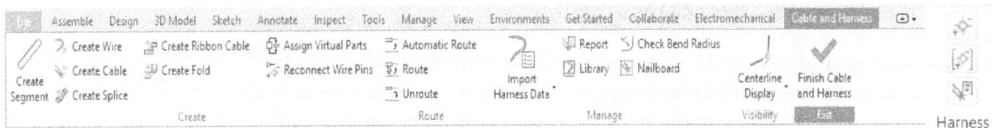

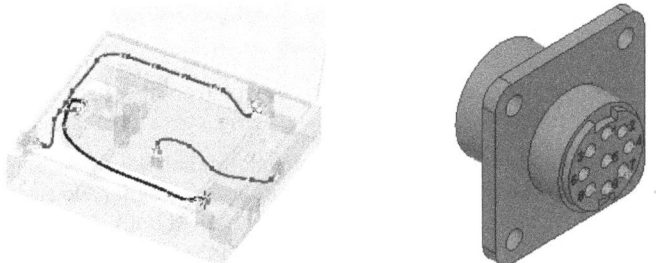

Wire, Cable, and Segment Display

You can display cables, wires, and segments in two different ways. You can have them display as thin lines at the center of their path or as rendered with the appropriate diameters. Each object and type of object can be set separate from the others. For example, you can have one wire display as rendered while all the other wires display as thin centerlines.

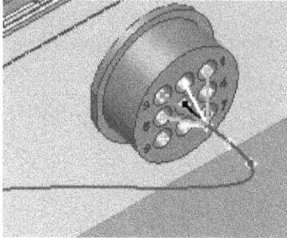

Centerline Display   Rendered Display   Mix of Centerline and Rendered Display

There are three different ways you can change the display between thin centerline and rendered. To change the display of a single object, you can toggle the display using the shortcut menu option or change the setting in the properties dialog box for that object. Using the display option in the Cable and Harness tab, in the Visibility panel, you can change the display for all the wires, cables, and segments in the active harness assembly. When you select the Custom Display option, the Custom Display dialog box opens. Within the dialog box, you set the display setting for all the objects of that type that are in the active harness assembly.

The following figure shows the display options being accessed in the ribbon when a harness assembly is active. It also shows the Custom Display dialog box, which opens by clicking Custom Display from the display list.

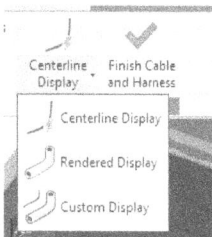

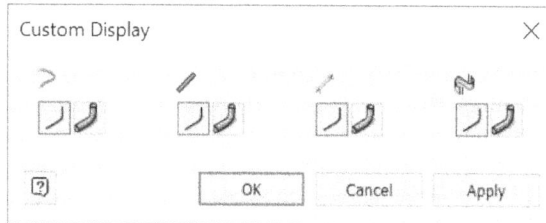

Cable and Harness Design Files

At a minimum, a harness design is composed of a harness assembly and a harness part within the harness assembly. The harness part is automatically created when you create the harness assembly. The harness objects like wires, cables, and segments are then added to the harness part or harness assembly.

You create a harness assembly from within a standard Autodesk Inventor assembly file. You can locate the harness anywhere in the assembly hierarchy except in another harness assembly. A standard Autodesk Inventor assembly can contain as many harness assemblies as required.

An electrical part is a part that has connecting pin information defined within it that enables you to connect wires and cables to it. Depending on your design, you either add electrical parts to the overall assembly, directly to a harness assembly, or a combination of both. You typically add connectors to the harness assembly when the connectors are a part of the harness. One example is a purchased cable with the end connector already attached to the wires.

The following figure shows a design consisting of multiple harness assemblies. On the right side of the figure, one of the harness assemblies is highlighted and identified. In this design, some of the connectors are in the overall assembly, some are positioned in subassemblies, and some were added directly to the harness assembly. The listing of folders within the harness part is dependent on the objects created in that harness assembly.

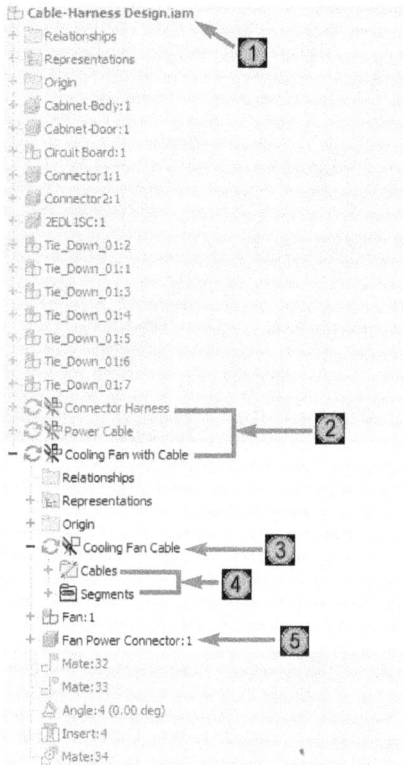

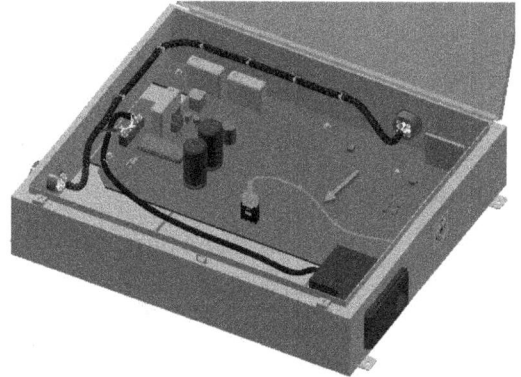

1. Overall standard Autodesk Inventor assembly file.

2. Individual harness assemblies.

3. Harness part within the active harness assembly.

4. Object folders for the types of objects created in the harness assembly and added to the harness part.

5. Parts added to the harness assembly that are defined with connector information.

Process: Creating a Cable and Harness Design

The following steps give an overview of creating a cable and harness design.

1. Place and constrain electrical parts in the assembly.

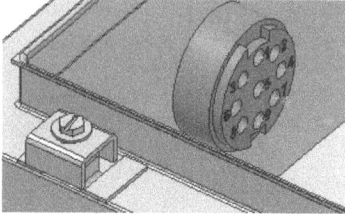

2. Add a harness assembly to the current assembly. If required, place and constrain electrical parts in the harness assembly.

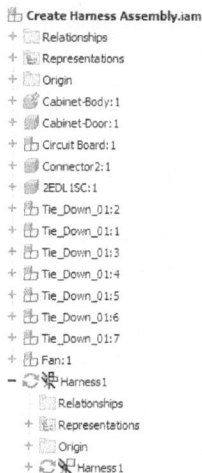

3. Add wires and cables to the active harness subassembly between pins on the electrical parts. Add cable and harness properties to the wires as required.

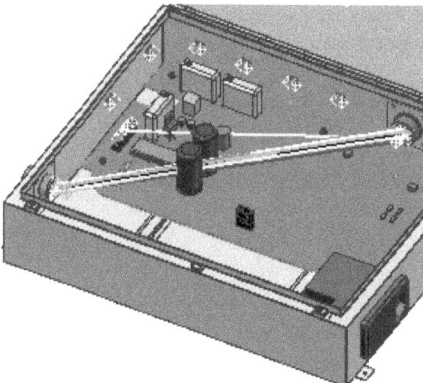

4. Create segments that define the possible wire paths through the assembly. Add cable and harness properties to the segments as required.

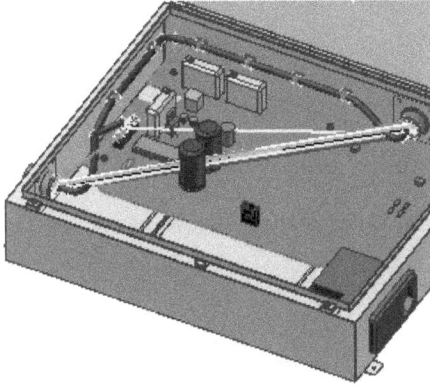

5. Route wires through the segments.

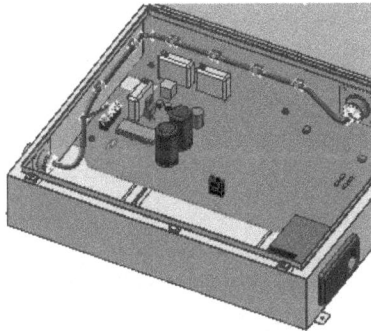

6. Document the harness assembly by creating drawing views of the assembly just as you would any other assembly.

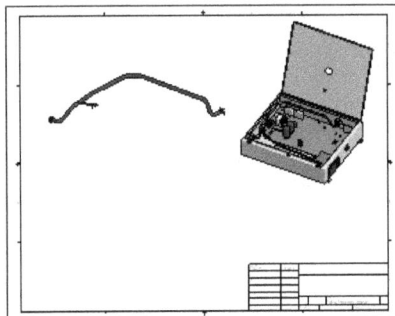

7. Use the Cable and Harness report generator to create reports on part count, wire lists, wire lengths, and other required electrical information.

8. Create a nailboard drawing showing a 2D layout of the 3D harness assembly.

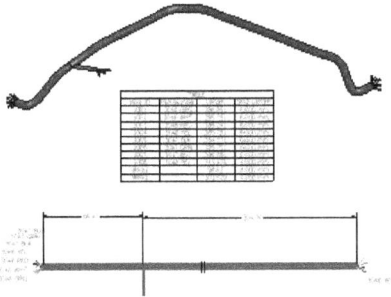

Creating a Harness Assembly

To add cable and harness content to your assembly designs, you must first create a harness assembly. To create a harness assembly in your design, you need to know where and how to create it.

In the following figure, the Browser for an assembly is shown before and after the creation of a harness assembly.

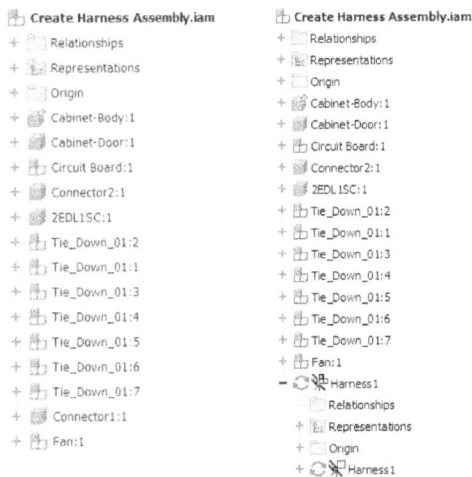

Access

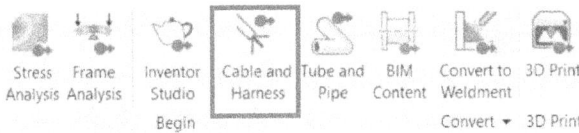

Ribbon: Environments>Begin panel

File Creation Options

You begin creating a cable and harness design by first creating a harness assembly in your assembly model. You create the harness assembly using the Create Harness tool. After you start the tool, the Create Harness dialog box displays enabling you to enter a unique name and location for the harness subassembly.

By default, the file is named *<assembly name>.Harness#.iam*, where <assembly name> is the name of the overall assembly file and where # is the next incremental number. The harness assembly file is saved to the location of the open assembly file in a folder of the same name as the assembly file. Along with the harness assembly file, a corresponding harness part is also created and saved. You can provide a different name and location.

Browser with new Harness

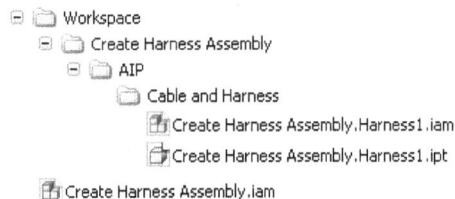

Folder and file relationship
for new harness assembly

Procedure: Creating a Harness Assembly

The following steps give an overview of creating a new harness assembly.

1. Open the assembly in which you want to create a harness assembly. Or, activate the overall assembly for editing.

2. Start the Cable and Harness tool.

3. In the Create Harness dialog box, set the harness assembly name and location. Accept the default name or enter a unique name.

Configuring Harness Settings

Each harness assembly that you create can have its own unique set of master settings. To change the default values for a harness assembly, you need to know where and how to access the settings.

Harness Settings Access

You change the master settings for a harness assembly in the Harness Settings dialog box. You display this dialog box by clicking Harness Settings in the shortcut menu. You access the Harness Settings shortcut menu by right-clicking on the browser name of the active harness assembly.

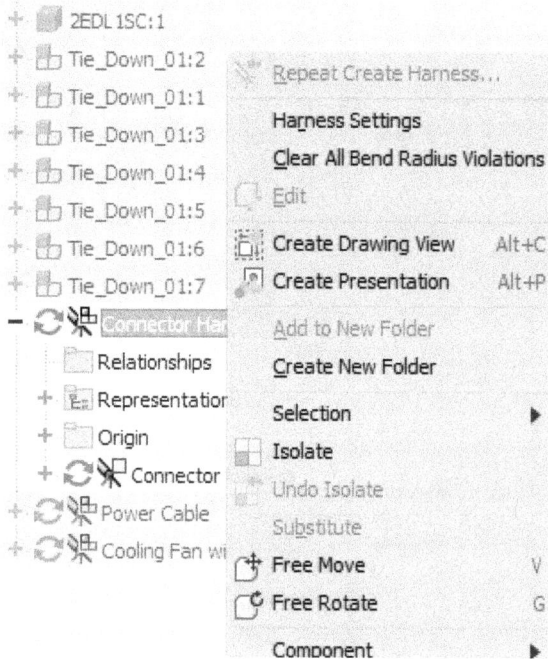

Harness Settings

The values you set in the Harness Settings dialog box control the creation and configuration of newly created wires, cables, splices, segments, and nailboard drawings for that specific harness assembly. The options and settings are split between multiple tabs based on what they control. The settings that are pertinent to all harness objects are located in the General tab and the File Locations tab. When you change the settings in the Harness Settings dialog box, those settings and values apply to newly created objects and information. The properties for existing objects do not update.

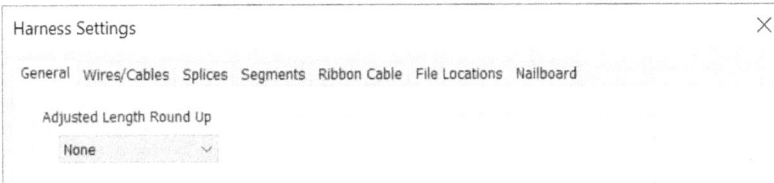

Harness Settings   ✕

General Wires/Cables Splices Segments Ribbon Cable File Locations Nailboard

Adjusted Length Round Up

None   ⌄

> After creating a new harness assembly and prior to creating the harness objects, review the harness settings for the harness assembly to ensure that the default settings match your requirements for newly created harness objects.

Harness Settings: General Tab

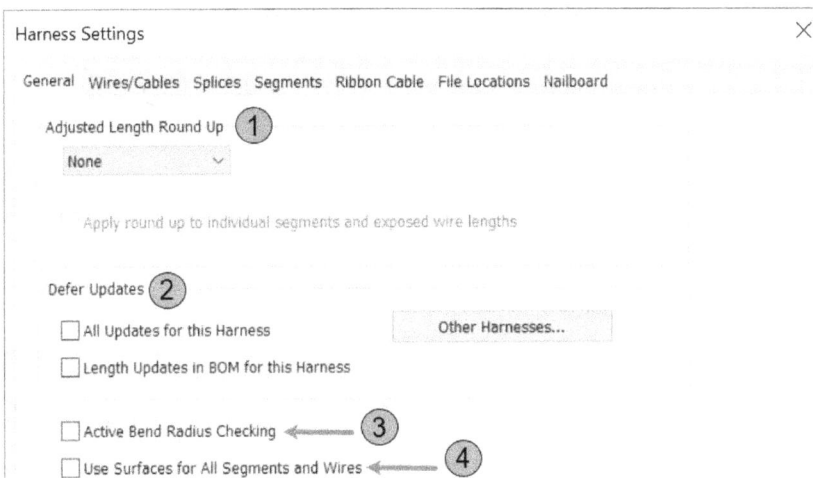

Harness Settings   ✕

General Wires/Cables Splices Segments Ribbon Cable File Locations Nailboard

Adjusted Length Round Up   ①

None   ⌄

Apply round up to individual segments and exposed wire lengths

Defer Updates ②

☐ All Updates for this Harness   Other Harnesses...

☐ Length Updates in BOM for this Harness

☐ Active Bend Radius Checking ⟵⟶ ③

☐ Use Surfaces for All Segments and Wires ⟵⟶ ④

1️⃣ Use to set the round up value that is required to be applied to the adjusted wire, cable, ribbon cable, and segment lengths.

2️⃣ Set if and how updates to the harness assembly should be deferred or not. Select to defer updates to improve performance when a large number of objects are being created and edited within the harness assembly.

3️⃣ Select to have all segments, wires, and cables automatically checked to see if they violate the minimum bend radius value for the style of that object.

4️⃣ Select to have wires and segments created as surfaces. Clear to have them created as solids. Set as surfaces for faster processing times. Set as solids for enhanced visual representation.

Harness Settings: File Locations Tab

The cable and harness library file that is used by the harness assembly is determined based on the setting in the File Locations tab. You can either select to use a specific library file, or you can use the library file that resides in the folder specified for the active project's design data location.

When the option is selected to use the project's design data location, the library that is used is based on what is located in the folder specified in the project file or the Application Options dialog box. When the project file is set to use [Default] for Design Data (Styles, etc.), then the path defined in the Application Options is used.

In the following figure, the design data configuration location in the project file is shown on the left and in the Application Options dialog box displays on the right.

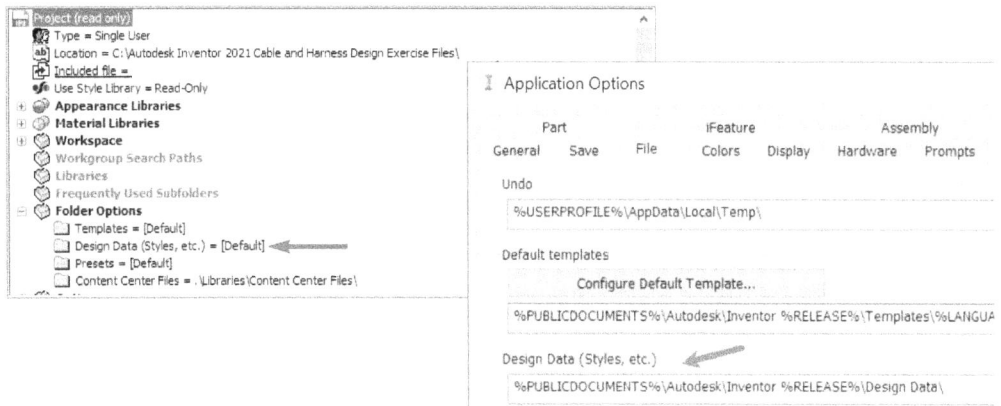

Procedure: Configuring Harness Settings

The following steps give an overview of configuring the harness settings for a harness assembly.

1. Activate the harness assembly for in-place editing.

2. In the Browser, right-click on the harness assembly name and click Harness Settings.

3. In the Harness Settings dialog box, set the default creation properties to match your requirements.

Inserting Electrical Parts

You place and constrain electrical parts in an assembly just as you would place and constrain standard Autodesk® Inventor® parts. To add the electrical parts to the correct location, you need to understand the options for inserting electrical parts and how to insert parts that can either originate from the Content Center or not originate there.

The following figure shows the default categories in the Content Center for cable and harness content and images of the initially available content in those categories.

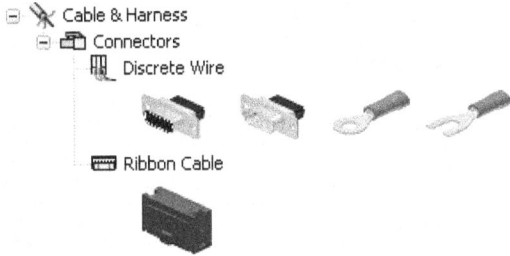

Characteristics of an Electrical Part

Electrical parts are standard Autodesk Inventor parts or iParts that have extended properties and one or more defined connection points, known as pins. Electrical parts include any parts to which you connect wires, such as connectors, terminal strips, PLC input/output terminal blocks, power supplies, switches, and indicator lamps.

The following figure shows just a few of the many possible electrical parts that can have cable and harness connection data associated with them.

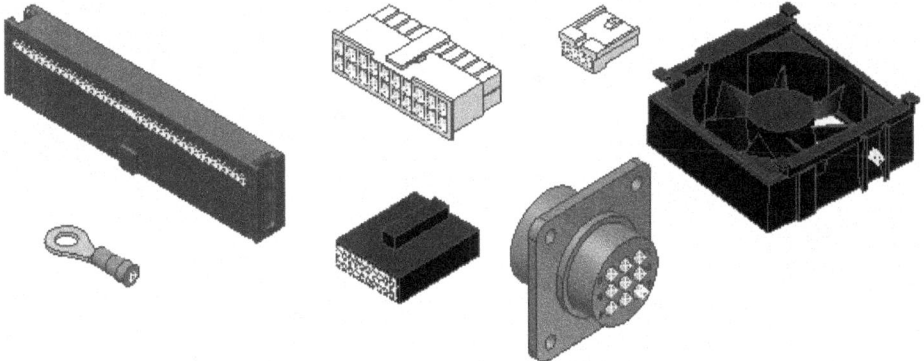

To create a wire or cable route, you select the pins in an electrical part that is already added to the assembly or to the harness assembly. Because the creation of wires and cables requires the pin information in electrical parts, you add the electrical parts to your design before creating the wires and cables.

Inserting Electrical Parts

You add an electrical part to an assembly or harness assembly using the Place Component tool or the Place Component from Content Center tool. If you have a harness assembly active for in-place editing, to add an electrical part to the harness assembly, select the Assemble panel to assemble the electrical part.

Insert Location for Electrical Parts

You place electrical parts either inside or outside of the harness assembly, depending on how you prefer to document the harness assembly. As a general rule, put the electrical connectors in the harness assembly if they are purchased that way, or if the connectors are assembled to the wires or cables before assembling it in the overall assembly design.

In the following figure, a portion of a design is shown where electrical connectors have been inserted inside and outside of a harness assembly.

To assemble electrical parts in a harness assembly to parts in the overall design, you must activate the overall assembly before adding the assembly constraints. Individual parts within the harness assembly constrain to the correct location because the harness assembly is set as adaptive.

> When a harness assembly is active for in-place editing, the selection priority defaults to the selection of sketch features. To move an electrical part in the harness assembly, change the selection priority to Part Priority so that you can click and drag the part to a new location.

Process: Inserting Electrical Parts

The following figure shows an overview of the steps for inserting electrical parts.

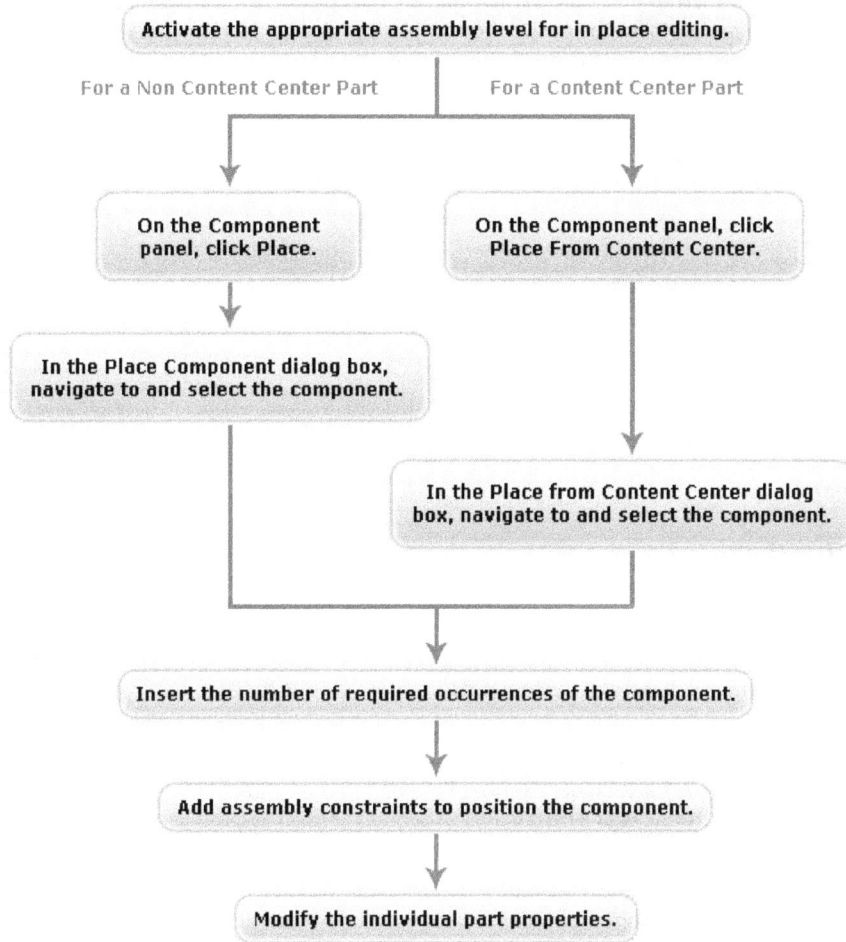

Activate the appropriate assembly level for in place editing.

For a Non Content Center Part   For a Content Center Part

On the Component panel, click Place.

On the Component panel, click Place From Content Center.

In the Place Component dialog box, navigate to and select the component.

In the Place from Content Center dialog box, navigate to and select the component.

Insert the number of required occurrences of the component.

Add assembly constraints to position the component.

Modify the individual part properties.

Setting Unique Part Properties for Electrical Parts

To create a complete electrical design, specific properties and values are added to electrical parts. These additional properties and values communicate the complete information about the design when you generate reports for the design. To complete your electrical designs with the information you require, you need to modify the properties of an electrical part occurrence, including its reference designator.

In the following figure, the Part Properties dialog box for an occurrence of the Fan Power Connector part displays. You enter a unique RefDes (reference designator) value.

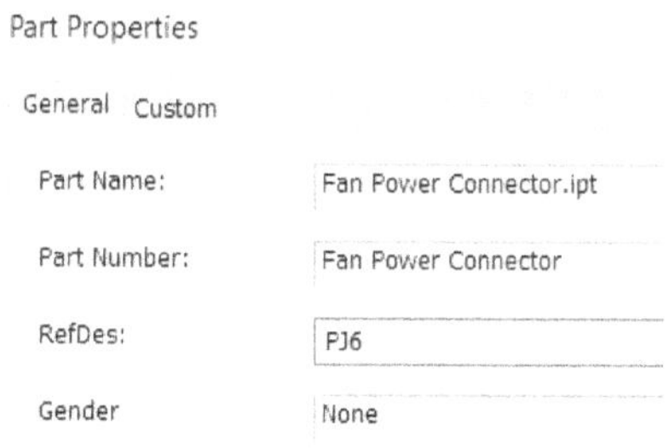

Part Properties

General   Custom

Part Name:	Fan Power Connector.ipt
Part Number:	Fan Power Connector
RefDes:	PJ6
Gender	None

Part Properties

When you insert an electrical part into a design, that part contains properties that are specific to that part file, and it contains properties that can be set unique for each occurrence. The part name and part number are set automatically based on the part file name and the Autodesk Inventor part number. The reference designator (RefDes) and custom properties are unique for each occurrence.

The reference designator is a unique identifier that maps the part to the schematic design. A typical electrical part has a placeholder identifier, such as U?, already set for its RefDes value. You then add a specific designator value for each occurrence of the part in the context of the assembly. For example, if you place three occurrences of a certain RS232 connector in an assembly, each occurrence must have a unique identifier, such as U1, U2, and U3.

You can add custom properties to the part to provide specific information to downstream processes, such as reporting. Most custom properties are not used by Autodesk Inventor. They are used to add data to the part so the information is available when you create a report of the design. Custom properties specific for electrical parts can include properties for current, resistance, temperature, voltage, and embedded length. The values for these custom properties often come from the data book for the component.

Part Property Access

To edit the properties of an electrical part, you must first activate the harness assembly. When the harness assembly is active, you select the part in the Browser or graphics window and then select Harness Properties in the shortcut menu. When the harness assembly is active, you can select any electrical part and select the Harness Properties menu option, regardless of where the electrical part is located in the model. After you select Harness Properties, the Part Properties dialog box opens, enabling you to change the RefDes value and add or edit custom properties.

In the following figure, the Harness Properties option is shown being accessed for electrical parts that are inside and outside of the active harness assembly.

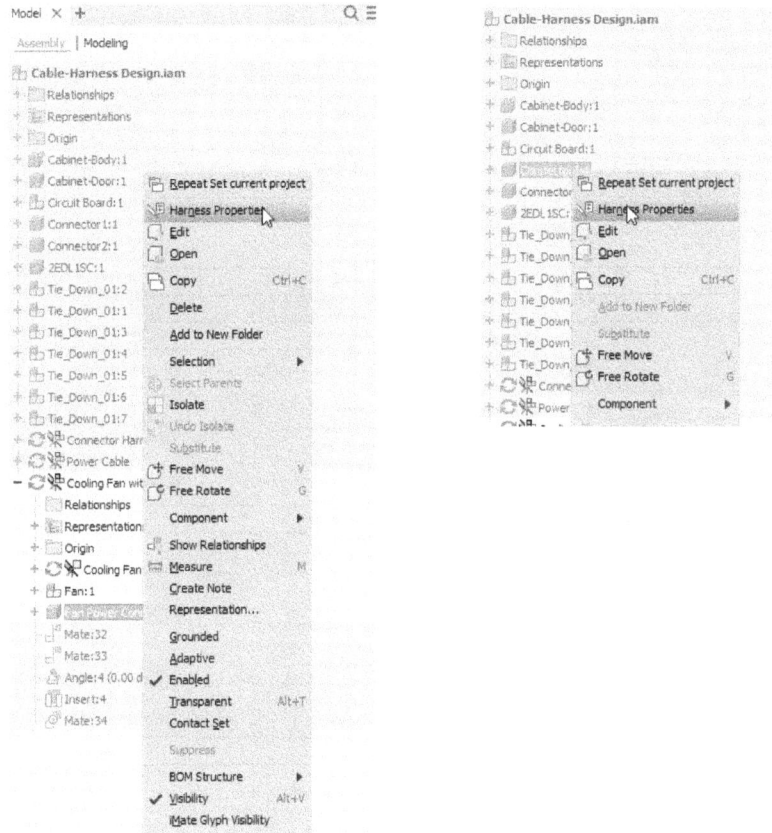

> To change the properties of an electrical part by selecting the part in the graphics window, after you activate a harness assembly for in-place editing, change the selection priority to Part Priority.

Procedure: Setting Unique Part Properties for Electrical Parts

The following steps give an overview of setting unique part properties for different occurrences of electrical parts.

1.   Activate a harness assembly for in-place editing.

2.   In the Browser or graphics window, right-click on the occurrence of the electrical part and click Harness Properties.

3.   In the Part Properties dialog box, enter a unique RefDes value or specify a custom property value.

Exercise: Review and Navigate a Design

In this exercise, you will identify and review the different aspects and properties of a cable and harness design.

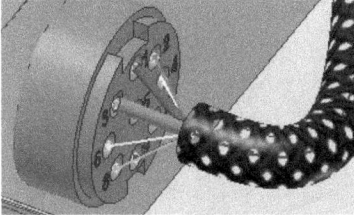

The completed exercise

Exercise Setup

Before you start this exercise, you will need to activate the Cable and Harness Design project.

1. Start the Autodesk Inventor software.

2. In the Get Started tab, in the Launch panel, click Projects.

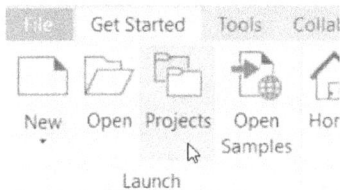

3. At the bottom of the Projects dialog box, click Browse.

- Browse to *C:\Autodesk Inventor 2021 Cable and Harness Design Exercise Files*.
- Click *Cable and Harness Design.ipj*.
- Click Open.
- Close the projects window.

Examine a Design

1. Open *Cable-Harness Design.iam*.

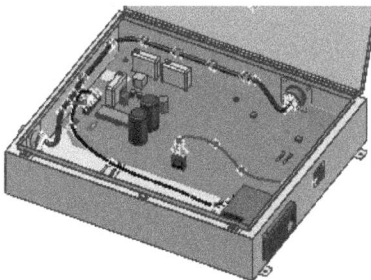

2. In the Browser, click each harness assembly and review what highlights in the graphics window.

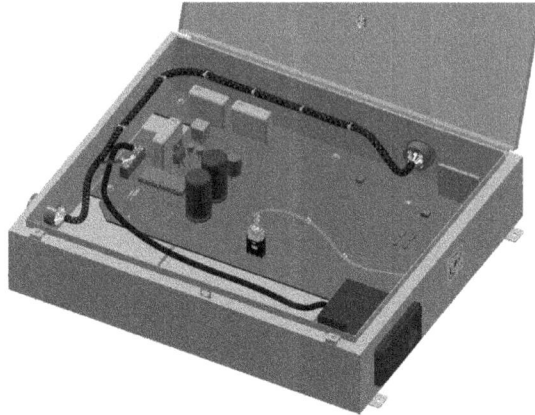

3. To begin reviewing the harness properties for an electrical connector, in the Browser, double-click on Connector1 to activate it for in-place editing.

4. In the Browser, right-click on the second connector pin work point. Click Harness Properties.

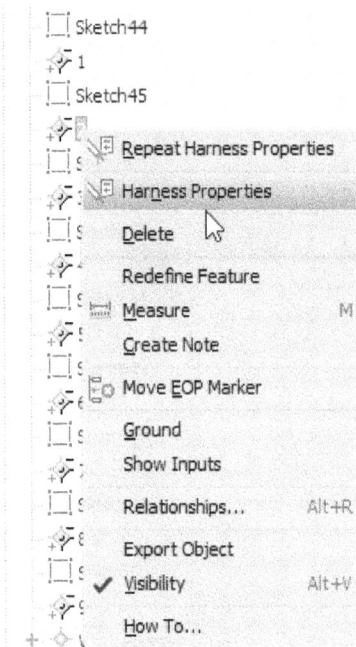

5. In the Connector Pin Properties dialog box:
    - Review the current name for this pin.
    - Click Cancel.

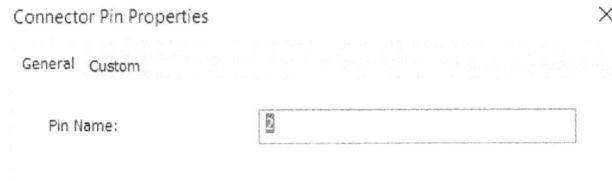

Connector Pin Properties   ✕

General   Custom

    Pin Name: [2]

6. Click Return in the ribbon.

7. In the Browser, double-click on Connector Harness to activate it for in-place editing.

8. In the Browser, expand the categories below the harness part to review the wires, segments, and virtual parts that compose the harness part.

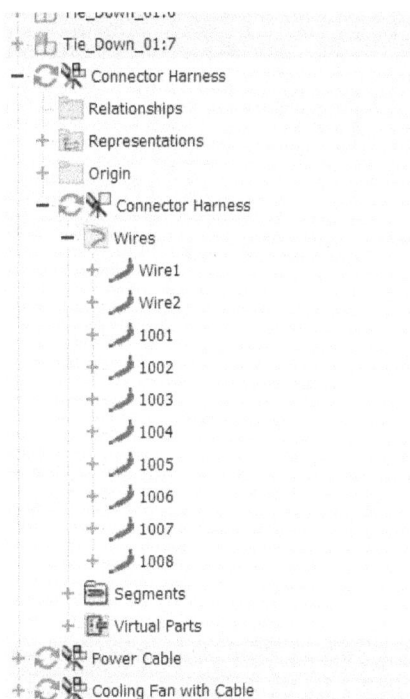

9. To begin reviewing the properties for the harness assembly, in the Browser, right-click on Connector Harness and click Harness Settings.

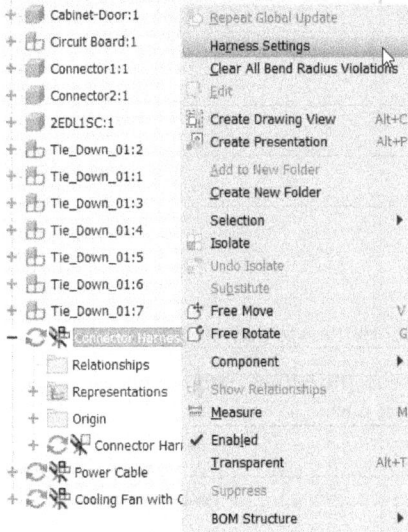

10. In the Harness Settings dialog box:

- Click the different tabs and review the available settings and options.
- To change the display for wires from centerline to rendered, select the Wires/Cables tab, and in the Default Display panel, click Rendered Display.
- Click OK.

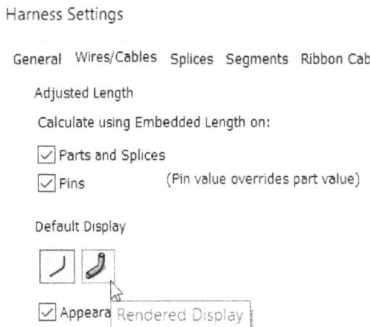

11. Zoom in to view the wires at Connector1.

Note that the wires are still displaying as thin lines at the center of the wire. The previous setting impacts only newly created wires.

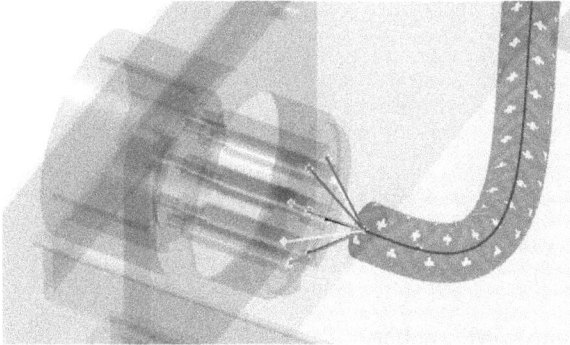

12. To begin changing harness properties for a single wire, in the browser, right-click on Wire1. Click Harness Properties.

13. In the Wire Properties dialog box:

- In the Occurrence tab, for Wire ID, enter **1000**.
- In the Display tab, in the Default Display panel, click Rendered Display.
- Click OK.

14. In the Browser and graphics window, review the changes to the wire name and its display.

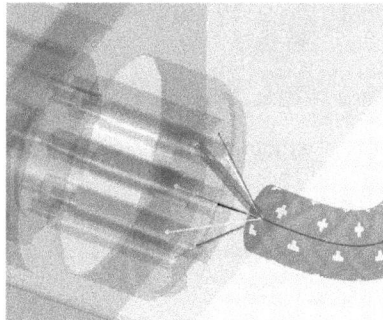

15. To toggle the display of a wire, in the Browser or graphics window, right-click on wire 1001. Click Display As Rendered.

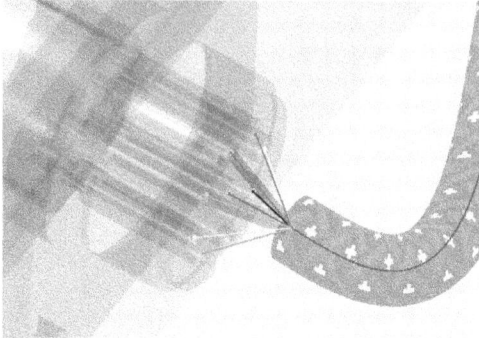

16. Click Finish Cable and Harness in the ribbon.

17. Close all files without saving changes.

Exercise: Create a Harness Assembly

In this exercise, you will create harness assemblies, add electrical parts, and set the properties of the electrical harness and one of the electrical parts.

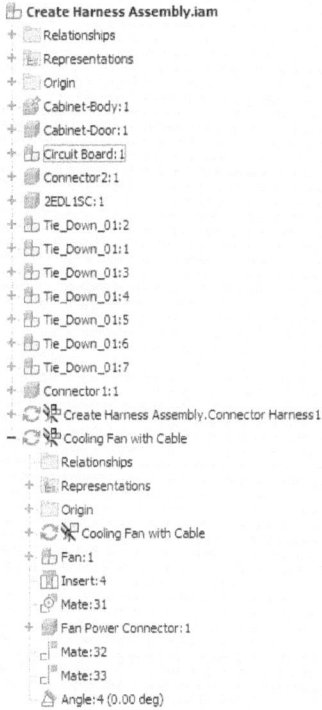

The completed exercise

1. Open *Create Harness Assembly.iam*.

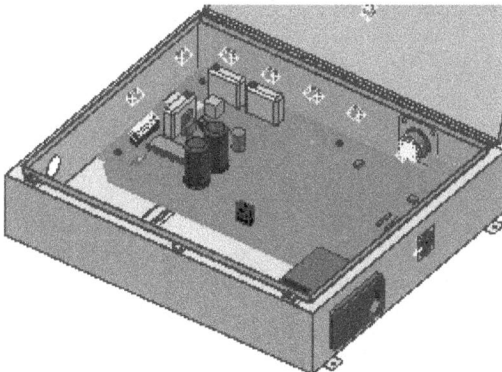

2. To add an electrical part to the assembly:
   - In the Assemble tab, in the Component panel, click Place.
   - In the Place Component dialog box, select *Connector1.ipt*.
   - Add a single occurrence as shown in the following figure.

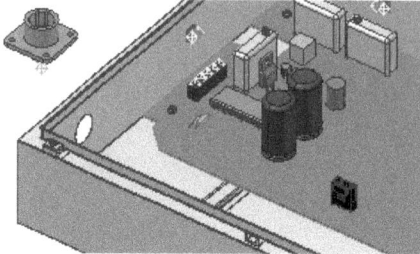

3. Add constraints (insert and an angle assembly constraint or a Rigid Joint to assemble the part as shown in the following figure.

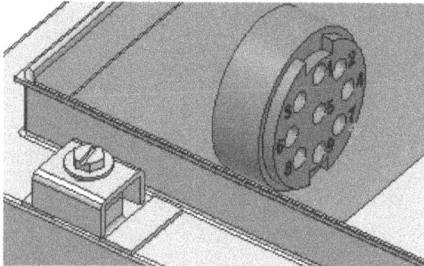

4. To begin creating a new harness assembly with its name having the assembly name as a prefix, in the ribbon, in the Environments tab, in the Begin panel, click Cable and Harness.

5. In the Create Harness dialog box:
   - In the Harness Assembly File Name field, change the name from *Create Harness Assembly.Harness1.iam* to **Create Harness Assembly.Connector Harness1.iam**.
   - In the Harness Assembly File Location field, review the default folder location where the assembly will be created.
   - Click OK.

6. In the Browser, review what was created and the corresponding folder and file names. Click Local Update, if required.

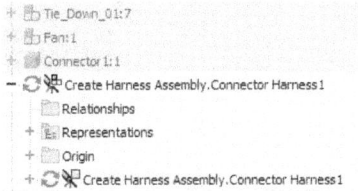

7. Click Finish Cable and Harness in the ribbon.

8. To create a harness assembly with a name that does not include the overall assembly name:

- In the Environments tab, in the Begin panel, click Cable and Harness.
- In the Create Harness dialog box, in the Harness Assembly File Name field, enter **Cooling Fan with Cable.iam**. Click Local Update, if required.
- Click OK.

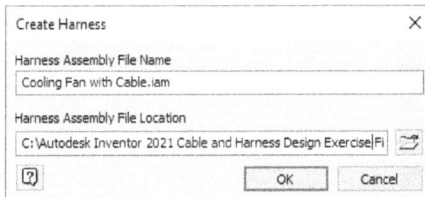

9. In the Browser, review what was created and the corresponding folder and file names.

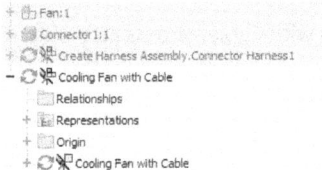

10. To restructure the fan so that it is in this new harness assembly instead of the overall assembly, in the Browser, drag and drop the Fan assembly below the Cooling Fan with Cable part as shown in the following figure.

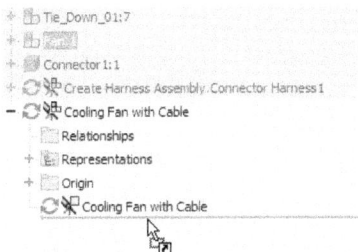

11. The assembly structure appears as shown in the following figure.

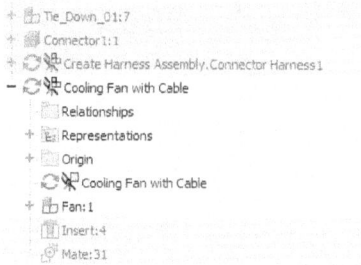

12. To add a connector directly to the harness assembly:

- In the Assemble tab, in the Components panel, click Place.
- In the Place Component dialog box, select *Fan Power Connector.ipt*.
- Add a single occurrence as shown in the following figure.

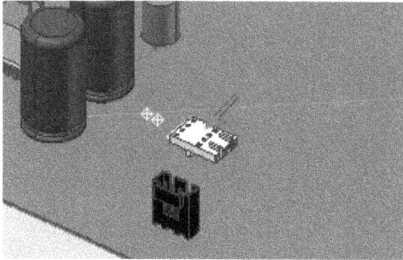

13. To begin configuring global settings for the harness before creating wires and cables:

- In the Browser, right-click on the Cooling Fan with Cable harness assembly.
- Click Harness Settings.

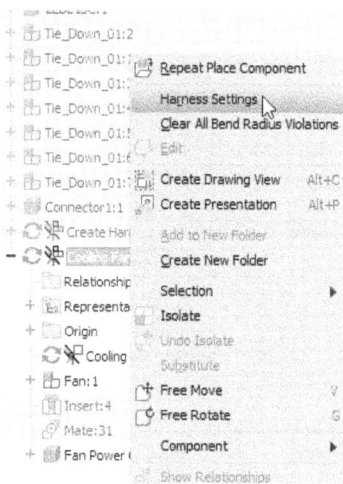

14. In the Harness Settings dialog box, General tab:

- In the Adjusted Length Round Up drop-down list, select 5.000 mm.
- Click the Apply round up to individual segments and exposed wire lengths check box.
- Click OK.

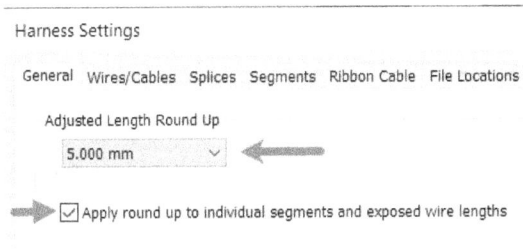

Harness Settings

General Wires/Cables Splices Segments Ribbon Cable File Locations

Adjusted Length Round Up

5.000 mm

☑ Apply round up to individual segments and exposed wire lengths

15. To begin setting the properties for the Fan Power Connector part:

- In the Browser, right-click on Fan Power Connector.
- Click Harness Properties.

16. In the Part Properties dialog box, in the General tab:

- In the RefDes field, enter **PJ6**.
- Click OK.

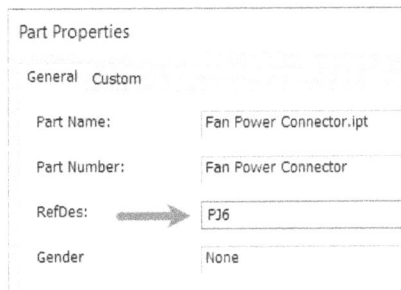

Part Properties

General Custom

Part Name:	Fan Power Connector.ipt
Part Number:	Fan Power Connector
RefDes:	PJ6
Gender	None

17. To begin assembling this connector to the connector on the circuit board, in the ribbon, click Finish Cable and Harness.

18. Add a mate assembly constraint between the selected faces as shown in the following figure.

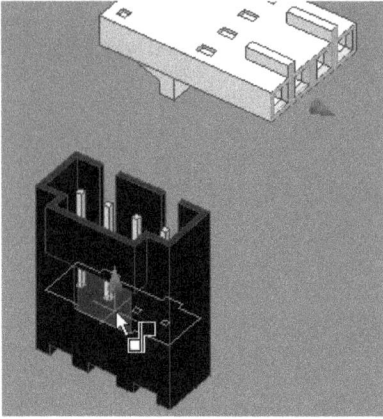

19. To add a mate assembly constraint to align the pins:

- Select the work point as shown in the following figure.
- In the Browser, under Circuit Board and under J9B1 Connector, select Pin 1 Center.
- Click Apply.

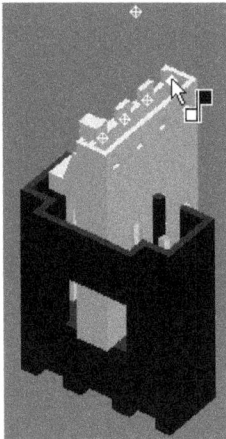

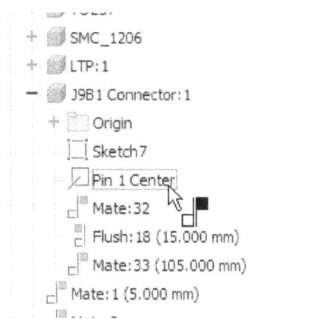

20. Add an angle constraint to align the part as shown in the following figure.

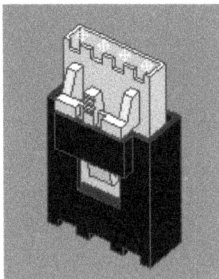

21. In the Browser, review what you just added and created in the overall assembly and what you added to the harness assembly.

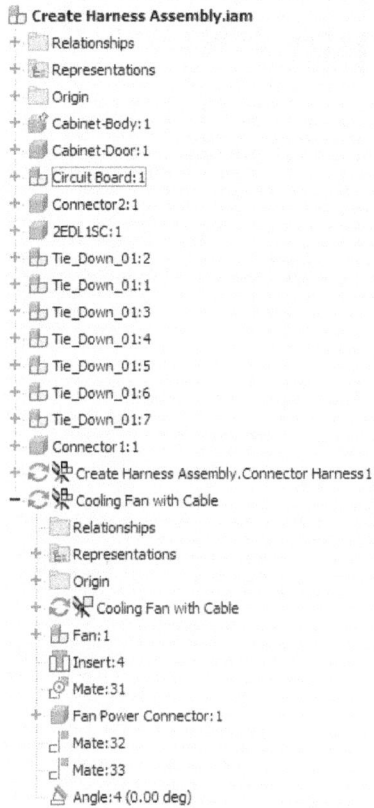

```
Create Harness Assembly.iam
 + Relationships
 + Representations
 + Origin
 + Cabinet-Body:1
 + Cabinet-Door:1
 + Circuit Board:1
 + Connector2:1
 + 2EDL1SC:1
 + Tie_Down_01:2
 + Tie_Down_01:1
 + Tie_Down_01:3
 + Tie_Down_01:4
 + Tie_Down_01:5
 + Tie_Down_01:6
 + Tie_Down_01:7
 + Connector1:1
 + Create Harness Assembly.Connector Harness1
 − Cooling Fan with Cable
      Relationships
 +    Representations
 +    Origin
 +    Cooling Fan with Cable
 +    Fan:1
      Insert:4
      Mate:31
 +    Fan Power Connector:1
      Mate:32
      Mate:33
      Angle:4 (0.00 deg)
```

22. Close all files without saving changes.

Chapter Summary

In this chapter, you learned about Autodesk Inventor Cable and Harness functionality and the basic workflow to create and document a design.

Having completed this chapter, you can:

- Describe the process for creating a complete cable and harness design, create a harness assembly in an assembly design, and insert electrical parts.

Wire a Harness Assembly

In this chapter, you learn to add wires and cables to a design. You then learn to create route segments and have the wires and cables follow those routes. You also learn to create ribbon cables and create wires and cables by importing the data.

Objectives

After completing this chapter, you will be able to:

- Add wires and cables between pins in electrical parts and connectors.
- Add route segments to a design and route existing wires or cables through the route segments.
- Import wire or cable data from an external file.
- Add ribbon cables between electrical connectors.

Lesson: Adding Wires and Cables

This lesson describes how to add the wires and cables that connect pins in electrical parts to a harness assembly.

Along with electronic connectors, wires and cables are at the core of an electronic design. After you have positioned the electronic connectors, the next step in creating and documenting your design is to add wires and cables between the pins on the connectors.

The following figure shows a design that is complete through the creation of the required wires and cables. After the wires and cables have been added, they can then be routed and modified to traverse through the assembly design as required.

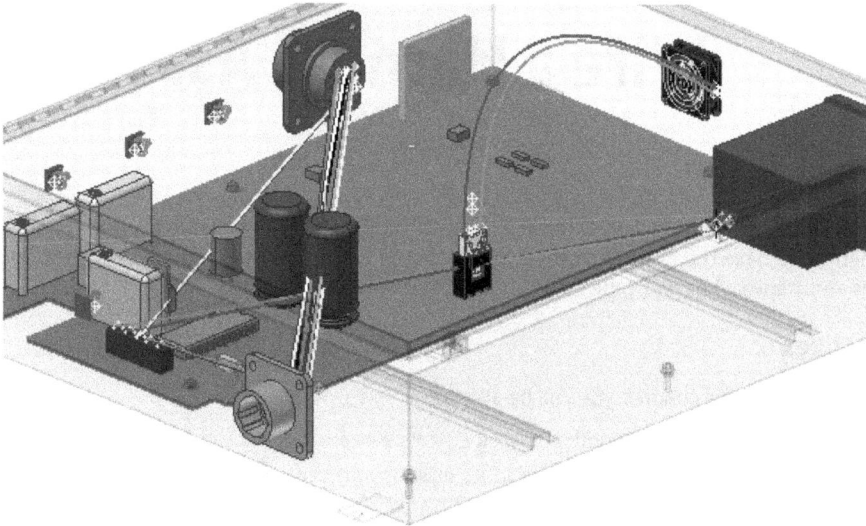

Objectives

After completing this lesson, you will be able to:

- Add wires to a harness assembly going between pins in electrical parts.
- Add cables to a harness assembly going between pins in electrical parts.
- Control the global property and display settings for wires and cables.

Adding Wires

After you have added electrical parts and created the harness assembly, your next step in creating a cable and harness design is to add wires and cables to the active harness assembly. To add the correct wires between the electrical parts where you require them, you need to know what tool to use and how to use it.

In the following figure, the design is shown before and after adding multiple wires between different electrical parts.

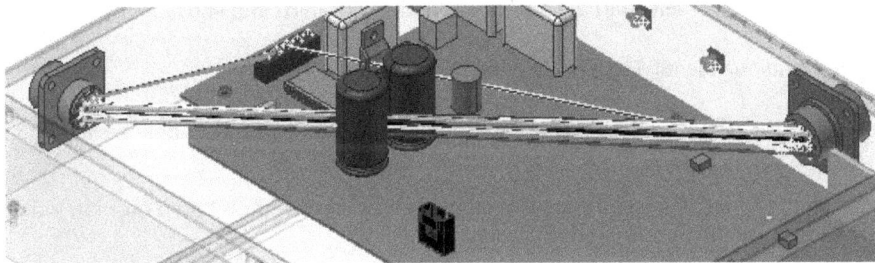

Access

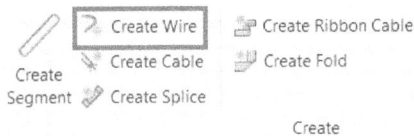

Ribbon: Cable and Harness tab>Create panel

Create Wire

When you create a wire in a harness assembly, you enter a unique identifying name for the wire, select the library category to use, and select the specific style. After you specify the properties and type of wire to create, you click the pins on the connectors that you want to have as the start and endpoints of the wire. The wire is added to the harness assembly only after you click OK or Apply in the Create Wire dialog box. Before clicking OK or Apply and after selecting the start and end pins, you can change what you have entered and selected for the wire ID, wire category, and name of the wire.

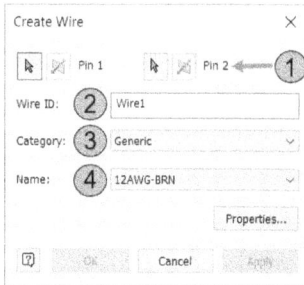

1. Select buttons for selecting the points where the wire starts and ends.

2. Enter a unique identifying name for the wire.

3. Select the wire category. The list of wire categories is based on what is defined in the cable and harness library file.

4. Select the name of the wire you want to create. The list of wires is based on what is defined in the library within the selected category.

Wires in the Browser

The wires you add to the active harness assembly are added to the harness part within that harness assembly. Each wire is listed separately in the Browser and organized within the Wires folder in the part. The start and end points of the wire list below the wire and identify the electrical part and pin number the wire is connected to.

In the following figure, three wires have been added to the harness part in the active harness assembly. The first two wires had specific unique wire identities entered while the third wire used the default automatic identifying name. The wire W101 connects between the electrical parts with reference designators U1 and J7. The wire connects to pin 1 on each of those components.

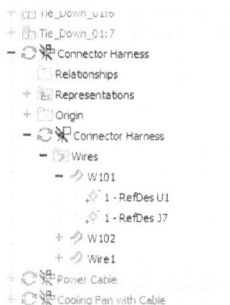

Procedure: Adding Wires

The following steps give an overview of adding a wire to a harness assembly.

1. Activate the harness assembly.

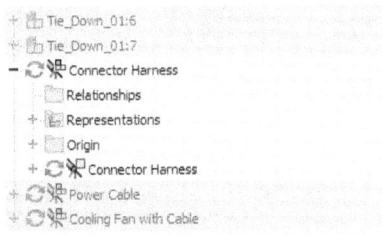

2. Start the Create Wire tool.

3. In the Create Wire dialog box, enter a wire ID for the new wire and select the type of wire to create by selecting the appropriate wire category and name.

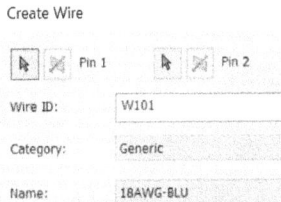

4. Select the pin work point on an electrical part where you want the wire to start.

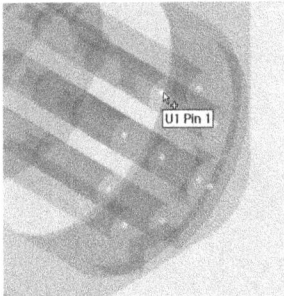

5. Select the pin work point on an electrical part where you want the wire to end.

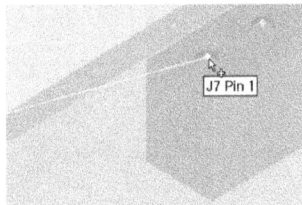

6. In the Create Wire dialog box, click Apply or OK to create the wire.

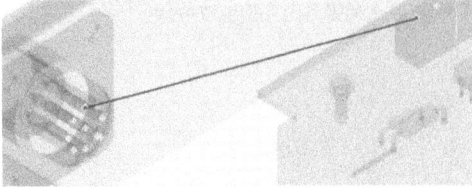

Adding Cables

The addition of cables to a harness design is very similar to the addition of wires. While the flow and options are very similar, there are a few unique aspects to creating a cable. To add cables to a harness assembly going between pins in electrical parts, you need to know what tool to use and how to use that tool.

In the following figure, the design is shown before and after adding a single cable between different electrical parts. In this case, the cable has only two conducting wires defined within its style.

Access

Ribbon: Cable and Harness tab>Create panel

Create Cable

When you create a cable in a harness assembly, you enter a unique identifying name for the cable, select the library category to use, and select the specific style within the library. After you specify the properties and type of cable to create, you click the pins on the connectors that you want to have as the start and end points for each wire in the cable. The cable is added to the harness assembly only after you click OK or Apply in the Create Cable dialog box.

The number of wires (conductors) within a cable varies depending on the style of cable that you select. The wire that is highlighted in the wire list in the Create Cable dialog box is the active wire for which you are selecting start and end pins when you select a pin work point on an electrical part. By default, you select the pin locations for the wires in the order that they are listed in the dialog box. To define the pin locations for a cable's wire in an order other than sequential, click that wire in the dialog box list and then select the pin work points. Because it is possible to create a cable without defining all of the start and end pins for each wire within the cable, it is good practice to click OK or Apply only after defining all start and end pins. By doing so, you do not have to go back at a later time and edit the cable to correct the missing connection locations.

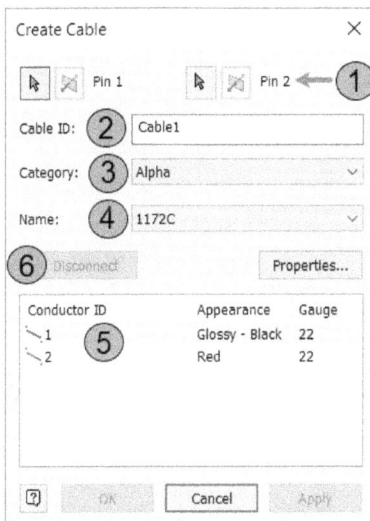

①   Select buttons to define the points where the selected wire within the cable starts and ends.

②   Enter a unique identifying name for the cable.

③   Select the cable category. The list of cable categories is based on what is defined in the cable and harness library file.

④   Select the name of the cable style you want to create. The list of cables is based on what is defined in the library within the selected category.

⑤   List of the wires within the cable. The highlighted conductor indicates the wire for which you want to set the pin connections, or the current selection that you want to clear. The icon to the left of the conductor ID indicates whether or not start and end pins have been specified.

⑥   Use to clear the pin selection for the highlighted connector to reselect its pin connections.

Cables in the Browser

The cables you add to the active harness assembly are added to the harness part within that harness assembly. Each cable lists separately in the Browser and is organized within the Cables folder in the part. Below the cable, each wire within the cable is listed. The start and end points of the wire then list below that to identify the electrical part and pin number the wire is connected to.

In the following figure, a single cable that consists of two wires has been added to the harness part in the active harness assembly. The first wire within the cable connects between pin 4 on electrical part J7 and pin 1 on part P1.

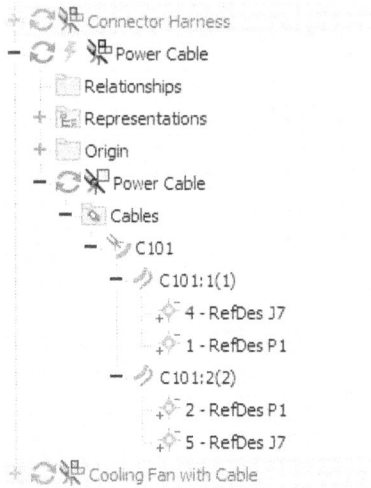

Procedure: Adding Cables

The following steps give an overview of adding a cable to a harness assembly.

1. Activate the harness assembly.

2. Start the Create Cable tool.

3. In the Create Cable dialog box, enter a unique ID for the new cable and select the type of cable to create by selecting the appropriate cable category and name.

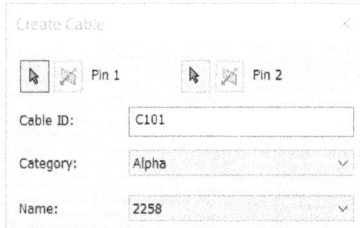

4. Select the pin work point on an electrical part where you want the first wire in the cable to start.

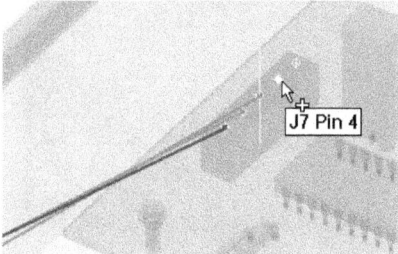

5. Select the pin work point on an electrical part where you want the first wire in the cable to end.

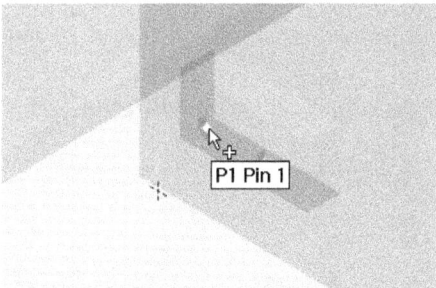

6. Select the start and end pin locations for the second wire in the cable.

7. If the cable contains more than two wires, continue to specify the start and end point locations for each wire in the cable.

8. In the Create Cable dialog box, click Apply or OK to create the wire.

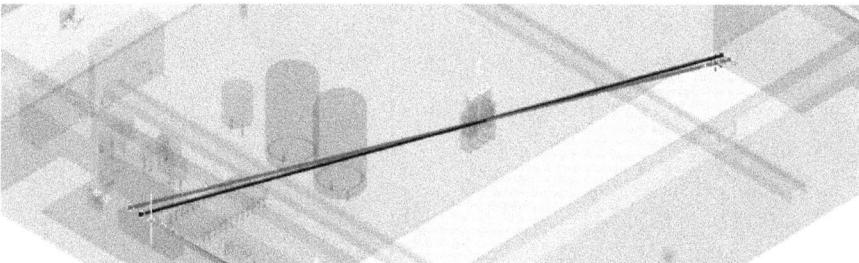

Global Settings

After you create a new harness assembly, you can change the settings that control the default properties of different objects that you can create in the harness assembly. To change the settings specific for the creation of wires and cables, you need to know where and how to access the options and which options are available to be set.

The following figure shows two different results for the creation of a cable consisting of two wires. The differences in the display were based on the differences in the default settings for wires and cables.

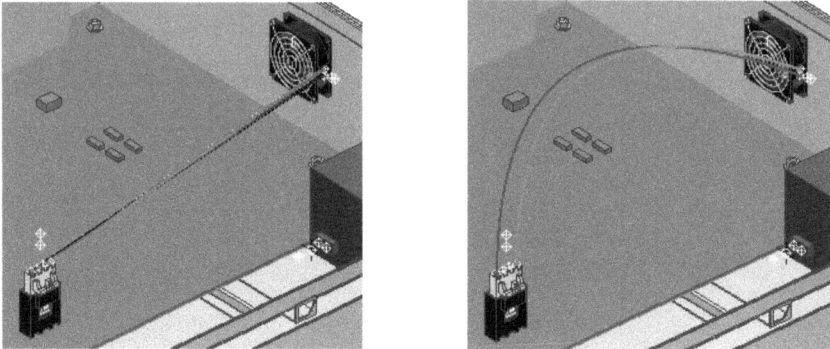

Harness Settings: Wires/Cables

You configure the default settings for a harness assembly in the Harness Settings dialog box. You configure the default settings for wires and cables for that harness assembly in the Wire/Cables tab of the Harness Settings dialog box.

Right-click on the active harness assembly in the Browser and then click Harness Settings to open the Harness Settings dialog box.

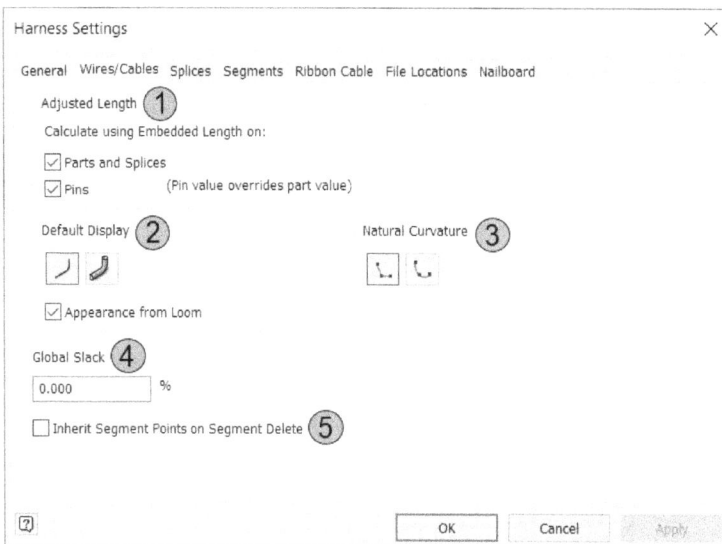

1. Use to increase the wire or cable length past the connector points based on the value of the custom properties Embedded Length or Embedded Length 2.

2. Set the default display type of a new wire or cable to display as a centerline or rendered. Use the Appearance from Loom option to control the default appearance of a wire or cable that has a loom property applied.

3. Toggle the default curvature calculation method for wires and cables. Set to Without Natural Curvature to create straight line segments from pin to pin. Set to With Natural Curvature to have the wires and cables arc to be tangent to the direction assigned to the connector.

4. Specify a percentage of the existing wire length to be added as extra to the wire or cable's overall length.

5. Select Inherit Segment Points on Segment Delete option to have routed wires or cables keep their shape and points when you delete the segment that was selected to route the wires or cables.

Exercise: Add Wires and Cables

In this exercise, you will review and set the default settings for existing harness assemblies, and you will add wires and cables to the harness assemblies.

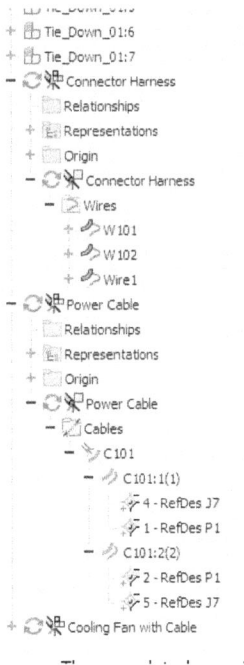

Add Wires

In this section of the exercise, you will add wires to an existing harness assembly.

1. Open *Cabinet-09-1.iam*.

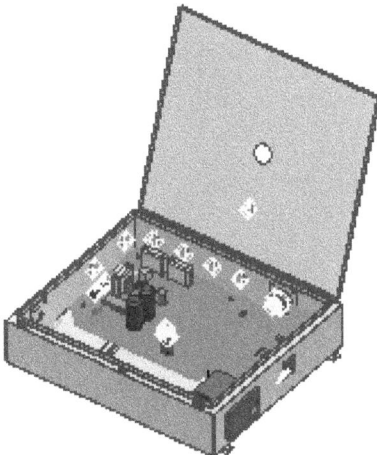

2. In the Browser, under Representations, activate the view representation Connector_01.

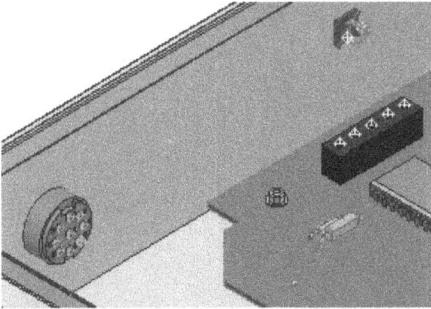

3. To activate the Connector Harness assembly so that wires can be created between the two connectors, in the Browser, double-click on Connector Harness.

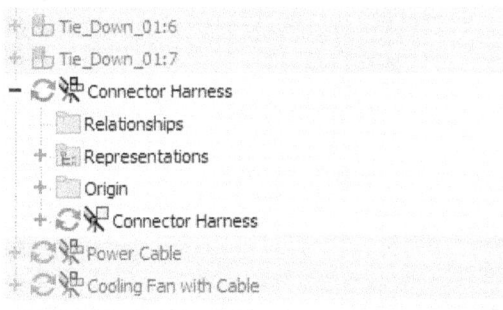

4. To review this harness assembly's current settings for wire creation:

- In the Browser, right-click on the Connector Harness assembly. Click Harness Settings.
- In the Harness Settings dialog box, in the Wires/Cables tab, note that in the Default Display area, the display is set to Centerline Display.
- Click Cancel.

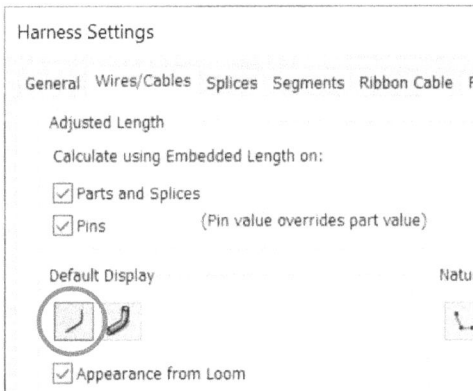

5. In the Cable and Harness tab, in the Create panel, click Create Wire.

6. In the Create Wire dialog box:
- In the Wire ID field, enter **W101**.
- In the Category list, select Generic.
- In the Name list, select 18AWG-BLU.

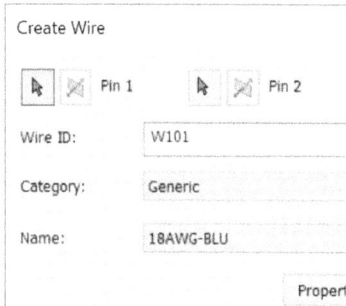

Create Wire

	Pin 1		Pin 2

Wire ID:	W101
Category:	Generic
Name:	18AWG-BLU

Propert

7. To specify the start pin for the wire, click the Pin 1 work point on Connector1 (RefDes U1) as shown in the following figure.

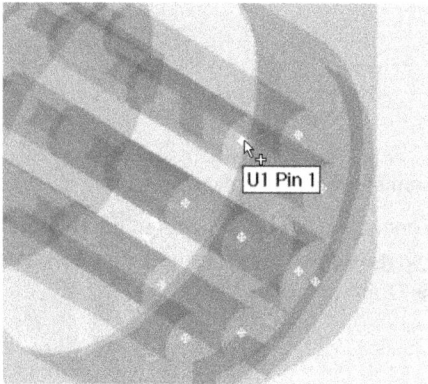

U1 Pin 1

8. To specify the end pin for the wire, click the Pin 1 work point on LTP (RefDes J7) as shown in the following figure.

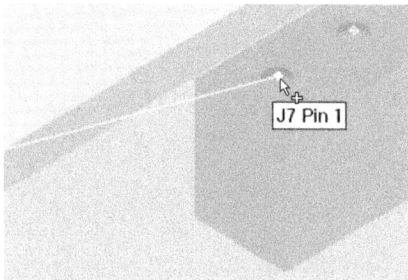

J7 Pin 1

9. In the Create Wire dialog box, click Apply. The assembly displays as shown in the following figure.

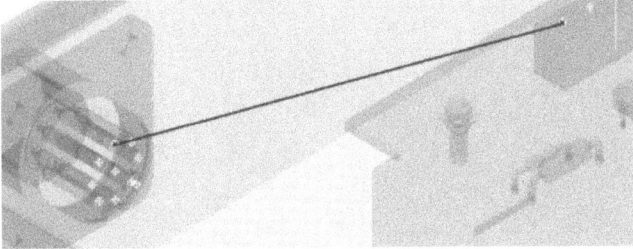

10. In the Create Wire dialog box:
    - In the Wire ID field, enter **W102**.
    - In the Name list, select 18AWG-GRN.

Create Wire

Pin 1   Pin 2

Wire ID: W102

Category: Generic

Name: 18AWG-GRN

Propertie:

11. Create a second wire starting at Pin 2 on Connector1 (U1) and ending at Pin 2 on LTP (J7) as shown in the following figure.

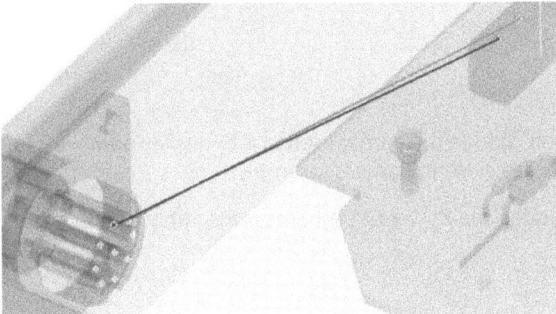

12. Create a third wire starting at Pin 4 on Connector1 and ending at Pin 3 on LTP, as shown (using the default settings). Close the Create Wire dialog box after creating the third wire.

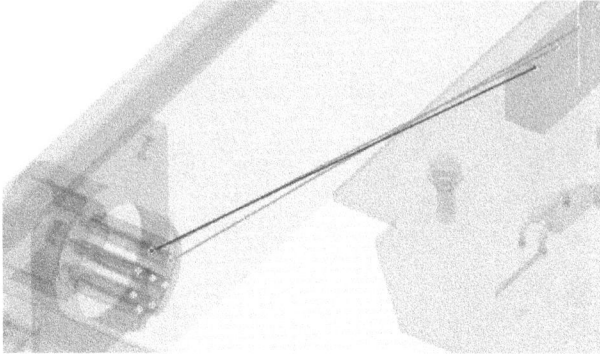

13. In the Browser under Connector Harness, expand the Wires category to review what was added to the Browser for these individual wires.

Add a Cable

In this section of the exercise, you change the harness settings to display new wires and cables as rendered and then add a cable to an existing harness assembly.

1. In the Browser, double-click on the Power Cable harness assembly to activate it.

2. To change this harness assembly's default settings for cable creation:

- In the Browser, right-click on Power Cable assembly and click Harness Settings.
- In the Harness Settings dialog box, in the Wires/Cables tab, in Default Display area, click Rendered Display.
- Click OK.

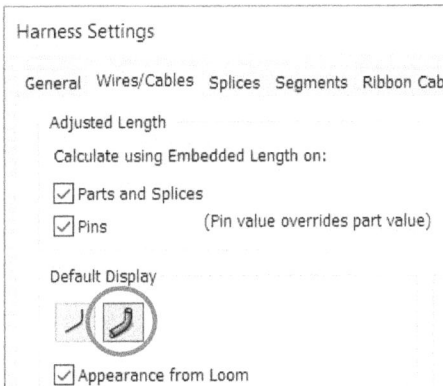

Harness Settings

General Wires/Cables Splices Segments Ribbon Cabl

Adjusted Length

Calculate using Embedded Length on:

☑ Parts and Splices

☑ Pins   (Pin value overrides part value)

Default Display

☑ Appearance from Loom

3. In the Cable and Harness tab, in the Create panel, click Create Cable.

4. In the Create Cable dialog box:

- In the Cable ID field, enter **C101**.
- In the Category list, select Alpha.
- In the Name list, select 2258.

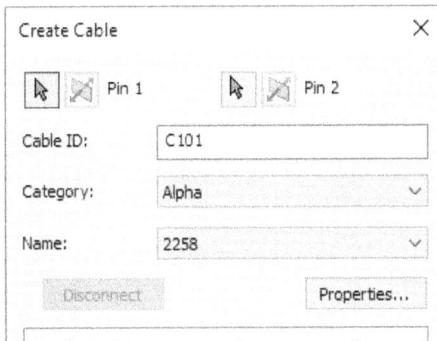

Create Cable   ✕

☐ ☒ Pin 1   ☐ ☒ Pin 2

Cable ID: C101

Category: Alpha   ⌄

Name: 2258   ⌄

Disconnect   Properties...

5. To specify the start point for the first wire in the cable, in the graphics window, click the Pin 4 work point on LTP as shown in the following figure.

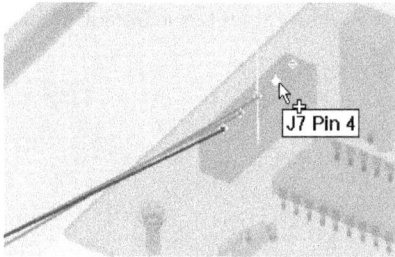

6. To specify the end point for the first wire in the cable, click the Pin 1 work point on the power supply (P1) as shown in the following figure. Do not click Apply.

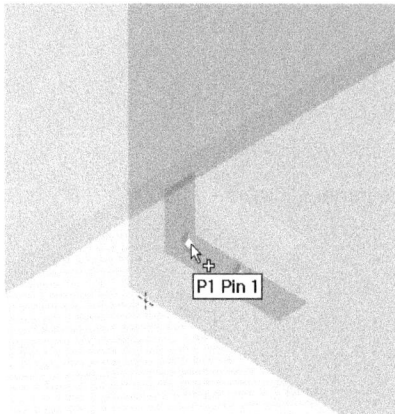

7. To define the second wire of the cable:

    ▪ On the power supply, click Pin 2.
    ▪ On the LTP connector, click Pin 5.
    ▪ In the Create Cable dialog box, click OK. The assembly displays as shown in the following figure.

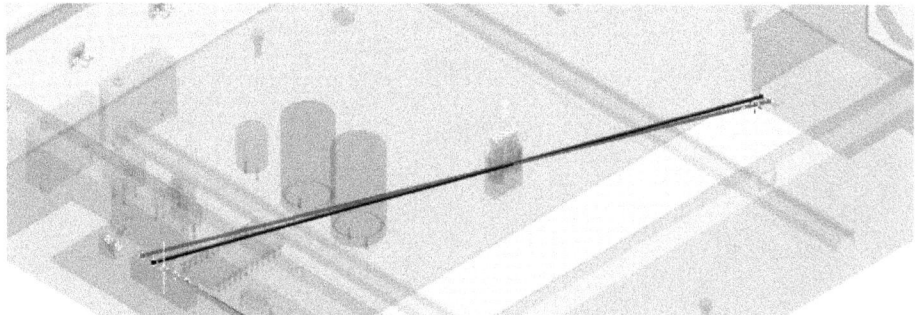

8. Zoom in to the connector to view the differences in their initial displays.

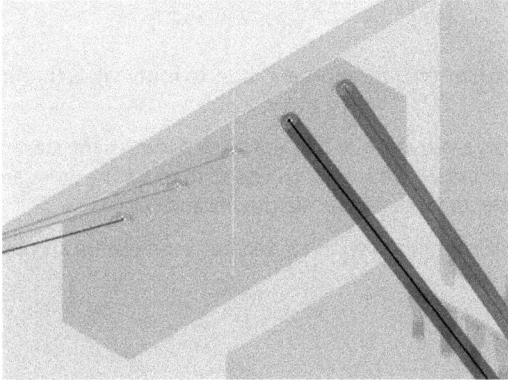

9. In the Browser under Power Cable, expand the Cables category to review what was added to the Browser for this cable.

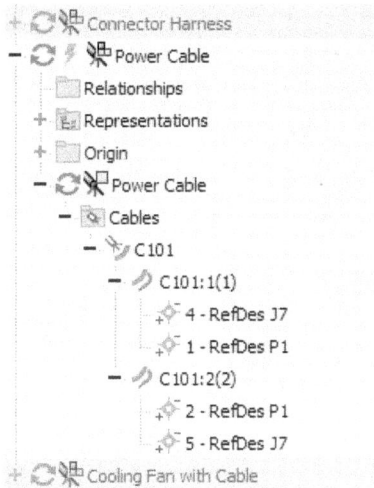

10. Click Finish Cable and Harness to return to the overall assembly.

11. Close all files without saving changes.

Lesson: Routing Wires and Cables

In this lesson, you learn how to create harness segments and how to route wires through harness segments.

Wires and cables added to an assembly are created in a straight line between the starting and ending connection points. To correctly design the wire harness, you need to route the wires around other components and through harness attachments such as tie-downs and clips.

The following figure shows a segment containing wires routed between electrical connectors in the assembly.

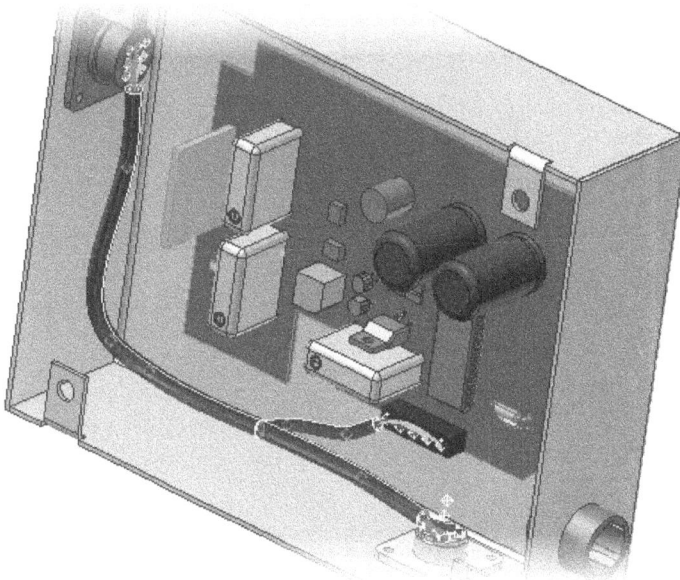

Objectives

After completing this lesson, you will be able to:

- Describe the purpose of route segments.
- Create a route segment.
- Create a segment that branches from an existing segment.
- Control the global property and display settings for segments.
- Manually route wires and cables through route segments.
- Route wires and cables automatically through route segments.
- View the path of a routed wire or cable.
- Unroute wires or cables from a route segment.

About Route Segments

A harness segment represents a virtual wire bundle path through an assembly.

The following figure shows wires in an assembly before and after routing the wires through segments.

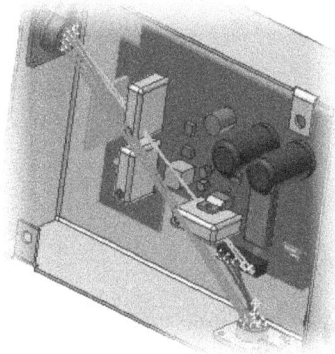

Wires added to assembly   Wires routed through segments

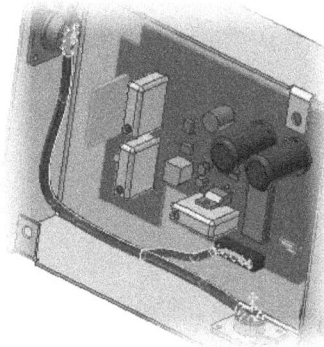

Definition of Route Segments

A segment represents a virtual bundle of wires and defines the paths or routings that a wire can take through an assembly. You use work points to define the segment path and reposition the work points to change the segment position and shape.

When you route a wire, you place unrouted wires into selected segments in the active harness using methods that range from manual to fully automatic. You typically use manual routing in a network of segments that contains gaps. You unroute wires to remove them from selected segments.

Example of Segments with Unrouted Wires

The following figure shows unrouted wires and the segments created to establish the wire harness path.

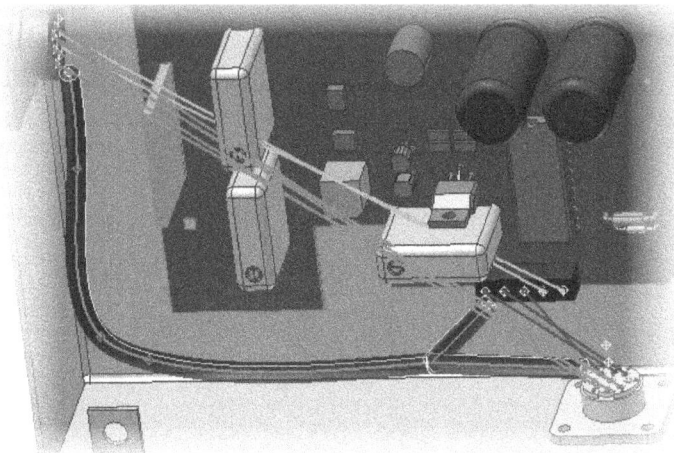

Creating Route Segments

You can define segment paths using work points, work features, offset distances, and other geometry, and make precise adjustments later.

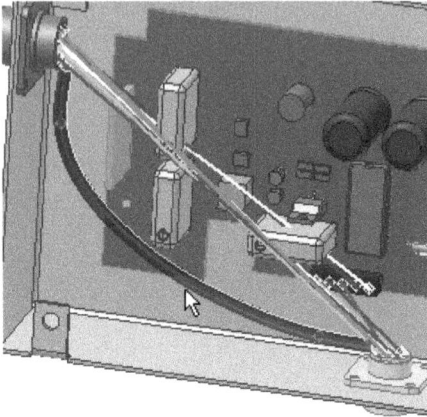

Initial segment with two work points

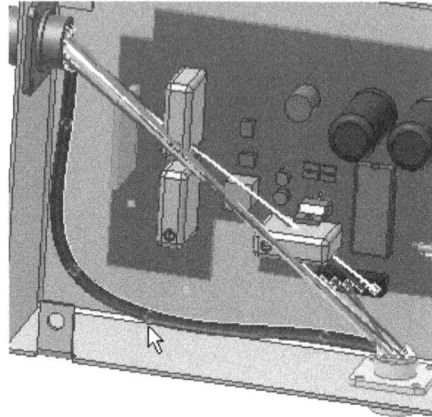

Segment with added work points

Creating Segments

To create a segment, you define at least two points consisting of the start and end points.

As you design, you can add segment work points where it is critical for the segment to adapt to changes in the assembly, or to control the direction of the segment around or through existing assembly geometry. Consider the number and position of work points when you place them.

To place segment work points precisely, define work features at critical locations before you insert the segment. Work features, such as work points and work axes, direct segments through tie-downs, clips, or other geometry. Segment work points associated to work features are updated when the model changes. Work features also create a more accurate approach to the connectors and direct the segment around geometry that you want to avoid.

Selecting Work Points for Segments

Like the points used to define pins on electrical parts, such as connectors, the points that you select for segments determine whether certain work points are updated when you make changes to the associated geometry. Segment work points that you create by selecting arbitrary points on a face are not updated with changes in the model geometry.

Segment work points based on the following geometry are updated when you make changes:

- Existing associative work points.
- Center points on any circular component such as a face, a hole, and cylindrical cuts or arc edges.
- Existing sketch points.
- Model vertices.

> Click Undo or press ESC while creating a segment to remove the last segment point that you created and end the operation.

Planning Segment Start Points and End Points

When multiple segments exist in an assembly, correct placement of the start point and endpoint of the segment in relation to the wire connection points is important. When you automatically route wires, the system checks for the harness segment ends that are closest to each end of the wire and then searches for the shortest path through the identified contiguous segments. Whenever possible, place the harness segments to avoid confusion about which segment is closest to the wire connection points.

Access

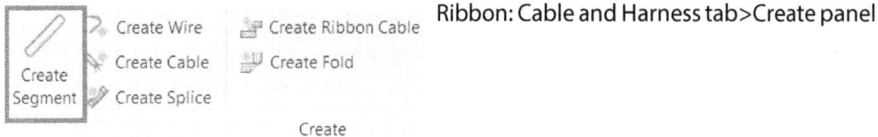

Create Segment

Create Wire
Create Cable
Create Splice

Create Ribbon Cable
Create Fold

Create

Ribbon: Cable and Harness tab>Create panel

Process: Creating Route Segments

The following steps give an overview of creating wire routing segments.

1. Activate the harness assembly for editing.

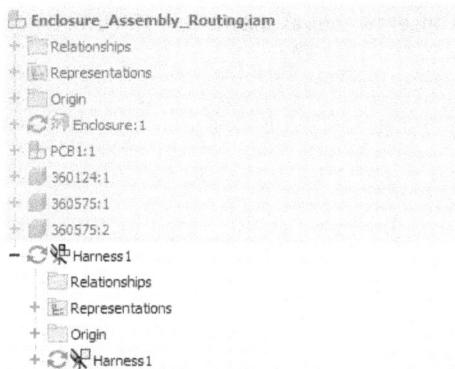

2. Click the Create Segment tool.

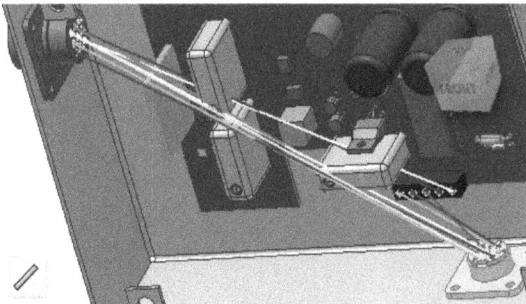

3. Select starting, intermediate, and endpoints for the segment, changing offset as required for each point.

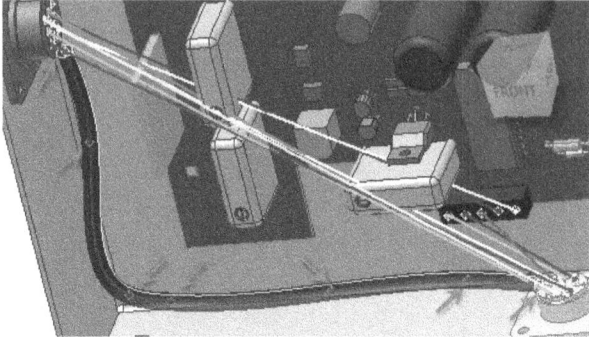

Applying Different Offset Distances

Arbitrary points that you select on a face are offset a specified distance from the selected geometry. Segment points that are based on existing geometry or work points are not offset.

A segment can require several offset distances throughout its length. To adjust the segment offset as you move through the assembly, right-click on the graphics window and click Edit Offset.

The offset length displays as a tooltip and offset symbol, as shown in the following figure.

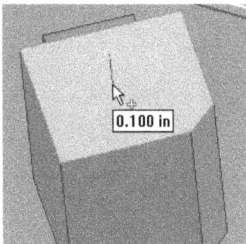

0.100 in

The offset distance is applied only when you create segments. It is not applied when you route wires through the segment, and it does not cause the diameter to be updated.

Creating Segment Branches

Segment branches and segments are created in a similar way. Branches automatically connect to existing segments. The following figure shows a segment with two branches.

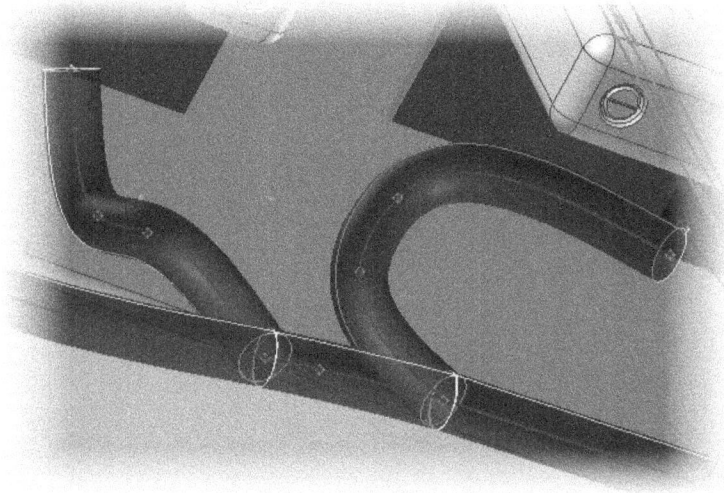

Adding Segment Branches

You make segment branches by starting or ending a new segment on an existing segment.

The original existing segment is broken into two segments at the intersecting point. When completed, all segments share a common endpoint. No tangent constraint is formed between the branch and the two original segments. All segments behave as separate entities.

The following figures show a completed branch and the Browser representation.

Graphical segment added

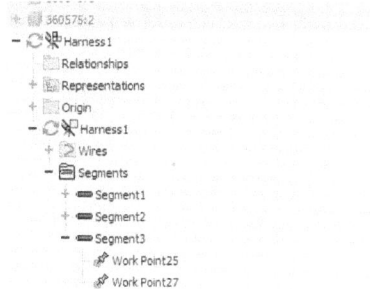

Segments created in tree view

When you route wires, each of the three segments behave as a separate entity and can assume different diameters.

Procedure: Creating Segment Branches

The following steps give an overview of how to add a branch to an existing segment.

1. Activate the harness assembly for editing.

    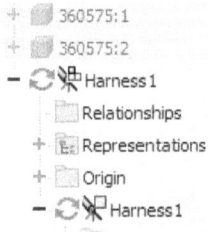

2. Start the Create Segment command.

3. Select a starting point for the segment on the existing segment. You can also end a segment on an existing segment.

4. Select reference points for the branch location.

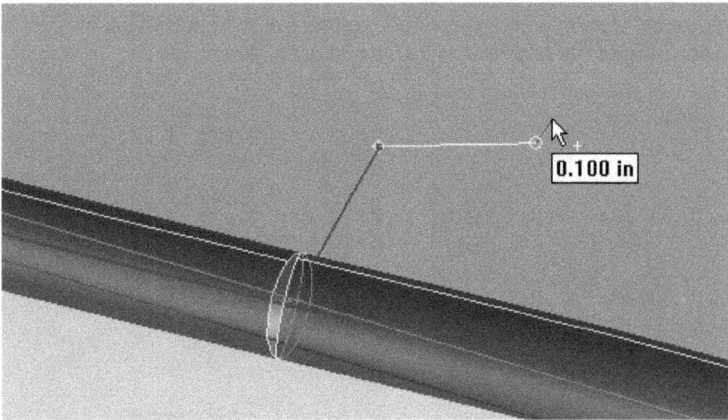

5. Right-click and click Finish. The existing segment is broken into two segments and the new segment is added to the assembly.

Segment Properties

Segment properties are stored in each individual segment occurrence. Available properties include automatic or fixed sizing of the segment, color, and physical dimensions.

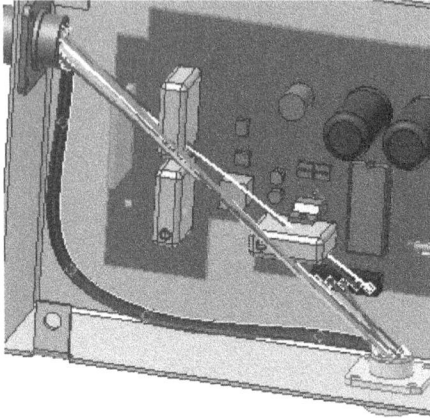

Default segment color blue

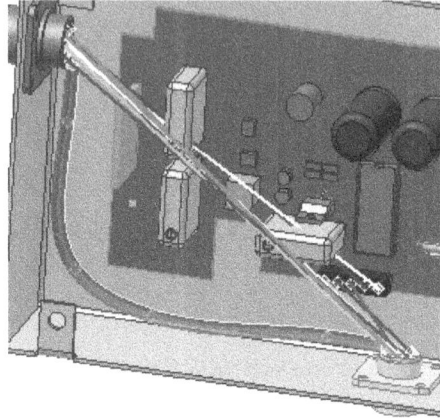

Segment color property set to red

Harness Settings: Segments

Like wires, segments contain a set of properties that provide a complete definition of the segment in the assembly. Unlike wires, segments do not exist in the context of a library and do not contain library-level properties. They contain only occurrence-level properties.

You can configure segments as fixed-diameter or variable-diameter segments. Fixed-diameter segments, such as semi-rigid tubing, do not change diameter as wires contained in it are routed, unrouted, or deleted. The diameters of variable segments are automatically updated as you add or remove wires.

The properties for a harness segment are established in the Segment Properties dialog box. Right-click on a segment and click Harness Properties to open the Segment Properties dialog box.

Occurrence Tab

The Occurrence tab in the Segment Properties dialog box lists properties related to the physical aspects of the segment.

① This area contains general options for the segment, including the segment name and various feature dimensions.

② The Bend Radius area has options for setting a fixed value for the radius or setting the radius from calculations based on the number and sizes of the wires routed through the segment.

③ The Diameter area has options for setting a fixed value for the diameter of the segment or setting the diameter from calculations based on the number and sizes of the wires routed through the segment.

Display Tab

The Display tab lists properties related to the appearance of the segment.

①   Sets or displays the segment Appearance.

②   Sets rendered or centerline display for the selected segment. This can also be toggled in the shortcut menu.

③   Displays the order in which the loom is placed when multiple looms are attached to the selected segment.

Harness Settings

You can set segment properties such as default diameter, display, bend radius, offset, and appearance in the Segments tab in the Harness Settings dialog box. These values are the defaults used in the creation of a segment and can be overridden in each segment occurrence.

In the Browser, right-click on the harness assembly and click Harness Settings to open the Harness Settings dialog box.

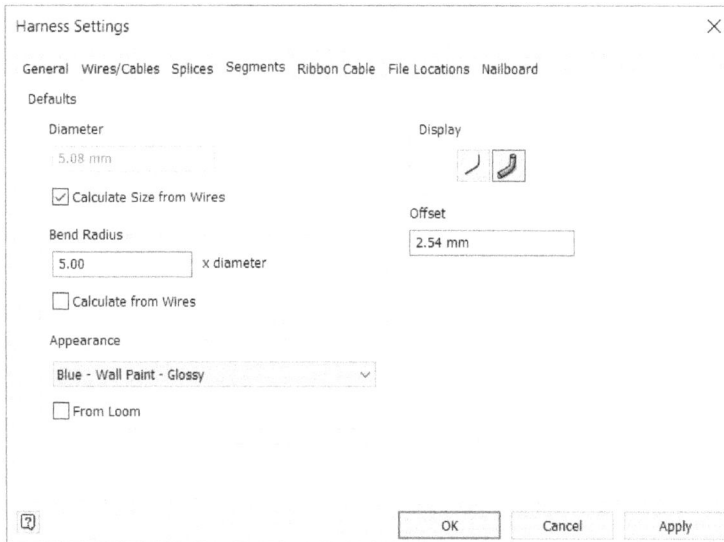

Manual Routing

Routing wires and cables manually provides methods for you to specify the individual segments for the program to use in order to establish the wire and cable paths through the assembly.

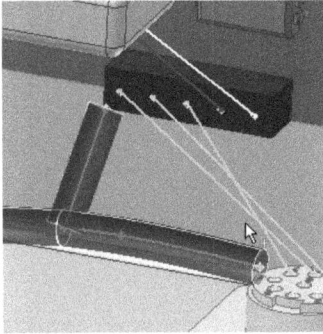

Individual wires selected for routing

Manual route completed

Manual Routing

When using the nonautomatic Route tool you have two options: semi-automatic routing or manual routing.

With the semi-automatic option, you route wires by selecting the starting and ending segments for the wire path. The software determines the shortest path for the wire through existing continuous segments. For the manual option, you must select each individual wire, and then manually select the individual segment or segments for the wires to be assigned to. Manual routing is most frequently used when there are gaps in the segments. When you route or place wires into segments, the wire lengths and segment diameters are calculated automatically by default. Wire lengths and segment diameters are also calculated automatically when you unroute wires or remove wires from segments. You can route wires only into segments that are in the active harness assembly.

> When you route or unroute wires, you can either select the wires before you begin or you can select the wires using the dialog box during the process.

Access

	Ribbon: Cable and Harness tab>Route panel

Automatic Route
Route
Unroute
Route

Manual Routing Options

There are two options available when manually routing wires. You can select the beginning and ending segments for the wire path. The software automatically calculates the path using the shortest distance through any intermediate segments. You can select the Single Segment option. When using this method, you select a single segment for the software to use. The wires are routed through this individual segment only; no other segments are included.

You select the manual routing method using options in the Route dialog box.

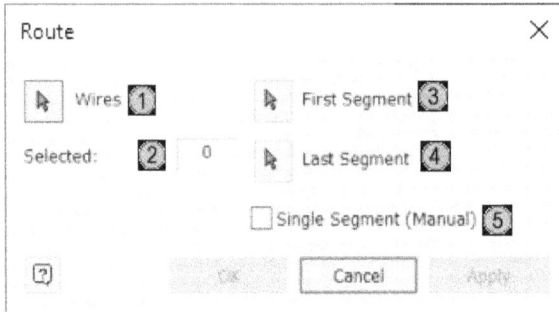

① Select Wires to individually select them.

② Displays the number of wires selected for routing.

③ Select First Segment to select the first segment in the path. This option is also used when Single Segment (Manual) is selected.

④ Select Last Segment to select the last segment in the path. This option is disabled when Single Segment (Manual) is selected.

⑤ Select Single Segment (Manual) to route the wires through a single segment.

Procedure: Manual Routing - Single Segment

The following steps give an overview of how to manually route wires through single segments.

1. Start the Route tool. In the Route dialog box, ensure that the Wires button is selected (default). Select the Single Segment (Manual) check box.

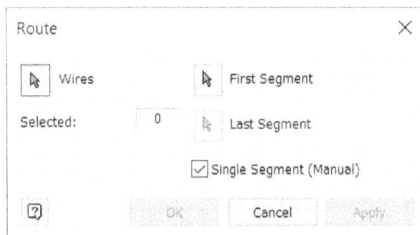

2. Select the wire or wires that you want to route through a segment.

3. In the Route dialog box, select First Segment.

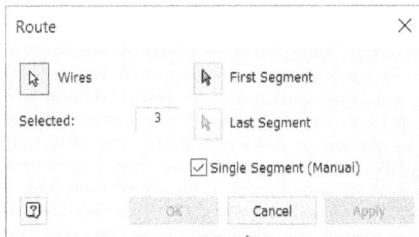

4. Select a single segment.

5. Click Apply to route the wires through the segment.

Tip: You can continue to route the same wires through additional segments, one at a time. The segments can be discontinuous and can be used for incremental routing to create networks with gaps.

Procedure: Manual Routing - Select Segments

The following steps give an overview of how to manually route wires by selecting the start and ending segments.

1. Start the Route tool. In the Route dialog box, ensure that the Wires button is selected (default). Be sure the Single Segment (Manual) check box is not selected.

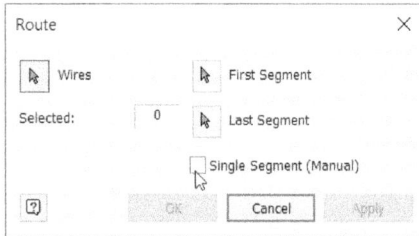

2. Select the wire or wires that you want to route.

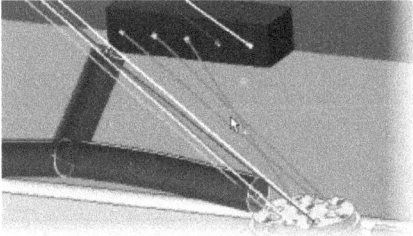

3. In the Route dialog box, select First Segment.

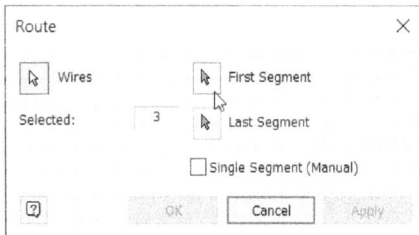

4. Select the starting segment for the wire routing.

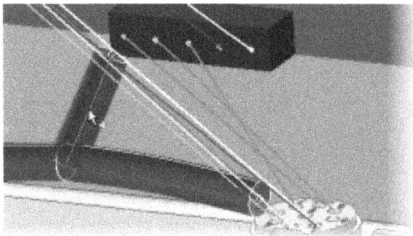

5. In the Route dialog box, select Last Segment (default).

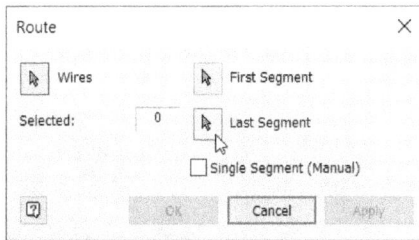

6. Select the ending segment for the wire routing.

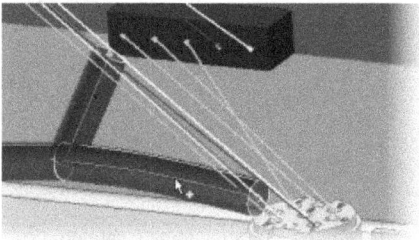

7. Click Apply to route the wires through the continuous segments that connect the selected segments in the network. The segment diameter and wire length are calculated automatically.

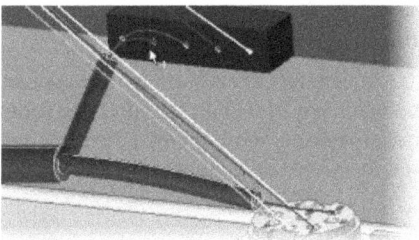

Automatic Routing

Use automatic routing to route one or more selected wires into segments based on the shortest path through the network, and the segment opening that is closest to the wire start point and endpoint.

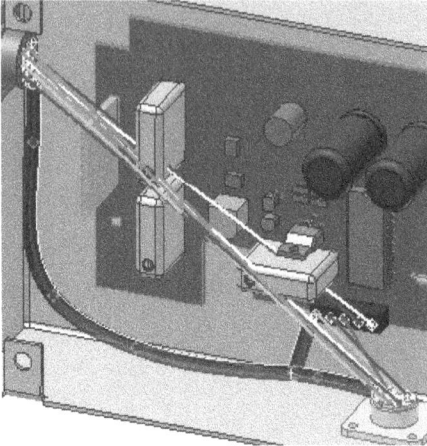

Wires and segments before automatic routing

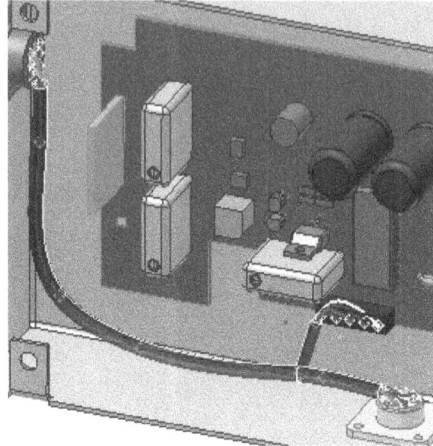

After automatic routing

You can automatically route all unrouted wires or selected wires.

When you automatically route wires, the system checks for the closest harness segment ends to each end of the wire. When the segment ends are identified, the system examines all segments found, looks for the shortest path, and then routes the wires.

If the harness segment endpoints are within 0.5 millimeters of each other, they are considered to be the same distance. If there is no connection between any identified start and end segment points, such as when the endpoints are from different harness segments or when the same segment point is identified for both the start point and endpoint, the route fails. In these cases, you can route the wires manually.

Access

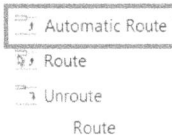

Ribbon: Cable and Harness tab>Route panel

Procedure: Automatic Routing

The following steps give an overview of how to automatically route wires through segments in your assembly.

1. Start the Automatic Route tool. In the Auto Route dialog box, select Wires to select individual wires, or select the All Unrouted Wires check box to select all unrouted wires in the assembly.

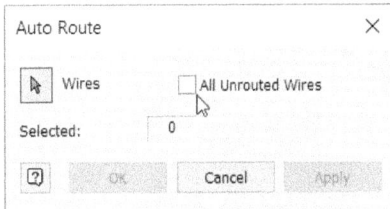

2. If required, select individual wires for routing.

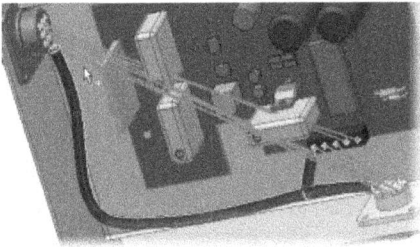

3. Click Apply to route all selected wires automatically through the nearest segment paths.

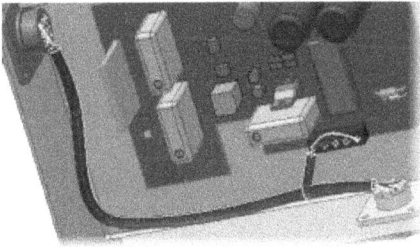

View Path Tool

In a complex assembly, wire paths are not always easy to see. The View Path tool displays the path of a selected wire or wires through all routed segments.

The following figure shows the path of a wire through a segment.

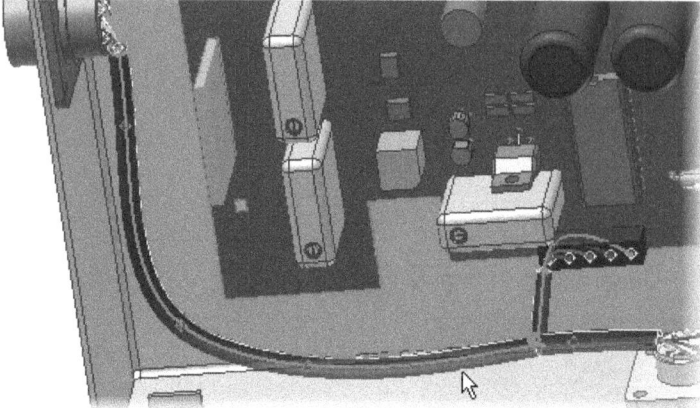

Highlighting a Wire Path

To highlight all of the segments that a routed wire passes through, right-click on the wire and select View Path. The segments remain highlighted until the next command operation.

The following figures show the View Path operation and results.

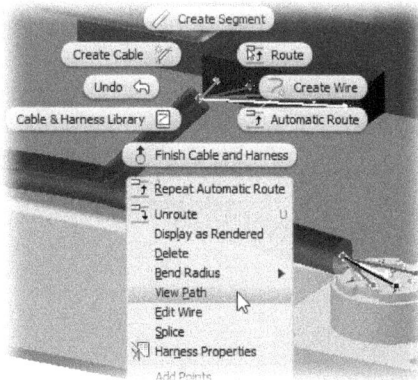

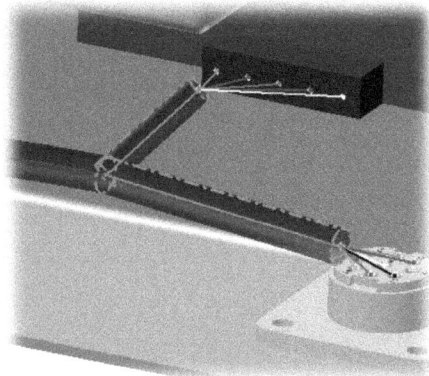

Unrouting Wires and Cables

When routing wire and cables into segments, you sometimes need to change the path of a wire. This requires that you unroute a wire, or wires, from a segment.

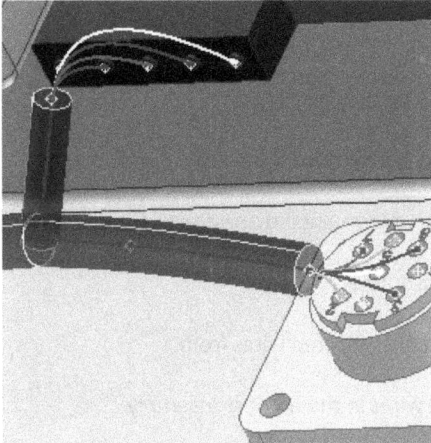
Before unrouting

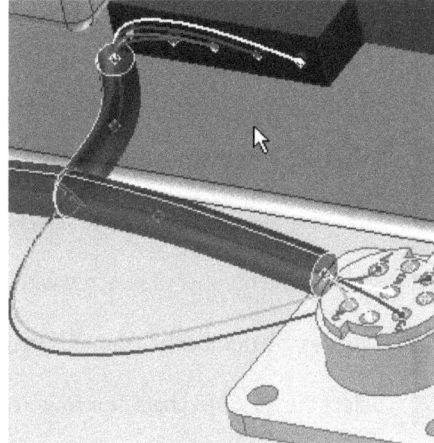
After unrouting

Access

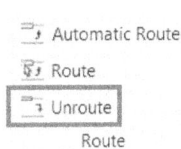

Ribbon: Cable and Harness tab>Route panel

Keyboard: U

Unroute Tool Options

You use the Unroute tool to unroute one, some, or all wires from a segment.

You can unroute:

- Selected wires from all segments (default).
- Selected wires from selected segments.
- All wires from selected segments.
- All wires from all segments.

> When the last wire is unrouted from a segment that is set to calculate size from wires, the segment diameter remains the same as its diameter with the last wire. When you unroute all wires at once, the current segment is not resized.

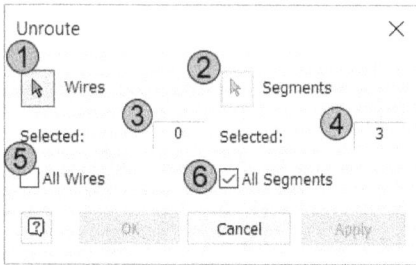

① Select the Wires button to select individual wires for unrouting.

② Select the Segments button to select individual segments to unroute the selected wires from.

③ Displays the number of selected wires for unrouting.

④ Displays the number of segments to unroute the selected wires from.

⑤ Select the All Wires check box to unroute all wires in the harness assembly.

⑥ Select the All Segments check box to unroute the selected wires from all segments in the harness assembly.

Procedure: Unrouting Wires and Cables

The following steps give an overview of how to unroute wires and cables.

1. Start the Unroute tool. Select the Wires button to select individual wires, or select the All Wires check box to select all wires in the active harness assembly.

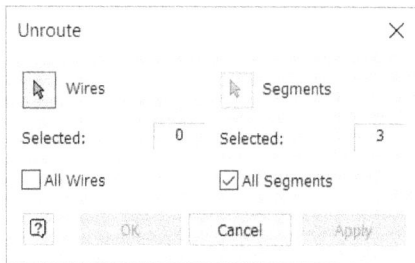

2. Select the wires to be unrouted in the drawing.

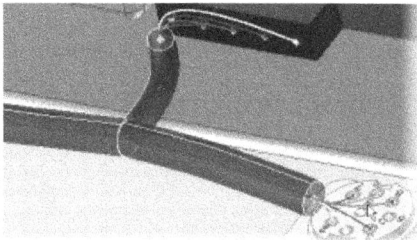

3. Select the Segments button to select individual segments to unroute the wires from, or select the All Segments check box to remove the wire routing from all segments.

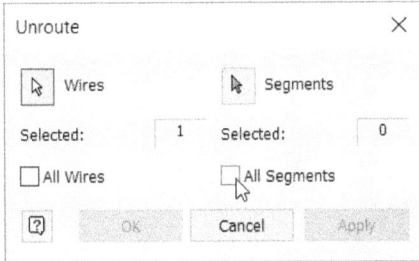

4. Select the segments to remove the wire routings from.

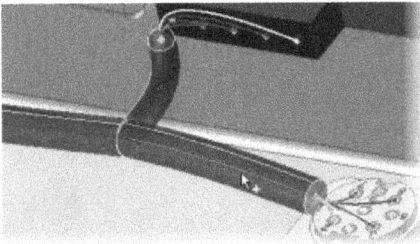

5. Click OK or Apply to unroute the wires from the selected segments.

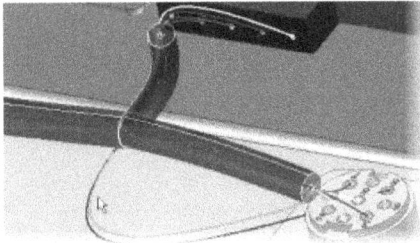

Exercise: Route Wires and Cables

In this exercise, you will route wires through an assembly. You will create segments, automatically route wires, unroute wires, and manually route wires into segments.

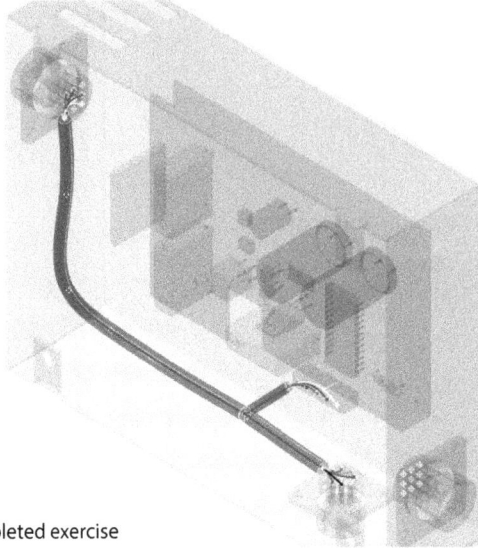

The completed exercise

Create Segments

In this portion of the exercise, you will prepare to route wires through an assembly. You will create a segment and a branch for the wire routings.

1. Open *Enclosure_Assembly_Routing.iam*. Note that the wires have interferences with components on the printed circuit board.

   Reorient the model as shown in the following figure.

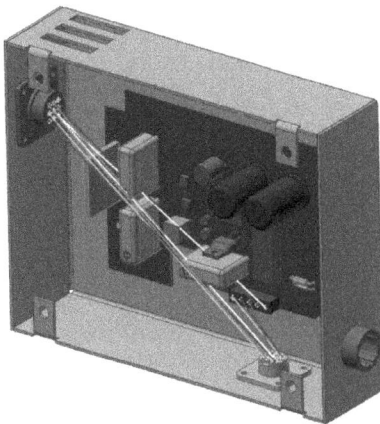

2. In the Browser, right-click on Harness1 and click Edit.

3. In the Cable and Harness tab, in the Create panel, click Create Segment.

4. In the graphics window, with the offset set to 2.54mm, select a point on the face of the blue connector, 360575:1.

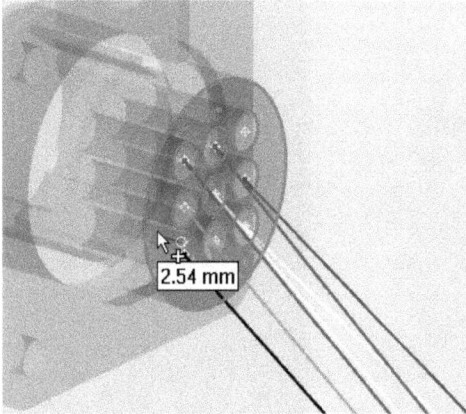

5. Right-click on the graphics window and click Edit Offset.

6. In Edit Offset dialog box, for Offset Distance, enter **12.00mm**. Click OK.

7. In the graphics window, select a point on the same enclosure face as the blue connector, about 1/4 of the distance from the connector to the enclosure corner.

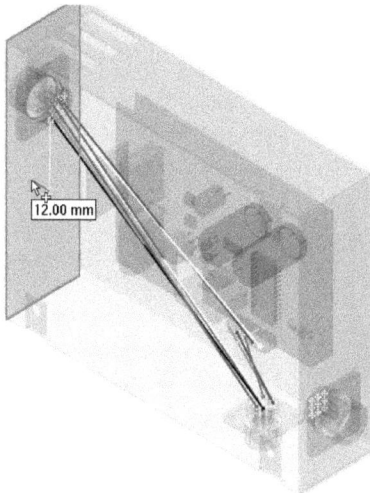

8. Select a second point on the same face about 3/4 of the distance from the connector to the enclosure corner.

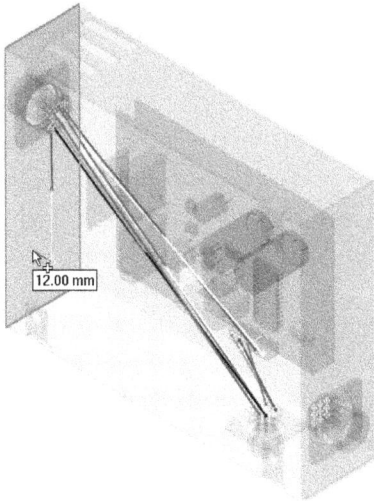

9. Select a point on the same enclosure face as the yellow connector, 360124:1, about 1/4 of the distance from the enclosure corner to the connector.

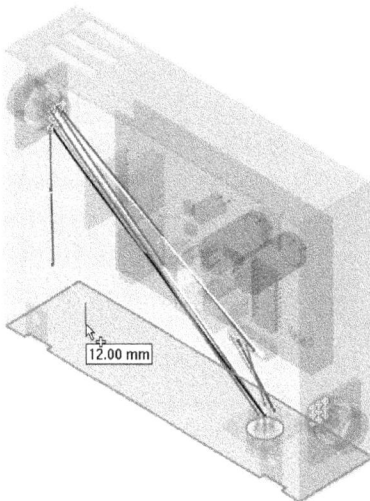

10. Select a second point on the same face about 3/4 of the distance from the enclosure corner to the connector.

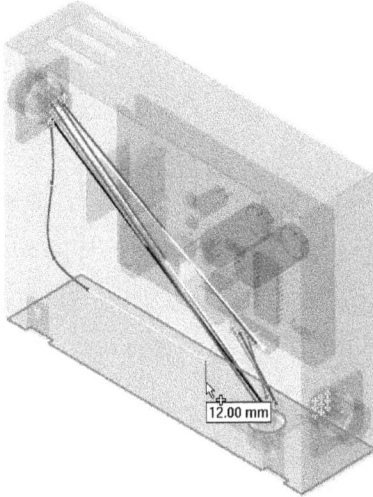

11. Right-click on the graphics window and click Edit Offset.

12. In the Edit Offset dialog box, for Offset Distance, enter **2.54mm**. Click OK.

13. Select a point on the face of the yellow connector, 360124:1.

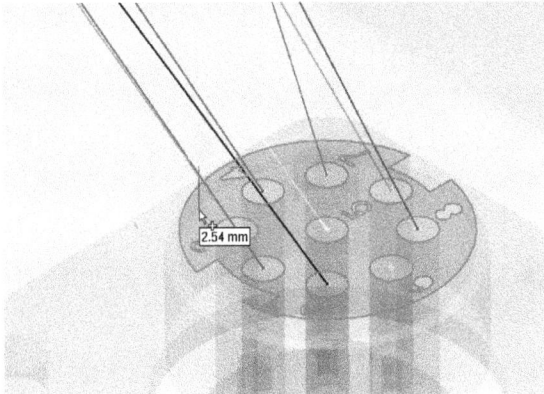

14. Right-click in the graphics window and click Finish.

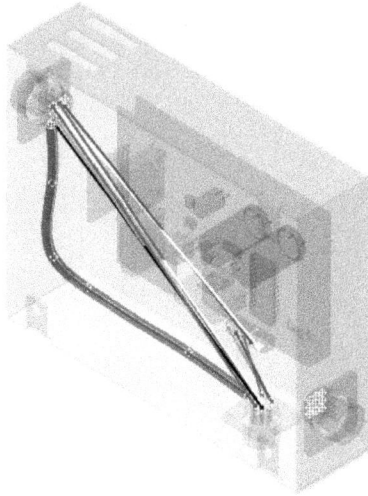

15. In the Cable and Harness tab, in the Create panel, click Create Segment.

16. In the graphics window, on the existing segment, select the work point closest to the yellow connector.

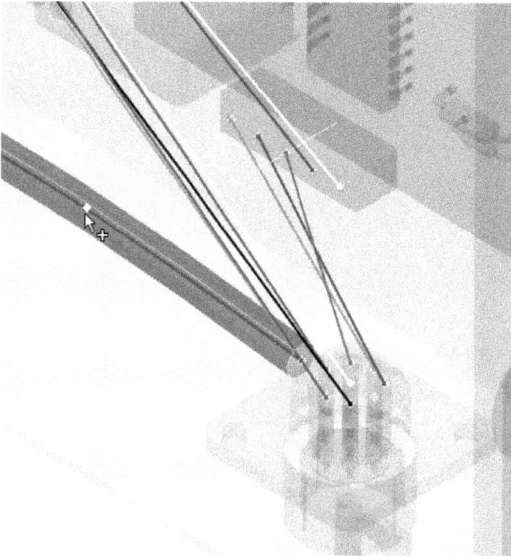

17. With the offset set to 2.54mm, select an ending point for the branch on the face of the terminal bar. Locate the point in the lower left corner of the face.

18. Right-click in the graphics window and click Finish.

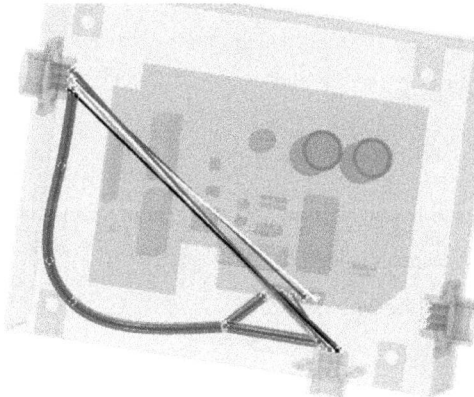

Route Wires

In this portion of the exercise, you automatically route all wires. Then, you unroute a wire and manually route it into a different segment.

1. On the Cable and Harness tab, on the Route panel, click Automatic Route.

2. In the Auto Route dialog box, click All Unrouted Wires. Click OK.

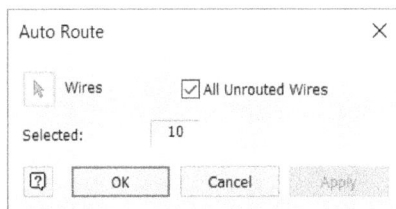

3. Zoom into the terminal bar and the yellow connector. Note that the white wire is automatically routed to the closest segment end. This should be routed into the branch with the other wires from the terminal bar. If the white wire routed correctly through the segment, you would not need to reroute it. To practice unrouting and rerouting, continue with the exercise regardless if it was automatically done correctly.

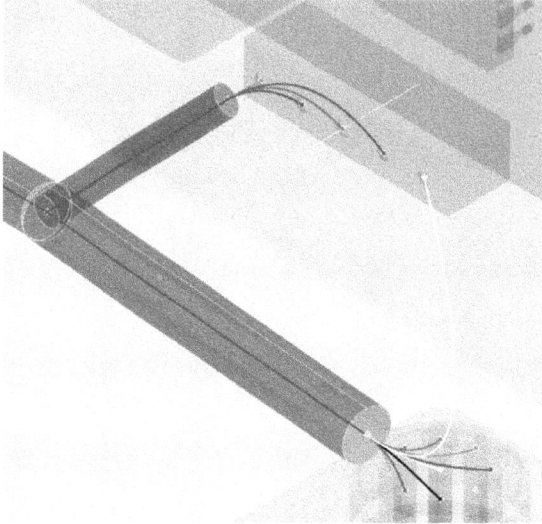

4. To reroute the white wire, in the Cable and Harness tab, in the Route panel, click Unroute.

5. In the Unroute dialog box, ensure Wires is selected.

6. In the graphics window, select the white wire.

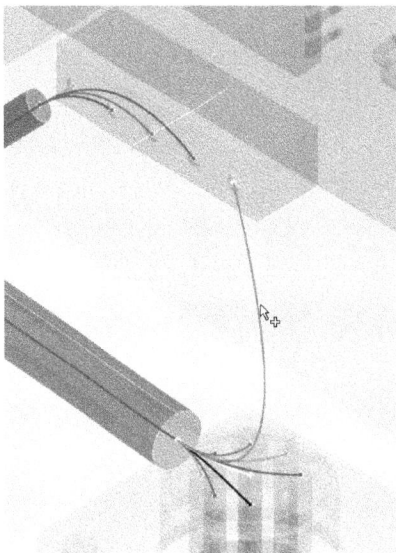

7. In the Unroute dialog box, click OK.

8. To manually route the white wire, in the Cable and Harness tab, in the Route panel, click Route.

9. In the Route dialog box, ensure Wires is selected.

10. In the graphics window, select the white wire.

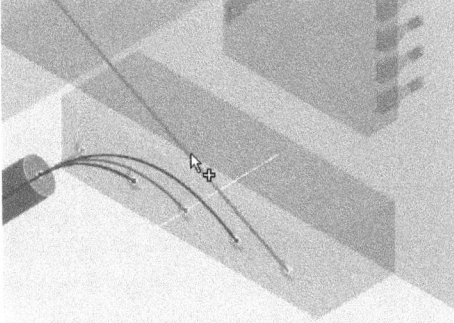

11. In the Route dialog box, select First Segment.

12. In the graphics window, select the segment branch nearest the terminal block.

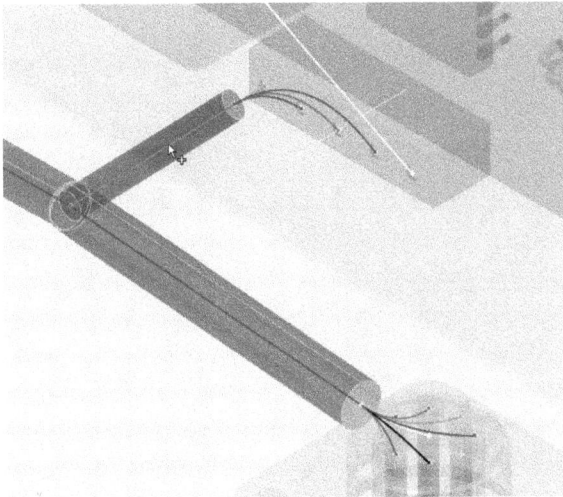

13. For the second segment, select the segment closest to the blue connector.

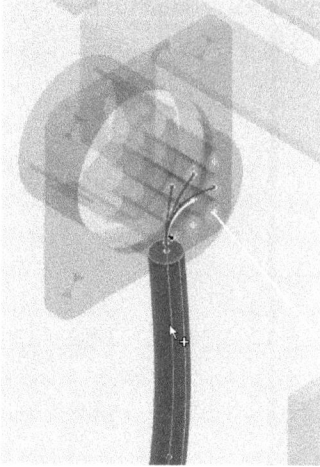

14. In the Route dialog box, click OK. The white wire is routed through the branch segment.

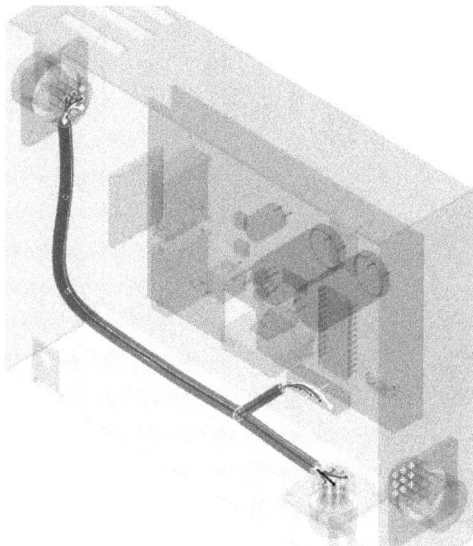

15. Close all files without saving changes.

Lesson: Importing Wire and Cable Data

In this lesson, you learn how to import harness data from an external file, correcting errors during the import process.

Many companies use software programs specifically for the design of electrical schematics and diagrams. Instead of creating each wire or cable individually, you can export design data from these programs and import it into an assembly using wire list data, automatically connecting to the electrical components in the assembly. This reduces design time and translation errors.

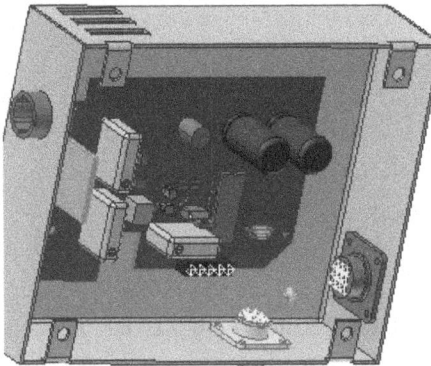

Assembly before importing wires

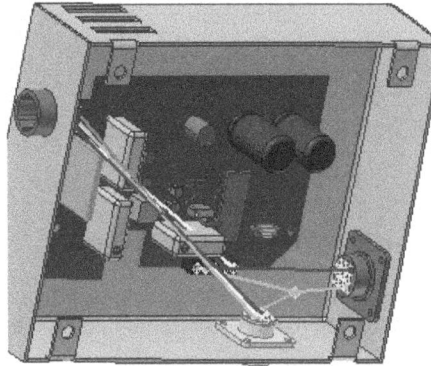

Assembly after importing wires

Objectives

After completing this lesson, you will be able to:

- Import wire and cable data.
- Review wire and cable data for issues prior to importing the data.
- Correct identified issues to successfully import wire and cable data.

Importing Wire and Cable Data

To import wire and cable data into your assembly, you need to know the methods and tools available for importing harness data files.

The following figures show examples of harness data files.

	WireListImport.csv							
	A	B	C	D	E	F	G	H
1	2201	3053-ORG		U3	1	U7	7	
2	2202	3053-WHT		U7	2	J12	4	
3	2203	3053-RED		U7	4	J12	5	
4	2204	3053-YEL		U7	9	U3	3	
5	2205	3053/1-BLK		U3	7	U7	5	
6	2206	3053/1-GRN		U3	8	U7	3	
7	2207	3053/1-BLU		U7	6	U3	4	

Import wire list: CSV format

```
<?xml version="1.0" encoding="UTF-16"
 - <HarnessData Context="C:\Inventor D
   - <Harness Name="Harness1" FullFileNa
     Harness\Enclosure_Assembly.H
     <PropertyDefinition Name="FAMILY"
     <PropertyDefinition Name="WDBLKN
   - <Library FullFileName="C:\Program
     Harness\Cable&HarnessDefaul
     <PropertyDefinition Name="Color"
     <PropertyDefinition Name="Insula
     <PropertyDefinition Name="Insula
     <PropertyDefinition Name="SAE
```

Import wire list: XML format

Importing Wire and Cable Data

Wire lists can be imported into Autodesk® Inventor® using two formats, either XML or CSV. Import files can be created manually or generated by other applications, such as AutoCAD® Electrical.

If the CSV file format is used, it must also be accompanied with a CFG or configuration file. If the XML file format is used, the configuration information is included with the file format. XML formatted files can also contain additional property data and can generate virtual parts.

During the import process, the software displays the import status in the Imported Harness Data dialog box. A log file is created containing the details of the import. Once imported, the data set automatically creates and connects wires and cable wires in the harness assembly. Existing wire and cable occurrence properties are not updated or changed during the import process.

> You can verify electrical part data prior to importing the harness data file using the Review Harness Data tool to create a report of all the electrical parts defined in the data file. Use this list to make corrections and insert missing parts.

> Neither XML nor CSV import files provide enough information to create and place electrical parts and splices in the harness assembly. For success with the import, these objects must already exist in the harness assembly.

Access

Report   Check Bend Radius
Import   Library   Nailboard
Harness Data
Manage

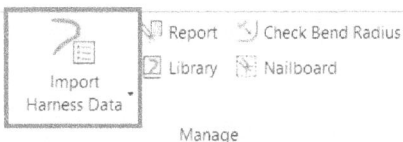

Ribbon: Cable and Harness tab>Manage panel>
Harness Data drop-down

Process: Importing Wire and Cable Data

The following figure shows an overview of importing wire and cable data from wire lists.

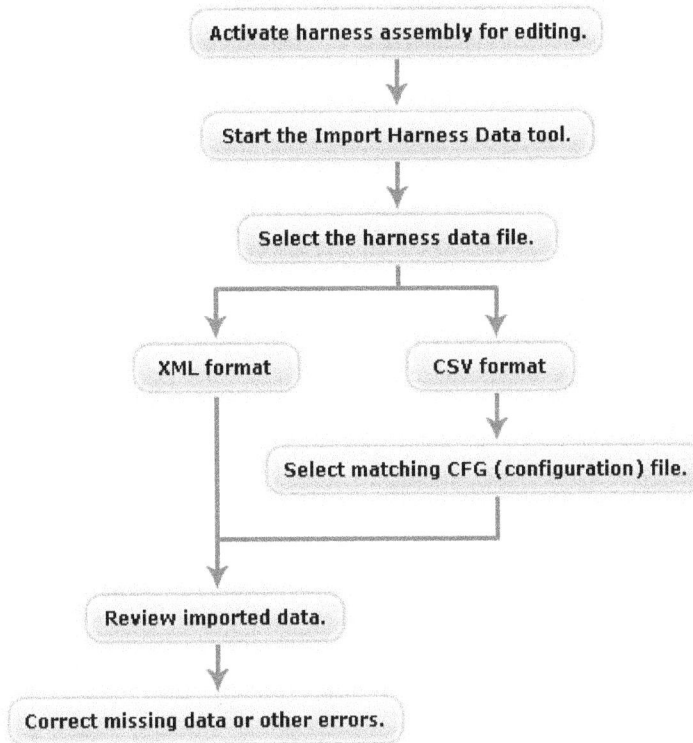

Guidelines

Use the following guidelines to ensure a successful import of wire lists.

- Electrical parts and splices must already exist in the assembly before importing wire lists.
- Reference designators must be assigned to the assembly components, and must match the appropriate components in the harness data file.
- Wire types listed in the harness data file must exist in the Cable & Harness Library.
- All wires must have a unique ID code (wire number) assigned to them.

Reviewing Data Before Import

You can review a harness data file before importing the file into a harness assembly. Using this method, you can locate potential errors before they occur during the import process.

The following figure shows an example of a harness data file open for review before importing.

RefDes	Part Number	Vendor	Circuits	Description
X1	3601243		9	AMP 3
X2	3605752		9	AMP
X3			5	
X4			3	
SP1			2	

Review Harness Data

The **Review Harness Data** tool creates a list of all electrical parts and electrical part properties included in the harness data file you want to import. Error conditions display for any part that does not have a RefDes in the active harness assembly. Use this list to check for and correct missing RefDes information and to verify that the required electrical parts exist in the harness assembly before importing the file.

You can filter the list to display only connectors, only splices, or all items. You can also copy the report to the Microsoft Windows clipboard, where you can paste the report data into other applications.

The following figure shows the Review Harness Data dialog box listing both verified electrical parts and parts in an error state that need editing or creation.

RefDes	Part Number	Vendor	Circuits	Description	Stock Number
X1	3601243		9	AMP 3	
X2	3605752		9	AMP	
X3			5		
! X4			3		
SP1			2		

Access

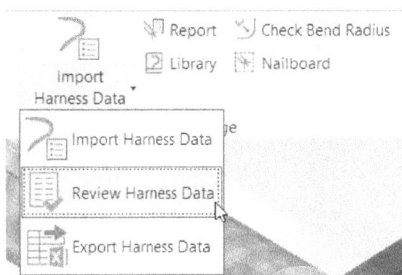

Ribbon: Cable and Harness tab>Manage panel> Harness Data drop-down

Procedure: Reviewing Data Before Import

The following steps give you an overview of how to review the harness data file information before importing the data.

1. Activate the harness for editing. Start the Review Harness Data tool.

2. Browse to the harness data file to be imported.

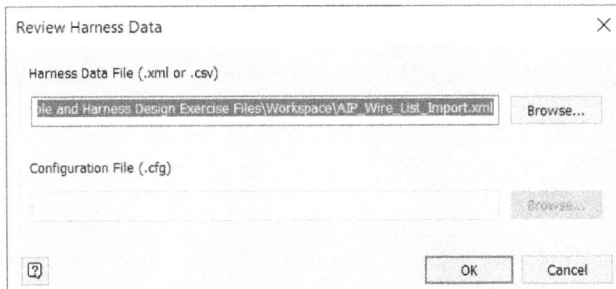

3. As required, filter the harness data information.

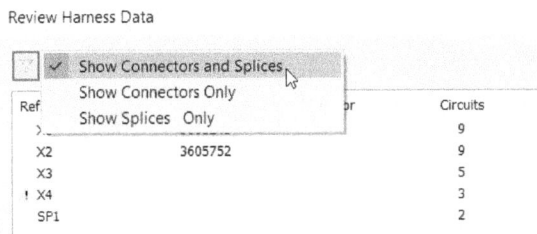

4. If appropriate, copy the information to the Windows Clipboard for further processing.

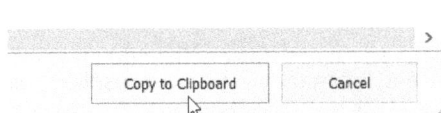

Correcting Import Issues

Imported harness data is often incomplete or incorrect. Sometimes data required to complete a harness definition in a 3D environment is missing. To complete the harness definition, you need to correct these errors.

The following figure shows the Imported Harness Data dialog box displaying the results of importing a harness data file that includes errors.

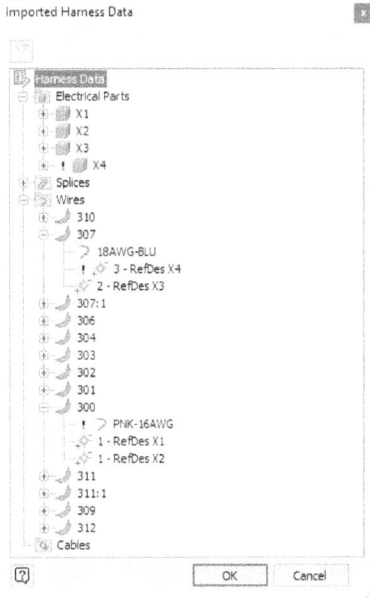

Correct Import Issues

You use the Import Harness Data tool to import a harness data file. After importing the harness data file, the Imported Harness Data dialog box opens, listing the electrical parts, splices, wires, and cable information defined in the harness data file. You use this dialog box to:

- View the imported data.
- Identify and correct any issues with the data.
- Add additional information to provide a complete definition.

The recommended way to correct any error conditions is to view the issue description and solutions, and then perform the recommended action. The usual corrective action is to create a reference from the imported data to definitions in the Cable & Harness library, or to electrical parts in the 3D model.

> Electrical parts and pins and their RefDes must exist in the assembly prior to importing harness data.

> Use the Review Harness Data tool to review and verify the existence of electrical parts and pins and their RefDes before importing the harness data file.

Options for Correcting Import Harness Data

In the Imported Harness Data dialog box, right-click on the error condition icon to display options for viewing error details and repair options. Different options are available for each of the four different imported data types, electrical parts, splices, wires, and cables.

The following figure shows the main options available for correcting an electrical part.

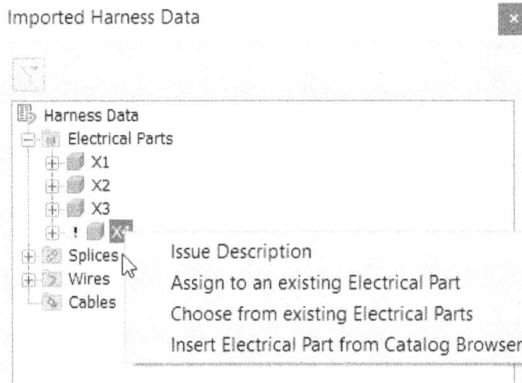

Option	Description
Issue Description	Describes the cause of the issue and how to correct it.
Assign to an existing Electrical Part	Displays the Select Electrical Part dialog box to assign the imported RefDes to an electrical part in the assembly. Only electrical parts that do not have a RefDes assigned to them are available.
Choose from existing Electrical Parts	Displays the Select Electrical Part dialog box to assign the RefDes of an existing electrical part to the imported electrical part.
Insert Electrical Part from Catalog Browser	Enables you to insert an electrical part from an installed catalog so that it can be assigned to the imported RefDes.

The following figure shows the main options available for correcting a wire.

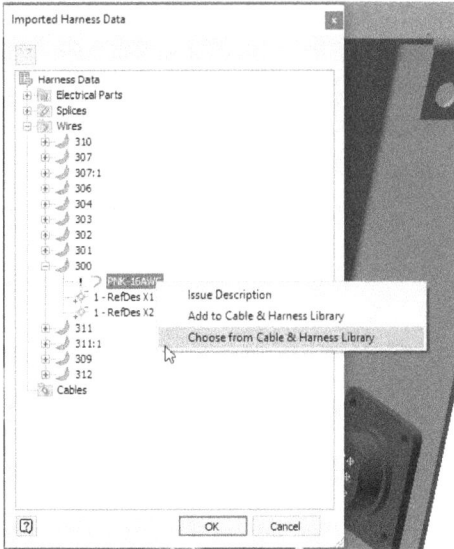

Option	Description
Issue Description	Describes the cause of the issue and how to correct it.
Add to Cable & Harness Library	Displays the Cable & Harness Library dialog box to add the imported wire definition to the library.
Choose from Cable & Harness Library	Displays the Cable & Harness Library dialog box to choose a wire definition from the library to replace the imported wire.

Process: Correcting Import Issues

The following steps give an overview of how to correct issues when importing a harness data file.

Exercise: Import Wire and Cable Data

In this exercise, you will import a harness data file. You will complete the following tasks:

- Import a harness data file.
- Assign a RefDes to an existing electrical part.
- Select a wire definition from the Cable & Harness library.

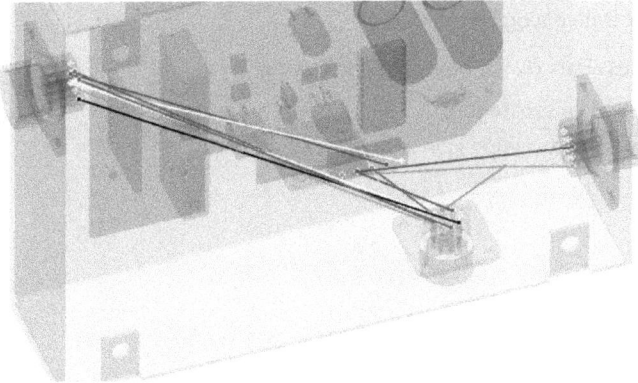

The completed exercise

1. Open *Enclosure_Assembly_Import.iam*.

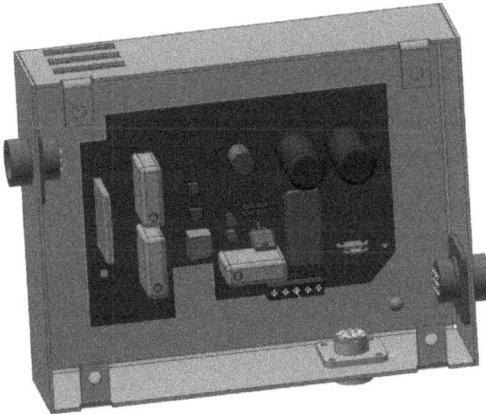

2. In the Browser, right-click on Enclosure_Assembly_Import.Harness1 and click Edit.

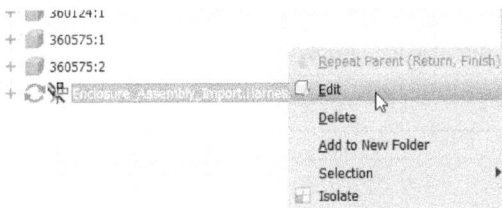

3. In the Cable and Harness tab, in the Manage panel, click Import Harness Data.

4. In the Import Harness Data dialog box, for Harness Data File, click Browse.

5. In the Select Wire List Data File dialog box, do the following,

- Browse to the Workspace folder.
- Select *AIP_Wire_List_Import.xml*.
- Click Open.

6. In the Import Harness Data dialog box, click OK.

7. In the Imported Harness Data dialog box, do the following:

- Expand the Electrical Parts category.
- Right-click on the error condition icon in front of X4.
- Click Issue Description.

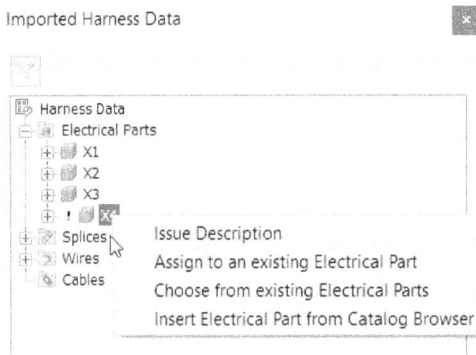

8. The issue description and suggested corrective action display.

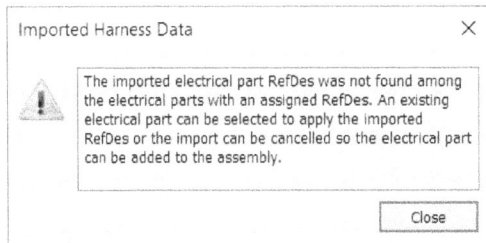

9. In the Imported Harness Data dialog box, click Close.

10. In the Imported Harness Data dialog box, do the following:

- Right-click on the error condition icon in front of X4.
- Click Assign to an existing Electrical Part.

11. In the Select Electrical Part dialog box, verify that Electrical Part is selected.

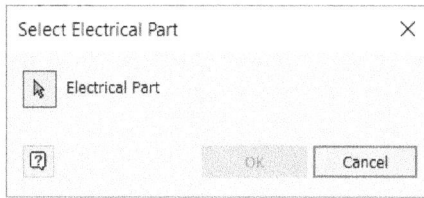

12. In the graphics window, select the blue connector, 360575:2, on the right face of the enclosure.

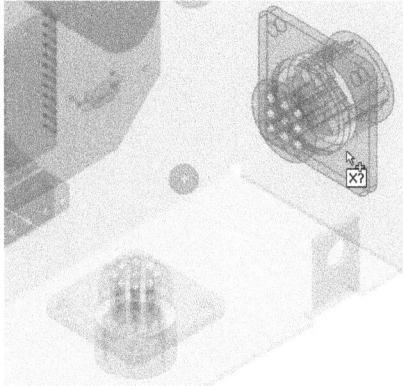

13. In the Select Electrical Part dialog box, click OK.

14. In the Imported Harness Data dialog box, do the following:

- Expand the Wires category.
- Expand wire number 300.
- Right-click on the error condition icon in front of PNK-16AWG and click Choose from Cable & Harness Library.

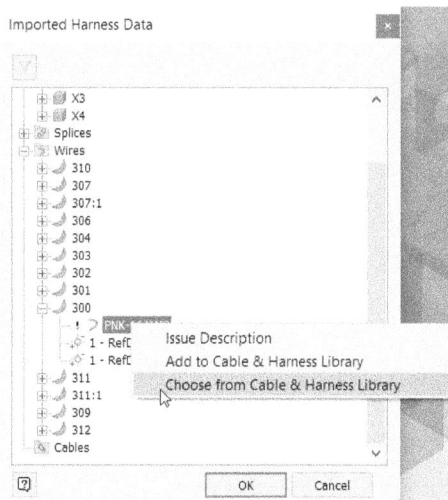

15. In the Cable & Harness Library dialog box, do the following:

- Expand the Generic category.
- Select 16AWG-RED.
- Click OK.

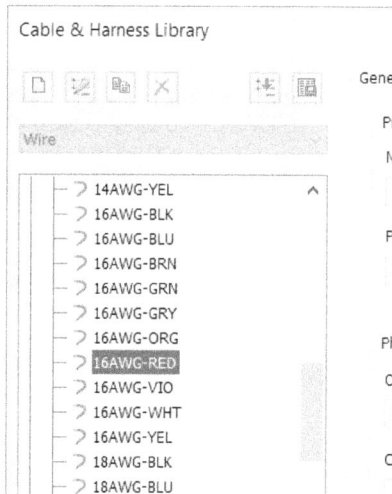

16. In the Imported Harness Data dialog box, click OK.

17. In the Imported Harness Data dialog box, click Close.

The import process is completed and the wire definitions from the harness data file are imported and connected to the appropriate electrical parts and pins.

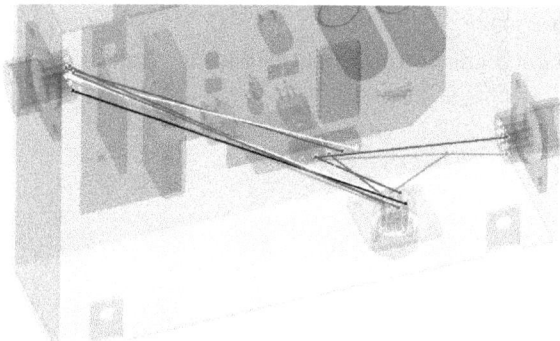

18. Close all files without saving changes.

Lesson: Adding Ribbon Cables

This lesson describes the creation of ribbon cables in a harness assembly between electrical connectors.

Ribbon cables are used frequently in electronic and other applications in which multiple wires run between connectors and enclosure space is limited.

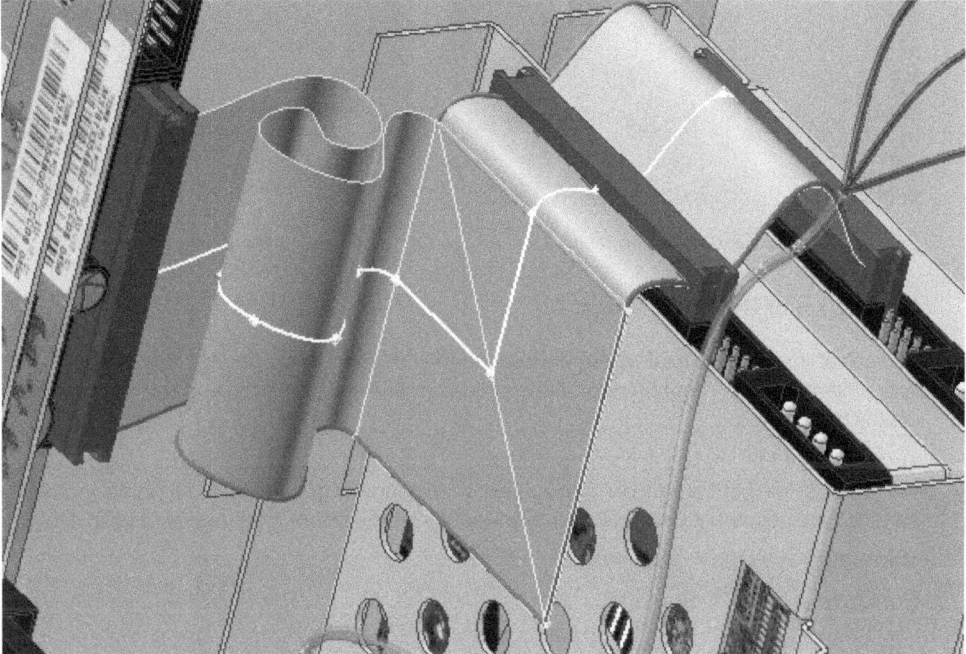

Ribbon cable between three connectors

Objectives

After completing this lesson, you will be able to:

- Describe the characteristics and use of ribbon cables.
- Add ribbon cables to a harness assembly.
- Add a fold to a ribbon cable.
- Change the twist of a ribbon cable.
- Control the global property and display settings for ribbon cables.

About Ribbon Cables

Ribbon cables are frequently found in electronic assemblies. To work with ribbon cables, you need to know what they are and how they are defined.

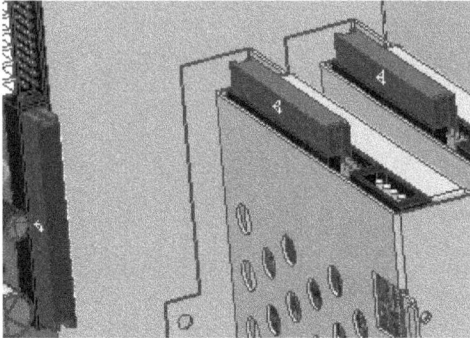

Before adding ribbon cable

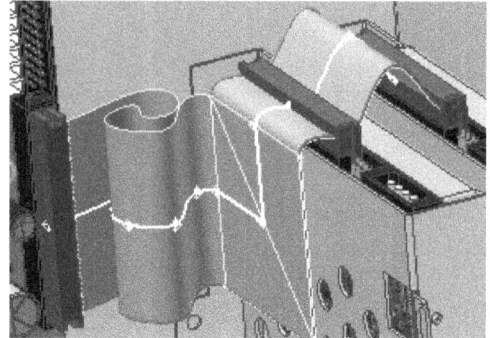

After adding ribbon cable

Definition of Ribbon Cables

Ribbon cables are a group of wires bundled together in a flat, single-level configuration. Ribbon cables in their simplest form contain two points, one on a starting connector, and the other on an ending connector.

You can add additional work points and folds to further define and control the shape and direction of the ribbon cable path around or through existing assembly geometry. Work points are offset from existing face geometry. Once created, work points on the ribbon path are used to add folds.

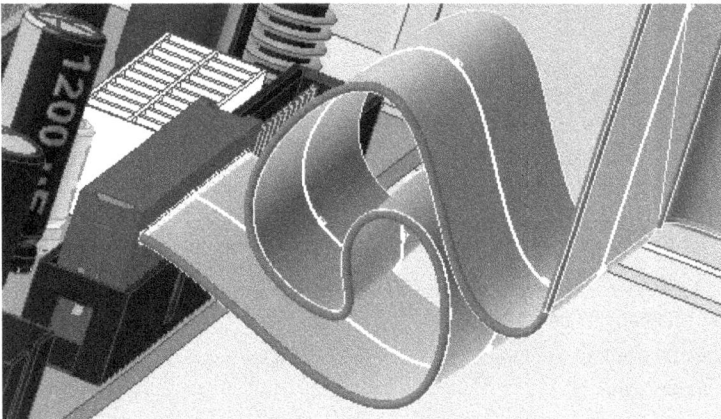

Example of a Ribbon Cable

Electronic equipment such as computers frequently uses ribbon cables to connect between the motherboard and other devices, including hard drives and CD drives within the computer case. The narrow form of the connector is easiest to fit into the tightly organized circuit board.

Adding Ribbon Cables

Ribbon cables are commonly used in some types of electrical designs. To add ribbon cables to your assembly, you need to know where the tools are located and the methods available for ribbon cable creation.

The following figure shows a ribbon cable running between two hard drives in a computer.

Access

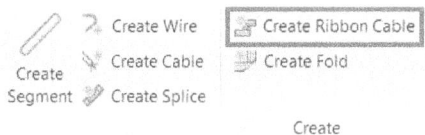

Ribbon: Cable and Harness tab>Create panel

Create Ribbon Cable

A ribbon cable links two ribbon cable connectors together with a flat wire bundle, called a ribbon. Between the starting and ending connectors you can add additional work points to manipulate the path of the ribbon cable through the assembly.

To add additional connectors to a ribbon cable, route the cable through the connector using work points. The additional connector or connectors are not recognized as part of the ribbon cable assembly, and do not have any connectivity to the ribbon cable.

Ribbon cable creation options are controlled by the Create Ribbon Cable dialog box.

① Click button to select the start connector.

② Set the starting pin number on the start connector.

③ Click to align the orientation of the wire connections to the start connector pins.

④ Click to toggle the outward direction of the ribbon cable from the start connector.

⑤ Click button to select the end connector.

⑥ Set the starting pin number on the end connector.

⑦ Click to align the orientation of the wire connections to the end connector pins.

⑧ Click to toggle the outward direction of the ribbon cable from the end connector.

⑨ Enter ribbon cable properties such as ID, Category, and Name.

You can create work points within the assembly before creating the ribbon cable, to precisely position the ribbon cable to key points in the assembly.

Only connectors authored as ribbon cable connectors can be selected when creating ribbon cables. Other types of connectors cannot be selected.

Procedure: Adding Ribbon Cables

The following steps give an overview of how to add a ribbon cable to your assembly.

1. Activate a harness. Start the Create Ribbon Cable tool.

2. Select the start connector.

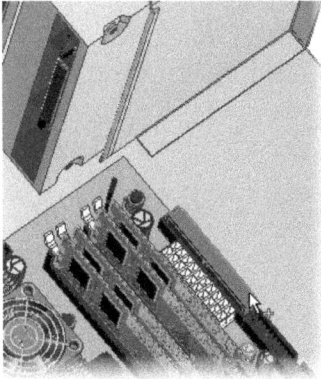

3. Select the end connector.

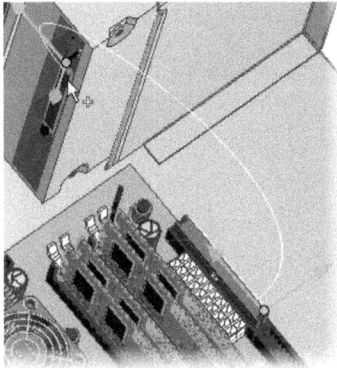

4. If required, change the cable direction.

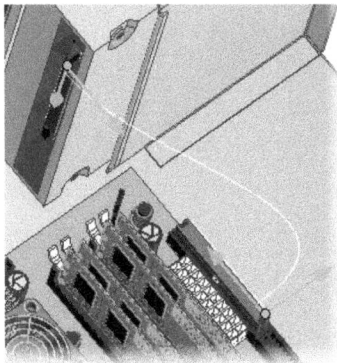

5. Specify the ribbon cable. Click OK.

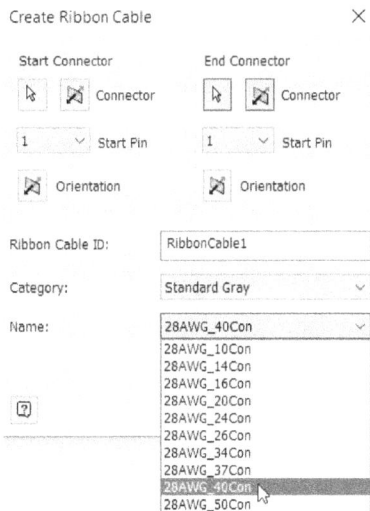

6. Route the ribbon cable.

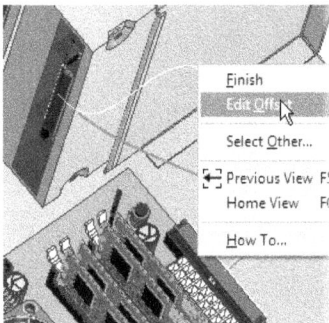

7. Finish the placement of the ribbon cable. Changes to the position of the cable can be made as required once it is placed to relocate it, if required.

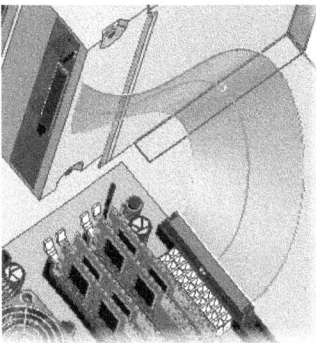

Adding a Fold

To set the direction of the path that a ribbon cable takes through the harness assembly, you can add single or double 90-degree folds at work points that exist along the ribbon cable path. To create folds, you need to know the tools and methods available for fold creation.

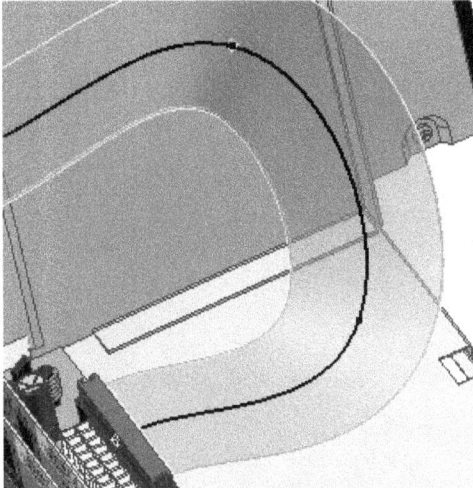
Ribbon cable before adding fold

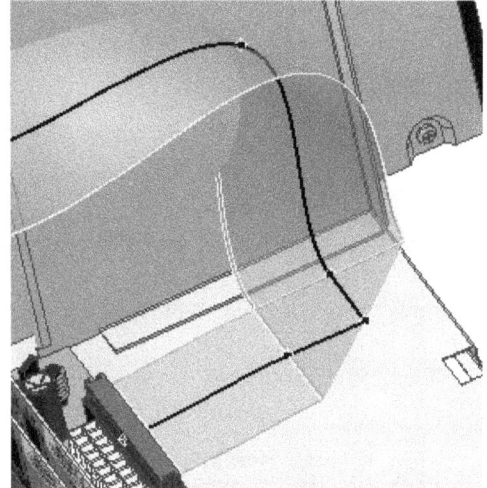
Ribbon cable after adding fold

Access

Ribbon: Cable and Harness tab>Create panel

Context menu: Create Fold

Create Fold

The Create Fold command is available in the ribbon's Create panel, or the shortcut menu when you right-click on a work point on the sweep path.

When you create a fold, the point you select for it is changed from a normal work point to a fold point. It also truncates the original path spline to the start of the fold and creates a new ribbon cable portion from the end of the fold to the other connector. Each of the involved entities (the original ribbon portion, the fold, and the new ribbon cable portion) has a node displayed in the Browser tree.

The default orientation of the fold is from the start connector pointing in the direction of the next work point on the path. Directional arrows display in the graphics window to guide your selections.

You can realign the fold using the two alignment buttons on the dialog box, and repeat the alignment as many times as required. No constraint is established by the alignment, and the fold is not associative with any of the faces you select during the alignment process.

You select between a single or double fold. The single fold folds back over itself at a 90 degree angle. The double fold first folds back 180 degrees onto itself before folding onto itself again at a 90 degree angle.

The options available for creating a fold are controlled by the Create Fold dialog box.

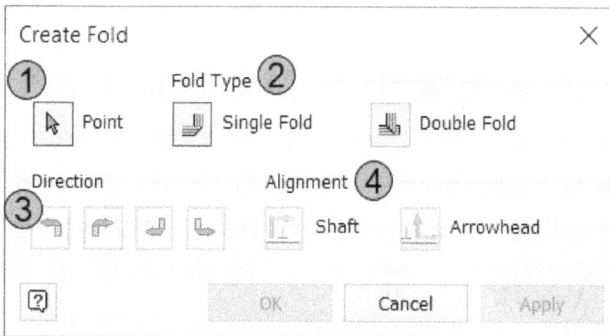

① Click to select the work point to use as the fold point.

② Select the type of fold to create, single or double.

③ Sets the direction of the fold. You can set the direction from the start connector to the left or right, or from the end connector to the left or right.

④ Aligns the fold perpendicular to a selected planar face. Select the portion of the arrow to align, and then select the geometry to use.

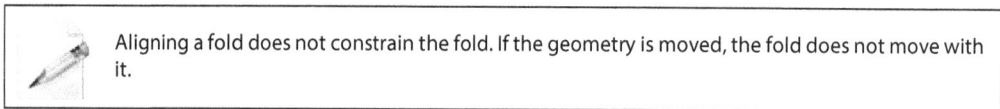

Aligning a fold does not constrain the fold. If the geometry is moved, the fold does not move with it.

Procedure: Adding a Fold to a Ribbon Cable

The following steps give an overview of how to add a fold to a ribbon cable.

1. In an active harness containing a ribbon cable, start the Create Fold tool. Select a work point on the ribbon cable.

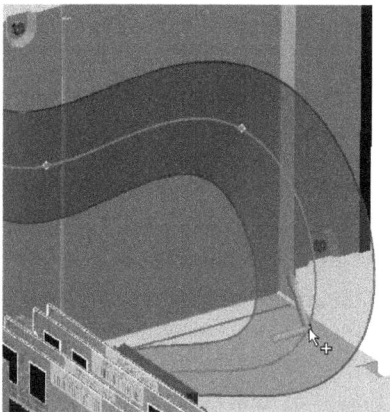

2. In the Create Fold dialog box, define the Fold Type.

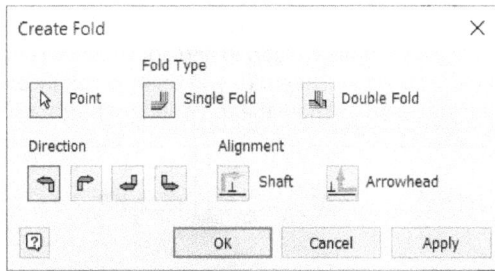

3. Use the Alignment tools to align the fold (Shaft and Arrowhead).

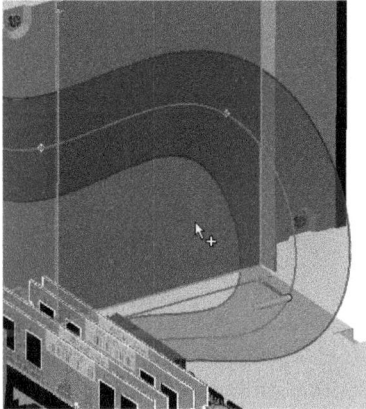

4. Add the fold to the cable.

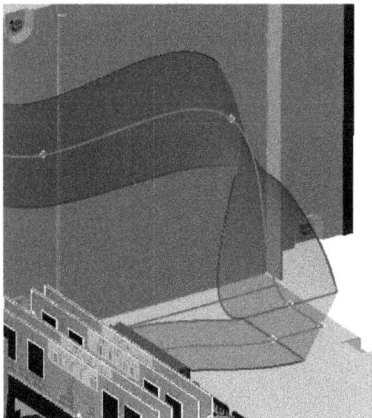

Editing a Twist

When a ribbon cable is created, there is a natural amount of twist added based on the path. As the harness changes, and folds and additional work points are added and adjusted, the twist is affected and may require adjustments to achieve the shape you need. To edit these naturally occurring twists to conform to your design requirements, you need to know the tools and methods available for editing a twist.

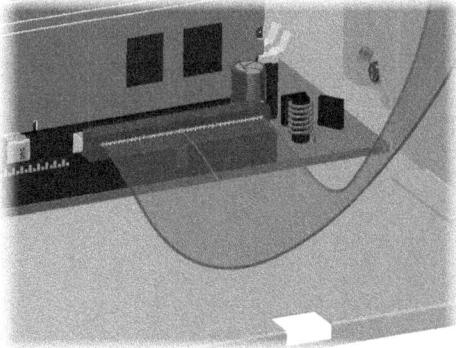

Before editing twist

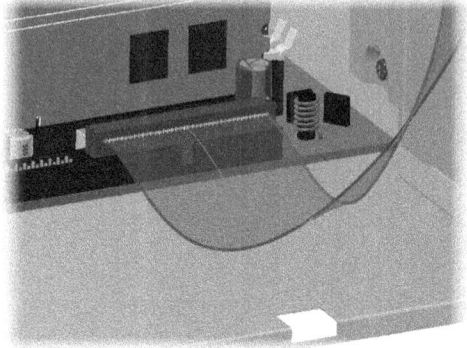

After editing twist

Edit Twist

You use the Edit Twist tool to select a work point on the ribbon cable path and interactively reposition it. You can also enter a specific angle. After you adjust the position of the twist tool and accept the angle, that angle is added to the work point as an internal attribute, and the ribbon cable is swept at the specified angle at that point. This attribute dictates the amount of natural twist the ribbon cable has on either side of the work point.

To remove the explicit angle at that particular point, you must delete the point and create another to replace it. The work points at which you can edit the twist angle are only the normal work points that control the shape of the spline. They are not the work points used for the start or end of a ribbon cable portion or for fold points.

When editing the twist on a ribbon cable, you can click and drag either of the two arrows displayed or right-click on one of the arrows and click Enter Angle. You then enter a precise angle to edit the ribbon twist.

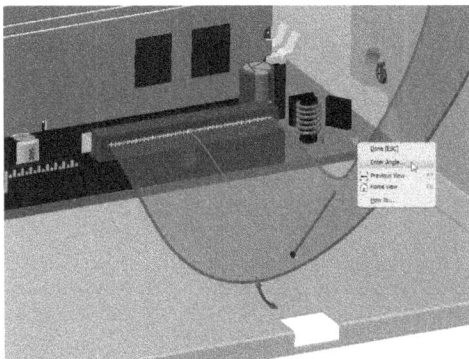

The Edit Twist tool consists of several elements.

Element	Description
Orientation Bar	Shows the surface orientation of the ribbon cable at the current location.
Conductor One Indicator	A sphere on the end of the Orientation Bar that indicates the position of the first conductor on the ribbon cable relative to the Twist Control tool.
Rotation Arrows	Shows the rotation angle possibilities for the ribbon cable, and enables unrestricted rotation around the displayed axis. Click and drag the arrows to rotate the axes. To enter a precise angle, move the cursor over the rotation handle arrow, right-click, and select Enter Angle.

You cannot edit the twist on a work point that represents the start or end of the ribbon cable path, or a fold point. The work point selected must be an ordinary work point.

The Edit Twist tool is unavailable if the sweep cannot be created for the ribbon cable, or if the ribbon cable displays as a centerline.

To resize the Edit Twist tool, use the plus sign (+) and the minus sign (-) keys on the keyboard.

Command Access

To access the Edit Twist tool to add or edit a ribbon cable twist, you right-click on a work point on the ribbon cable path, and select Edit Twist from the shortcut menu.

Procedure: Editing a Twist

The following steps give an overview of how to edit the twist of a work point on a ribbon cable.

1. In an active harness containing a ribbon cable, right-click on a work point on the cable and click Edit Twist.

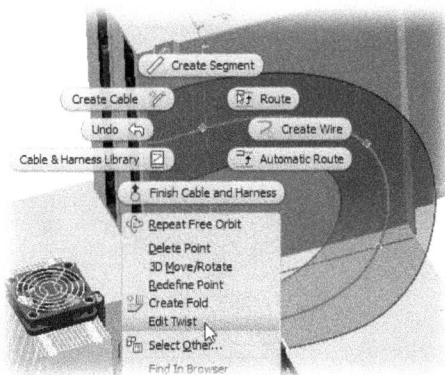

2. Either drag the rotation arrow to a new location or enter a precise twist angle. To enter a precise angle, right-click on the rotation arrow and click Enter Angle.

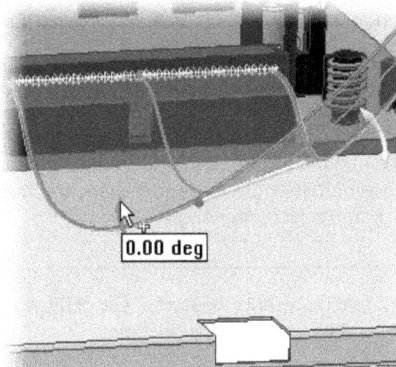

3. Right-click and click Apply.

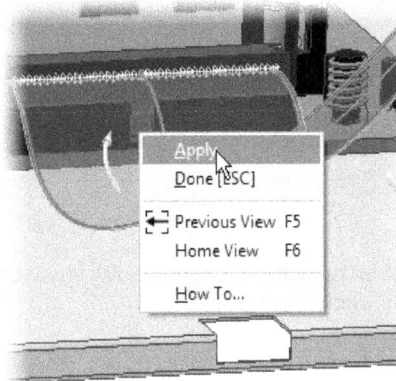

4. The new twist angle is applied to the ribbon cable.

Ribbon Cable Properties

Ribbon cable properties are mostly controlled by settings defined in the Cable and Harness library. Default creation settings are established by the Harness Settings values. In order to create ribbon cables that meet your design requirements, you need to know where these settings are located and how to change them.

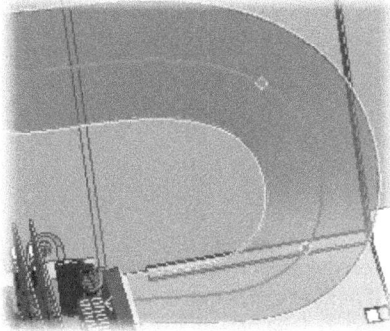

Default ribbon cable

Ribbon cable display changed using library

Harness Settings: Ribbon Cable

Default settings for the creation of a new ribbon cable are determined by the values selected in the Harness Settings dialog box.

Display properties for a ribbon cable are established by the Cable & Harness library selection, and cannot be set at the occurrence level. To change the display of a ribbon cable, edit the cable and select a different ribbon cable definition from the library.

In the Browser, right-click on the harness assembly and click Harness Settings to open the Harness Settings dialog box.

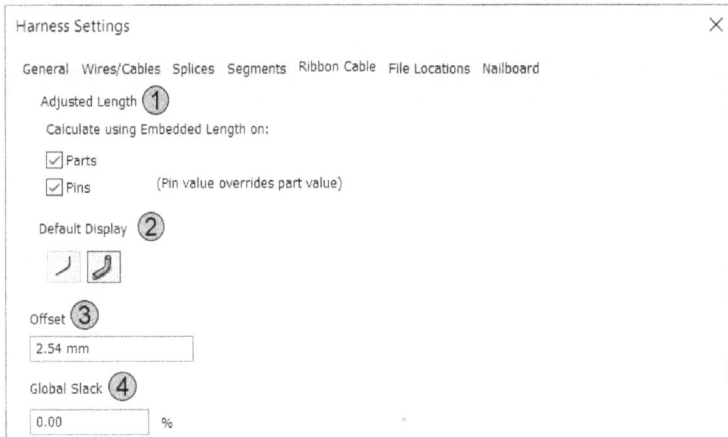

① Sets how to adjust the ribbon cable length based on the amount of ribbon cable used beyond the point where the cable enters the connector. If neither check box is selected, there is no adjustment. The Embedded Length property added to a pin or part is used when one or both check boxes are selected.

② Sets display for creating all ribbon cables.

③ Sets the default offset distance for ribbon cable work points.

④ Sets the extra length to add to ribbon cables in the harness assembly. The value is a percentage of the existing ribbon cable length.

Ribbon Cable Properties

The Ribbon Cable Properties dialog box displays all the current property settings for the selected ribbon cable, and enables you to edit the Ribbon Cable ID and Custom properties. All other properties for a ribbon cable are determined by the library selection for the type of ribbon cable.

Right-click on the centerline of a ribbon cable and click Harness Properties to open the Ribbon Cable Properties dialog box.

Ribbon Cable Properties: Occurrence Tab

Select the Occurrence tab to display the Ribbon Cable ID (editable) and the length properties for the ribbon cable.

Ribbon Cable Properties: General Tab

Select the General tab to display properties for the ribbon cable. These settings are determined by the Cable & Harness library and are not editable.

Ribbon Cable Properties	✕
Occurrence **General** Display Custom	
Name:	28AWG_40Con
Category:	Standard Gray
Part Number:	28AWG_40Con
Number of Conductors:	40
Pitch:	1.27 mm
Height:	0.89 mm
Width:	50.80 mm
Gauge:	28

Ribbon Cable Properties: Display Tab

Select the Display tab to change the default display of the ribbon cable between Centerline and Rendered display modes.

Ribbon Cable Properties	✕
Occurrence General **Display** Custom	
Default Display	

Ribbon Cable Properties: Custom Tab

Select the Custom tab to manage custom properties for the ribbon cable. You can add and edit the values for the custom properties.

Ribbon Cable Properties	✕
Occurrence General Display **Custom**	
Name:	⌄	Add
Type:	Text ⌄	Delete
Value:		

Name	Value	Type

Exercise: Add a Ribbon Cable

In this exercise, you will add a ribbon cable between a computer motherboard and a CD-ROM drive. Then you will edit the cable, changing the ribbon cable twist.

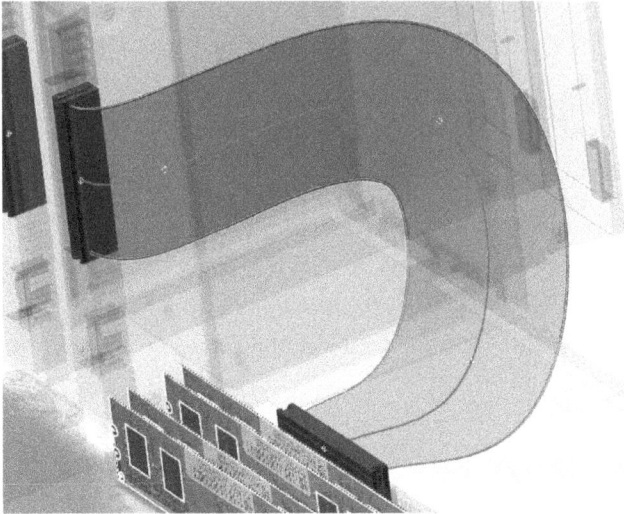

The completed exercise

1. Open *Computer.iam*.

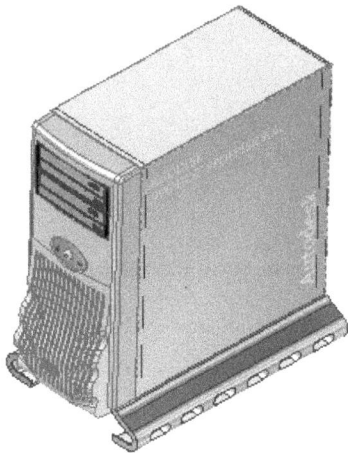

2. Orient the model as shown to display the upper right corner of the motherboard and the connectors on the CD-ROM drives.

3. To simplify the viewing of the assembly, do the following:

- In the Browser, expand Representations.
- Expand Level of Detail: Master.
- Right-click on CDROM Ribbon Cable Creation and click Activate.

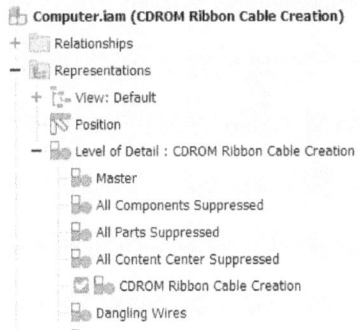

4. The simplified view of the assembly displays.

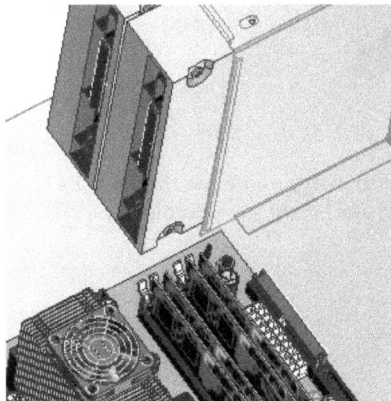

5. To activate the harness assembly for editing, in the Browser, right-click on CDROM Ribbon Cable and click Edit.

6. In the Cable and Harness tab, in the Create panel, click Create Ribbon Cable.

7. For the Start Connector, in the graphics window, select the connector on the upper right corner of the motherboard.

8. For the End Connector, in the graphics window, select the connector on the CD-ROM closest to the motherboard.

9. To reverse the side on which to create the ribbon cable entering the CD-ROM connector, in the Create Ribbon Cable dialog box, under End Connector, click Connector.

10. To select a 40 conductor ribbon cable from the Cable & Harness library, do the following:

- For Name, select the drop-down arrow.
- Select 28AWG_40Con from the list.
- Click OK.

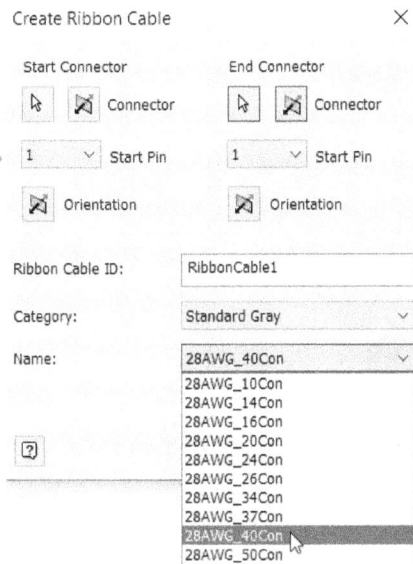

11. The sweep operation fails. In the Cable & Harness dialog box, click OK.

12. To change the ribbon cable offset, right-click in the graphics window and click Edit Offset.

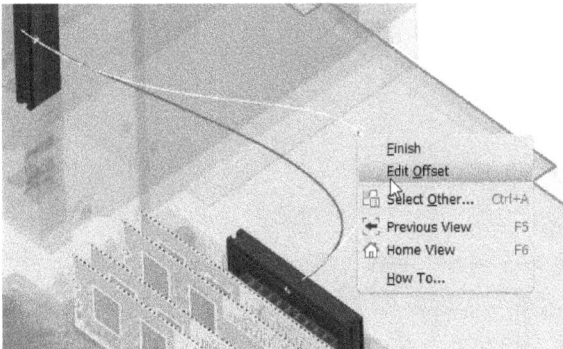

13. In the Edit Offset dialog box, for Offset Distance, enter **18mm**. Click OK.

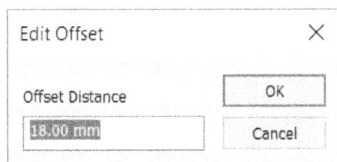

14. Select a point on the cabinet base plate, straight out from connector, approximately 3/4 distance to edge of base.

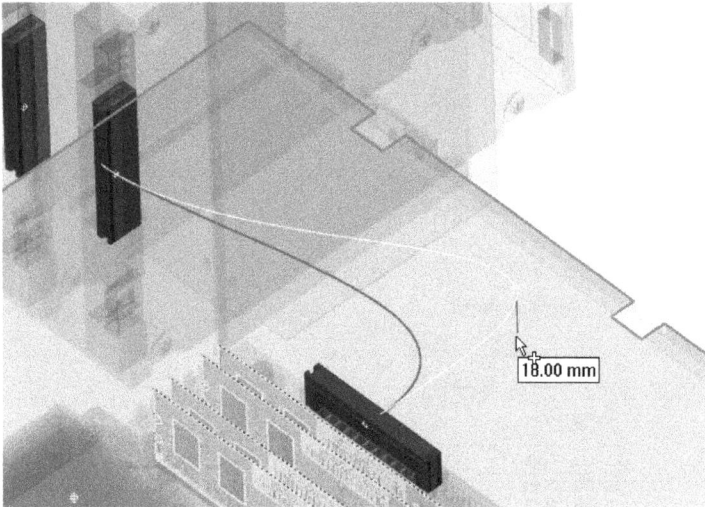

15. Select a second point on the CD-ROM mounting bracket, aligned with both the CD-ROM connector and the previously placed work point.

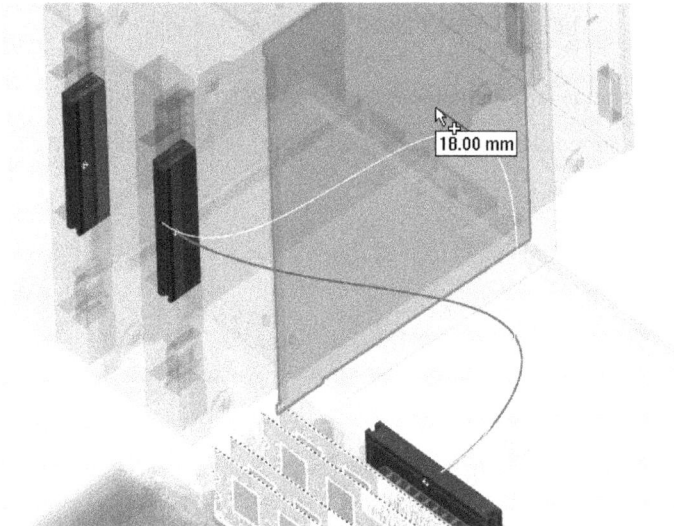

16. Select a third point on the CD-ROM aligned with the CD-ROM connector and assembly screw nearest the connector end of the CD- ROM.

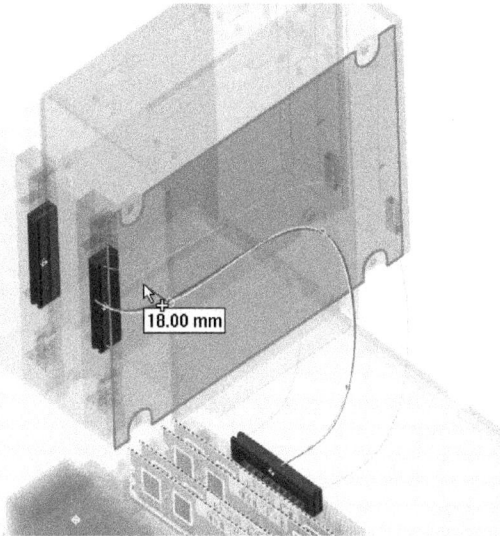

17. Right-click in the graphics window and click Finish.

18. Right-click on the centerline of the ribbon and click Display as Rendered, if not already displayed as rendered.

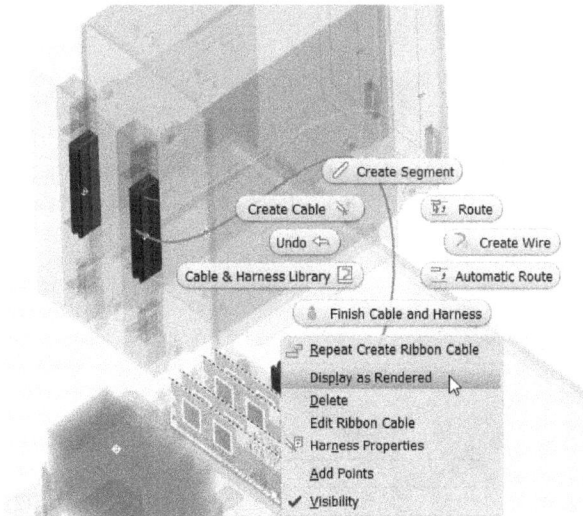

19. To edit the twist of cable entering the CD-ROM connector, right-click over the work point nearest to the CD-ROM connector and select Edit Twist.

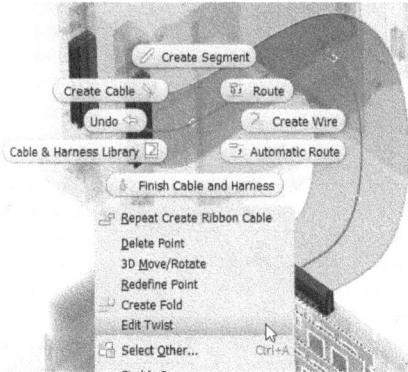

20. Right-click on the direction arrow and click Enter Angle.

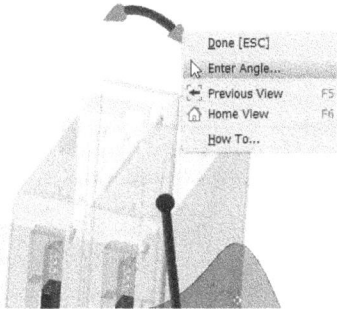

21. In the Enter Angle dialog box, enter **5**.

22. Right-click in the graphics window and click Apply. Depending on the placement of points, the cable may extend through the geometry of the CD-ROM casing. In the next exercise, this will be resolved.

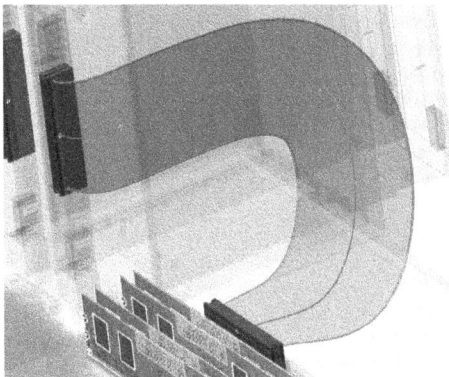

23. Close all files without saving changes.

Exercise: Add Ribbon Cable Folds

In this exercise, you will add folds to an existing ribbon cable. Next, you will edit the folds, streamlining the route of the ribbon cable through the assembly.

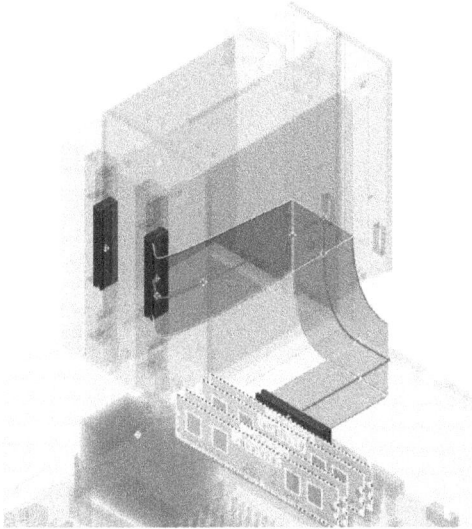

The completed exercise

1. Open *Computer_Fold.iam*.

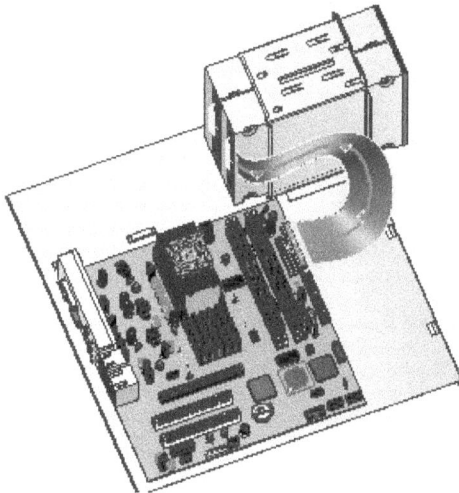

2. To activate the harness for editing, right-click on CD-ROM Ribbon Cable Fold and click Edit.

3. In the ribbon, in the Cable and Harness tab, in the Create panel, click Create Fold.

4. In the graphics window, select the work point closest to the connector on the motherboard.

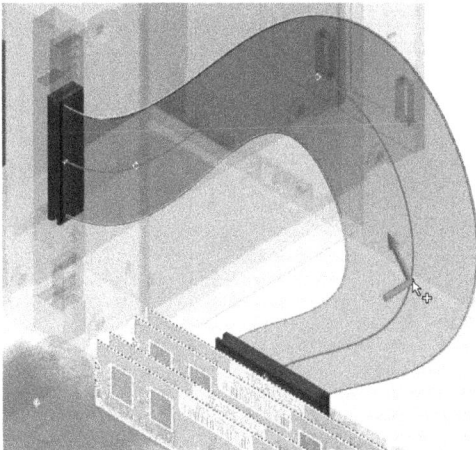

5. In the Create Fold dialog box, do the following:

- In Fold Type area, click Single Fold.
- In Alignment area, click Shaft.

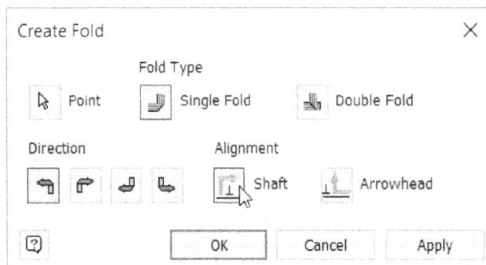

---

6. In the graphics window, select a face of the connector receptacle parallel to the ribbon cable direction.

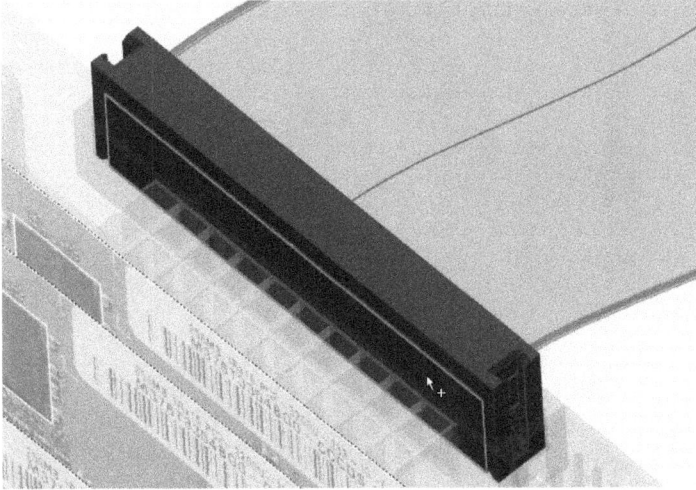

7. In the Create Fold dialog box, under Alignment, click Arrowhead.

8. In the graphics window, select the side face of the CD-ROM mounting bracket.

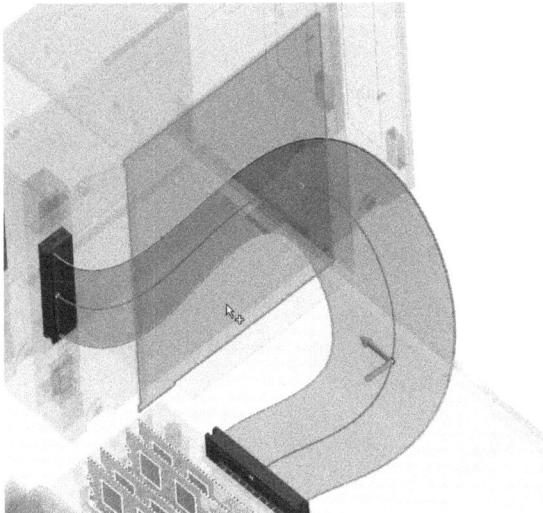

9. In the Create Fold dialog box, click Apply.

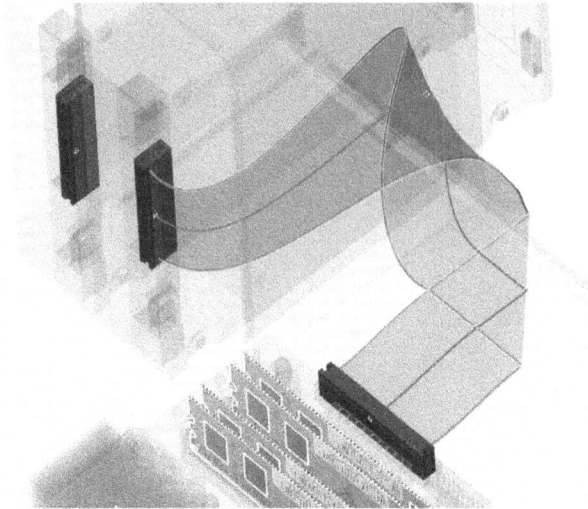

10. In the graphics window, select the middle work point on the CD-ROM ribbon cable.

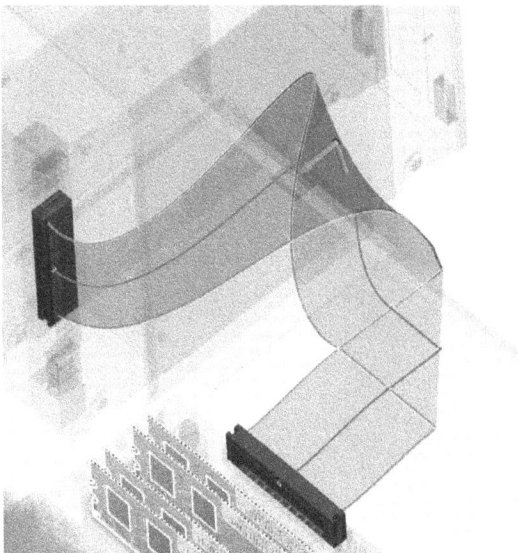

11. In the Create Fold dialog box, do the following:

- In Fold Type area, click Double Fold.
- In Alignment area, click Shaft.

12. In the graphics window, select the bottom back plate of the computer.

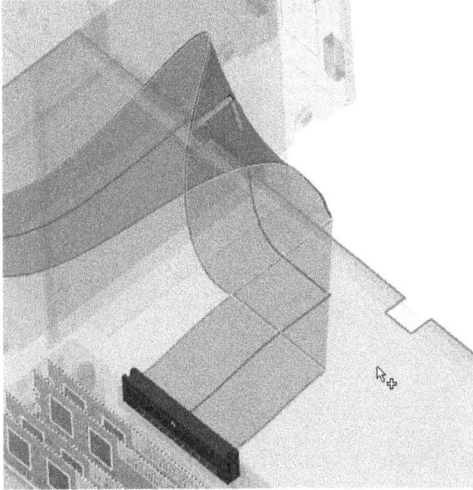

13. In the Create Fold dialog box, click Arrowhead.

14. In the graphics window, select the front face of the CD-ROM drive.

15. In the Create Fold dialog box, click OK.

16. In the message dialog box indicating the sweep operation failed, click OK.

17. To adjust the position of the work point at the first fold:

   - Right-click on the work point at the first fold and click 3D Move/Rotate.
   - Move the point further from the CD-ROM drives as shown looking down at the motherboard and click Apply.

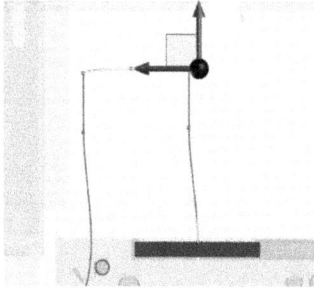

18. To adjust the position of the work point at the second fold:

   - Click the second work point.
   - Move the point up and further from the motherboard as shown and click OK.

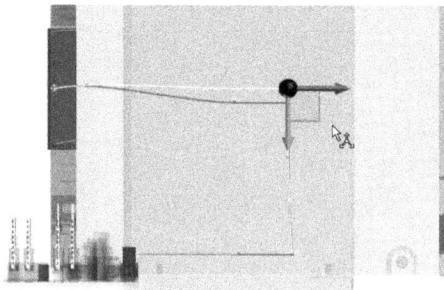

19. When the sweep operation succeeds, right-click on the centerline of ribbon cable and click Display as Rendered.

   Note: If the sweep did not succeed at this point, edit the position of the points again. All points should be approximately perpendicular to one another.

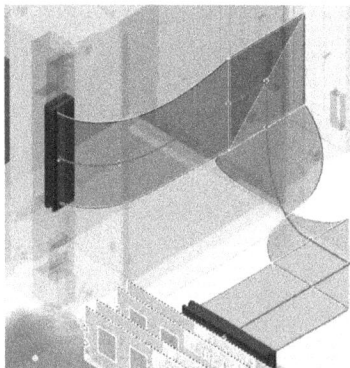

20. In the graphics window, right-click on the second fold work point and click Edit Fold.

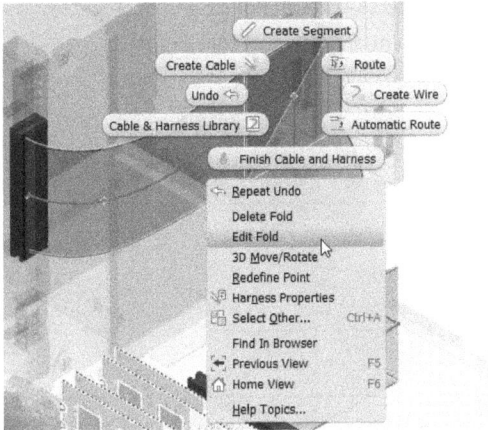

21. To correct the fold direction and turn, in the Edit Fold dialog box, do the following:

- In Fold Type area, click Single Fold.
- In Direction area, select down-left.

22. Click OK.

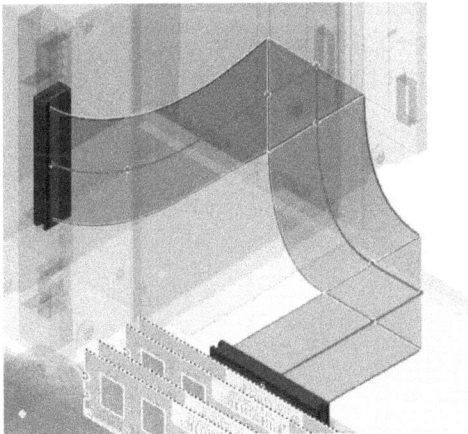

23. To fix how the cable connects to the end connector, add a point to the cable centerline.

   ▪ Right-click on the cable centerline and select Add Points.
   ▪ Add a new point between the last point and the end connector.
   ▪ Press ESC to end new point placement.

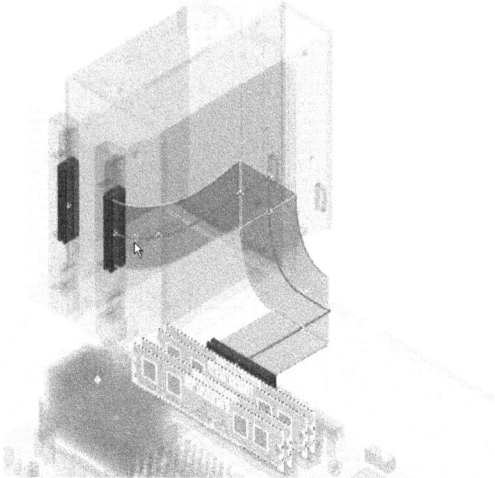

24. Use the 3D Move/Rotate tool to adjust the location of the new point.

   ▪ Right-click on the new point and select 3D Move/Rotate.
   ▪ Select the red arrowhead and drag the point to reposition it.

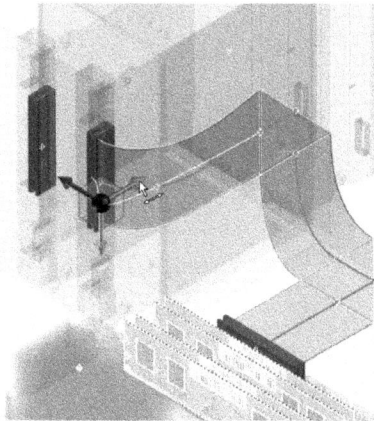

25. Right-click and select OK. The cable should be repositioned similar to that shown in the following figure. If the cable fails, you can edit the position of the work points as required, to resolve the failure.

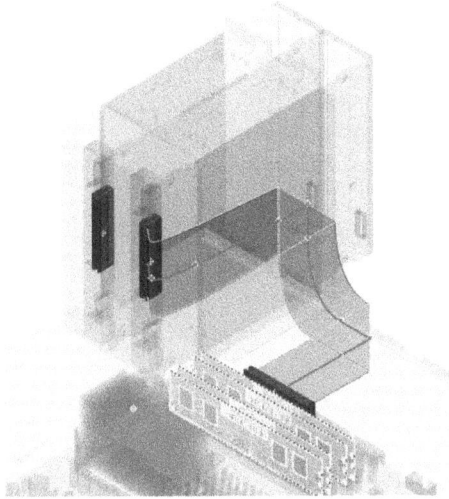

26. Close all files without saving changes.

Chapter Summary

In this chapter, you learned to add wires and cables to a design. You then learned to create route segments and have the wires and cables follow those routes. You also learned to create ribbon cables and create wires and cables by importing the data.

Having completed this chapter, you can:

- Add wires and cables between pins in electrical parts and connectors.
- Add route segments to a design and route existing wires or cables through the route segments.
- Import wire or cable data from an external file.
- Add ribbon cables between electrical connectors.

Refine a Cable and Harness Design

In this chapter, you learn how to refine a cable and harness design by editing the current content and adding additional content. You learn how to edit your existing design content of wires, cables, route segments, and cable ribbons. You also learn how to add and edit splices and virtual parts.

Objectives

After completing this chapter, you will be able to:

- Edit the properties, connections, and positions of wires, cables, ribbon cables, and route segments.
- Add splices to a harness assembly and edit a splice.
- Add and edit virtual parts.
- Create 2D drawings and nailboards of a harness design.

Lesson: Modifying Wires, Cables, Segments, and Ribbon Cables

This lesson describes the common tools and techniques for modifying wires, cables, route segments, and ribbon cables.

Design changes frequently require the editing of existing components and assemblies. To complete the design in the most effective manner, you need to know the tools available for modifying wires, cables, and segments, and how to use them.

The following figure displays the Cable & Harness ribbon with the available editing tools highlighted.

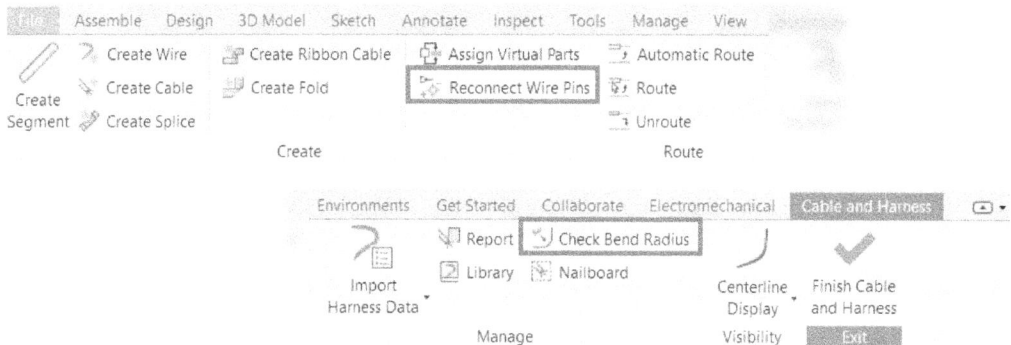

Objectives

After completing this lesson, you will be able to:

- State the types of edits that are common between wires, cables, route segments, and ribbon cables.
- Toggle the display between rendered and only centerline.
- Change which definitions are used and the start and end connections for wires, cables, and ribbon cables.
- Delete wires, cables, cable ribbons, and route segments.
- Add, delete, move, and redefine points in a wire, cable, route segment, and ribbon cable.
- Check a harness assembly for bend radius violations.
- Copy a design and make it a unique adaptive design.

Common Edits

There are multiple tools and procedures that you can use to modify wires, cables, and segments. Tools are accessed from either the panel bar or shortcut menus.

The following figure shows the shortcut menu displayed when right-clicking a wire.

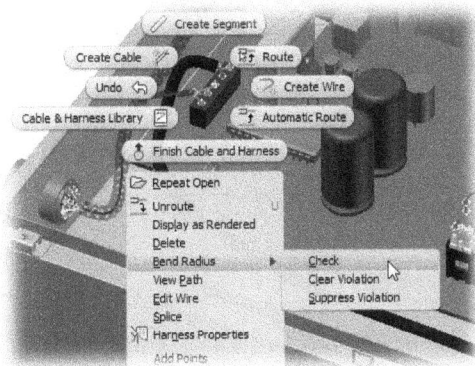

Common Edits

To perform modifications to existing harness components, you must activate the harness assembly for editing in the browser. Many of the editing tools for Cable and Harness objects are accessed by selecting the component and right-clicking to access a specific shortcut menu. However, general editing commands are also available from the ribbon.

The following is a list of the common editing tasks used to modify harness assembly components:

- Toggle display from a simple centerline to a rendered display.
- Edit definitions and connection points.
- Delete harness components such as wires, cables, ribbon cables, and route segments.
- Add and modify points.
- Check bend radiuses.
- Copy a design.

> To display the shortcut menu for editing harness components, either right-click on the component in the browser, or right-click on the centerline of the rendered component in the graphics window.

Toggling Display as Rendered

You can display wires as either rendered or centerline. Centerline display is the default. Use it for optimal performance while creating and routing wires.

If you select rendered, the wire is drawn as a 3D shaded solid, which is similar to how the physical wire appears. With centerline display, wires are drawn as lines, making it easier to see and work on existing model geometry.

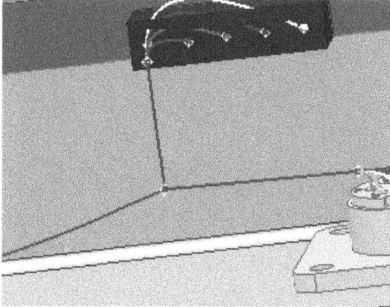

Segment with Display as Rendered toggled off | Segment with Display as Rendered toggled on

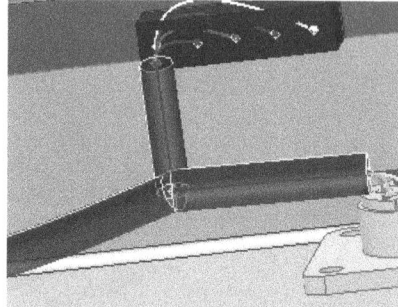

Display as Rendered

The display preference can be set in several ways, either with the shortcut menu, the appropriate properties dialog box, the Harness Settings dialog box, or the display settings on the Visibility panel of the ribbon. The occurrence level display settings always override the current display state.

The Centerline option sets wires and cables to display the centerline of the geometry. This applies to unrouted wires and cables, and the pieces of a routed component that do not lie in the segments. The Rendered option sets wires and cables to display as three-dimensional shaded solids.

You can change the display for all or individual segments, cables, wires, and ribbon cables depending on what is active when the display setting is selected. You can also control the display for each object independently. Segments and ribbon cables display as Rendered by default, and cables and wires display as Centerline.

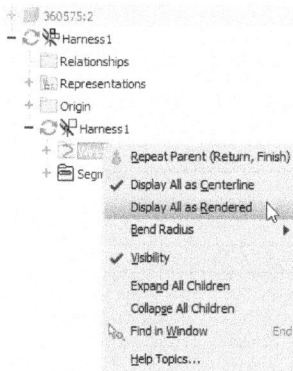

Folder-level display settings in Browser | Occurrence-level display setting in Browser

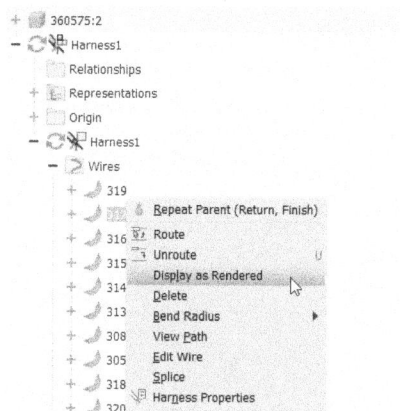

You can also change the display setting at the occurrence level in the graphics window. Right-click on the individual component and toggle the display setting in the shortcut menu.

Procedure: Toggling Display as Rendered for Individual Components

Use the following steps to change the display for individual wires, cables, cable wires, ribbon cables, and segments.

1. Double-click on the harness assembly to activate it.

2. In the Browser or graphics window, right-click on a wire, cable, cable wire, segment, or ribbon cable, and then toggle the display setting from the shortcut menu.

3. Optionally, you can right-click and click Harness Properties, and then set the appropriate display from the related dialog box.

Procedure: Setting Display as Rendered for All Components

Use the following steps to change the display for all wires, cables, ribbon cables, and segments.

1. Double-click on the harness assembly to activate it.

2. In the Browser, right-click on the Segments, Cables, Wires, or Ribbon Cables folder, and click the display setting from the shortcut menu.

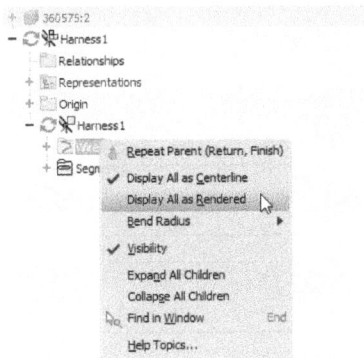

3. You can also select the Display Settings from the Cable and Harness toolbar.

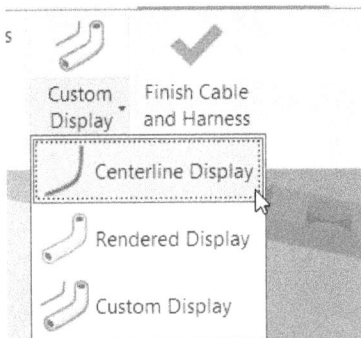

Procedure: Setting Custom Display Settings

Use the following steps to use the custom display settings to select different display options for all object types.

1. Double-click on the harness assembly to activate it.

2. In the ribbon, select Custom Display from the list.

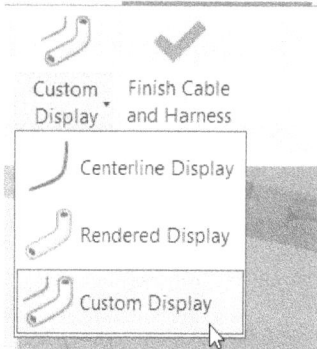

3. In the Custom Display dialog box, click the buttons to set the appropriate display for segments, cables, wires, and ribbon cables independent of one another.

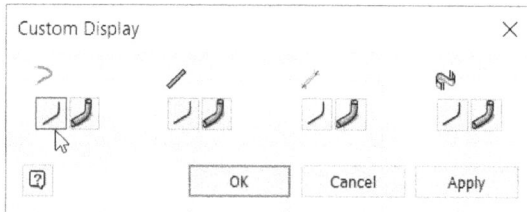

Changing Definitions and Connection Points

The design process frequently requires changes to existing harness components such as wires, cables, and ribbon cables. To make these changes you need to know where the commands are located, and how to use them.

The following figures show examples of the Edit Wire and Edit Cable command locations.

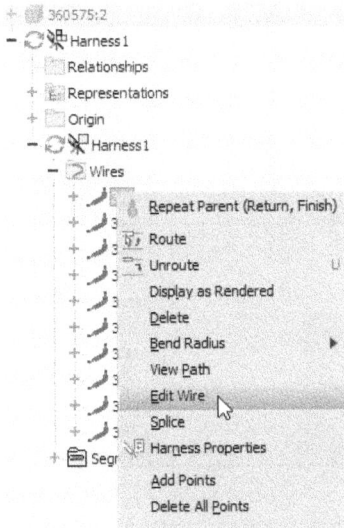

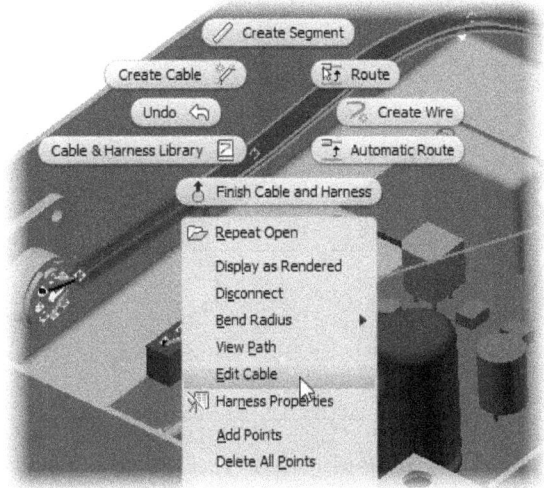

Harness Edit Commands

You can display the same dialog box to edit a wire, cable, or ribbon cable that was displayed when you initially created the wire, cable, or ribbon cable. You display the dialog box by selecting the wire or cable in the browser or graphics window, right-clicking, and then clicking the edit option associated to that wire or cable, such as Edit Wire, Edit Cable, or Edit Ribbon Cable.

Edit Wire

Use the Edit Wire dialog box to change the starting pin, ending pin, wire category, and wire name. The Properties button opens the Library Wire dialog box where you can review wire library information.

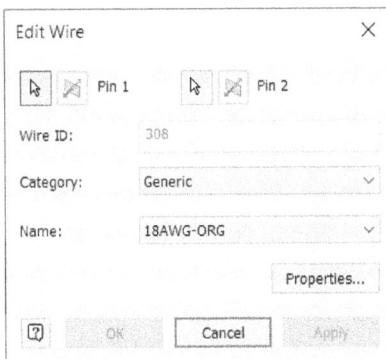

Edit Cable

Use the Edit Cable dialog box to change the starting pin and ending pin for the wires in the cable. Select a wire from the list to edit the wire endpoints.

The Properties button displays the Library Cable dialog box where you can review cable library information.

Edit Ribbon Cable

Use the Edit Ribbon Cable dialog box to change the connector assignments and settings for the starting and ending connectors for an existing ribbon cable. You can also edit the ribbon cable category and name.

The Properties button displays the Library Ribbon Cable dialog box where you can review ribbon cable library information.

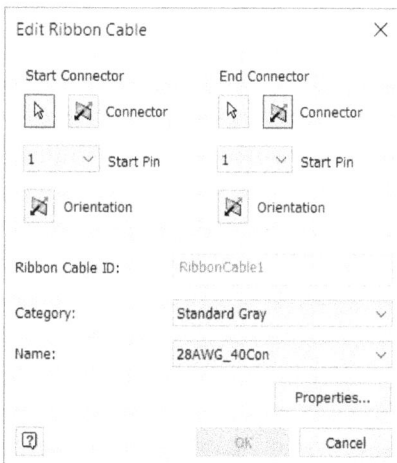

Procedure: Changing Definitions and Connection Points

The following steps give an overview of changing a wire, cable, or ribbon cable to use a different definition, start connection, or end connection.

1. Activate the harness assembly for editing.

2. In the Browser or graphics window, right-click on the centerline of the required harness component and click the Edit Wire, Edit Cable, or Edit Ribbon Cable command.

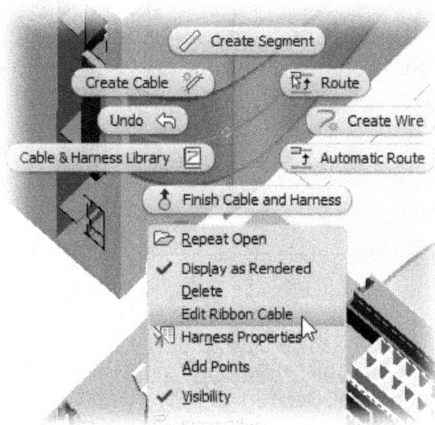

3. In the dialog box, make the required setting and definition changes.

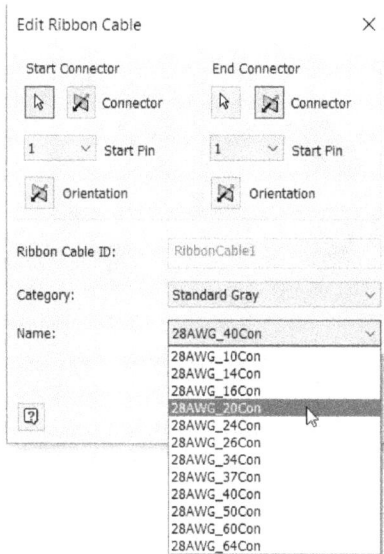

Deleting Wires, Cables, Ribbon Cables, or Route Segments

As the design process continues, sometimes it is necessary to remove or delete wires, cables, ribbon cables, or route segments from the harness assembly.

The following figure shows a harness assembly before and after deleting a route segment and wires.

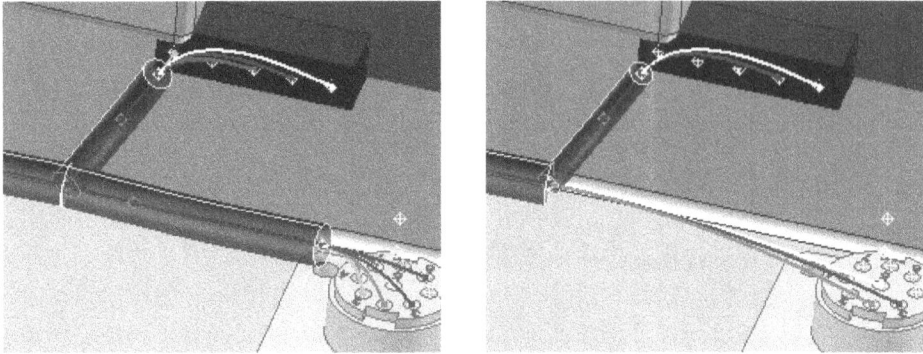

Access

To access the Delete command for a wire, ribbon cable, or segment, right-click on the component in either the Browser or the graphics window, and click Delete.

To access the Delete command for a cable, right-click on the cable in the Browser only, and click Delete.

The following figures show the Delete option in the Browser for a route segment, and the Disconnect option for a cable wire in the graphics window.

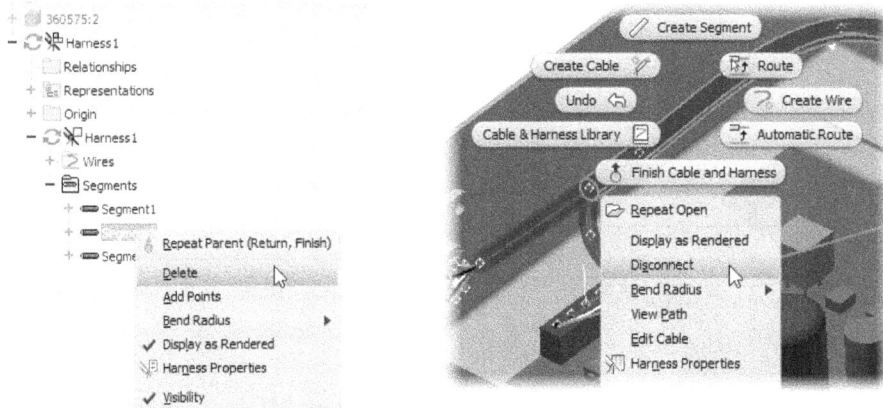

You cannot delete a cable wire. You can either disconnect the cable wire so that it is not displayed, or you can delete the entire cable.

To disconnect a cable wire, right-click on the individual wire in either the Browser or the graphics window, and click Disconnect from the shortcut menu.

Procedure: Deleting Wires, Cables, Ribbon Cables, or Route Segments

The following steps give an overview of how to delete wires, cables, ribbon cables, or route segments from a harness assembly.

1. Activate the harness assembly for editing.

2. For a wire, ribbon cable, or segment, right-click on the component in either the Browser or in the graphics window, and click Delete.

3. For a cable, right-click on the cable in the Browser, and click Delete.

4. Optionally, to disconnect an individual cable wire, right-click on the wire in either the Browser or the graphics window, and click Disconnect.

Adding and Modifying Points

In addition to the starting and ending points of a wire, cable, route segment, or ribbon cable, other work points can be used to define the path and location of the components. To work with the additional points, you need to know how to add, delete, move, or redefine points in wires, cables, route segments, or ribbon cables.

The following figure shows a route segment before and after adding work points to change the segment path.

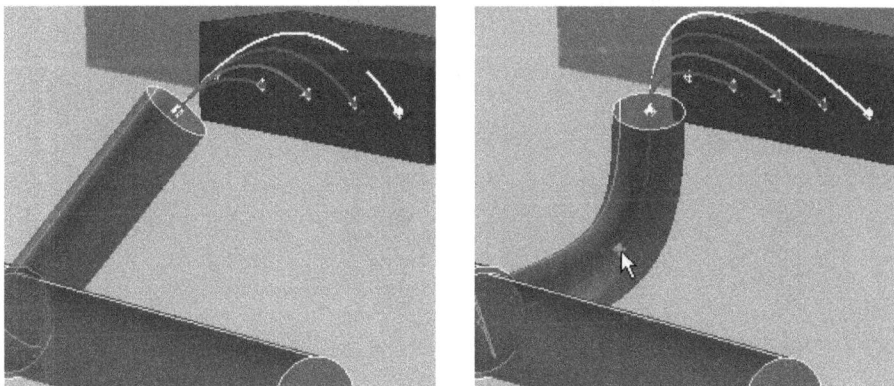

Access to Adding and Modifying Points

The commands for adding, deleting, and modifying points to wires, ribbon cables, route segments, and cable wires are available in the shortcut menu. To access the shortcut menu, right-click on the harness component in the Browser or in the graphics window.

Procedure: Adding a Point

The following steps describe an overview of adding points to a wire, ribbon cable, route segment, or cable wire.

1. Activate the harness assembly for editing.

2. In the Browser or graphics window, right-click on the wire, ribbon cable, route segment, or cable wire and click Add Points.

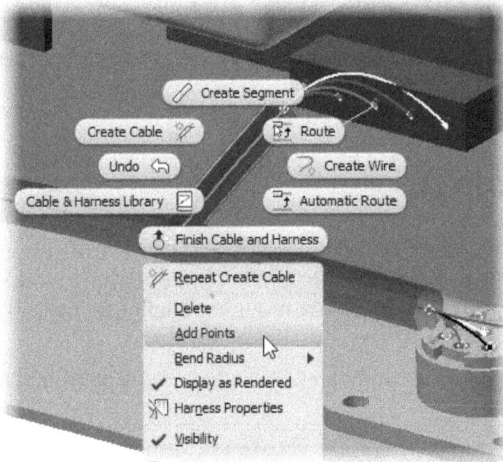

3. Select locations for the points on the centerline of the selected component.

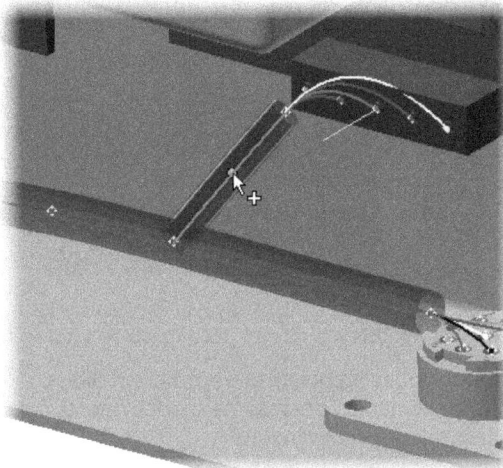

> You cannot add points to cables or disconnected cable wires.

Procedure: Deleting a Point

The following steps describe an overview of deleting points from a wire, ribbon cable, route segment, or cable wire.

1. Activate the harness assembly for editing.

2. In the Browser or graphics window, right-click on the point and click Delete Point in the shortcut menu.

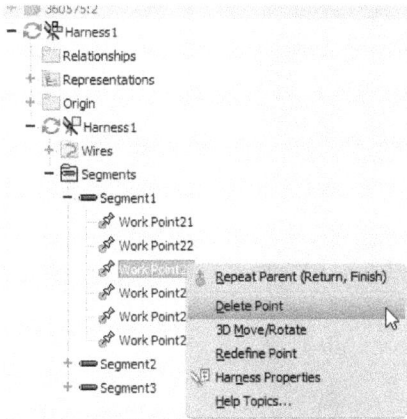

3. Optionally, to delete all points from a wire or cable wire, in the Browser or graphics window, right-click on the wire and click Delete All Points.

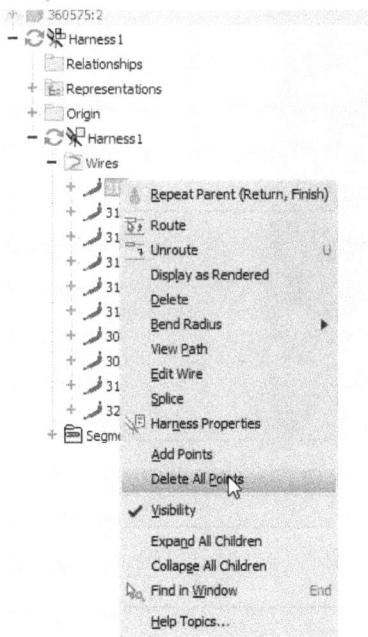

Procedure: Moving One or More Points

The following steps describe an overview of moving points in a wire, ribbon cable, route segment, or cable wire.

1. Activate the harness assembly for editing. In the Browser or graphics window, right-click on the point and click 3D Move/Rotate in the shortcut menu.

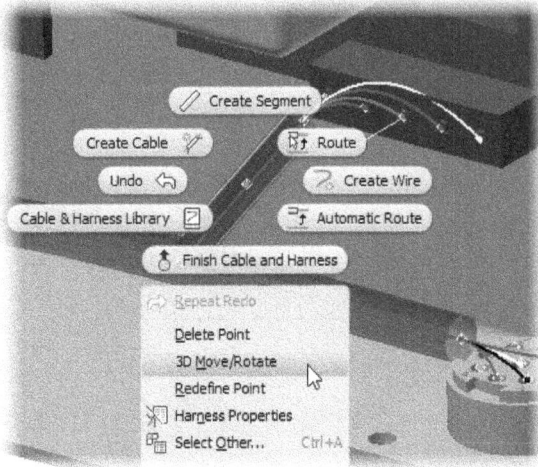

2. Use the triad to dynamically move the point.

3. Alternately, enter distances and angles in the mini-toolbar.

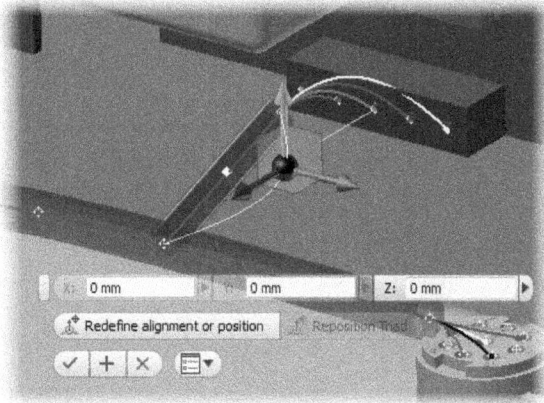

> To move multiple points in tandem, press CTRL or SHIFT and click each point. Right-click and click 3D Move/Rotate.

Procedure: Redefining a Point

The following steps describe an overview of redefining points in a wire, ribbon cable, route segment, or cable wire.

1. Activate the harness assembly for editing. In the Browser or graphics window, right-click on the point and click Redefine Point in the shortcut menu.

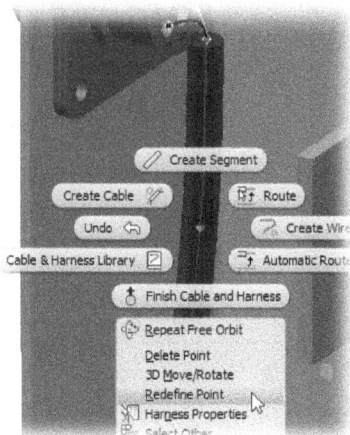

2. If the offset distance requires editing, you can right-click on the point and click Edit Offset.

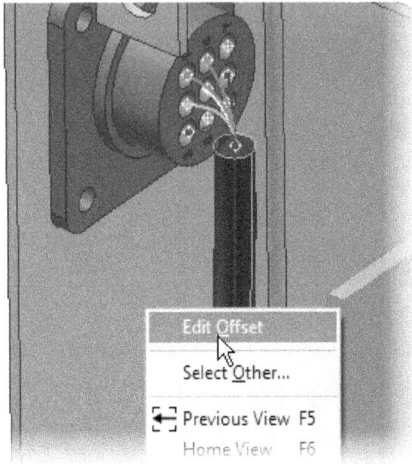

3. Edit the offset distance as required.

4. In the graphics window, select a new location for the point.

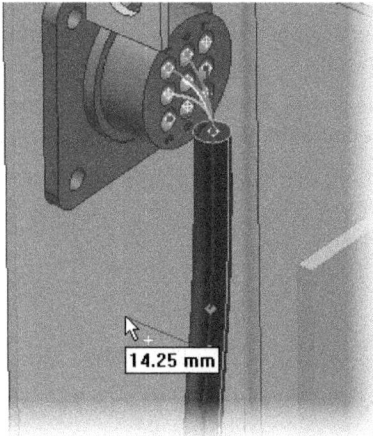

> To lengthen a route segment and have control points along the lengthened part, use the Redefine Point option to change the endpoint of the segment. Then add points along the added portion of the segment. Redefine the added points to position the points as required.

Checking Bend Radius

The position of segments and routed and unrouted wires in a harness assembly can sometimes violate the specified minimum bend radius. To correct this issue, you need to know how to check a harness assembly for bend radius violations and how to view the results.

The following figure displays an example of the Bend Radius shortcut menu for a segment.

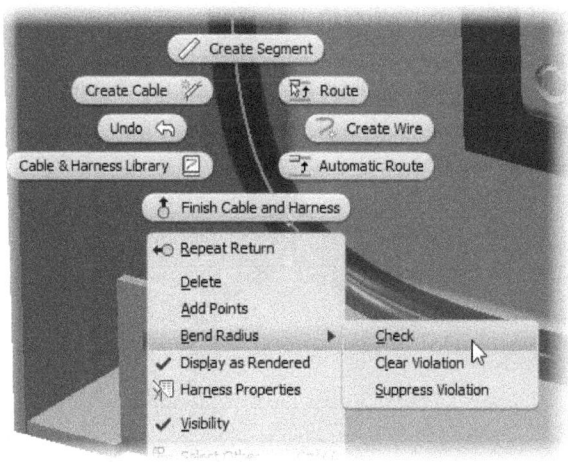

Bend Radius Check Tool

The minimum bend radius for a cable or wire is the smallest radius to which a cable or wire can be bent. This value varies depending on the cable and material types. The values for the minimum bend radius are set in Harness Properties for a wire or cable object.

You can set the bend radius for cables as a multiple of the cable diameter, or select the Calculate from Wires check box to make the cable bend radius depend on the wires setting.

The following figure displays the Bend Radius options as harness properties for segments.

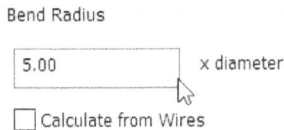

Bend Radius

| 5.00 | x diameter |

☐ Calculate from Wires

Access

Ribbon: Cable and Harness tab>Manage panel

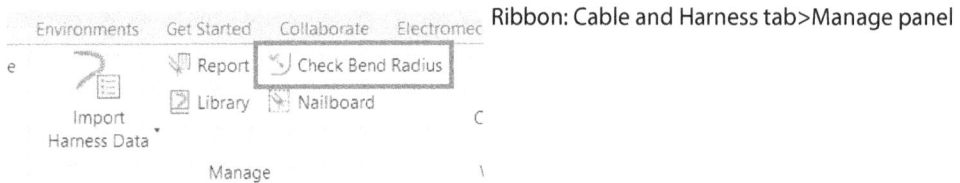

Checking Bend Radius

To check for bend radius violations, select one, some, or all objects in the harness assembly, and run the bend radius check. Icons display in the Browser alerting you to any violations. You can also show violations to view additional details and highlight the point or points that are causing the failure.

You can adjust the wire or segment position to fix a violation, or you can continue working and adjust them later. You can also suppress or clear violation errors in the Browser.

When active checking is enabled, objects that are affected by an operation and all objects that previously failed the bend radius check are automatically checked under certain conditions.

The following figure shows an example of the bend radius options available from the shortcut menu for a segment with a bend radius violation.

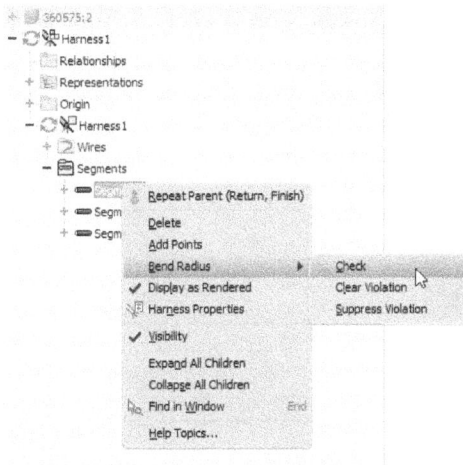

Use the following options with the Check Bend Radius tool.

Option	Description
Check	Checks for bends that do not meet the specified minimum bend radius on segments, wires, and cables in the active assembly.
Clear Violation	Removes the Bend Radius violations for the selected harness component.
Suppress Violation	Ignores all bend radius violations for the object during bend radius checks. The browser icon also updates to indicate the suppressed state.

Procedure: Checking Bend Radius

The following steps describe an overview of using the Bend Radius tool.

1. Activate the harness assembly for editing. In the Browser or graphics window, select the harness component.

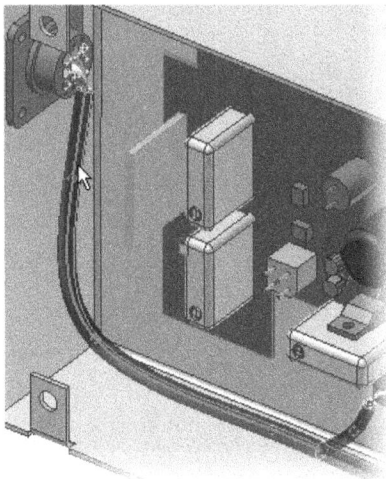

2. Start the Check Bend Radius tool. You can access the tool from the ribbon or by right-clicking and selecting from the shortcut menu.

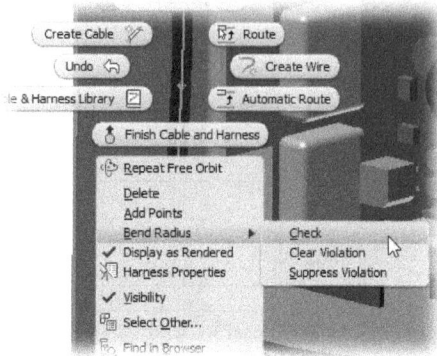

Copying a Design

Once a harness design is completed, you might want to reuse the design in the same or different drawings.

The following figure shows an example of a copied harness assembly.

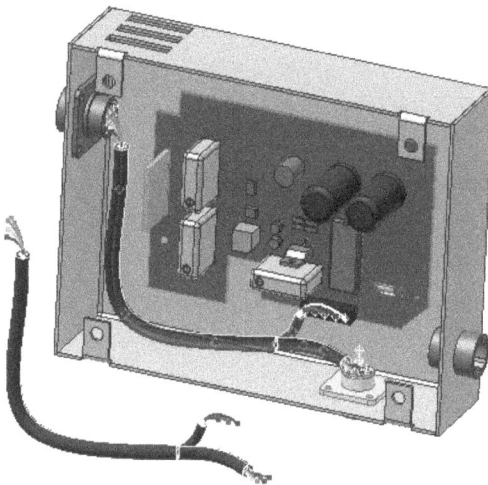

Copying a Harness Design

Once a harness design has been created, you can reuse the design in the current model assembly or in different model assemblies.

To copy the harness design existing in the active assembly, you can drag and drop the existing harness design from the Browser into the graphics window, or you can use the Place Component tool to browse to the external harness assembly definition and insert it into the active model assembly.

Make Harness Assembly Adaptive

Harness assemblies that are copied and placed in the assembly are dependent on the primary or original occurrence. Changes to the primary occurrence automatically updates all copied or secondary occurrences. These secondary occurrences can be constrained as a rigid body in the assembly, but cannot be edited. To reuse these occurrences and make them available for edits, you can use the Make Adaptive option. Adaptive occurrences can be edited in the Cable and Harness environment and update to assembly changes.

When you use the Make Adaptive tool on a secondary occurrence, the harness assembly and harness part are essentially transitioned to a new adaptive and primary occurrence. This occurrence is independent of the original and can be edited in the Cable and Harness environment.

Procedure: Copying a Design from the Same Assembly

The following steps describe an overview of the steps required to copy a harness design from the same overall assembly.

1. Make the overall assembly active for editing.

2. Drag and drop the harness assembly to be copied from the Browser to the graphics window.

   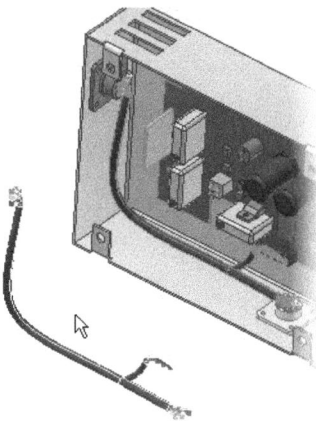

3. In the Browser, right-click on the new occurrence of the harness assembly and click Make Adaptive. Click Yes and save the new assembly.

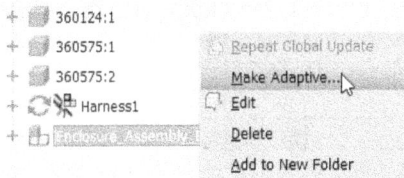

```
+  360124:1
+  360575:1
+  360575:2                 Repeat Global Update
+  Harness1                  Make Adaptive...
+  Enclosure_Assembly_       Edit
                             Delete
                             Add to New Folder
```

4. In the Make Adaptive dialog box, specify the name and location for the new harness assembly and part.

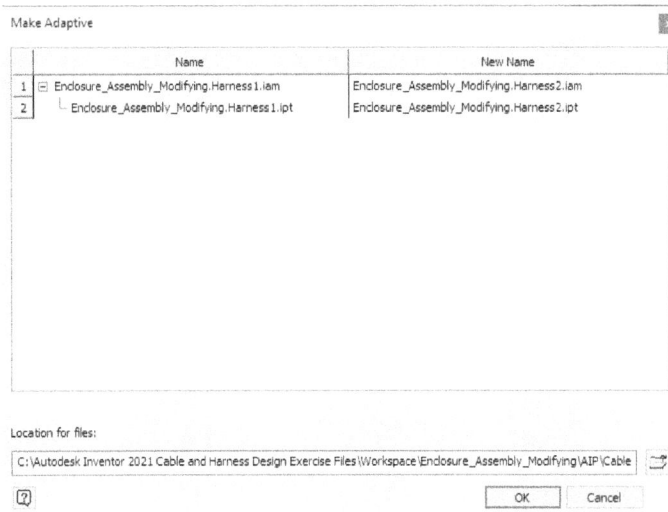

Make Adaptive

	Name	New Name
1	⊟ Enclosure_Assembly_Modifying.Harness1.iam	Enclosure_Assembly_Modifying.Harness2.iam
2	└ Enclosure_Assembly_Modifying.Harness1.ipt	Enclosure_Assembly_Modifying.Harness2.ipt

Location for files:

C:\Autodesk Inventor 2021 Cable and Harness Design Exercise Files\Workspace\Enclosure_Assembly_Modifying\AIP\Cable

OK   Cancel

Procedure: Copying a Design from a Different Assembly

The following steps describe an overview of the steps required to copy a harness design from a different assembly into the active assembly.

1. Make the overall assembly active for editing.

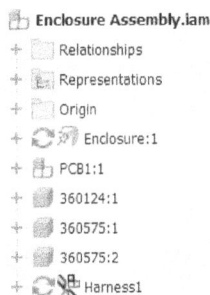

```
   Enclosure Assembly.iam
+  Relationships
+  Representations
+  Origin
+  Enclosure:1
+  PCB1:1
+  360124:1
+  360575:1
+  360575:2
+  Harness1
```

2. Start the Place Component tool.

3. In the Place Component dialog box, browse to and select the harness assembly to be copied.

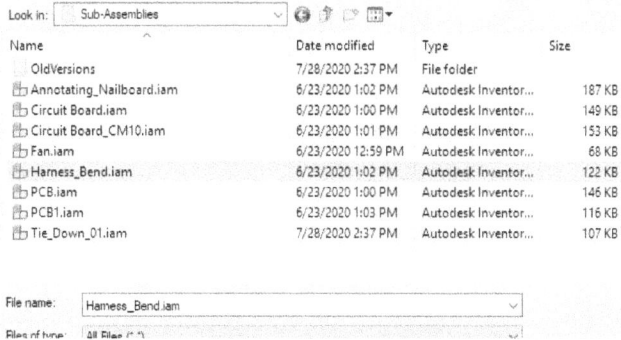

4. In the graphics window, select a location for the copied harness assembly.

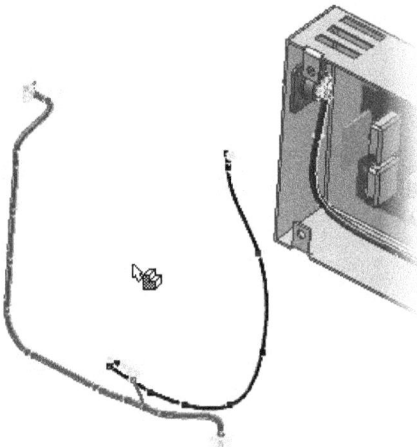

5. In the Browser, right-click on the new occurrence of the harness assembly and click Make Adaptive. Click Yes and save the new assembly.

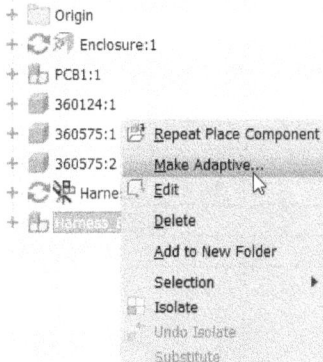

6. In the Make Adaptive dialog box, specify the name and location for the new harness assembly and part.

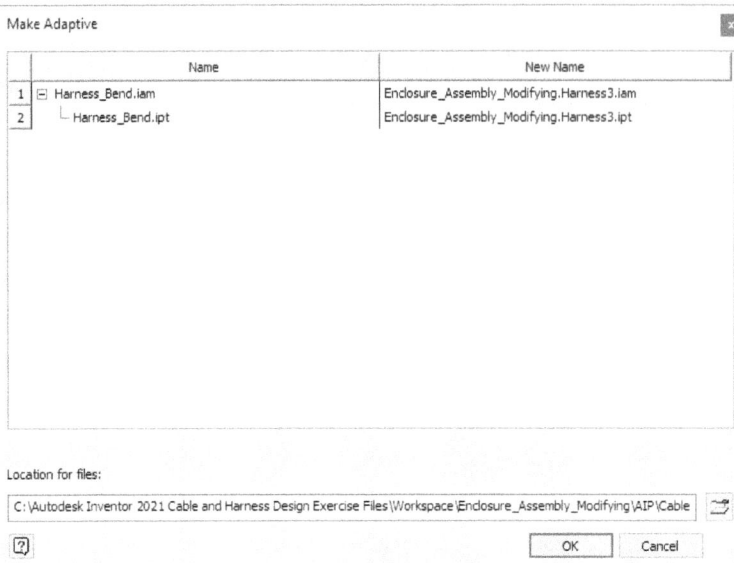

	Name	New Name
1	⊟ Harness_Bend.iam	Enclosure_Assembly_Modifying.Harness3.iam
2	└ Harness_Bend.ipt	Enclosure_Assembly_Modifying.Harness3.ipt

Make Adaptive

Location for files:

C:\Autodesk Inventor 2021 Cable and Harness Design Exercise Files\Workspace\Enclosure_Assembly_Modifying\AIP\Cable

OK   Cancel

Exercise: Edit Display, Settings, and Properties

In this exercise, you edit an existing harness assembly. You complete the following tasks:

- Change Harness Settings.
- Change display of all wires.
- Change display of only one wire.
- Change occurrence properties for a wire.
- Delete a route segment.

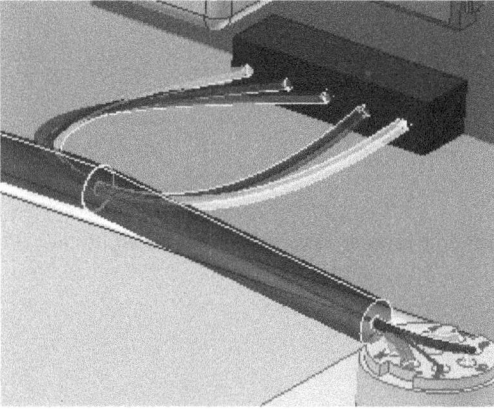

The completed exercise

1. Open *Enclosure_Assembly_Modifying.iam*.

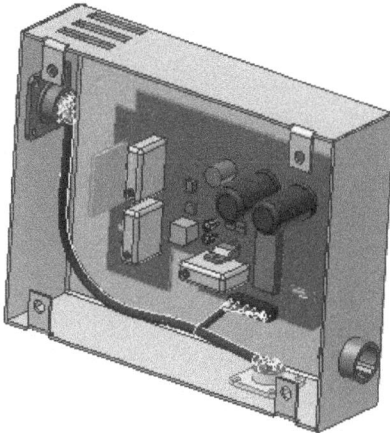

2. In the Browser, double-click on Harness1 to activate it for editing.

3. Zoom in to the two connectors and wires in the lower right corner of the enclosure.

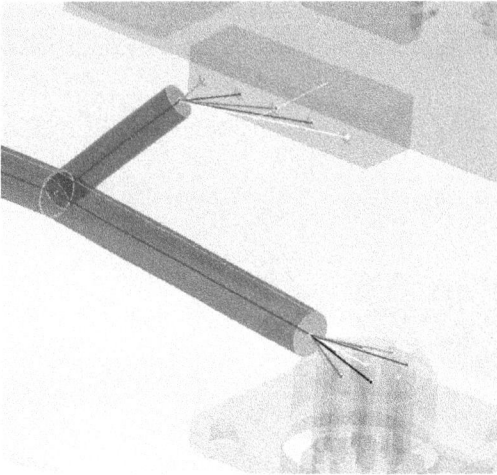

4. To change the curvature display of wires in the assembly, in the Browser, right-click on Harness1 and click Harness Settings.

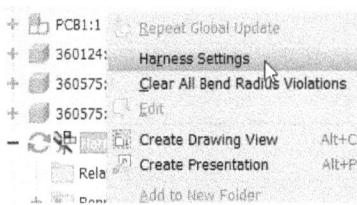

5. In the Harness Settings dialog box, in the Wires/Cables tab, in Natural Curvature area, click the With Natural Curvature tool. Click OK.

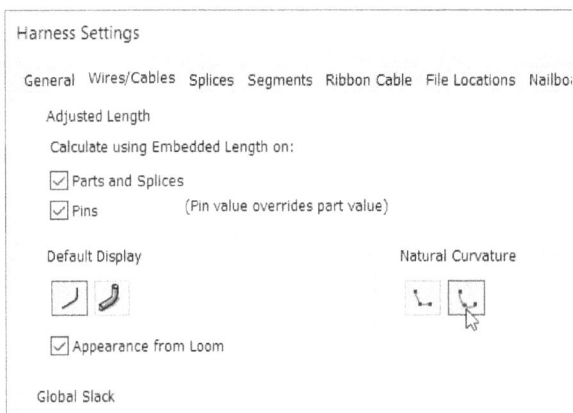

6. Review the display of the wires. Their display changed to include the curvature.

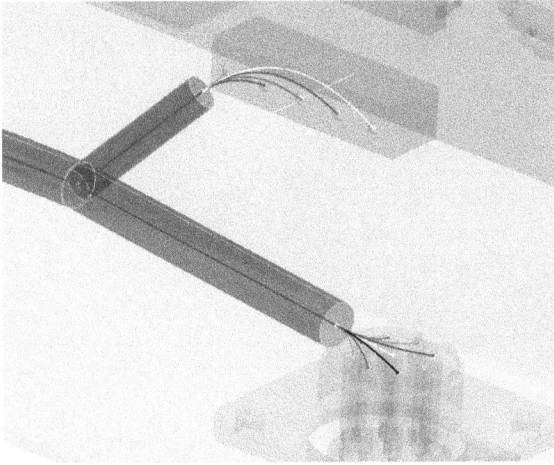

7. To change the display of all wires in the assembly to Rendered, in the Browser, do the following:

- Expand Harness1.
- Right-click on the Wires folder.
- In the shortcut menu, click Display All as Rendered.

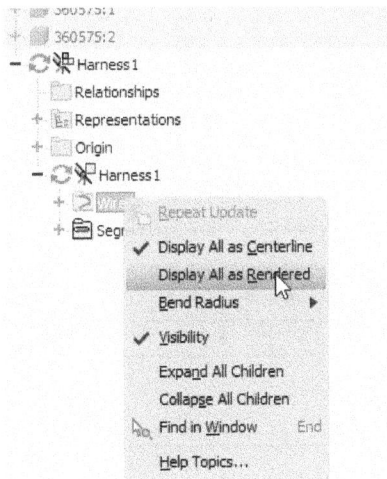

8. Review the display for all wires in the harness assembly. They now all display as rendered.

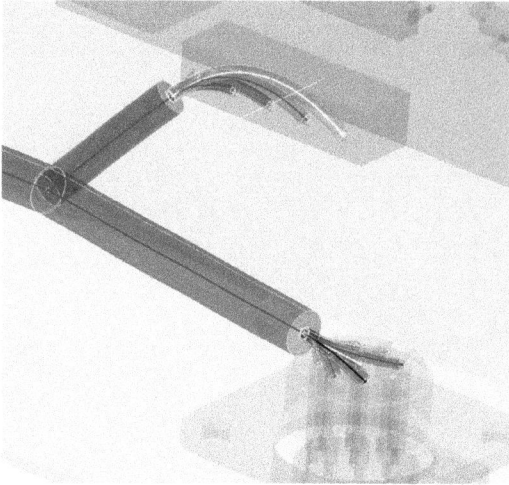

9. Zoom in to the wires on connector 360124:1.

10. To change the display of a single wire to Centerline display, in the graphics window, right-click on the centerline of the black wire. Click Display as Rendered to clear its selection.

11. To delete a route segment, in the graphics window, zoom out to view the two connectors.

12. Right-click on the centerline of the segment connected to the blue connector and click Delete.

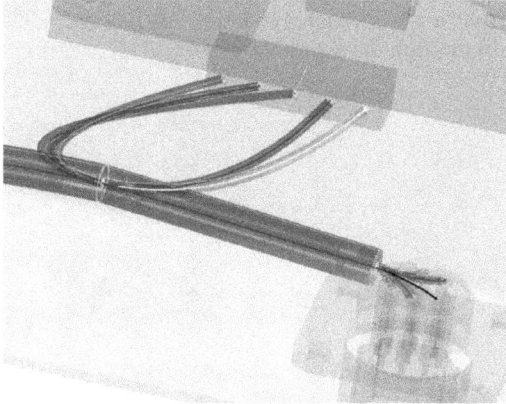

13. Undo the change.

14. Close all files without saving.

Exercise: Add and Modify Points

In this exercise, you will modify multiple points of a segment and then change the update settings so that they are deferred to when you will make additional changes. You will also add and delete points on segments to modify the path through the assembly.

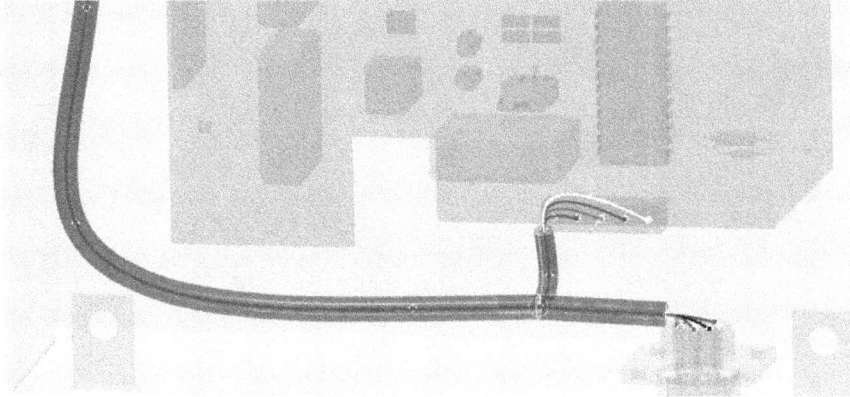

The completed exercise

1.   Open *Enclosure_Assembly_Points.iam*.

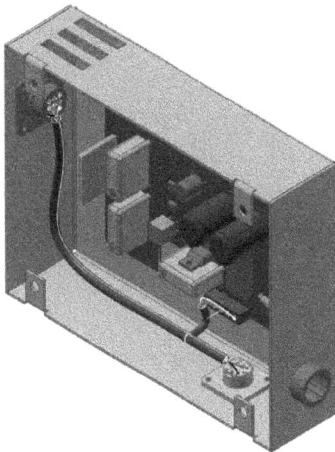

2.   In the Browser, double-click on Harness1 to activate it for editing.

3. Zoom in to the lower left corner as shown in the following figure. Note how the segment crosses the corner of the circuit board.

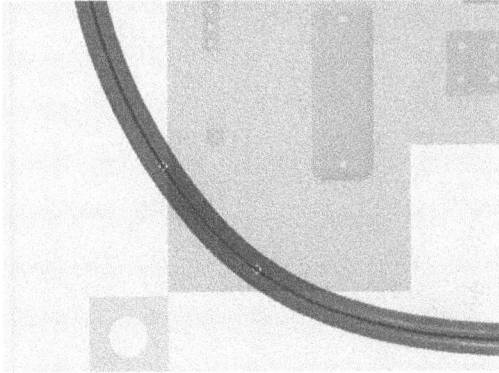

4. CTRL+ select the two node points as shown in the following figure.

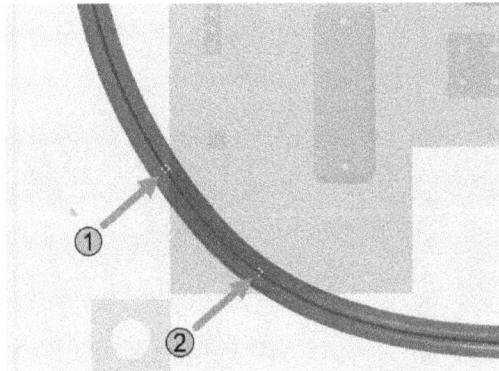

5. Right-click on one of the nodes and click 3D Move/Rotate.

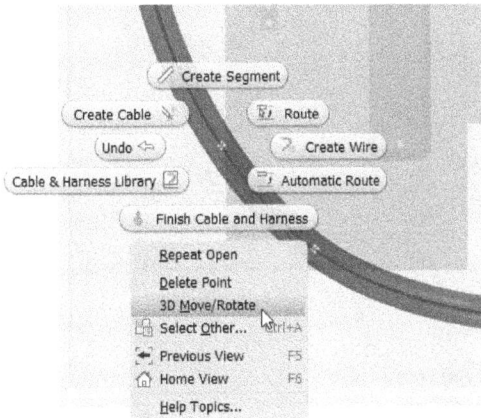

6. Click and drag the X linear axis and the Y linear axis to reposition the nodes as shown in the following figure. Note how each of the two nodes is repositioned at the same time.

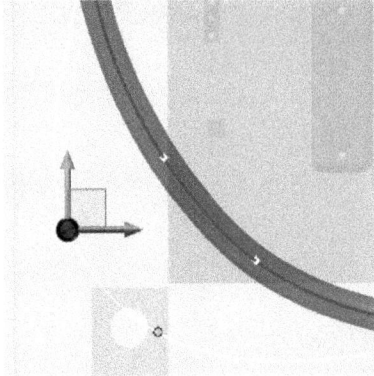

7. In the 3D Move/Rotate mini-toolbar, click OK to execute the change.

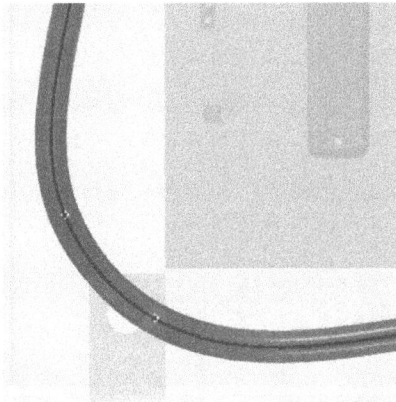

8. Zoom out to view the entire harness assembly.

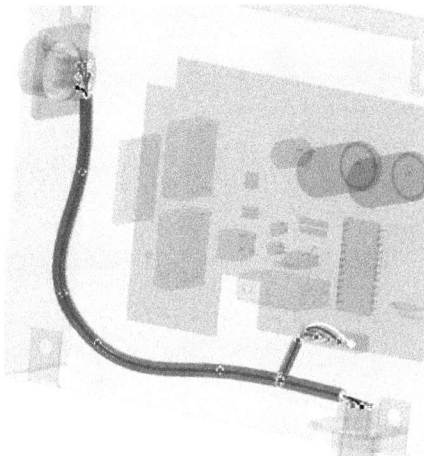

9. To set Harness1 to defer all updates, in the Browser, right-click on Harness1 and click Harness Settings.

10. In the Harness Settings dialog box, in the General tab, in Defer Updates area, click All Updates for this Harness. Click OK.

   Observe that the harness display is suppressed.

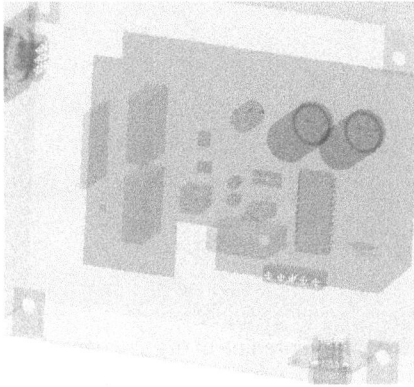

11. Observe the glyph in the Browser indicating that Harness1 has its updates deferred.

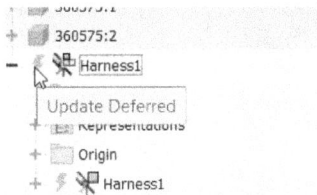

12. To display Harness1:

   - In the browser, right-click on Harness1.
   - Click Harness Settings.
   - In the Harness Settings dialog box, in the General tab, in Defer Updates area, clear the All Updates for this Harness checkbox.
   - Click OK to save the change and close the Harness Settings dialog box. The harness is redisplayed.

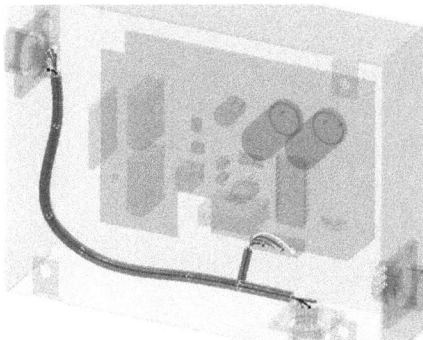

13. Zoom in to the short segment attached to the connector on the PCB.

Observe how the natural curve of the wire passes through the connector due to the angle of the segment.

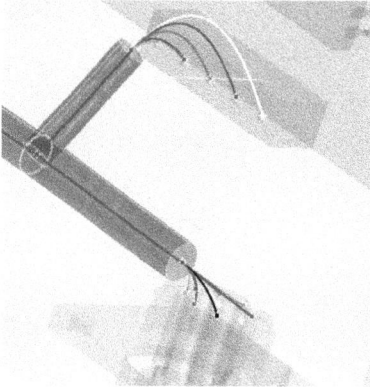

14. To add a point to the segment, right-click on the centerline of the segment and click Add Points.

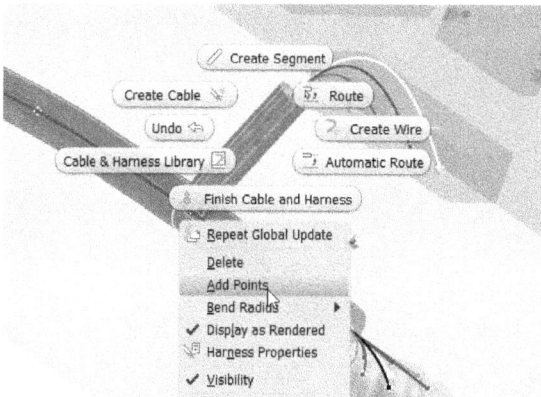

15. In the graphics window, select a location approximately at the midpoint of the segment centerline.

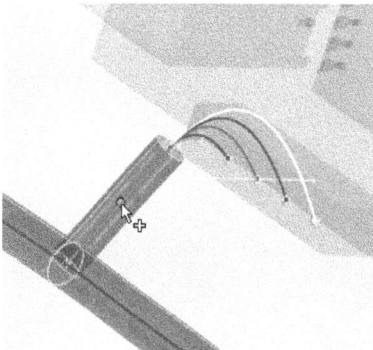

16. Right-click in the graphics window and click Finish.

17. Right-click on the newly added point and click 3D Move/Rotate.

18. Click and drag the Y (towards the side casing) and Z (towards PCB) linear axes to relocate the point to the approximate position as shown in the following figure.

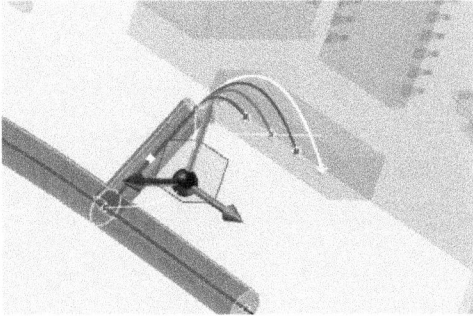

19. In the 3D Move/Rotate mini-toolbar, click OK.

Observe how the relocation of the point changes the entry angle to the segment. The natural curve of the wires now misses the connector.

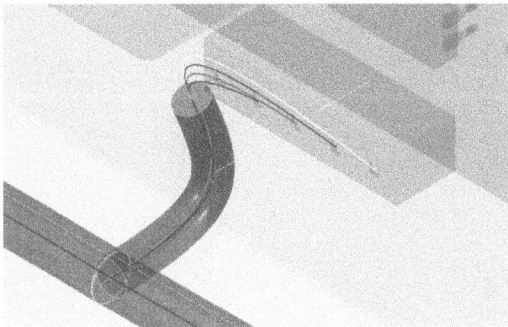

20. Zoom out to view entire harness.

21. Right-click on the point of the segment as indicated.

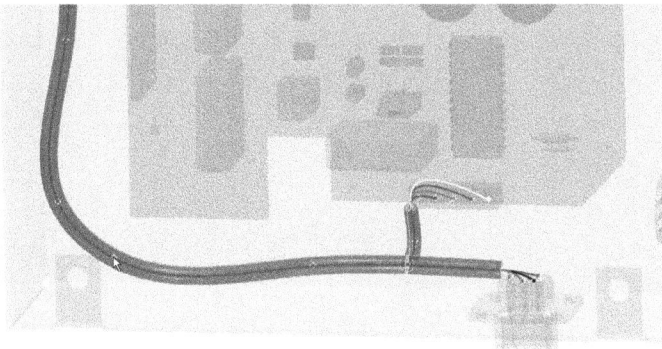

22. Click Delete Point.

Observe how the path of the segment is changed when the point is removed.

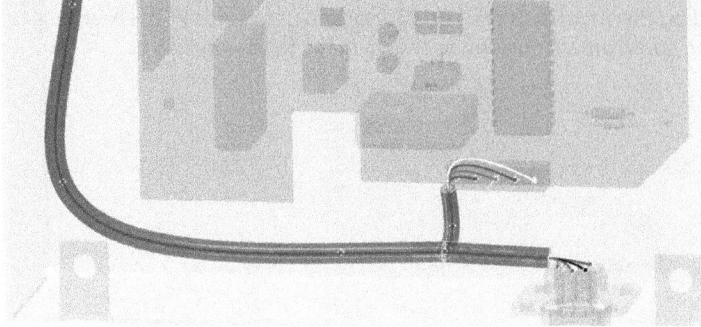

23. Close all files without saving.

Exercise: Check the Bend Radius

In this exercise, you will check the bend radius for a segment, change the radius setting for the segment, and review the results of the changes.

- + 360124:1
- + 360575:1
- + 360575:2
- − Harness1
  - Relationships
  - + Representations
  - + Origin
  - − Harness1
    - + Wires
    - − Segments
      - + Segment1
      - + Segment2
      - + Segment3

The completed exercise

1. Open *Enclosure_Assembly_Bend.iam*.

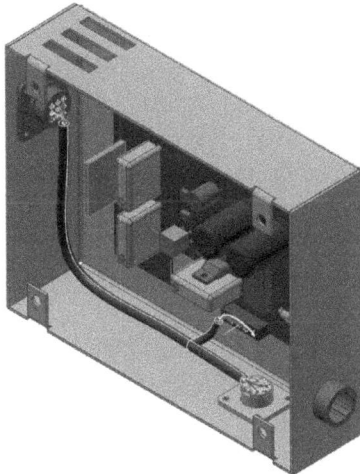

2. Activate Harness1 for editing. Expand Harness1 to display segments.

3. To initiate a bend radius check:

   - Right-click on Segment1 and click Bend Radius>Check.
   - In the alert dialog box, click OK.

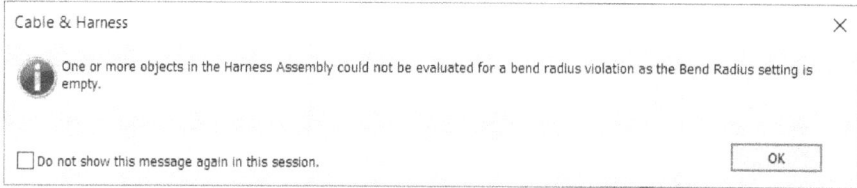

Cable & Harness   ✕

ⓘ One or more objects in the Harness Assembly could not be evaluated for a bend radius violation as the Bend Radius setting is empty.

☐ Do not show this message again in this session.   OK

---

4. In the Browser, review the entry for Segment1. An information icon displays beside Segment1.

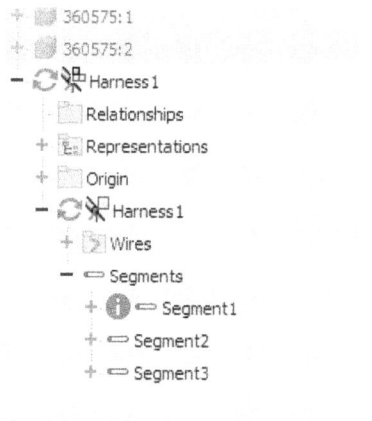

   360575:1
   360575:2
   Harness1
     Relationships
     Representations
     Origin
     Harness1
       Wires
       Segments
         ⓘ Segment1
         Segment2
         Segment3

5. To display information about the Segment1 icon, in the Browser, move the cursor over the icon.

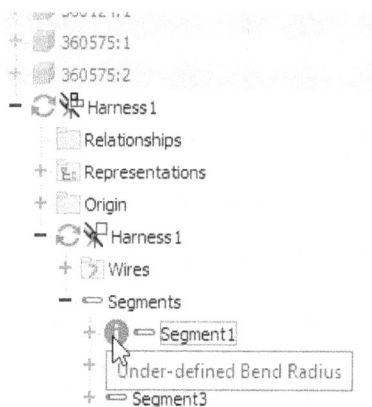

   360575:1
   360575:2
   Harness1
     Relationships
     Representations
     Origin
     Harness1
       Wires
       Segments
         Segment1
         Under-defined Bend Radius
         Segment3

6. In the Browser, right-click on Segment1 and click Harness Properties.

---

7. In the Segment Properties dialog box, in the Occurrence tab, for Bend Radius, enter **5.0**. Click OK.

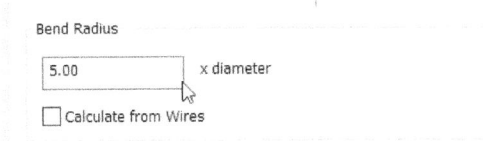

8. In the Browser, right-click on Segment1 and click Bend Radius>Check. The information icon changes to a yellow triangle.

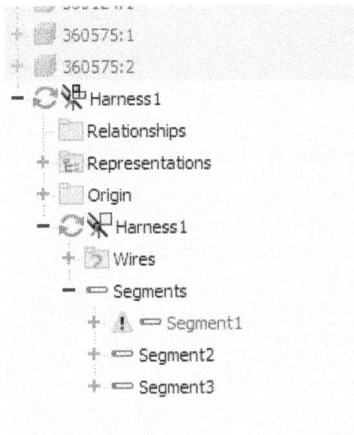

9. Right-click on Segment1and select Bend Radius>Show Violations. The Show Violations dialog box displays the approximate location of the violation.

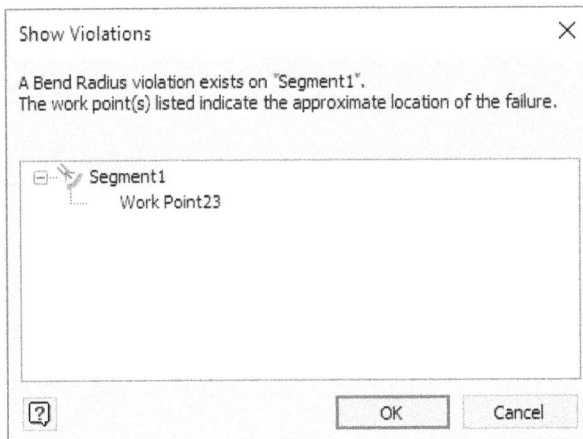

10. Zoom in to the end of the segment that displays the violation.

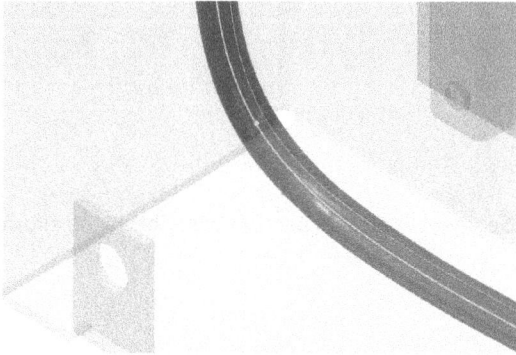

11. In the Show Violations dialog box, click OK.

12. In the Browser, right-click on Segment1and click Bend Radius>Clear Violation.

13. In the Browser, right-click on Segment1and click Harness Properties.

14. In the Segment Properties dialog box, in the Occurrence tab, for Bend Radius, enter **3.0**. Click OK.

Bend Radius

| 3.0 | x diameter |

☐ Calculate from Wires

15. In the Browser, right-click on Segment1and click Bend Radius>Check. No violations are reported.

16. Click Finish Cable and Harness.

17. Close all files without saving.

Lesson: Working with Splices

In this lesson, you learn to identify, add, and edit splices within a wiring harness.

Splices are an integral part of a wiring harness design. Identifying locations, as well as adding and editing splices, enables you to efficiently design your wiring harness.

In the following figure, two splices are used to wire a connector. The first splice is used to run a single wire from the main harness. Then, a second splice is used to distribute power among the three connectors.

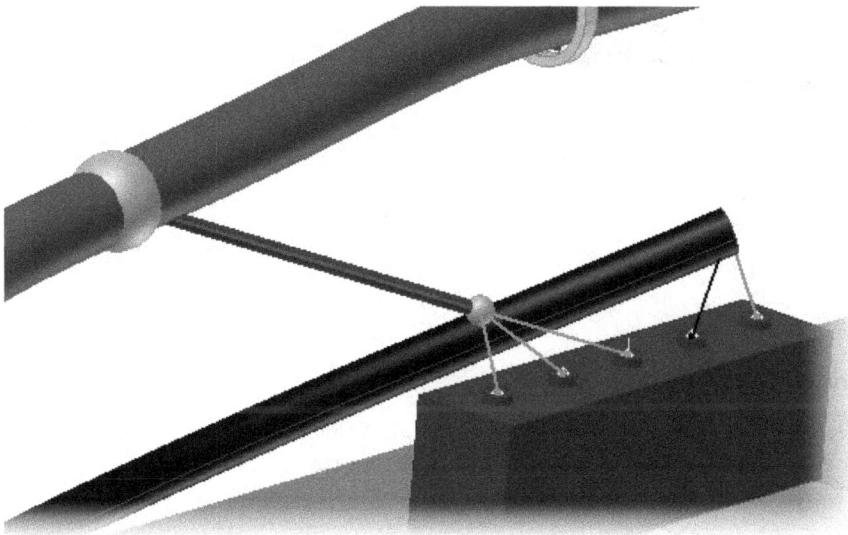

Objectives

After completing this lesson, you will be able to:

- Describe the purpose, characteristics, and types of splices.
- Add a splice offset from a face or into a wire or route segment.
- List the different ways splices can be modified.
- Edit a wire to splice it to an existing splice.

About Splices

A splice in a wiring harness enables a complete electrical circuit to be created without running wires the full path of the circuit. Reducing the amount of wiring to complete a circuit reduces material cost and weight, and can also aid when performing diagnostics on the wiring harness.

In the following figure, a wire is being added to a splice in the wiring harness.

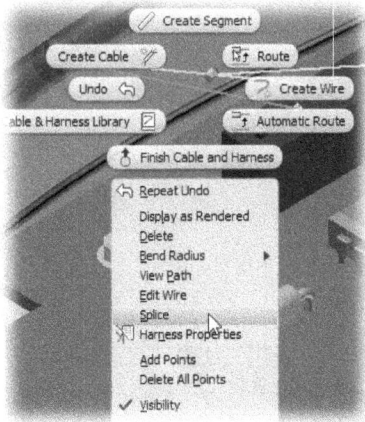

Definition of Splices

A splice is a union or junction of two objects. In Autodesk® Inventor® Cable and Harness, a splice is a modifiable object that enables two or more wires to create a path that completes a circuit for the flow of electricity.

Example Splices

A splice is added to the power wire out of the power supply. A wire is run from the splice to a small light next to the power supply indicating that power is flowing from the power supply.

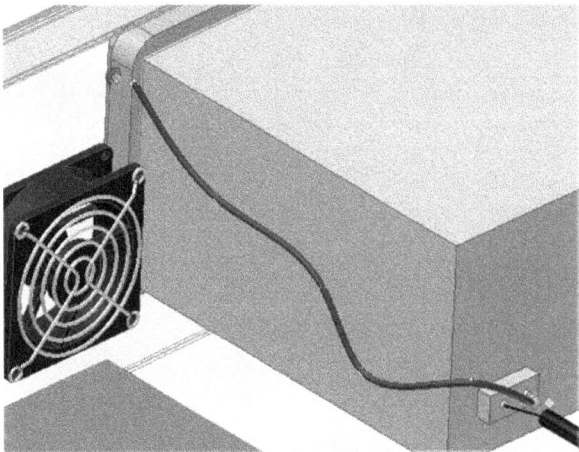

Adding a Splice

If you know where a splice will be located, you can add the splice before creating wires. Then, when wires are added to the harness, they can be routed using the splice. To locate a splice before creating wires, you start the Create Splice tool and select a face. The splice is offset from the selected face.

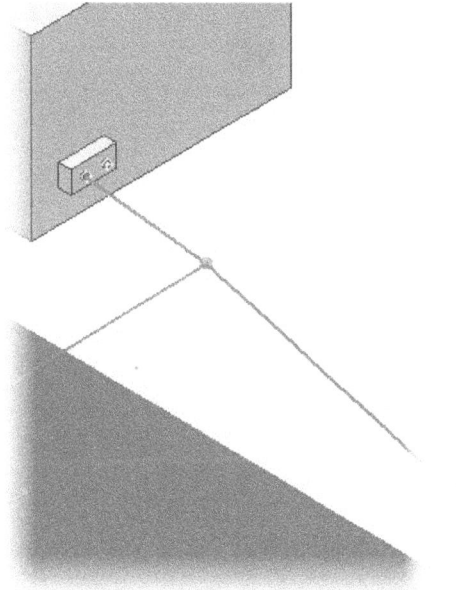

If you want to add a splice after creating wires, you start the Splice tool and select a wire. After creating the splice, you can splice existing wires to the splice, or route new wires through it.

In the following figure, a splice is offset from a face, and then wires are routed through the splice.

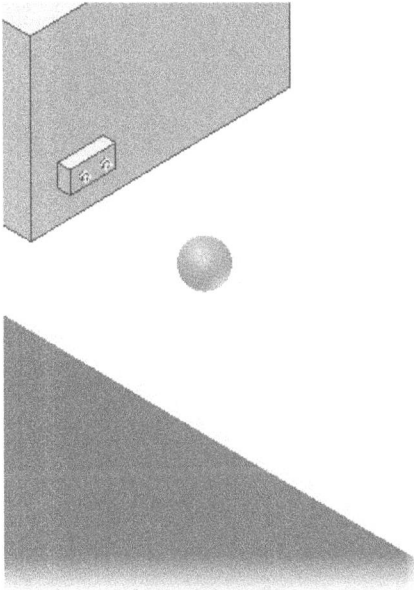

Splice offset from face | Wires routed through the splice

Access

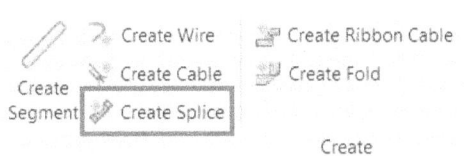

Ribbon: Cable and Harness tab>Create panel

Create Splice Options

Each splice added to a harness requires a unique identifier to map the splice to the schematic design. When you start the Splice tool, the Create Splice dialog box displays. In the Create Splice dialog box, you specify this identifier. You can accept the default name or specify your own name. The name specified displays in the Browser under Splices.

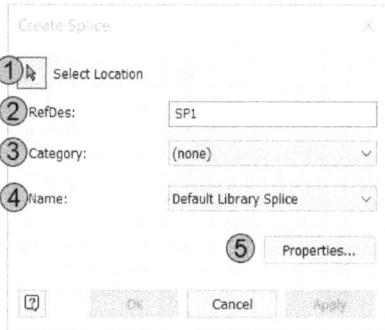

[1] **Select Location** - Use to locate the splice on the wiring harness.

[2] **RefDes** - Use to specify a unique identifier that maps the splice in the schematic diagram. A RefDes is required for each splice.

[3] **Category** - (Optional) Use to specify the category where the splice is located.

[4] **Name** - Use to select the name in the Cable and Harness Library. If no name is selected, the Default Library Splice is used. The last selected name becomes the default name.

[5] **Properties** - Use to display the Library Splice dialog box.

Procedure: Adding a Splice

The following steps describe how to add a splice to a wiring harness.

1. With a wiring harness active, start the Create Splice tool.

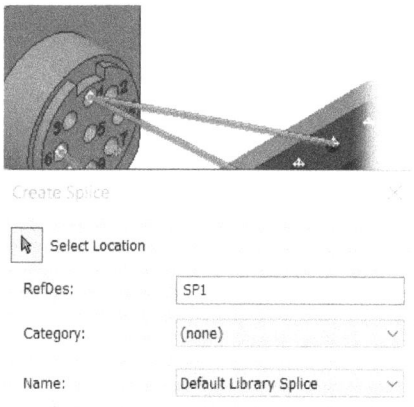

2. Enter the required information in the Create Splice dialog box.

3. Select a segment splice or wire. Click Apply to add additional splices. Click OK to exit the tool.

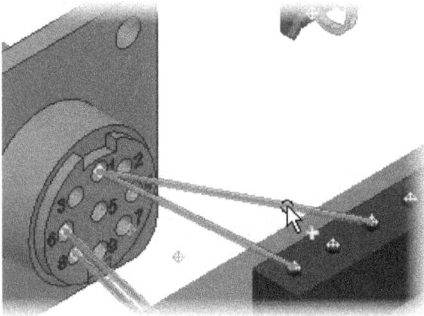

Splice Modifications

After a splice has been added to a harness assembly, there are several options or operations that can be performed to modify the splice. Each of these can be accessed by right-clicking the splice. This can be done in the browser or the graphics window.

In the following figure, a splice in the wiring harness is modified. In this instance, the offset distance of the splice is updated.

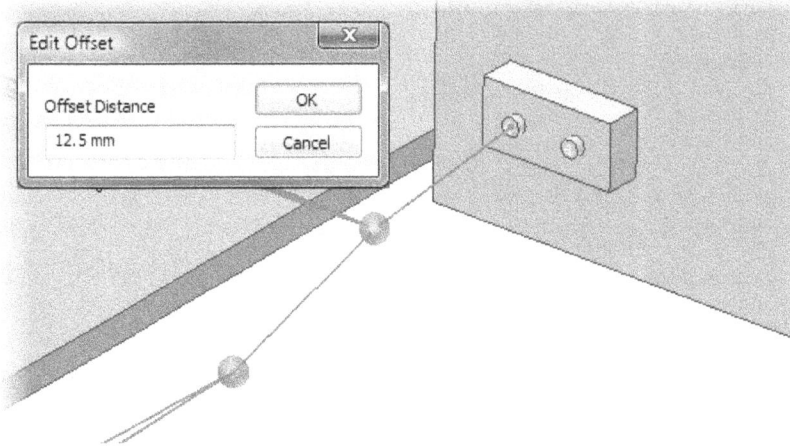

Access

To access options to modify a splice, in the browser or graphics window, right-click on the wire or the splice.

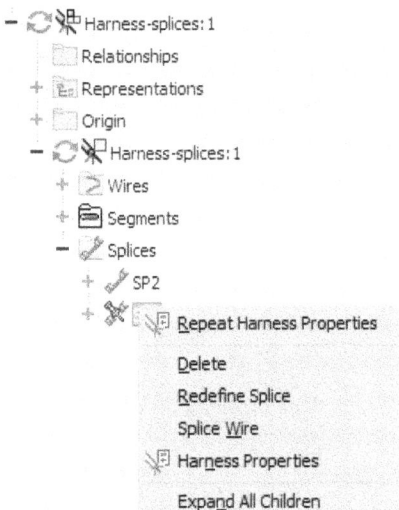

Use the following options to modify splices when you right-click on the splice.

Option	Description
Delete	Use this option to remove a splice from a wiring harness. If two wires are attached, the wires combine and form a single wire. If three or more wires are attached, the logical connections for the wires are maintained.
Redefine Splice	Use this option to redefine a new location on the current wire or move to a new wire. Also use this option to redefine the offset value.
Splice Wire	Use this option to add a wire to the splice.
Harness Options	Use this option to access the Splice Properties dialog box. In the Occurrence tab, you can specify a new value for RefDes.

Redefining Offset Value

To redefine the offset value, right-click on the splice and click Redefine Splice. Then, right-click in an open area of the graphics window and click Edit Offset.

Editing a Wire to a Splice

If you determine that a splice is required to be added after you have already created wires, you might edit a wire to add to that splice. You can add a wire to a splice by working with either the wire or the splice. In the Browser or the graphics window, you select the object and select Splice Wire from the shortcut menu.

If adding the wire to the splice results in a redundancy in the harness, you are prompted that the redundant wire will be removed from the harness when the wires are spliced.

In the following figure, wires are added to multiple splices in a wiring harness.

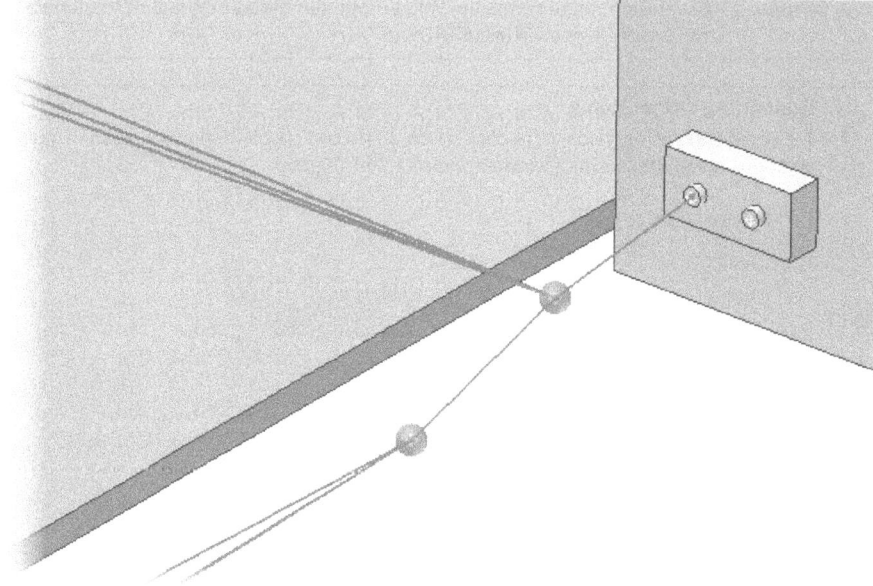

Access

To edit a wire to a splice, in the Browser or graphics window, right-click on the wire or the splice and click Splice.

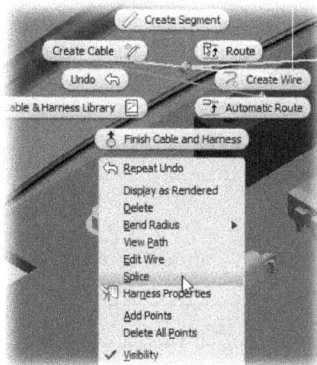

Procedure: Editing a Wire to a Splice

The following steps describe editing a wire to a splice.

1. Right-click on the wire and click Splice.

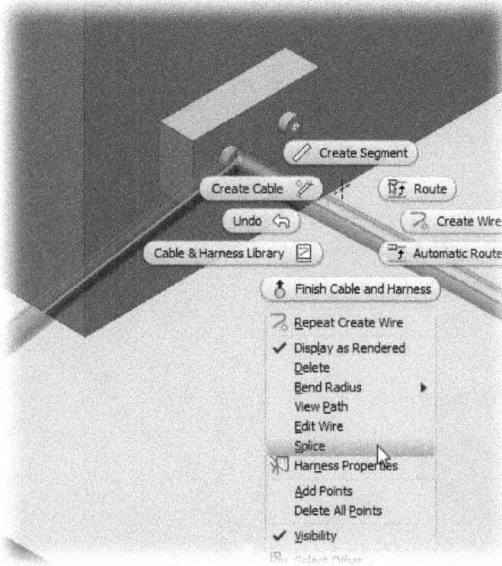

2. Select the splice. Alternatively, you can select a splice, right-click and select Splice Wire, and select the wire to splice.

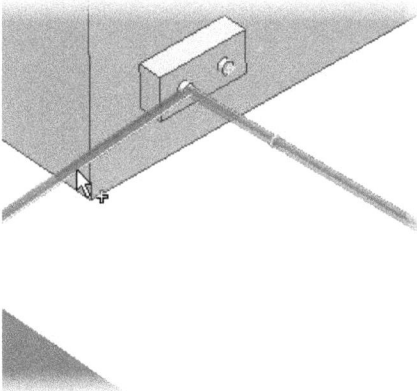

3. Note the warning that redundant wires are going to be removed.

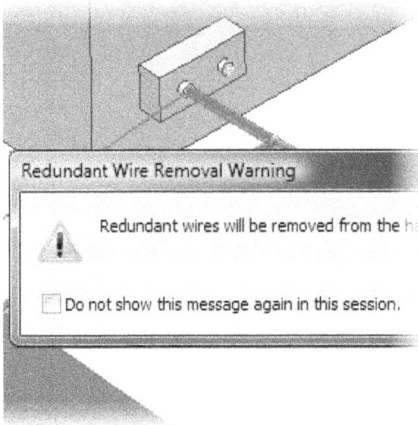

4. The end of the wire is moved to the splice.

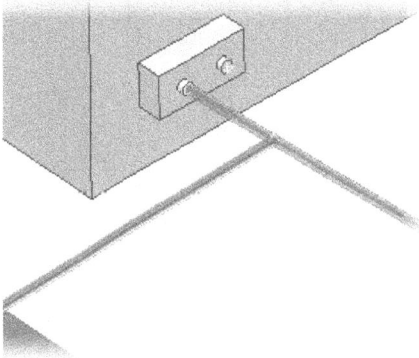

Exercise: Working with Splices

In this exercise, you will add and edit splices in a wiring harness. In addition, you will explore the properties of a splice.

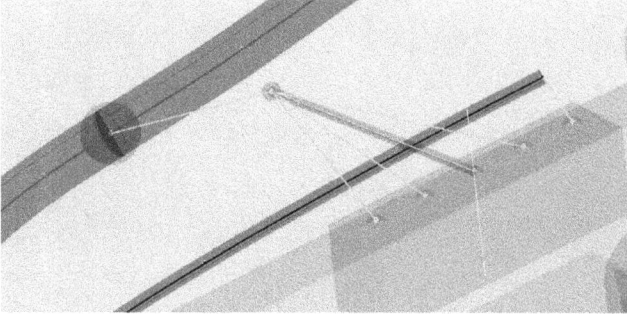

The completed exercise

1. Open *Working_with_Splices.iam*.

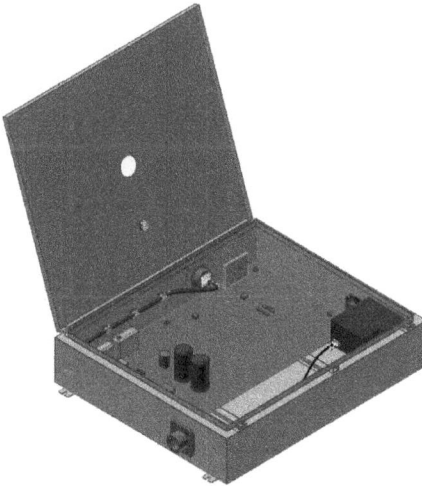

2. To activate the Cable and Harness environment, in the Browser, double-click on Harness-splices.

3. Rotate the assembly to view the components on the left inner side of the cabinet. Zoom in to see the three wires going from the main harness to the connector.

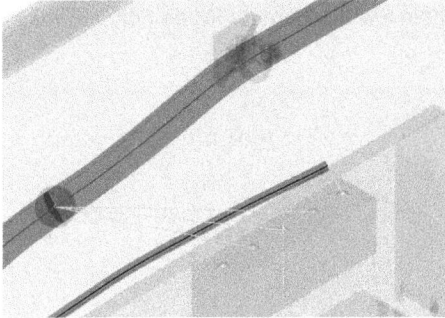

4. To add a splice to a wire:
- In the Cable and Harness tab, in the Create panel, click Create Splice.
- In the Create Splice dialog box, note the default value for RefDes: SP1.
- Click near the midpoint of the wire going to the center pin. Click OK.

Note: The wire is divided into two segments.

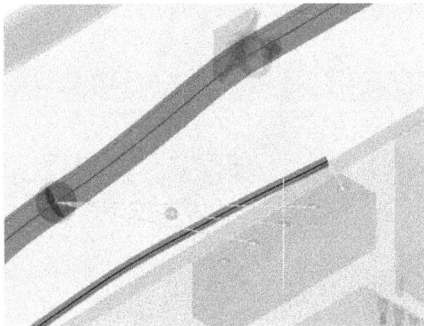

5. To add a wire to the splice:
- Right-click in the splice.
- Click Splice Wire.
- Select the third wire on the block.
- In the Redundant Wire Removal Warning message box, click OK.

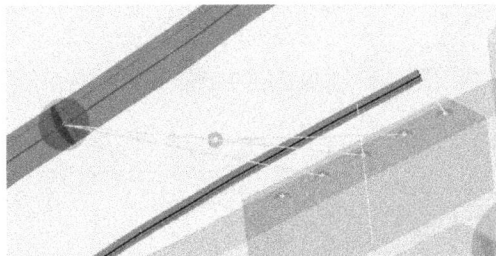

6. To add additional wires to the splice:
- Right-click on the first wire.
- Click Splice.
- Select the splice.
- In the Redundant Wire Removal Warning message box, click OK.

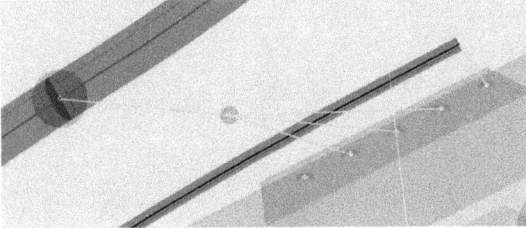

7. To add a new wire to the splice:
- Click Create Wire.
- Select Pin1 on the connector.
- Select the splice.
- In the Select Splice Pin dialog box, click OK.
- In the Create Wire dialog box, click OK.

8. In the Browser, expand the harness assembly to view the splices.

9. To view splice properties:
   - Right-click on splice SP1and click Harness Properties.
   - In the Occurrence tab, for RefDes, enter **Splice_1**.
   - Click Apply.

   Note: The Browser changes.

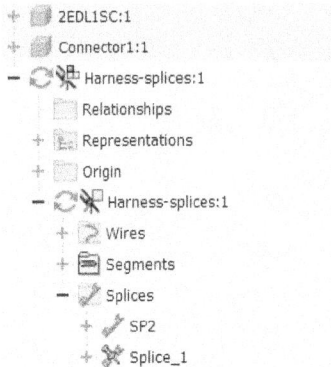

   - 2EDL1SC:1
   - Connector1:1
   - Harness-splices:1
     - Relationships
     - Representations
     - Origin
     - Harness-splices:1
       - Wires
       - Segments
       - Splices
         - SP2
         - Splice_1

10. To view properties of the wires connected to the splice:
    - In the Splice Properties dialog box, click the Wires tab.
    - Double-click on Wire1.
    - Click the Display tab.
    - Under Default Display, click Rendered Display. Click OK.
    - In the Splice Properties dialog box, click OK.

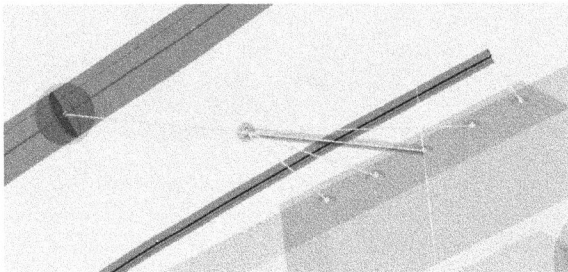

11. To relocate the splice:

    ■ In the graphics window, right-click on the splice and click Redefine Splice.
    ■ Right-click and click Edit Offset.
    ■ In the Edit Offset dialog box, for Offset Distance, enter **14 mm**. Click OK.
    ■ Click the inside of the cabinet as shown in the following figure.

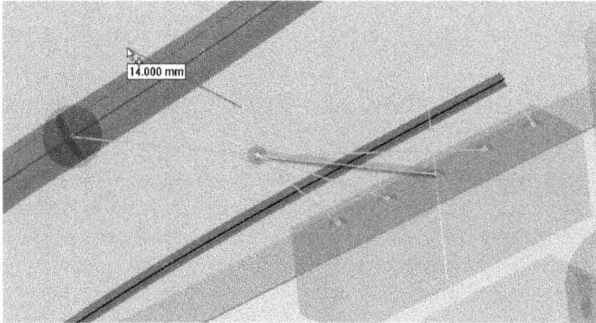

12. Note that the location of the splice is updated.

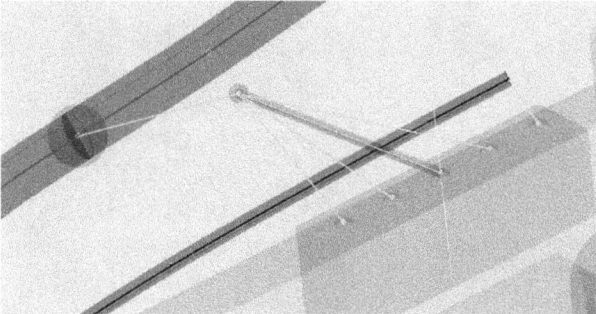

13. To delete the splice:

    ■ Right-click on the splice and click Delete.

    Note that all four wires go to the next logical connection.

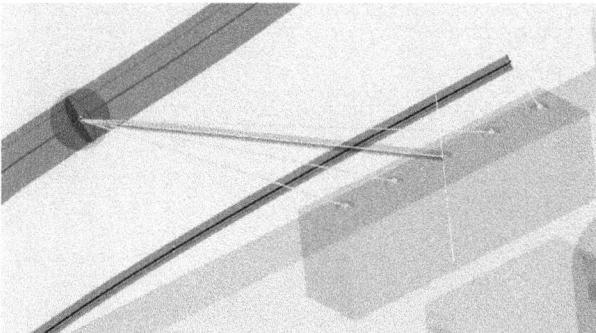

14. Close all files without saving changes.

Lesson: Working with Virtual Parts

In many instances, components of a design need to be counted, but they would not be worthwhile to model. In these cases, you can assign an object as a virtual part. A virtual part contains the required information to be included in a bill of materials, but is not a model in the design. A few examples of virtual parts include paint, wire ties, tie downs, or other items that might be purchased in bulk and used to complete the assembly. By assigning objects as virtual parts, you can refine your cable and harness designs.

Virtual parts enable you to refine your cable and harness designs by assigning bill of material information to cable and harness objects.

The following figure shows a harness design before and after the assignment of virtual parts. In this example, a loom has been assigned to the segment. With a style applied to the loom virtual part, you see the change displayed in the graphics window. However, many virtual parts are not displayed graphically. In addition to a loom, a plug has been assigned to the unused slot in the connector (number nine) to keep dust and debris from collecting.

Virtual parts not assigned   Virtual parts assigned

Objectives

After completing this lesson, you will be able to:

- Describe the purpose of a virtual part.
- Add virtual parts to your design by assigning them to cable and harness objects.
- Edit the properties of a virtual part.

About Virtual Parts

Virtual parts in cable and harness designs are non-solid models with assigned property information that enables them to represent a cable and harness object. Assigning this information to a cable and harness object enables that object to be counted in the bill of materials without actually modeling the object. Objects commonly assigned a virtual part status are terminals, seals, plugs, labels, and looms.

In the following figure, items 6 through 10 are virtual parts that have been added to the harness assembly. Adding these parts to the harness assembly enables their inclusion in the bill of materials.

Item		Part Number	Stock Number	BOM Structure	Unit QTY
	1	.Wire1		Normal	98.6200...
	2	3047-BLK.1005		Normal	384.3713...
	3	3047-BLU.1007		Normal	386.8814...
	4	3048-BLK.1009		Normal	302.8535...
	5	3048-RED.1010		Normal	302.3394...
	6	.Default Library Terminal		Normal	Each
	7	.Default Library Seal		Normal	Each
	8	.Default Library Plug		Normal	Each
	9	.Default Library Label		Normal	Each
	10	.Loom1		Normal	304.3027...
	11	3048-WHT.1002		Normal	385.7510...
	12	3048-YEL.1004		Normal	385.7510...
	13	3047-GRN.1006		Normal	385.7510...

Example of Virtual Parts

A cable and harness connector pin can be assigned as a Terminal, Seal, or Plug virtual part in a cable and harness design. Objects such as wires, cable wires, and segments are classified as Loom virtual parts. Wire pins, cable wire pins, and segment work points are considered Label virtual parts.

In the following figure, Assign Virtual Parts is used to assign a connector pin as a Terminal virtual part.

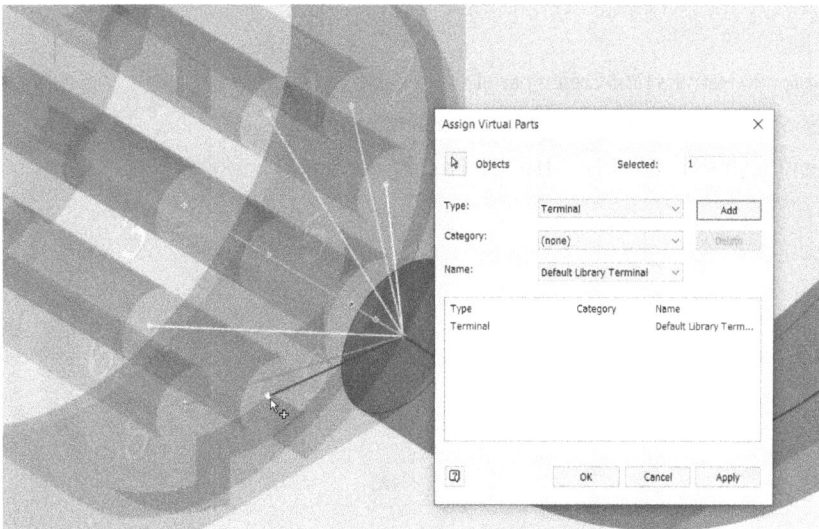

Assigning Virtual Parts

To assign a virtual part to a cable and harness object, you have to be in the cable and harness environment. You start the Assign Virtual Parts tool and select specific cable and harness objects. Depending on the object selected, you specify a Type, Category, and Name, then add the component to the virtual parts list.

In the following figure, a cable and harness wire segment is assigned the Loom virtual part type.

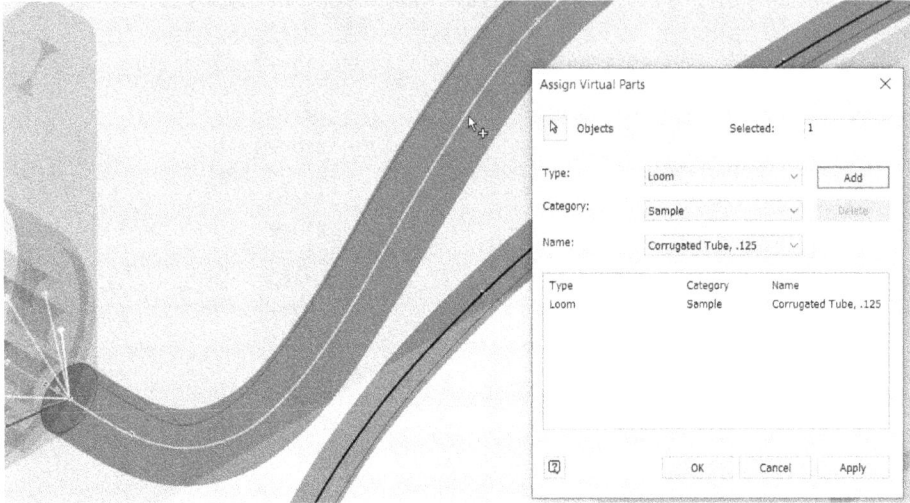

Access

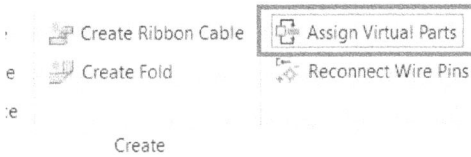

Ribbon: Cable and Harness tab>Create panel

Keyboard Shortcut: V (when cable and harness environment is active)

Context Menu: Right-click on object>Harness Properties>Virtual Parts tab

Assign Virtual Parts Options

The following options are available when assigning virtual parts in the cable and harness environment.

① **Objects** - Use to select harness objects to assign virtual parts. When multiple parts are assigned, an occurrence of the virtual part is created for each object.

② **Type** - Assigns the type of virtual part based on the object selected.

③ **Category** - (Optional) Assigns the virtual part to a category.

④ **Name** - Use to select the name of the virtual part in the Cable and Harness Library.

⑤ **Add** - Use to assign the virtual part to the selected object.

⑥ **Delete** - Use to remove selected objects from the virtual parts list.

⑦ **Virtual Parts List** - List the virtual parts assigned including their type, category, and name.

Procedure: Assigning Virtual Parts

The following steps describe creating a virtual part in a cable and harness design.

1. In the cable and harness environment, start the Assign Virtual Parts tool. Select a cable and harness object.

2. If required, select information for the Type, Category, or Name.

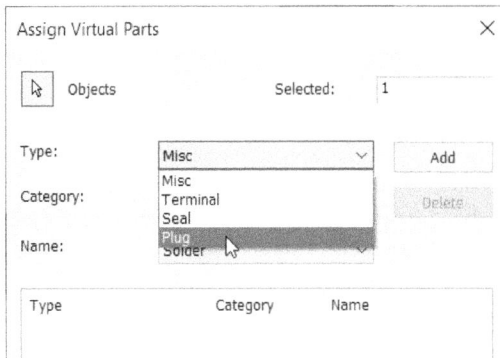

3. Add the virtual part to the list.

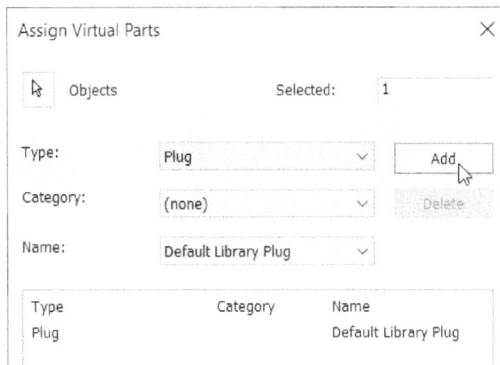

Editing Virtual Parts

You edit virtual parts by editing the harness properties. To access the virtual part properties, you locate the virtual part in the Browser, right-click and select Harness Properties in the menu. The appropriate dialog box displays based on the type of virtual part that is selected.

In the following figure, a Loom virtual part is accessed in the Browser and selected for edit using the Loom Properties dialog box.

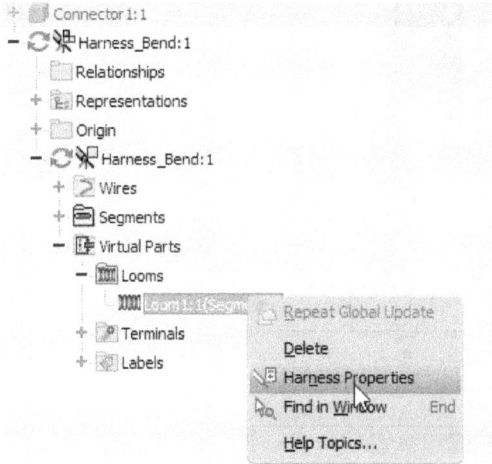

Access

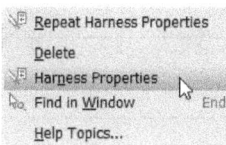

Context Menu: In the Browser, right-click on the virtual part>Harness Properties

Procedure: Editing Virtual Parts

The following steps describe editing a virtual part in a harness design.

1. With the cable and harness environment active, in the Browser, locate the virtual part. Right-click and click Harness Properties.

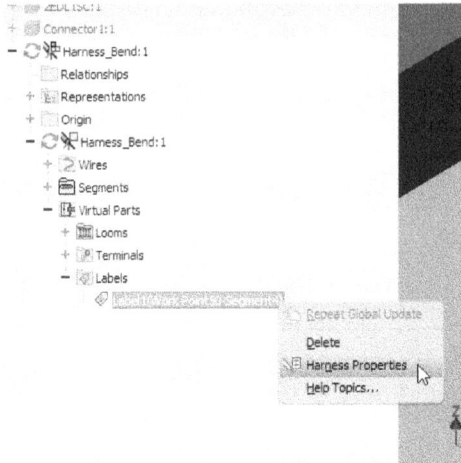

2. In the dialog box that displays, make the required changes. Click Apply.

3. The changes are applied to the virtual part.

Exercise: Work with Virtual Parts

In this exercise, you will add different virtual parts to a harness design. You will then edit a virtual part and review the virtual parts in the bill of materials.

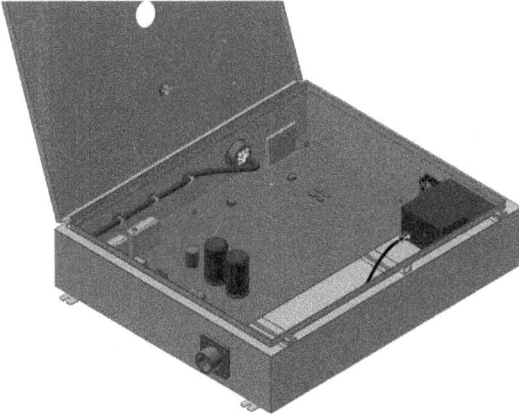

The completed exercise

1. Open *Virtual_Parts.iam*.

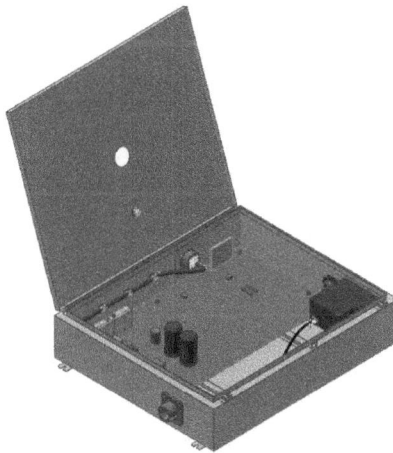

2. Zoom in to view the connector and wiring at the back of the cabinet.

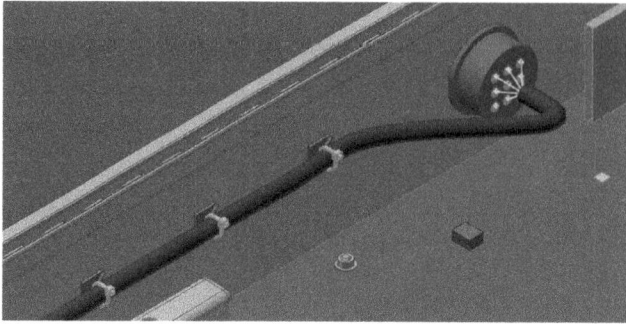

3. In the Browser, double-click on Harness_Bend to edit it.

4. To begin to create a virtual part:

- In the Cable and Harness tab, in the Create panel, click Assign Virtual Parts.
- Select the line defining the segment path as shown in the following figure.

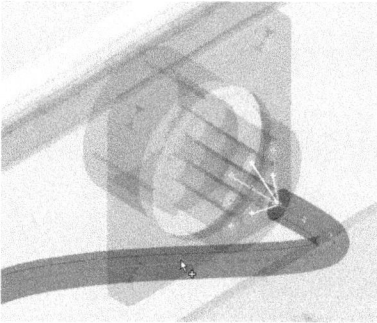

5. To define the virtual part, in the Assign Virtual Parts dialog box:

- For Type, select Loom.
- For Name, select Wire Sleeve.
- Click Add.

6. In the Assign Virtual Parts dialog box, click OK.

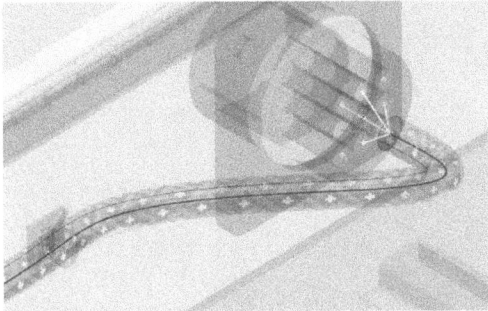

7. To begin to assign a terminal virtual part:
- In the Cable and Harness tab, in the Create panel, click Assign Virtual Parts.
- On the connector, select the number nine pin (arrow).

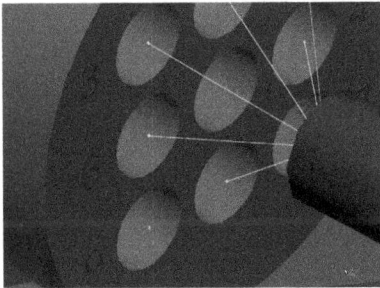

8. To define the Terminal virtual part:
- In the Assign Virtual Parts dialog box, for Type, select Terminal.
- Click Add.
- Click OK.

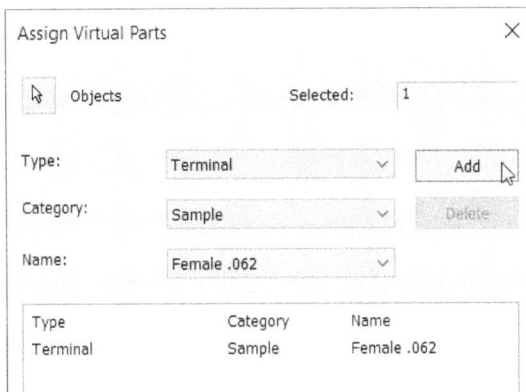

9. Change your view to display the power pack inside the cabinet.

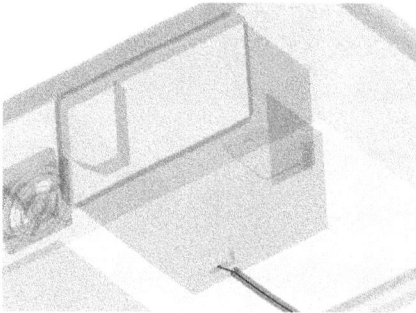

10. To begin to assign a label to a virtual part:
    - In the Cable and Harness tab, in the Create panel, click Assign Virtual Parts.
    - Select the point where the wire connects at the segment.

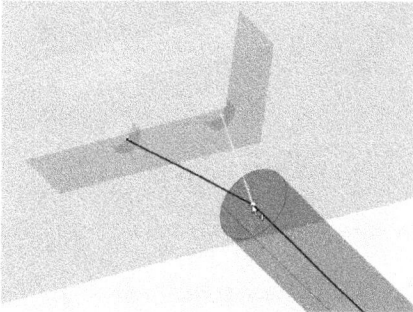

11. In the Assign Virtual Parts dialog box:
    - For Type, select Label.
    - For Name, select Default Library Label.
    - Click Add and OK.

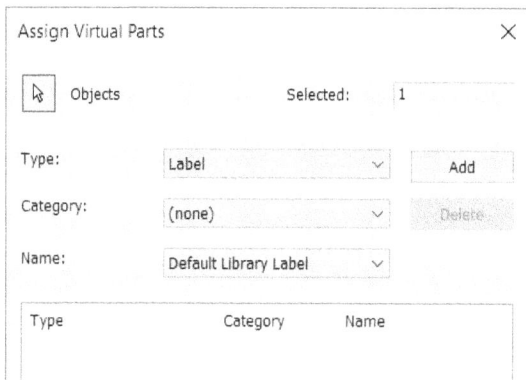

    - Click on local update if required.

---

12. In the Browser, expand the harness until the Virtual Parts folder displays. Expand the Labels folder.

13. To edit a virtual part:

- In the Browser, right-click on Label1(Work Point50-Segment4).
- Click Harness Properties.
- In the Label Properties dialog box, in the Occurrence tab, for Name, enter **Safety Warning Label_1**.

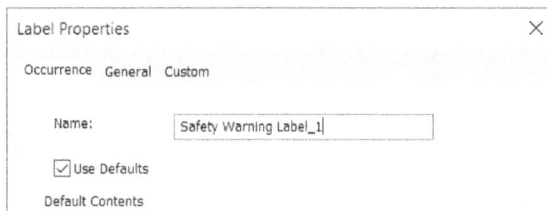

14. To apply the changes:

- Click OK.
- Review the Browser entry.

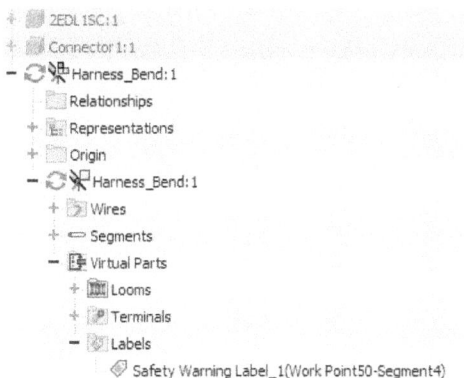

15. To review the BOM information:

- In the Manage tab, in the Manage panel, click Bill of Materials.
- In the Bill of Materials dialog box, select the Structured tab.
- Right-click on the Structured tab and click Enable BOM View.
- Review the virtual parts included.
- Click Done.

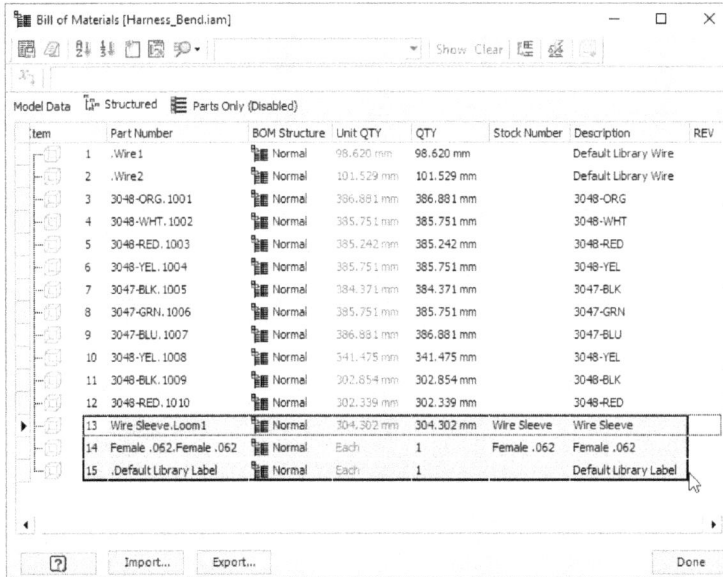

16. Click Home View.

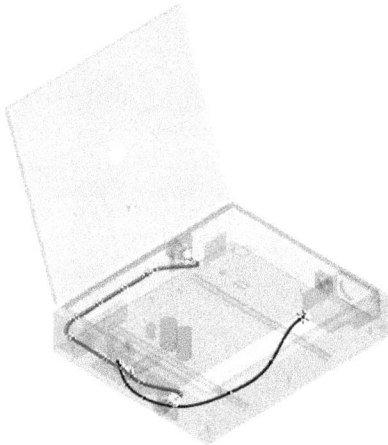

17. Close all files without saving changes.

Chapter Summary

In this chapter, you learned how to refine a cable and harness design by editing the current content and adding additional content. You learned how to edit your existing design content of wires, cables, route segments, and cable ribbons. You also learned how to add and edit splices and virtual parts.

Having completed this chapter, you can:

- Edit the properties, connections, and positions of wires, cables, ribbon cables, and route segments.
- Add splices to a harness assembly and edit a splice.
- Add and edit virtual parts.

Communicate the Design

In this chapter, you learn the tools and techniques for communicating your cable and harness design to others by creating and annotating 2D drawings and exporting the design data.

Objectives

After completing this chapter, you will be able to:

- Create 2D drawings and nailboards of a harness design.
- Annotate nailboards with dimensions and table information.
- Create reports and export the data for a cable and harness design.

Lesson: Creating Drawing Views of Cable and Harness Designs

This lesson describes the tools and techniques you use to create and edit drawing views of cable and harness designs.

Proper documentation is critical to any design. When documenting cable and harness drawings, it is important to understand the function and application of the tools used to document your designs.

The following figure shows the progression of a cable and harness wiring design. In view 1, the wiring harness is designed around the other components in the design. View 2 shows the harness isolated from the rest of the design, but still in 3D configuration. View 3 is the nailboard view of the same harness.

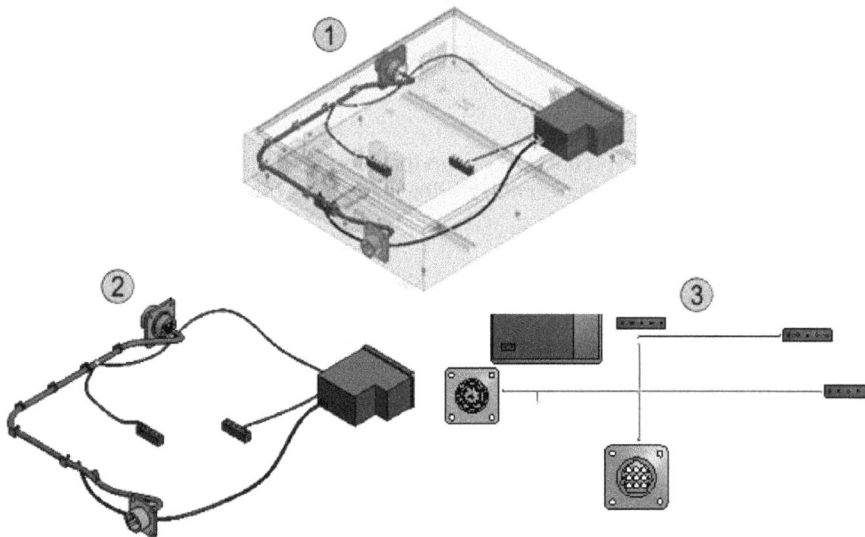

Objectives

After completing this lesson, you will be able to:

- Describe the types of views that can be created for a cable and harness design.
- Create a nailboard drawing view.
- Modify a nailboard view by pivoting sections, fanning in and out wires, breaking the sketch, and displaying wires at actual diameter.
- Add drawing views of the associated connectors.

Creating 2D Drawings

You use a combination of standard Autodesk® Inventor® drawing tools specific to Cable and Harness to document your cable and harness designs. In addition to standard drawing views, you can also create and edit nailboard drawing views, as well as add connector views.

The following figure shows two drawings of the same wiring harness for a computer power supply. The left image is an isometric view of the harness as it is installed in the computer case. The image on the right shows the 2D nailboard representation of the same wiring harness. This nailboard view includes views of the connectors used in the harness.

3D Isometric view of a power supply wiring harness   2D Nailboard view of a power supply wiring harness

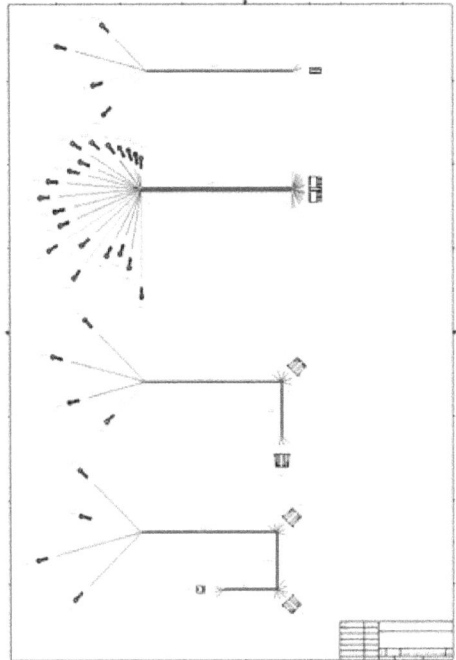

Description of 2D Cable and Harness Drawings

There are two primary methods for documenting a cable and harness design on a drawing sheet. Using standard Autodesk Inventor drawing tools you can create base, projected, isometric, and detailed views of the 3D design geometry just as you do for any part or assembly model. Alternatively, you can create a flattened-out representation of the cable and harness. This flattened-out view type is referred to as a nailboard drawing view. With a nailboard drawing view, you can add annotations to the view to document it for manufacturing.

<table>
<tr><td>

View Wires in Drawing Views

To display wires in drawing views, in the harness assembly, the wires must be set to Display as Rendered.
</td></tr>
</table>

<table>
<tr><td>

Representations

To improve performance, and to isolate harness views in an assembly, incorporate level of detail and view representations into your designs. Using level of detail representations enables you to suppress all components except those required in the view, and improves performance. View representations enable you to control settings such as color, visibility, and viewing angles.
</td></tr>
</table>

Process: Creating 2D Cable and Harness Drawings

The following figure shows an overview of creating 2D cable and harness drawings.

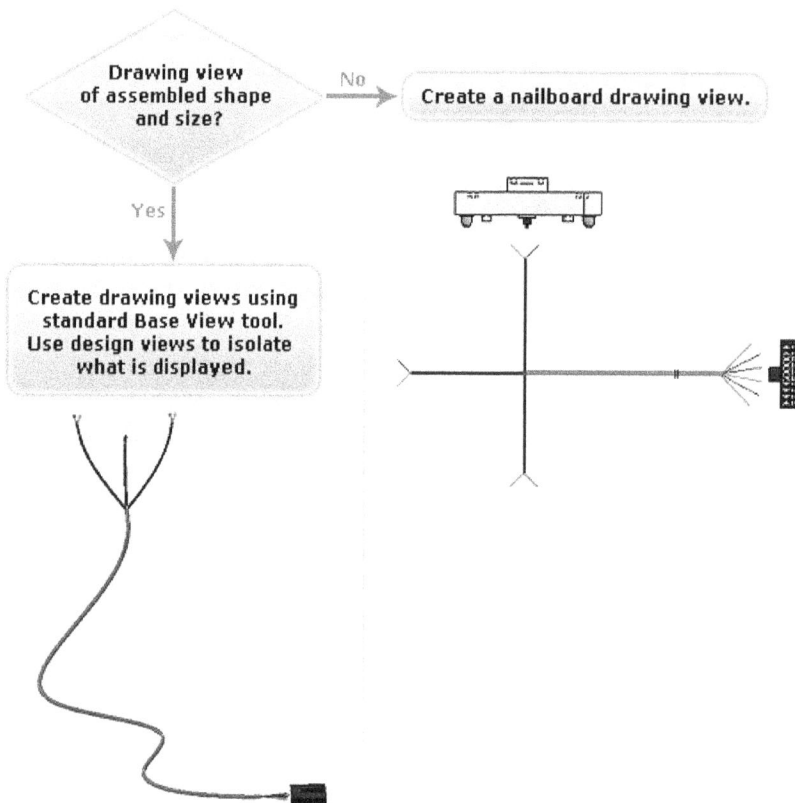

There is an option to quickly filter out surface and mesh bodies during drawing view creation. It affects segments of cable and harness assemblies, as the segments do not display by default. To display segments, as shown on the right in the following illustration, select Include Surface Bodies in the Recovery Options tab, in Drawing View window.

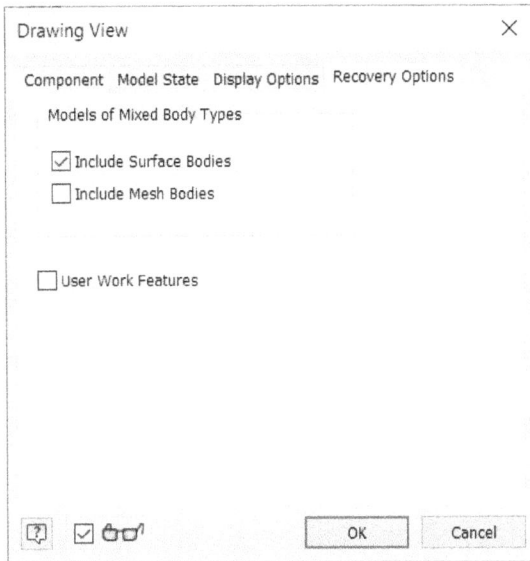

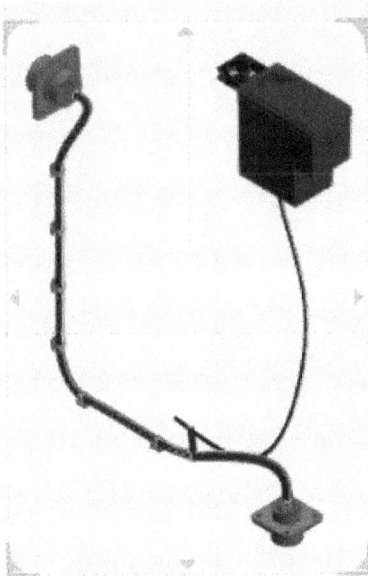

Segments displayed (with Include Surface Bodies selected)

Segments missing (default)

Creating Nailboard Drawing Views

To correctly document a harness assembly, you need to understand the options and steps required to create a nailboard view.

A nailboard view is a 2D, flattened view of a 3D wire harness. The wiring harness is unfolded, and straight segments are used to represent the harness. These segments are representative of the harness, but do not follow the exact path the way a 3D drawing view of the harness would. Once the nailboard view is added, it can be annotated to document the wire harness. Only one nailboard view per drawing file can be created.

The following figure shows two views of a wiring harness. The figure on the left shows the wiring harness as it is designed to fit around the other components in the assembly. The image on the right shows the flattened nailboard view of the same harness.

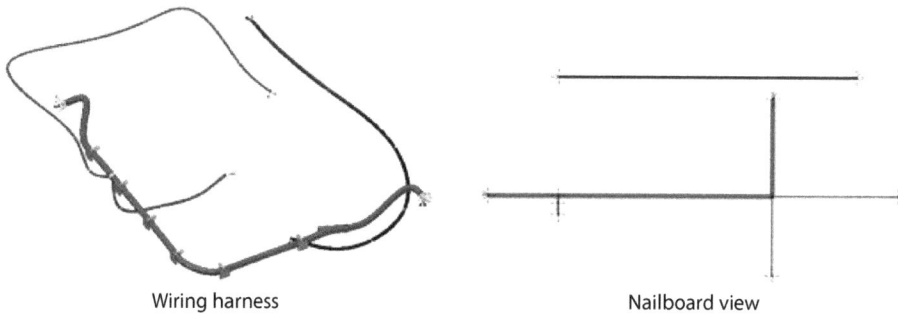

Wiring harness

Nailboard view

Access

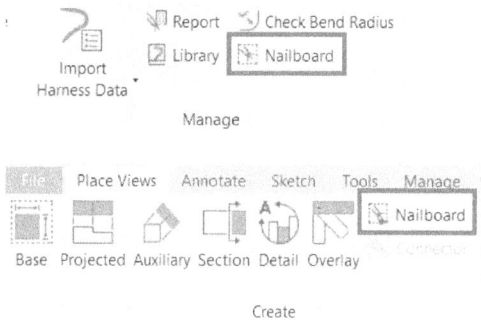

Ribbon: Cable and Harness tab>Manage panel

Ribbon: Place Views tab>Create panel

Nailboard View Dialog Box

When you create a nailboard view from within a drawing file, the Nailboard View dialog box displays, enabling you to specify properties of the nailboard view as it is created. If the assembly has multiple harnesses, you can specify which harness is used to create the view. If the nailboard view is initiated from the assembly file, the view is created based on the currently active harness.

The following options are available when creating a nailboard view.

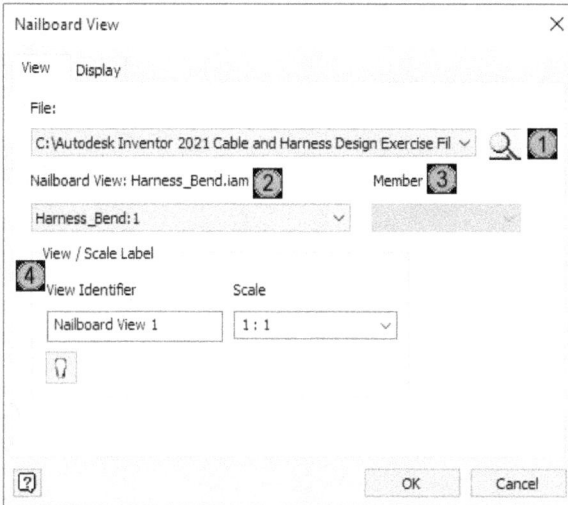

1. Use to select the assembly file that contains harness assemblies.

2. If an assembly contains multiple harness assemblies, use this list to specify the harness assembly for the nailboard view.

3. Use to select the iAssembly member to use for the nailboard view.

4. Use to specify a label and scale factor for the nailboard view. Also toggles the display of the label and scale factor.

Procedure: Creating Nailboard Drawing Views

You can create nailboard views from the Drawing or Cable and Harness environments. When starting from the Cable and Harness environment, you first specify the drawing template to be used. The view placed is based on the active harness. Once the template is selected, the nailboard view is placed on the drawing sheet.

When you create a nailboard view from within a drawing file, you specify options for the view in the Nailboard View dialog box. In the Nailboard View dialog box, you can specify different properties of the view.

The following steps describe creating a nailboard drawing view of a wire harness in the drawing environment.

1. Start the Nailboard View tool.

2. Specify the file, Nailboard view label, and scale.

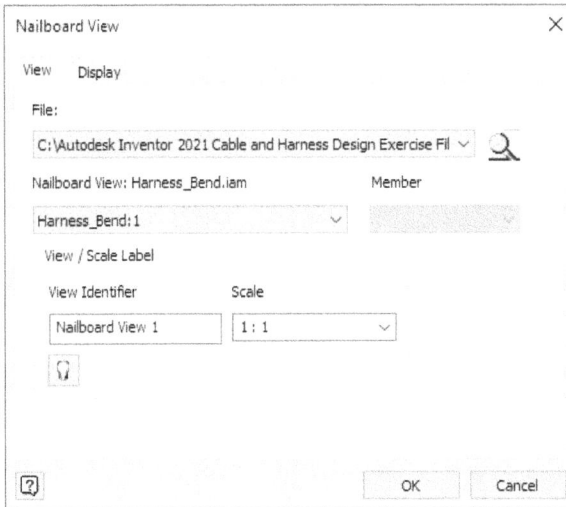

3. Set display options.

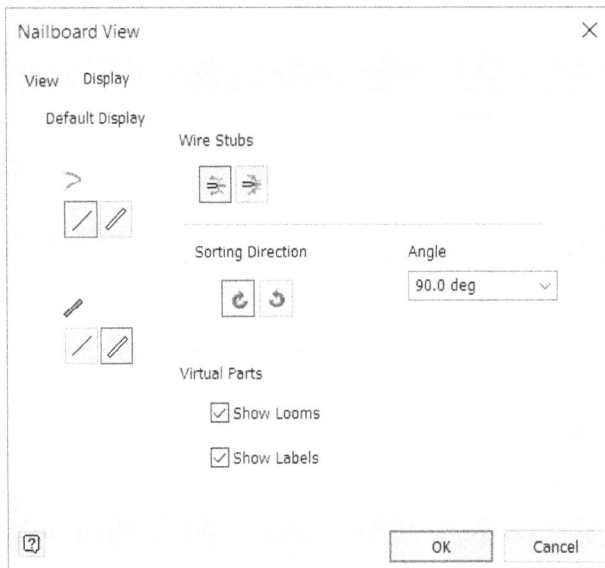

4. Click OK to create the view.

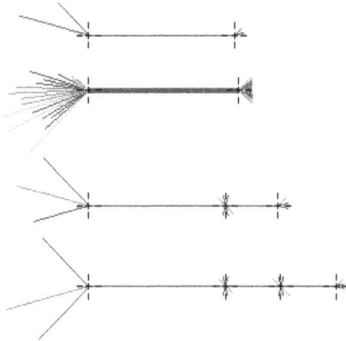

Browser and Panel Bar for Nailboard Views

Once a nailboard view is created, the Browser and ribbon change to the Nailboard environment.

The Nailboard ribbon displays tools that enable you to annotate, dimension, specify property displays, and generate reports based on the nailboard view. The Browser displays the harness name and the harness contents.

The following figures show the Nailboard Browser and ribbon after a nailboard view is created and is being edited.

Model | Cable & Harness

Harness_Bend: 1
- Segments
  - + Segment1
  - + Segment2
  - + Segment3
  - + Segment4
- Virtual Parts
  - + Looms
- Wires
  - + Wire8
  - + Wire7
  - + Wire9
  - + Wire6
  - + Wire4
  - + Wire5
  - + Wire3
  - + Wire2
  - + Wire1
  - + Wire10
  - + Wire12
  - + Wire11

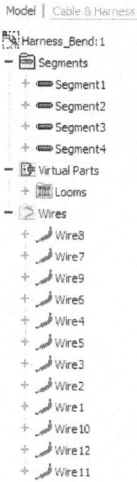

Browser nailboard view

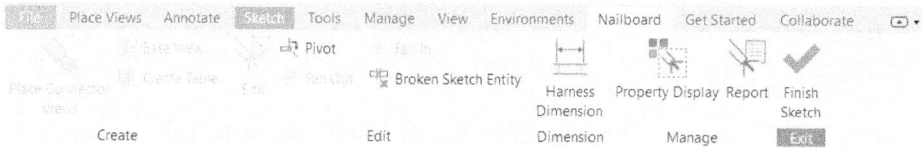

| | Place Views | Annotate | Sketch | Tools | Manage | View | Environments | Nailboard | Get Started | Collaborate | |

Base View   Pivot   Fan In
Create Table   Broken Sketch Entity   Harness   Property Display   Report   Finish
Place Connector   Fan Out   Dimension   Sketch
Views

Create   Edit   Dimension   Manage   Exit

Nailboard ribbon (when editing the sketch)

Modifying a Nailboard View

After you have created your nailboard view, editing tools in the Nailboard ribbon enable you to edit the display of the view. To change the display, you can pivot sections, break the sketch, display wires at actual diameter, and fan wires in or out.

The following figure shows a before and after view of a wiring harness. The left image shows the wire segment in a half nailboard drawing view in the original position. The right image shows the same nailboard view with harness segment pivoted to a new position.

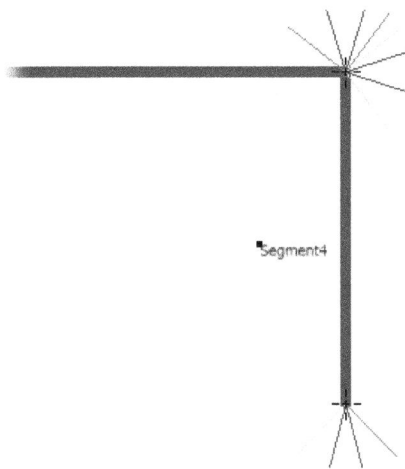

Original position   Segment pivoted

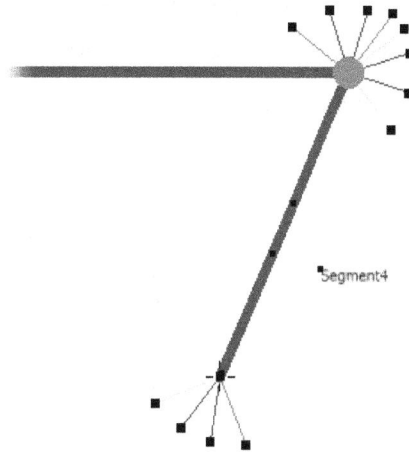

Description of Nailboard Editing Tools

The following tools are used to modify the display of a nailboard drawing view.

Icon	Option	Description
	Edit Nailboard Sketch	Use to activate the sketch environment for editing the nailboard view. You can also activate the sketch environment by double-clicking a harness object.
	Pivot	Use to fix one end of a harness in a nailboard view, and then drag the opposite end to rotate the segment. The harness rotates about the fixed position.
	Fan Out	Use to change the array of the wires at the end of segments. If the wires are fanned in, you can use this tool to fan them out. If they are fanned out, you can use this tool to change the angle of the fanned out wires. You can also select a wire and right-click to access this tool.
	Fan In	Use to fan in the wires at the end of the harness. The wires display as though they are enclosed with the segment. You can also select a wire and right-click to access this tool.
	Broken Sketch Entity	Use to shorten the display of a segment. You select a point on the segment as your first break point. Then select a second point. You can accept this distance or enter a precise value.
	Display as Actual Diameter	Use this tool to toggle the display of the wire. Right-click the wire and click Display as Actual Diameter. When the display is set to actual diameter, a checkmark displays next to the option in the menu.

Procedure: Changing the Fan Out Angle

The following steps describe changing the Fan Out angle for wires in a harness.

1. Double-click on a wire or segment to activate the nailboard sketch.

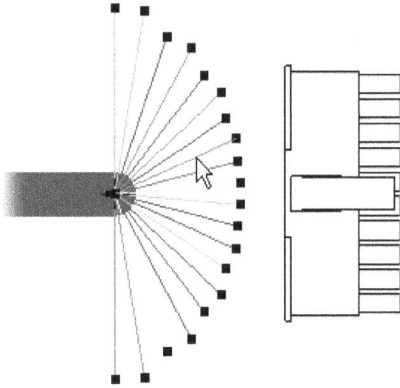

2. Right-click on the connection point of the wires and click Fan In/Out>Fan Out.

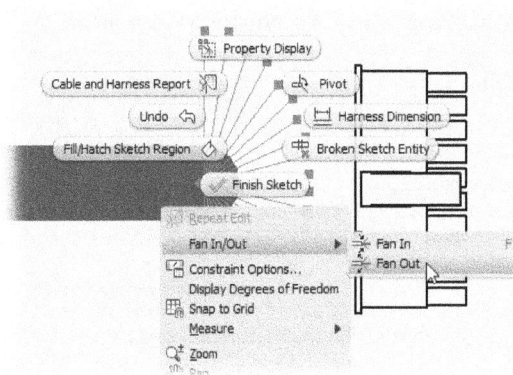

3. Enter the new angle.

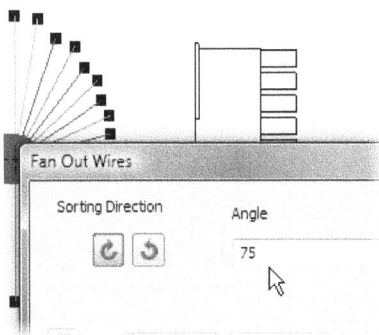

4. Apply the changes.

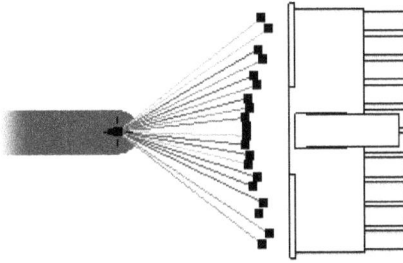

Procedure: Displaying the Wire as Actual Diameter

The following steps describe the steps to display a wire as actual diameter.

1. Double-click on a wire or segment to activate the nailboard sketch.

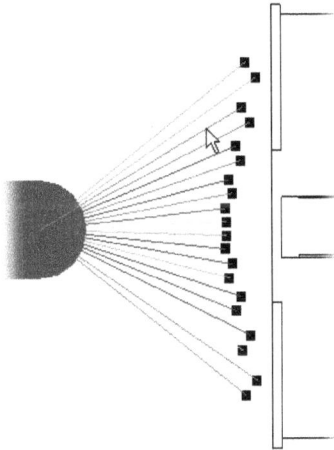

2. Right-click on the wire to change the display and click Display as Actual Diameter.

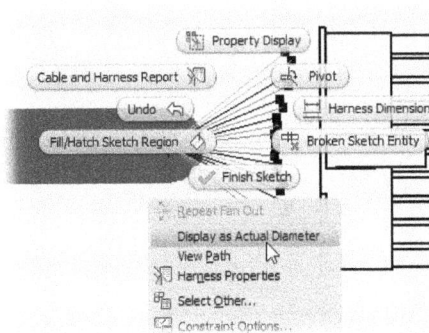

---

3. The display of the wire is changed.

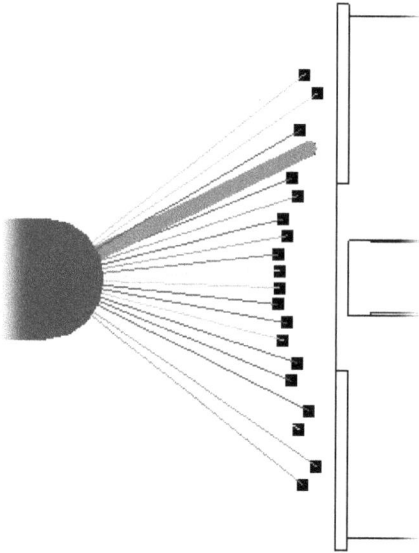

Adding Connector Views

The wiring harness connectors used in your designs are not included when you place a nailboard view. Connectors are added to nailboard views using the Place Connector View tool. When placing connectors, you specify which connectors in the harness display and other options including orientation, scale, and style.

The following figure shows before and after views of a simple wiring harness. The left image shows the nailboard drawing. The right image shows the same nailboard view with harness connectors added to the drawing.

Access

Ribbon: Nailboard tab>Create panel

Place Connector Views	After placing a nailboard view, you must select Finish Sketch for the Place Connector Views tool to be available.

Place Connector Views

The Place Connector Views dialog box enables you to specify which connectors in the harness display, and to adjust properties regarding them. Specific to the connector views are the Offset value and list of connectors. The Offset value sets the distance for the placement of the base view of the connector from the associated wire stubs. In the list of connectors associated with a harness, a checkmark indicates that the connector displays. You clear the checkmark to omit that connector from being displayed.

Other options such as Orientation, Scale, and Style are common for the display of Autodesk Inventor views.

The following figure shows the Place Connector Views dialog box.

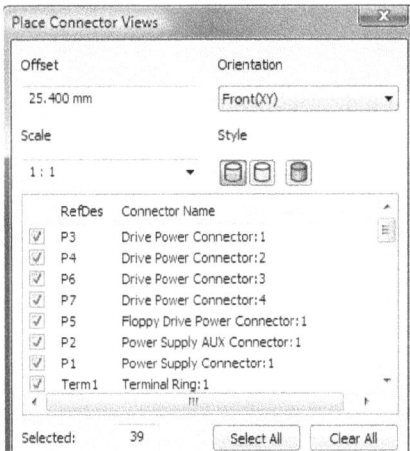

Procedure: Adding Connector Views

The following steps describe adding connector views to a nailboard drawing view.

1. Start the Place Connector View tool.

2. In the Place Connector Views dialog box, select the connector to be displayed and set the required display options.

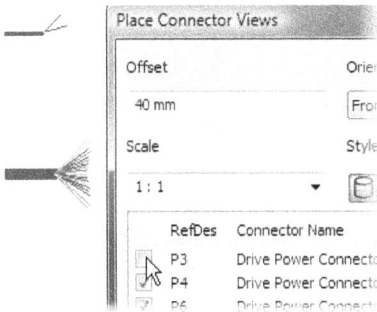

3. Click OK to display the connectors in the nailboard view.

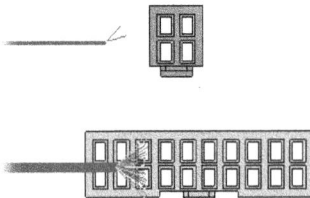

Exercise: Create Drawing Views of a Cable and Harness Design

In this exercise, you will create 2D drawing views of Autodesk Inventor Cable and Harness objects. You will use standard Autodesk Inventor view creation tools to create views of the 3D model. You will also create and edit nailboard drawing views.

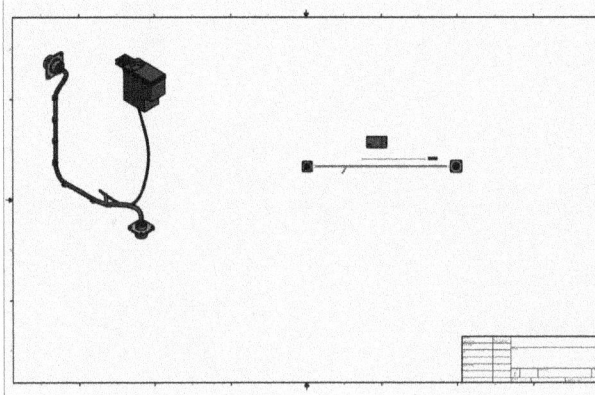

The completed exercise

1. Open *Create_2D_Harness_Drawings.iam*.

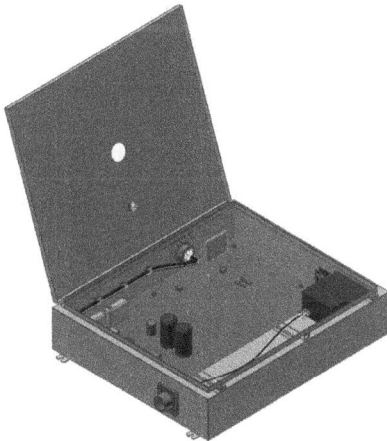

2. Create a new drawing file based on the *ANSI (mm).idw*.

3. To create a nailboard view of the wiring harness:

- In the Place Views tab, in the Create panel, click Nailboard.
- In the Nailboard View dialog box, in the View tab, in the View/Scale Label area, for Scale, select 1/2. Also, ensure the correct drawing is being referenced if you have multiple windows open.
- Click OK.
- Right-click and click Finish Sketch.

4. To reposition the nailboard view:
   - Move the cursor to the view.
   - When the move glyph displays, click and drag the view to the right side of the sheet.

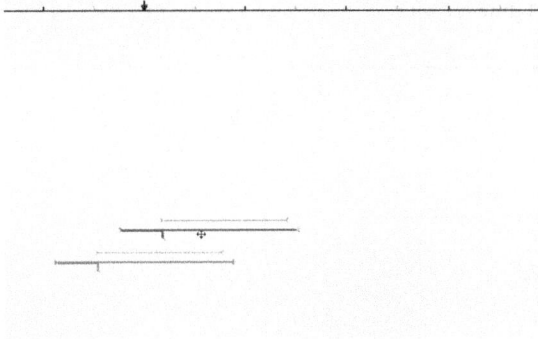

5. Zoom in to the left side of the nailboard view.

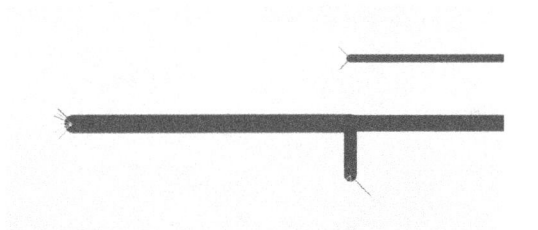

6. To pivot a segment of the harness in the nailboard view:
   - In the Nailboard tab, in the Edit panel, click Edit.
   - In the Nailboard tab, in the Edit panel, click Pivot. Alternatively, while remaining in the Sketch tab, right-click in the graphics window and click Pivot. Select the intersection of the segment as shown (1).
   - Click the end of the short segment (2) and drag to the left. Release when the angle is approximately 45 degrees, as shown in the following figure.
   - Right-click in the graphics window and click Finish.

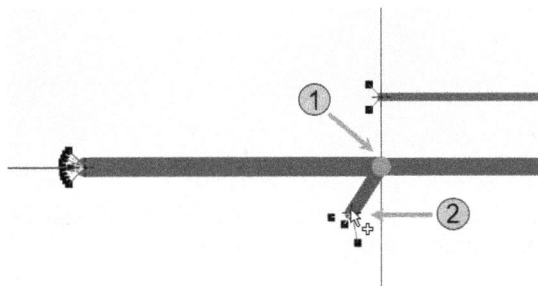

7. To shorten a segment:

- In the Nailboard tab, Edit panel, click Broken Sketch Entity. Alternatively, if still in the Sketch tab, right-click in the graphics window and click Broken Sketch Entity.
- Click the top segment of the harness sketch near the middle (1).
- Move the cursor to the right, approximately half the distance to the end (2).
- In the Edit Break dialog box, enter **90**. Click the green checkmark.

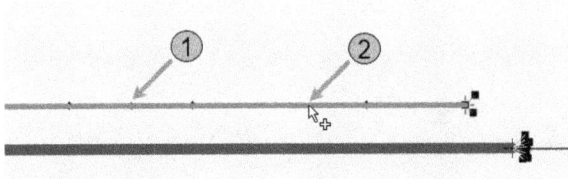

8. Select Finish Sketch.

9. To add connector views:

- In the Nailboard tab, in the Create panel, click Place Connector Views.
- In the Place Connector Views dialog box, for Offset, enter **20**.
- For Scale, select 1/2.
- For Style, click the Shaded tool.
- Click OK.

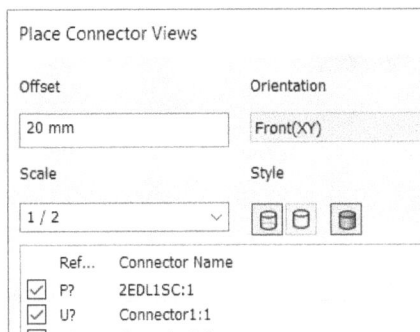

10. To relocate a connector view:

   - Move the cursor to the left connector.
   - When the connector view is highlighted, click and drag the view above the segment as shown in the following figure.

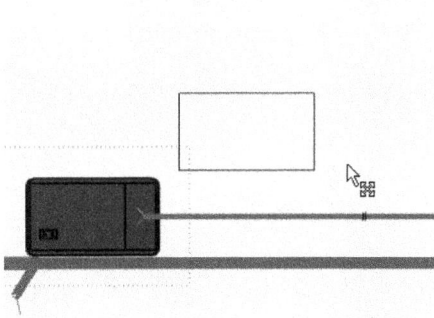

11. To begin to fan in wires:

   - On the keyboard, press E.
   - Zoom in to the wires at the angled segment.
   - Use a crossing window selection to select all of the wires.

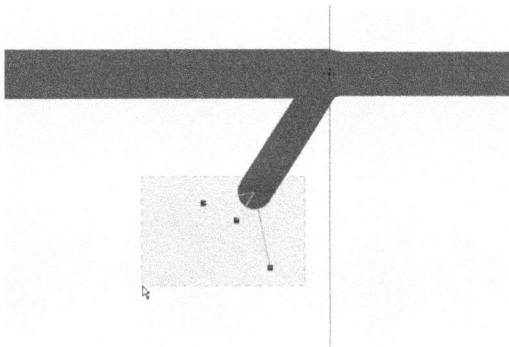

12. Right-click on any wire and click Fan In/Out>Fan In.

13. Pan to the right end of the segment.

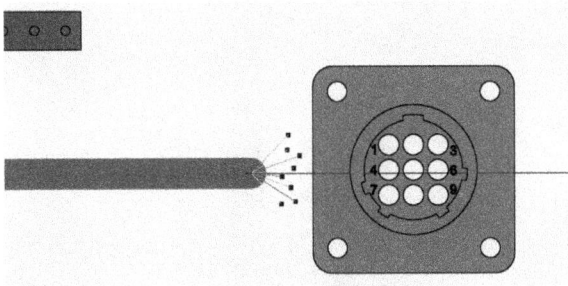

14. To begin to change the Fan Out angle:

- Window-select the wires next to the nine- pin connector.
- Right-click on any wire and click Fan In/Out>Fan Out.

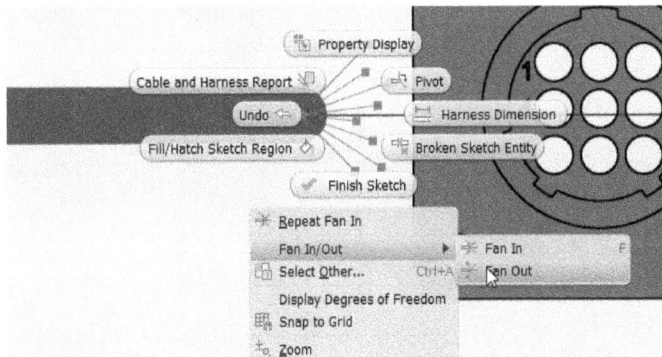

15. To change the Fan Out angle:

- In the Fan Out Wires dialog box, for Angle, enter **60**.
- Click OK.

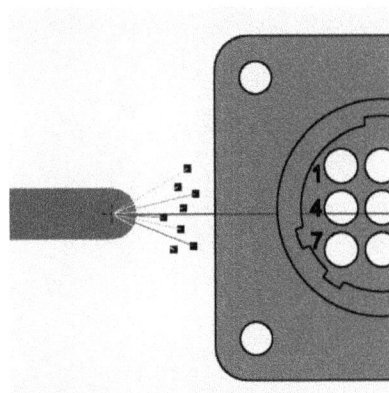

16. To display wires as actual diameter:

- Right-click on the top wire at the nine-pin connector.
- Click Display as Actual Diameter.

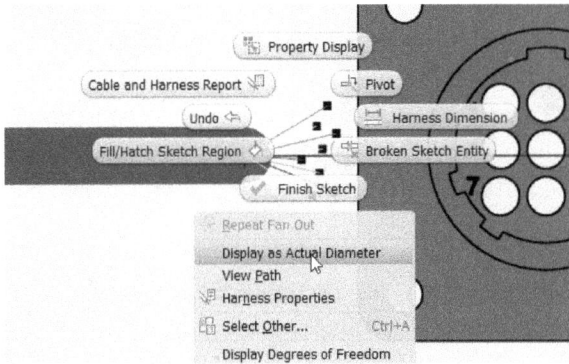

17. Repeat for the remaining wires at the nine-pin connector.

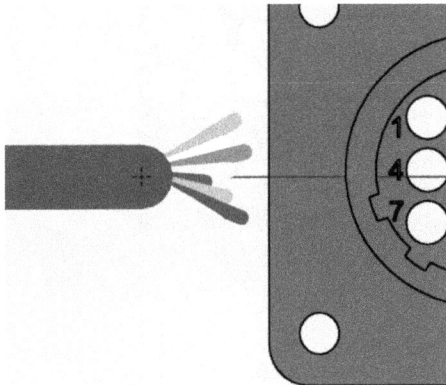

18. Select Finish Sketch.

19. To create a 3D drawing view of the harness:

   - In the Nailboard tab, in the Create panel, click Base View.
   - In the Drawing View dialog box, under Level of Detail, select Harness.
   - For Style, click Shaded icon.
   - Change the scale to 1:1.
   - Use the ViewCube to change the orientation similar to that shown in the following figure.
   - To display segments, select Include Surface Bodies in the Recovery Options tab in Drawing view window.
   - Click in the upper left area of the drawing to place the view.
   - Click OK.

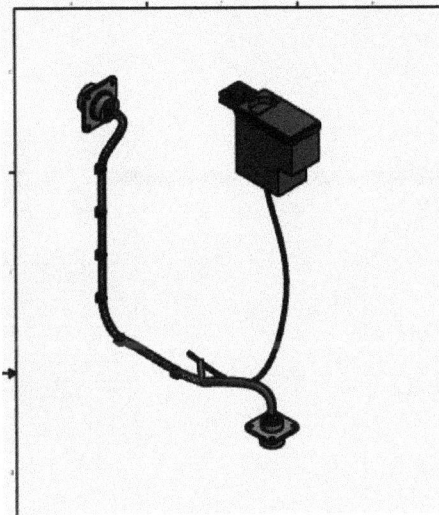

20. Close all files without saving changes.

Lesson: Annotating Nailboards

This lesson describes the tools and techniques for annotating nailboard drawing views with dimensions and property data. It also describes the options for setting the display of the design geometry and adding design data to the drawing sheet in a table format.

You annotate nailboard drawing views to communicate cable and harness design information for manufacturing.

The following figure shows an annotated nailboard drawing view. The wires have been set to display at actual diameter. Labels are applied to terminal connectors, and data has been imported from an external file and displayed in a table.

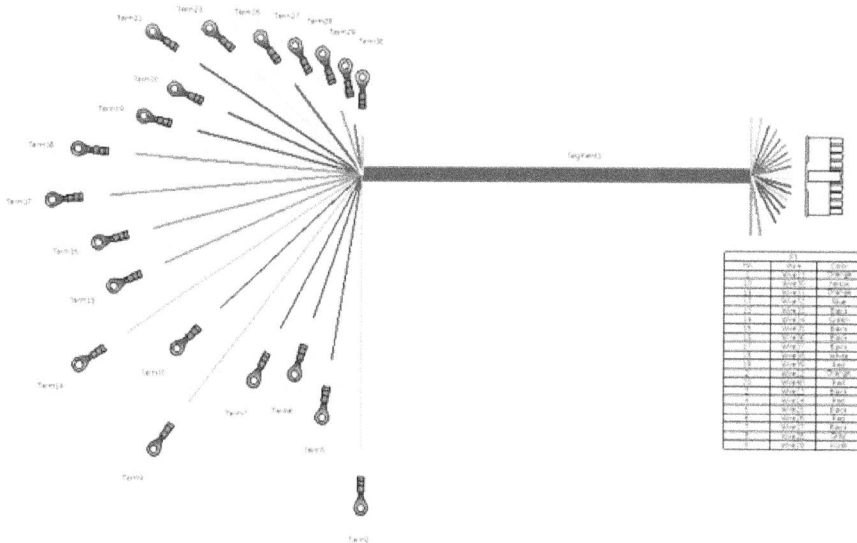

Objectives

After completing this lesson, you will be able to:

- Add harness dimensions to a nailboard drawing view.
- Add property information for components in a harness assembly as text to a nailboard drawing view.
- Toggle the display in a nailboard drawing view of looms and labels for virtual parts.
- Toggle between thin line and actual diameter display.
- Add a table of data to the drawing by selecting an external source file for the data.

Adding Harness Dimensions

There are two tools available for adding dimensions to nailboard views. You use the Harness Dimension tool in the Nailboard tab of the ribbon to add a driven dimension between two points on wires or segments. You use the General Dimension tool to dimension geometry not created in the nailboard view.

In the following figure, harness dimensions are added to the nailboard view.

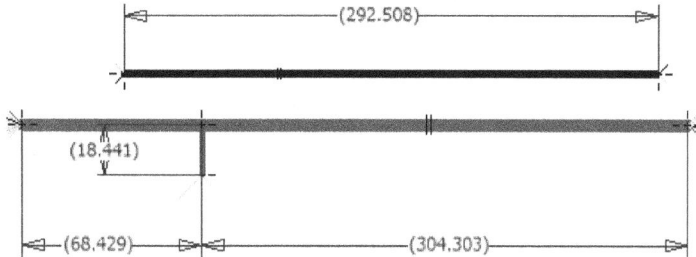

Description of Harness Dimensions

You use the Harness Dimension tool to create aligned dimensions between two points in a nailboard view. The points selected can be between wires and segments and can include the use of any intermediate wire work point. For nailboard views containing ribbon cables with folds, you can dimension to the start of the ribbon cable and to the fold lines to generate length values. You can also dimension to intermediate work points and the angular fold line.

Wires and segments in nailboard views are created as spline objects. Therefore, when dimensioning nailboard views, you must select two distinct points. The calculated or adjusted length considers several factors that affect final length such as service loops, global slack, and embedded length.

Harness dimensions are added directly to the nailboard sketch. To add dimensions to a nailboard view, you must be in the nailboard sketch editing environment.

Access

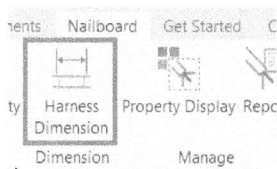

Ribbon: Nailboard tab>Dimension panel

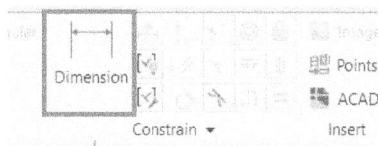

Ribbon: Sketch tab>Constrain panel (General Dimension)

Keyboard Shortcut: D

Procedure: Adding Harness Dimensions

The following steps describe adding harness dimensions to a nailboard drawing view.

1. Start the Harness Dimension tool.

2. Select the first point on the wire or segment.

    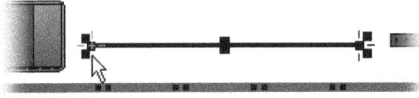

3. Select the second point on the wire or segment.

4. Locate the dimension. Repeat steps two and three to add additional dimensions, or right-click and click Done.

    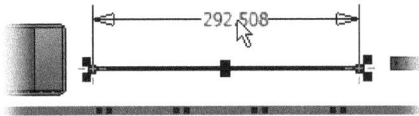

Displaying Harness Properties

The components of a cable and harness design possess data that you often need to communicate to others. To add this data to a nailboard drawing view, you need to know how to access this information. You can display harness properties for any wires, cable wires, pins, and segments displayed in the nailboard view. You can also display properties for the parts containing the pins.

The following figure shows the 3D and nailboard views of a harness design. Wire pin property information displays on the nailboard view to match the connections in the 3D design.

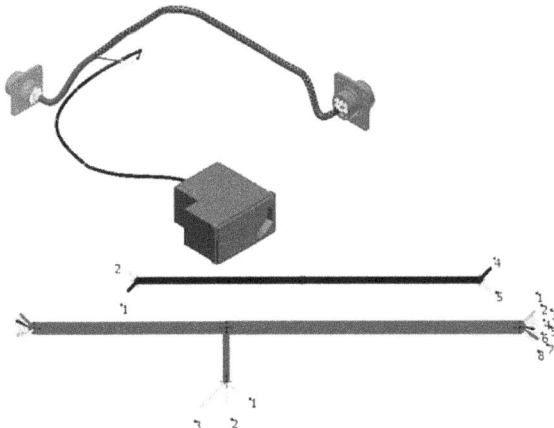

Access

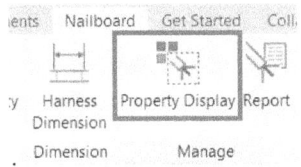

Ribbon: Nailboard tab>Manage panel

Property Display Dialog Box

The Property Display tool is available only when the nailboard sketch is active. You use the Selection Filter area to manually select objects in the nailboard view, or use one of the included filter options to automate the selection.

As you select a filter or objects in the view, a list of the available properties displays in the Property Name area on the right side of the dialog box. The Property Name area of the dialog box initially displays blank. The list is populated as objects are selected, and the options available are determined by the objects selected. If you select a filter, and the nailboard view does not contain that particular object, the list remains blank.

Once the Property Name is determined, you select your display options. Use Apply to display the properties, and then specify another selection set. Use OK to display the properties and exit the tool.

The following options are available in the Property Display dialog box.

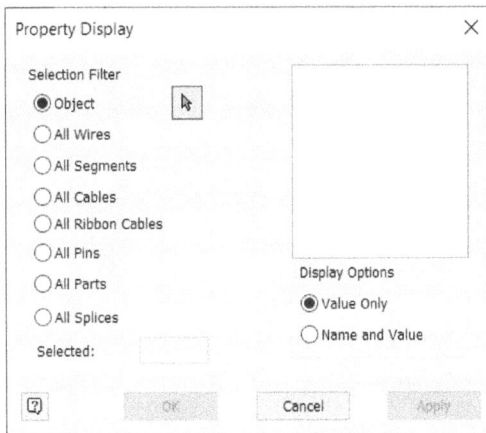

Examples of Property Display

The following figures show some of the different properties that can be displayed in a nailboard view.

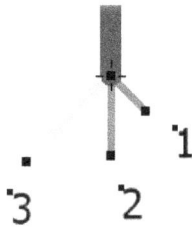

Pin name

Wire color

Gauge

Procedure: Displaying Harness Properties

The following steps describe displaying properties of a wire harness in a nailboard view.

1. Start the Property Display tool. Select the objects in the view or the required filter.

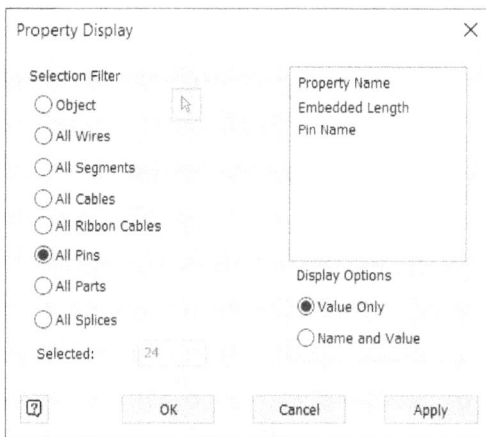

2. Select the property name. Click Apply.

3. Select the component and position the property.

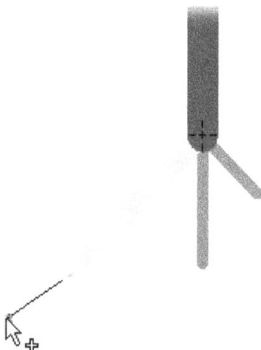

4. The property displays in the nailboard view.

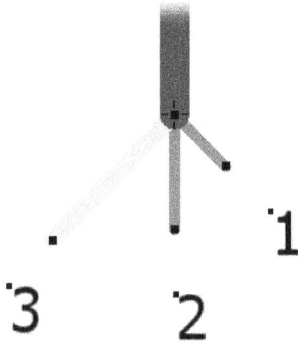

Loom and Label Virtual Parts

When annotating nailboard drawing views, you might want to display virtual parts that have been added to the design. You can toggle the display of loom and label virtual parts in a nailboard view.

In the following figure, the visibility of a loom is being toggled off in the nailboard view. The loom selected is highlighted in the view.

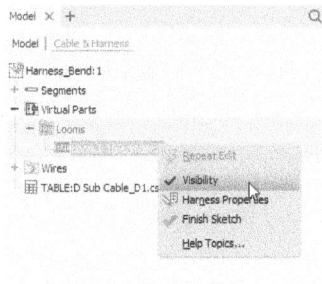

Nailboard Settings for Virtual Parts

The Nailboard Settings dialog box contains an area for globally controlling the visibility of looms and labels in nailboard views.

Right-click on the drawing name in the Browser and click Nailboard Settings to open the Nailboard Settings dialog box.

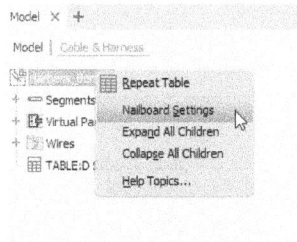

Nailboard Settings Dialog Box

The following figure shows the Nailboard Settings dialog box. To control the display of loom and label virtual parts in a nailboard view, you open the Nailboard Settings dialog box and in Virtual Parts area, place a checkmark next to the required option.

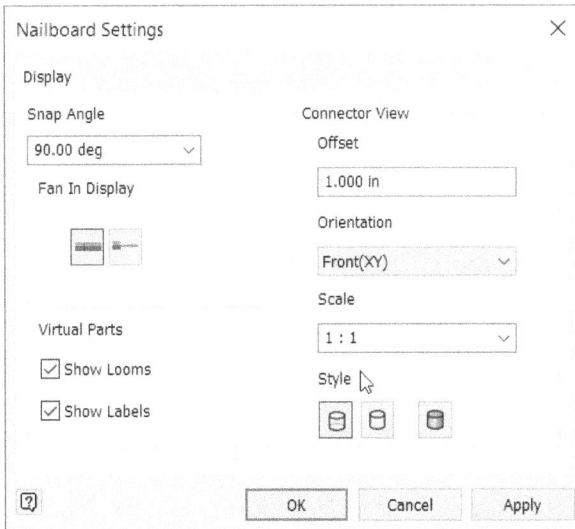

Display As Loom Option

Once the global display of virtual parts has been enabled in the Nailboard Settings dialog box, you can also control the display of individual looms and labels. To control the display, you expand the Virtual Parts folder in the Browser. Each label and loom in the nailboard view displays under the respective Labels or Looms folder. Right-click on the individual label or loom and click Visibility in the shortcut menu. A checkmark next to Visibility indicates that the label or loom displays in the nailboard view. If the Visibility option is grayed out in the menu, then the options for virtual parts display has not been selected in the Nailboard Settings dialog box.

The following figure shows two views of the same nailboard view. On the left, the visibility of all looms is toggled on. On the right, the individual visibility of the loom is toggled off.

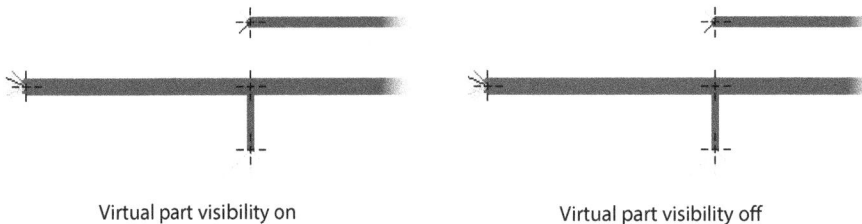

Virtual part visibility on   Virtual part visibility off

Display as Actual Diameter

You might want to display the wires and segments in a nailboard view at their actual diameter. You can achieve this on a global or individual basis by editing the respective folder in the Browser, or by editing the individual objects in the nailboard view.

Access

To access the options to display wires and segments as actual diameters or as thin lines, the nailboard sketch must be active. You then select the options to control the display from a shortcut menu.

You can set the display for individual wires or segments, or for all wires or segments. To set the display individually, right-click on the individual wire or segment from the Browser or graphics window. To set the display for all wires or segments, right-click on the Wires or Segments folder name in the Browser. The following figure shows the shortcut menu when you right-click on the Wires folder in the Browser.

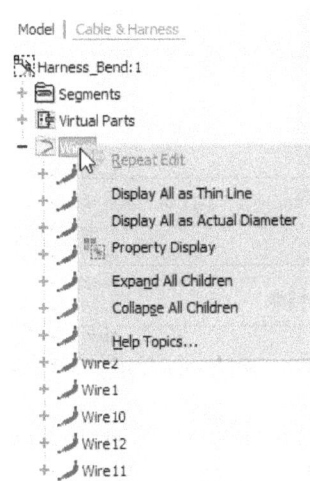

You can select multiple wires in the Browser or in the graphics window. In the Browser, use CTRL or SHIFT to select multiple segments wires. In the graphics window, a selection window or crossing window enables you to select multiple segments or wires.

Display Options

When you initially place a nailboard view, the default setting for segment display is to show all segments as actual diameter. For wires, the initial display setting is to show all wires as thin lines.

The following figure shows two views of a nailboard drawing view. On the left, the nailboard view with the default settings of the segments is shown as actual diameter, and the wires as thin lines. On the right, the display of the wires has been set to Display as Actual Diameter.

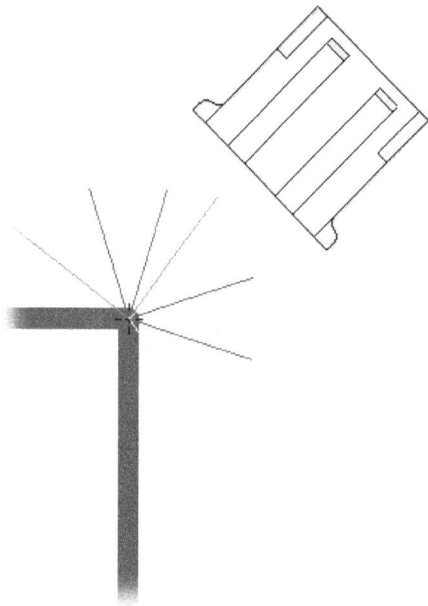

Default nailboard display

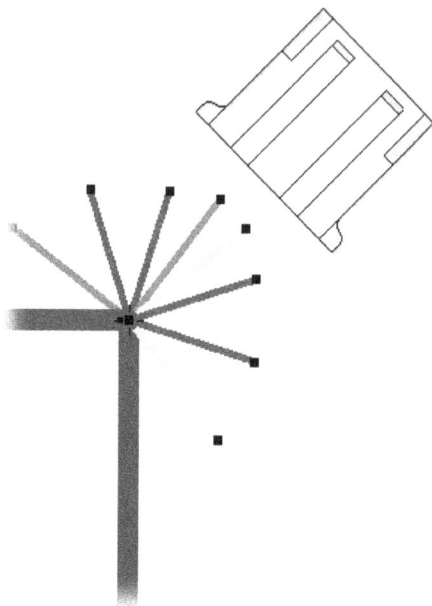

Wire display set to Actual Diameter

Adding Tables with Data from Another File

Data from an external source file can be inserted into a nailboard drawing view using the Table tool to annotate your design.

In the following figure, the table layout of an inserted table is edited to add additional rows and columns. Also, the default table name was changed to match the information in the table.

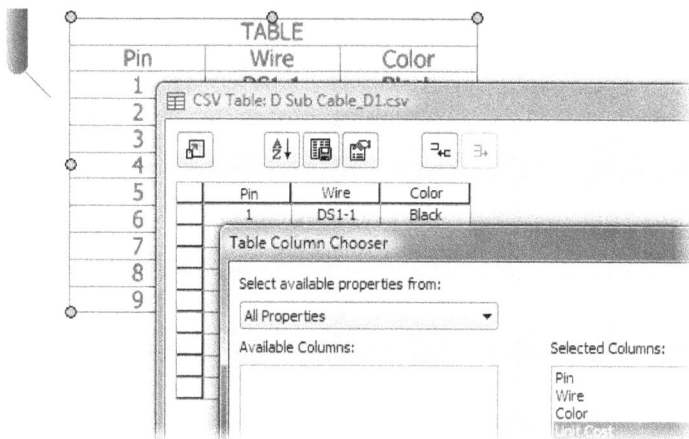

Description of Table Data

The Table tool enables you to import data into your nailboard drawing view. The data can come from a variety of sources; however, for cable and harness designs, a common source of data is from reports generated from the 3D design.

The data imported from external sources is not linked to the original source file. However, you can edit the table to add, change, or delete information for your design. Double-clicking the table in the nailboard view displays the table in a dialog box format that enables you to edit the table. In the dialog box, you can add, remove, or create new columns. You can also sort the table, export the table data, or add rows to the table. The layout of the table can be changed using the Table Layout tool. In the Table Layout dialog box, you can specify text styles, heading location, text wrapping, and line spacing. You can also change the default table name in the Table Layout dialog box.

Access

Ribbon: Nailboard tab>Create panel

Procedure: Adding Tables with Data from Another File

The following steps describe importing data from an external source file into a nailboard drawing view.

1. Start the Table tool. Browse to and select the external file.

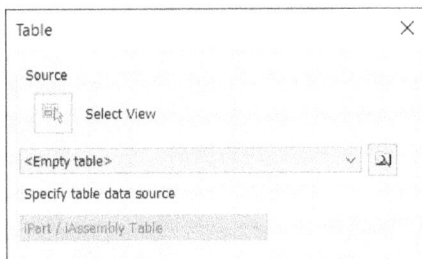

2. Click OK. Place the table on the sheet.

TABLE		
Pin	Wire	Color
1	DS1-1	Black
2	DS1-2	Red
3	DS1-3	White
4	DS1-4	Green
5	DS1-5	Orange
6	DS1-6	Blue
7	DS1-7	Brown
8	DS1-8	Yellow
9	DS1-9	Violet

Exercise: Annotate Nailboards

In this exercise, you will annotate a nailboard drawing view using harness dimensions, tables, harness properties, and virtual part display.

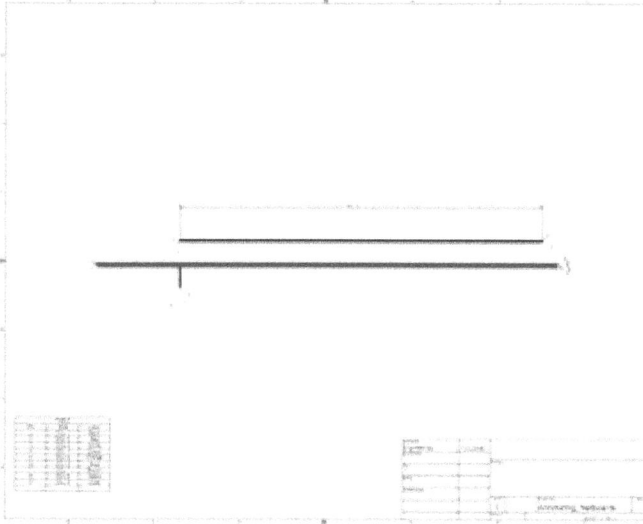

The completed exercise

1. Open *Annotating_Nailboard.idw*.

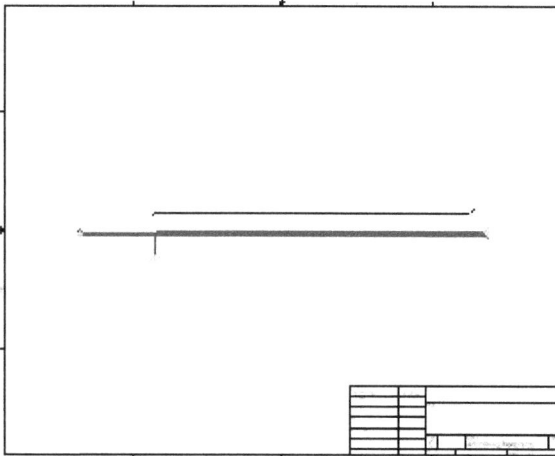

2. In the Nailboard tab, in the Edit panel, click Edit.

3. To dimension a harness segment:

- In the Nailboard tab, in the Dimension panel, click Harness Dimension.
- Click the left end of the top segment (1).
- Click the right end of the top segment (2).
- Place the dimension above the segment.

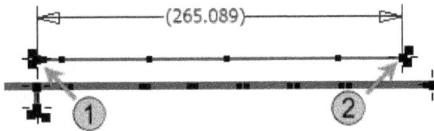

4. Zoom to the left end of the harness.

5. To begin to display harness properties:

- In the Nailboard tab, in the Manage panel, click Property Display.
- In the Property Display dialog box, in Selection Filter area, click All Pins.
- Under Property Name, select Pin Name.
- Under Display Options, click Value Only.

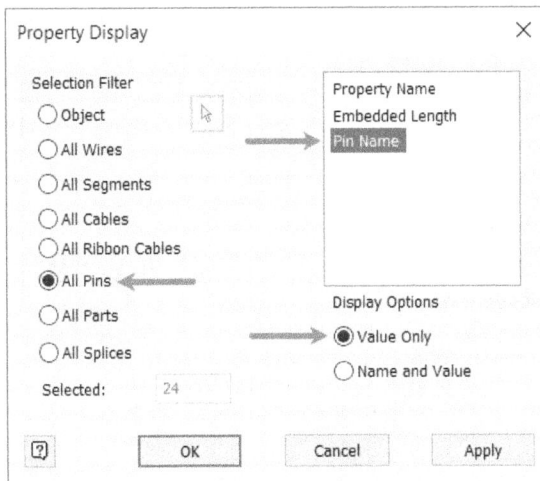

6. To display the property:
   - In the Property Display dialog box, click OK.
   - With the rubber band displayed, click above the wires.

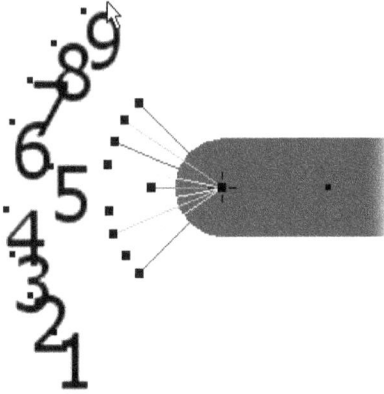

7. Zoom to the short vertical segment.

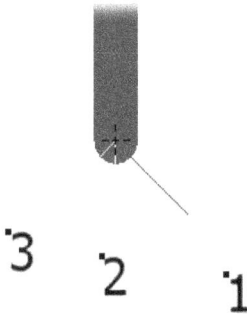

8. To display the wires as actual diameter:
   - Press CTRL and select the three wires displayed at the end of the short segment.
   - Right-click in the graphics window.
   - Click Display as Actual Diameter.

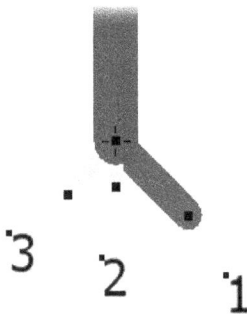

9. To exit the sketch, right-click and click Finish Sketch.

10. To begin to insert data from an external file:

- In the Nailboard tab, in the Create panel, click Create Table.
- In the Table dialog box, under Source, select Browse for File.
- Navigate to *C:\Autodesk Inventor 2021 Cable and Harness Design Exercise Files\Workspace* and select D Sub Cable_D1.csv.

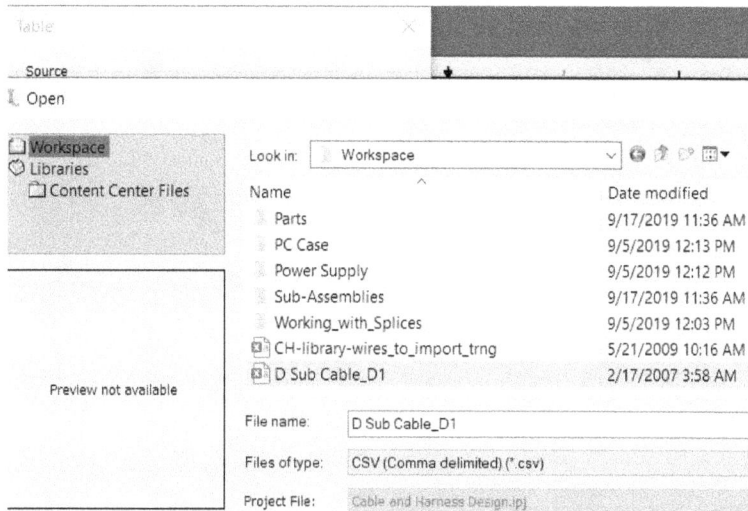

Table		×	
Source			
Open			

Workspace	Look in:	Workspace	⊙ 🔍 ▭ ⊞▾
Libraries			
Content Center Files	Name	^	Date modified
	Parts		9/17/2019 11:36 AM
	PC Case		9/5/2019 12:13 PM
	Power Supply		9/5/2019 12:12 PM
	Sub-Assemblies		9/17/2019 11:36 AM
	Working_with_Splices		9/5/2019 12:03 PM
	CH-library-wires_to_import_trng		5/21/2009 10:16 AM
Preview not available	D Sub Cable_D1		2/17/2007 3:58 AM
	File name:	D Sub Cable_D1	
	Files of type:	CSV (Comma delimited) (*.csv)	
	Project File:	Cable and Harness Design.ipj	

11. To place the table on the sheet:

- In the Open dialog box, click Open.
- In the Table dialog box, click OK.
- Click near the lower left corner of the sheet to place the table as shown in the following figure.

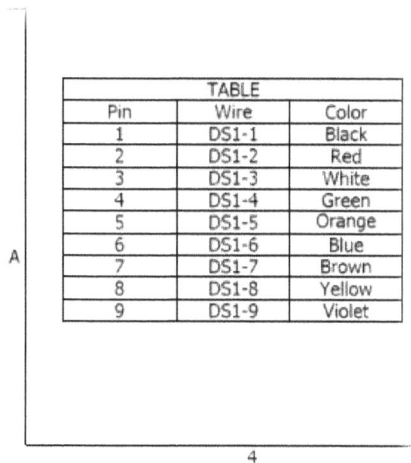

TABLE		
Pin	Wire	Color
1	DS1-1	Black
2	DS1-2	Red
3	DS1-3	White
4	DS1-4	Green
5	DS1-5	Orange
6	DS1-6	Blue
7	DS1-7	Brown
8	DS1-8	Yellow
9	DS1-9	Violet

A

4

12. To edit the table:
    - In the graphics window, double-click on the table.
    - In the CSV Table dialog box, click the box for Pin 9 (arrow).
    - Click Insert Row to add a row for future information.

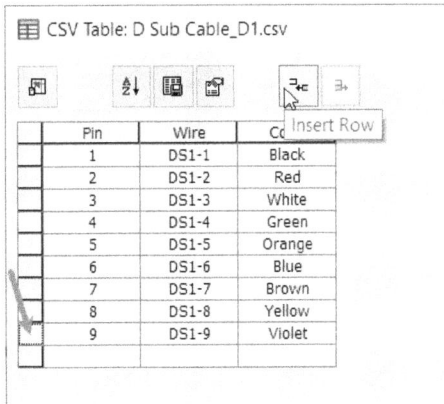

CSV Table: D Sub Cable_D1.csv

Pin	Wire	Co...
1	DS1-1	Black
2	DS1-2	Red
3	DS1-3	White
4	DS1-4	Green
5	DS1-5	Orange
6	DS1-6	Blue
7	DS1-7	Brown
8	DS1-8	Yellow
9	DS1-9	Violet

13. Click OK.

TABLE		
Pin	Wire	Color
1	DS1-1	Black
2	DS1-2	Red
3	DS1-3	White
4	DS1-4	Green
5	DS1-5	Orange
6	DS1-6	Blue
7	DS1-7	Brown
8	DS1-8	Yellow
9	DS1-9	Violet

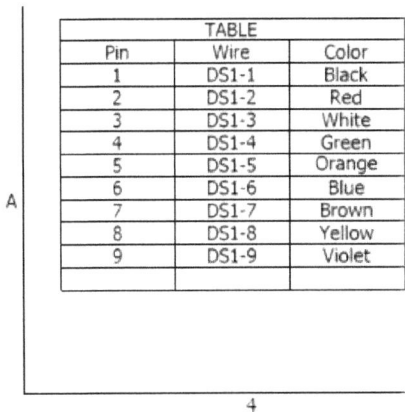

14. In the Browser, switch to the Cable and Harness view.

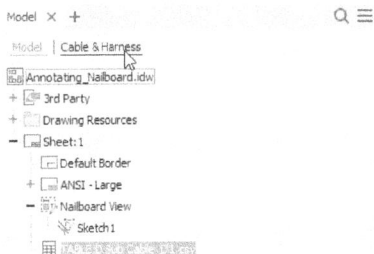

Model | Cable & Harness

Annotating_Nailboard.idw
+ 3rd Party
+ Drawing Resources
− Sheet: 1
  Default Border
  + ANSI - Large
  − Nailboard View
    Sketch 1
    TABLE D SUB CABLE D1.CSV

15. To begin to display virtual parts in the nailboard view:

  ▪ In the Browser, right-click on Harness_Bend.
  ▪ Click Nailboard Settings.

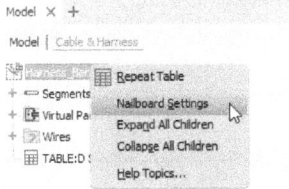

Model ✕ +

Model | Cable & Harness

- Harness_Bend
  - ⊞ Repeat Table
  - Nailboard Settings
  - Expand All Children
  - Collapse All Children
  - Help Topics...

+ ⟵ Segments
+ 🔲 Virtual Pa
+ 🔲 Wires
  ⊞ TABLE:D

16. To globally activate the display of virtual parts:

  ▪ In the Nailboard Settings dialog box, in Virtual Parts area, click Show Looms check box.
  ▪ Click OK.

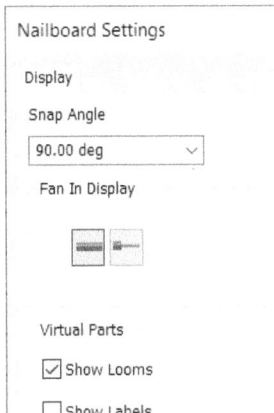

Nailboard Settings

Display

Snap Angle

90.00 deg

Fan In Display

Virtual Parts

☑ Show Looms

☐ Show Labels

17. Zoom to the area shown.

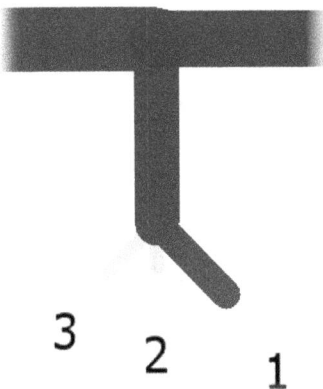

3   2   1

18. In the Nailboard tab, in the Edit panel, click Edit.

19. To individually control the display of virtual parts:

- In the Browser, fully expand the virtual parts folder.
- Right-click on Loom1:1(Segment1) and click Visibility to clear it.

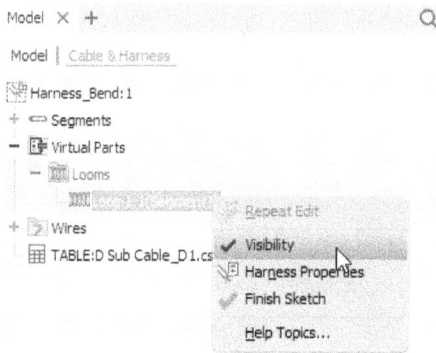

20. Right-click in a blank area of the graphics window and click Finish Sketch.

21. Close all files without saving changes.

Lesson: Exporting and Reporting Design Data

This lesson describes the creation of external files of cable and harness design data through the direct exporting of the data and through creation of reports.

As you add different components to your design, information regarding them is added to your drawings. To gather this information in a logical manner and share it with others, you need to understand how to report and export design data.

The following figure shows data created from a cable and harness design. In the background, a neutral XML file format is created from cable and harness data. The spreadsheet displays a report generated from a nailboard drawing view. In the foreground is the original report as it is being created in the Report Generator.

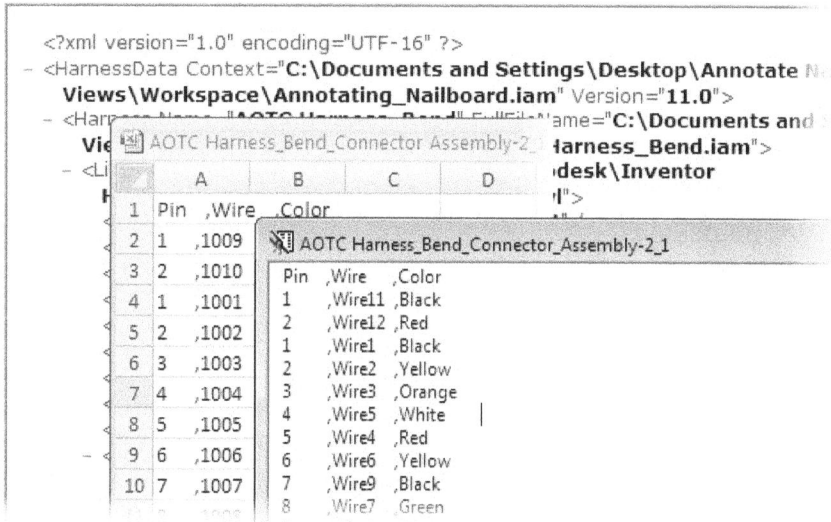

Objectives

After completing this lesson, you will be able to:

- Describe the purpose and benefits of exported harness design data.
- Export harness assembly design data to an XML file.
- Create CSV report files consisting of specified harness design data.

About Exported Data

You can generate several standard report types in the cable and harness environment. Reports can be used to centralize data and then can be shared with others in your organization. The information reported is based on the properties set for the harness components during the design process.

In the following figure, a table of a connector view in a nailboard drawing displays. The data for the table was created by exporting data from the assembly file. Then the data from the exported file is used to populate the table. By leveraging the data from the design, the amount of effort in creating the table is reduced, and the chance for data entry error is also reduced.

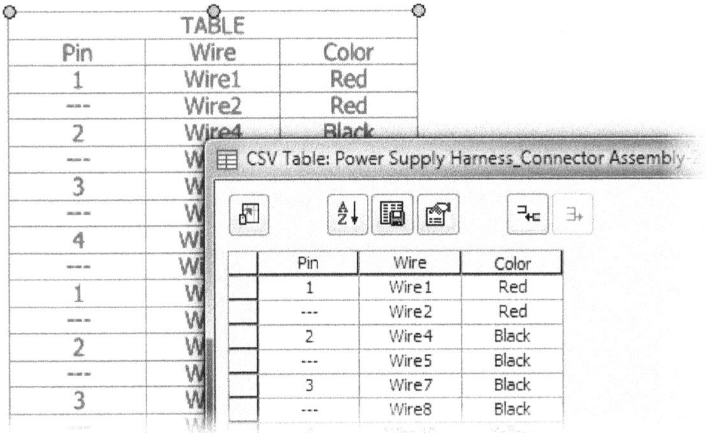

Definition of Exported Data

A report is created by gathering information and then assembling it in a logical and organized manner so that the intended audience can easily interpret the data. Exported data is information obtained from the design and organized into a formatted report, put into a common file format to be shared with others.

Example of Exported Data

In today's global environment, it is common for different components of a design to be worked on in many different locations, using many different tools. The ability to leverage the data within a design and export it to others on the design team, as well as to other departments, ensures that everyone is working with the same data.

An example is an electronic component with multiple wires connected to it. While one company or division designs the electronic component, another might be designing the wiring harness to connect the component to the rest of the system. During the design of the component, pin numbers are assigned to component connectors. The pin number data can be exported from the component design, then imported to the wiring harness design, to ensure compatibility early in the design process.

Exporting Data

You export harness assembly design data to share with others in the design project, as well as with customers and vendors. When you export data from your cable and harness assembly, you create a neutral XML file that can be imported into other programs. The file created contains the names of known cable and harness properties.

In the following figure, a cable and harness data file is exported in a neutral XML file format.

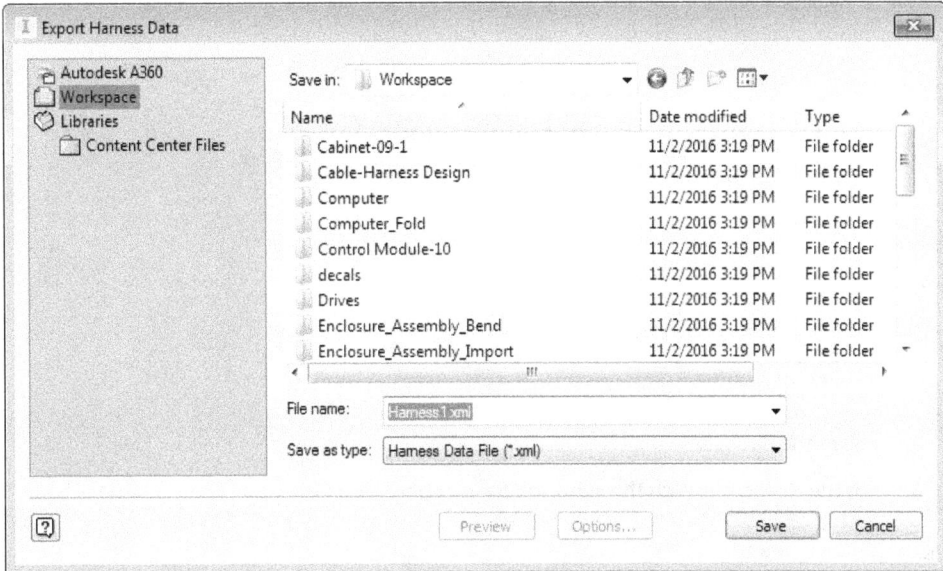

Access

Ribbon: Cable and Harness tab>Manage panel, click Harness Data drop-down

Cable and Harness Environment

To access the Export Harness Design tool, the Cable and Harness environment must be active. To activate the cable and harness environment, in the Browser, double-click on the harness assembly.

Procedure: Exporting Harness Assembly Design Data

The following steps describe exporting cable and harness data from an assembly to an XML file format.

1. In the assembly file, activate the Cable and Harness environment. Start the Export Harness Data tool. Rename the file or accept the default name.

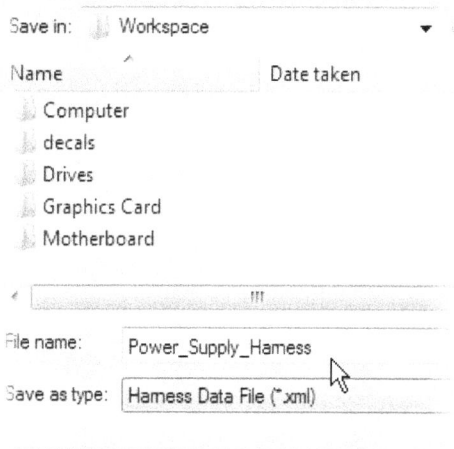

2. Save the file.

3. In the dialog box with the exported file location, click OK.

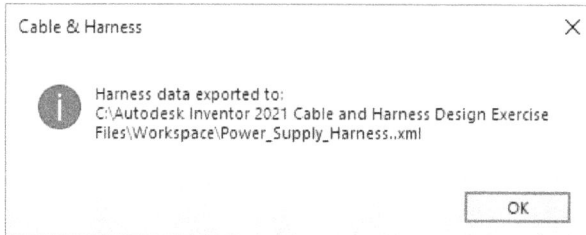

Generating Report Data

To create reports from a cable and harness nailboard drawing view, the sketch environment must be active. From the nailboard sketch environment, you display the Report Generator dialog box. From the Report Generator dialog box, you access the Create Report tool.

To create a report, you open a configuration file to format the report. Once the configuration file is specified, you can create the report using the default name, or double-click on the output file and specify a new name. The default name consists of the harness name combined with the configuration file name.

In the following figure, a configuration file is selected for use in the creation of a nailboard drawing view report.

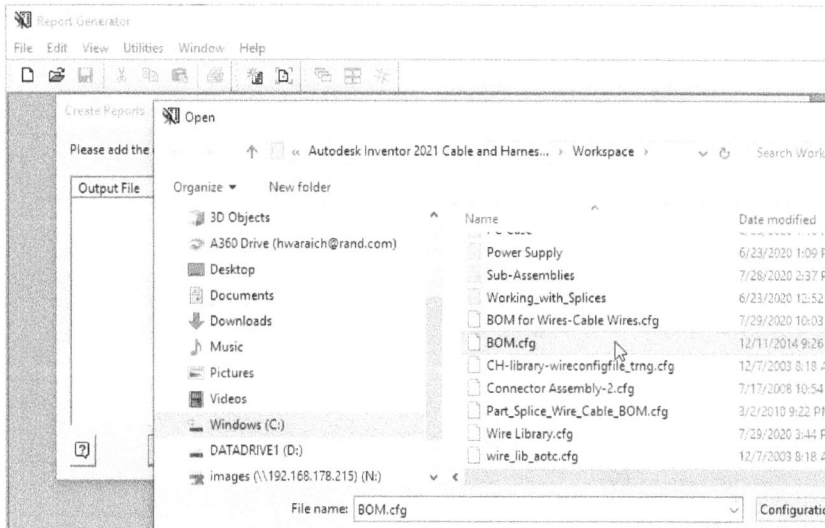

Access

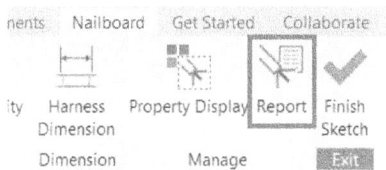

Ribbon: Nailboard tab>Manage panel

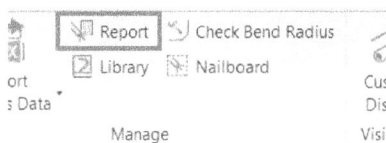

Ribbon: Cable and Harness tab>Manage panel

Report Generator Dialog Box

The following figure shows the Report Generator dialog box. The primary function of the Report Generator dialog box is to enable you to create reports and edit configuration files. In addition you can also create and edit text files and organize information using standard Windows tools such as Copy, Paste, and Print.

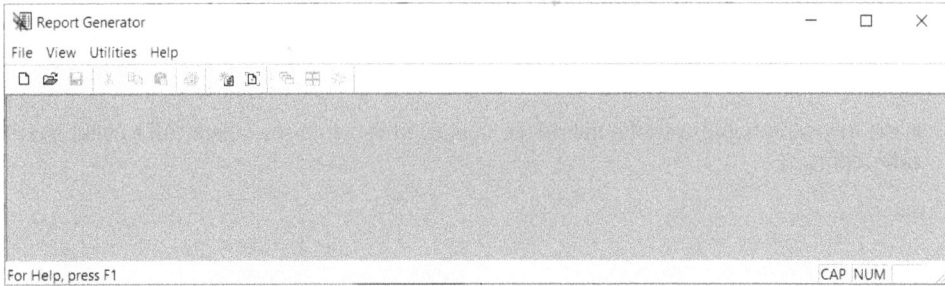

Procedure: Generating Report Data

The following steps describe creating a report in a CSV format.

1. Start the Report tool. In the Report Generator dialog box, click Create Report. Alternatively, click Utilities>Create Report.

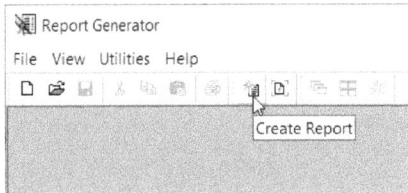

2. In the Create Reports dialog box, click Add File to List.

3. Select the CFG (configuration) file.

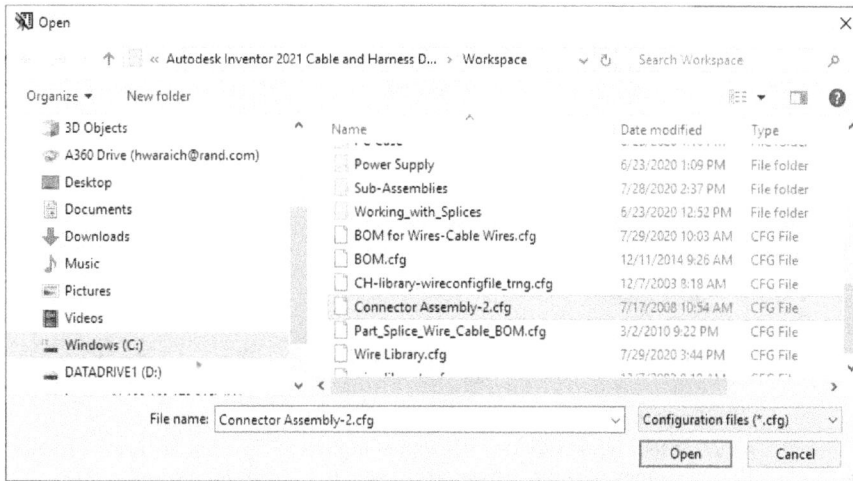

4. To rename the file, under Output File, double-click on the path file name.

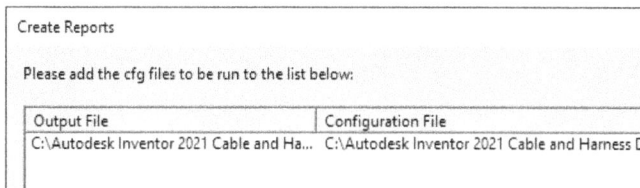

5. In the Select File for Report Output dialog box, for File, enter a new name and extension. Click Open.

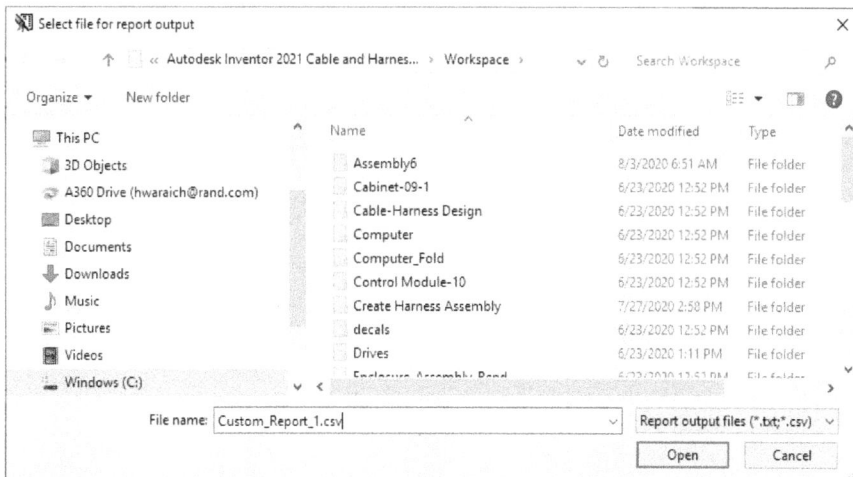

6. In the Create Reports dialog box, click OK.

```
Custom_Report_1
Pin  ,Wire    ,Color
1    ,Wire1   ,Red
---  ,Wire2   ,Red
2    ,Wire4   ,Black
---  ,Wire5   ,Black
3    ,Wire7   ,Black
---  ,Wire8   ,Black
4    ,Wire10  ,Yellow
---  ,Wire11  ,Yellow
1    ,Wire2   ,Red
---  ,Wire3   ,Red
```

CSV Report File vs. CSV Library Export File

A CSV file for a report is different in format from a CSV file associated with exported library data. The only common feature between the two is the CSV file format extension.

Exercise: Create External Files of Exported and Reported Data

In this exercise, you will export data from a cable and harness assembly and create a report from a nailboard drawing view.

Harness1_BOM_1.csv		
Part Number	,Vendor	,Quantity
12AWG-BLK	,---	,117.554 mm
2EDL1SC	,Syntek	, 1
3047-BLK	,Alpha	,385.573 mm
3047-BLU	,Alpha	,389.078 mm
3047-GRN	,Alpha	,387.443 mm
3048-BLK	,Alpha	,276.489 mm
3048-ORG	,Alpha	,389.106 mm
3048-RED	,Alpha	,661.359 mm
3048-WHT	,Alpha	,387.407 mm
3048-YEL	,Alpha	,815.861 mm
3605752	,---	, 1
AOTC-3605752	,AMP	, 1
LTP	,Molex	, 1

The completed exercise

1. Open *Export_Data_Create_Reports.iam*.

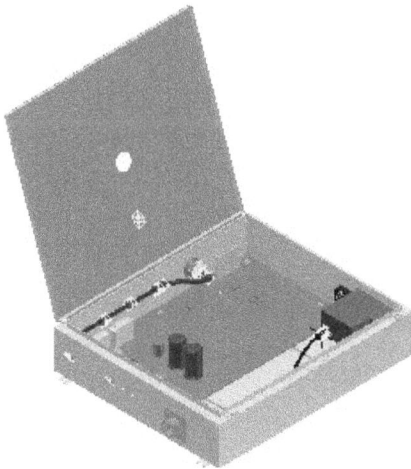

2. To activate the Cable and Harness environment, in the Browser, double-click on Harness1.

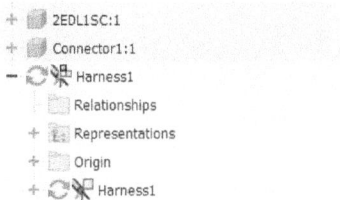

3. To begin to export data in an XML format, in the Cable and Harness tab, in the Manage panel, open the Harness Data drop- down list and click Export Harness Data.

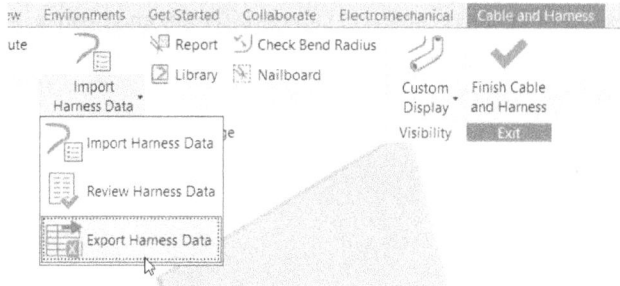

4. In the Export Harness Data dialog box:

- For File name, enter **My_Report**.
- Click Save.
- In the Cable and Harness message box, click OK.

5. Open *Export_Data_Create_Reports.idw*.

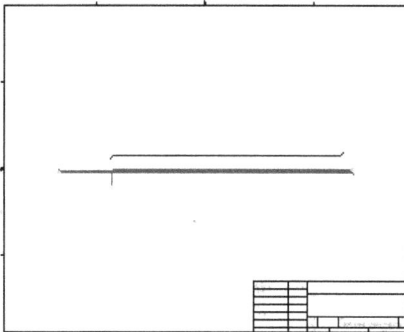

6. To activate the nailboard sketch, in the Nailboard tab, in the Edit panel, click Edit.

7. To begin creating a report in a CSV format:

- In the Nailboard tab, in the Manage panel, click Report.
- In the Report Generator dialog box, click Create Report. Alternatively, click Utilities>Create Report.

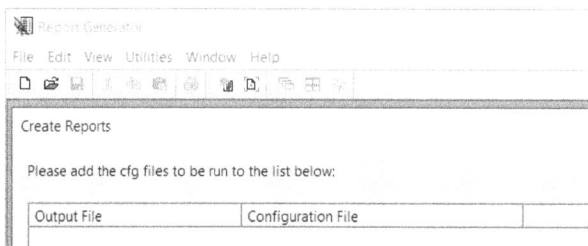

8. In the Create Reports dialog box:
   - Click Add File to List.
   - In the Open dialog box, select *BOM.cfg*.
   - Click Open.

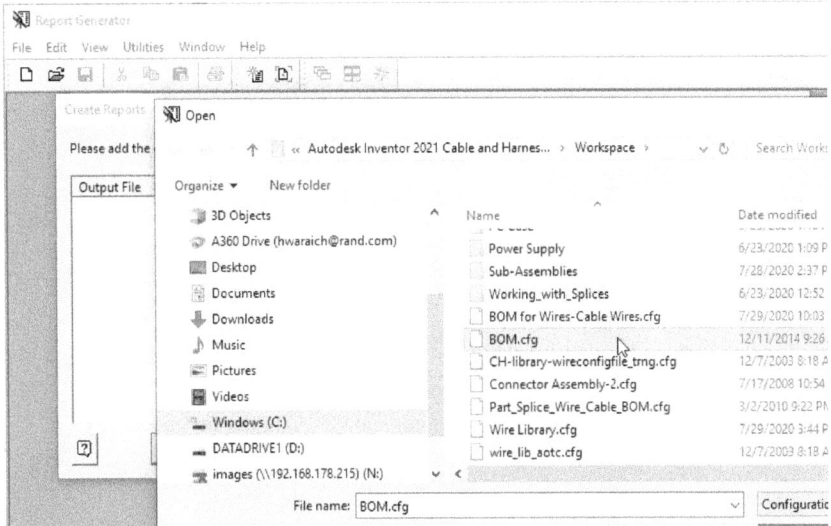

9. In the Create Reports dialog box, under Output File, double-click on the path listed.

10. To rename the file:
    - In the Select File for Report Output dialog box, for File Name, enter **My_Report**.
    - Click Open.
    - In the Create Reports dialog box, click OK.

11. Review the generated report.

Part Number	Vendor	Quantity
12AWG-BLK	---	117.553 mm
2EDL1SC	Syntek	1
3047-BLK	Alpha	385.572 mm
3047-BLU	Alpha	389.076 mm
3047-GRN	Alpha	387.441 mm
3048-BLK	Alpha	276.489 mm
3048-ORG	Alpha	389.104 mm
3048-RED	Alpha	661.357 mm
3048-WHT	Alpha	387.405 mm
3048-YEL	Alpha	815.858 mm
3605752	---	1
AOTC-3605752	AMP	1
LTP	Molex	1

12. Close all files without saving.

Chapter Summary

In this chapter, you learned the tools and techniques for communicating your cable and harness design to others by creating and annotating 2D drawings and exporting the design data.

Having completed this chapter, you can:

- Create 2D drawings and nailboards of a harness design.
- Annotate nailboards with dimensions and table information.
- Create reports and export the data for a cable and harness design.

Configure Library and Report Configuration Files

In this chapter, you learn how to add and edit library definitions and manage the cable and harness library file. You also learn how to create and edit the configuration files used for generating reports and for importing and exporting wire library data.

Objectives

After completing this chapter, you will be able to:

- Add and edit library definitions and manage the cable and harness library file.
- Create and edit the configuration files used for generating reports and the import and export of library data.

Lesson: Library Definitions and Library Files

This lesson describes the cable and harness library file, adding and editing library definitions, and management of the library file.

The cable and harness library is pivotal in the adding of wires, cables, and other objects to your designs. To save time during the creation of your designs, you should preconfigure the cable and harness library so that it includes the content you require. This also ensures that the content contains the properties required for later documentation of the design. For safety and further efficiency, after spending time customizing the library file, you should back up the file. If you are working in a team of designers, you can make your changes, or the entire library, available to others.

In the following figure, a portion of the default library list for wires is shown on the left. A modified version of the wire list that includes only the required wires is shown on the right.

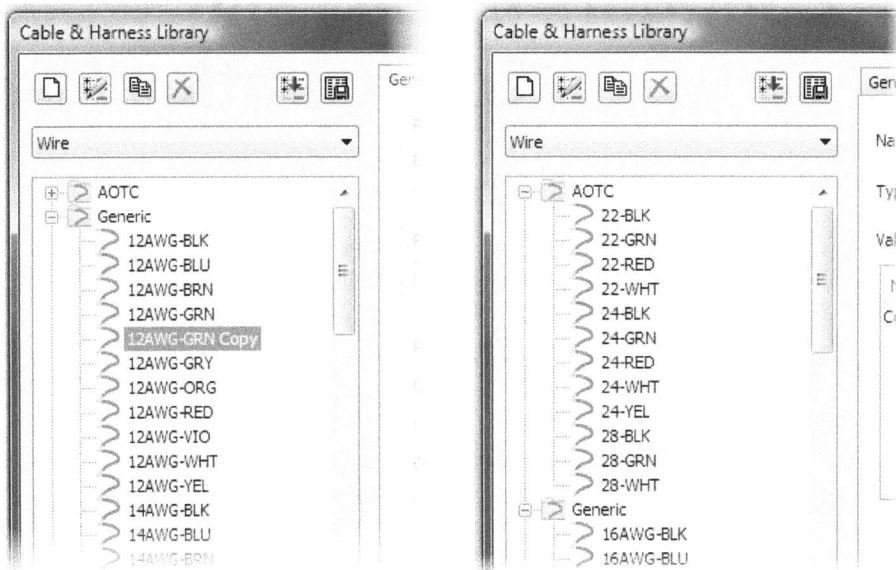

Objectives

After completing this lesson, you will be able to:

- Describe the purpose of the Cable and Harness Library and the location of the library file.
- Add a new library type to the library.
- Add a library definition to a library type.
- Export and import library objects from a neutral CSV file.
- State the format and organization of data for a CSV data file.

About the Cable and Harness Library

To ensure that you are able to add the cable and harness wires, cables, and other objects to your design that meet your requirements and with the properties you require, you need to know the purpose of the Cable and Harness Library, how to access it, and how to control where it is referenced from. Knowing where the library file is located and how it is referenced are essential. By knowing the file's location, you can make backup copies of the files, send the library file to others to use, or locate the file on a central server so multiple people in a design team can access the same custom library.

In the following figure, a wire definition that was initially created by copying an existing wire is in the process of being edited to set unique properties.

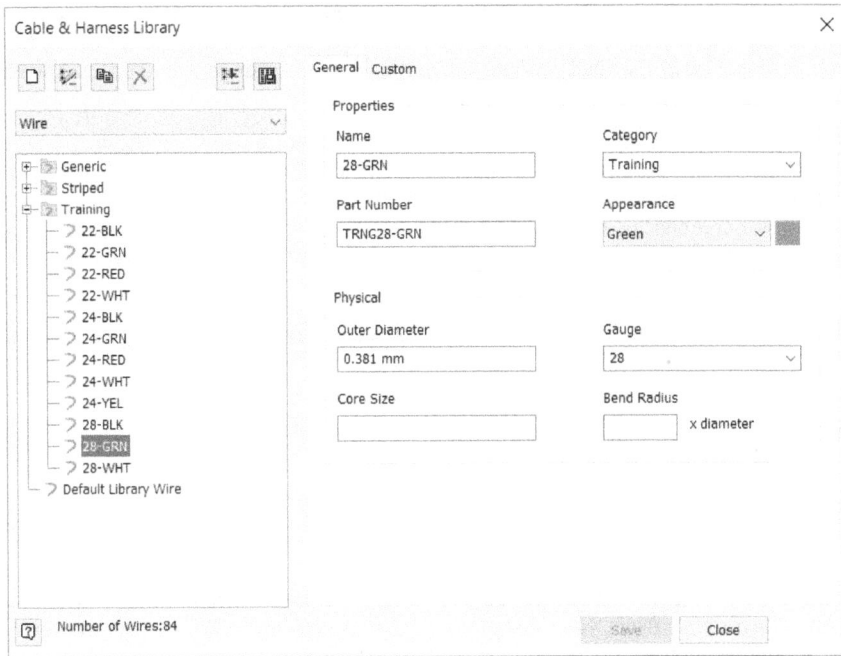

Definition of the Cable and Harness Library

The Cable and Harness Library contains the standard wire data that you use to create wires and cables in a harness assembly. These wires do not have a physical representation and exist only in the library file. You select from this list to insert wires and cables in the harness assembly.

You can use any standard wire definition that is in the library or add your own definitions. You can also modify and remove existing wires. To add a large set of library definitions, you can import wires and cables using an ASCII file.

With the library tools you can:

- View the basic properties for a selected wire or cable.
- Find the total number of wires and cables in the library.
- Modify, copy, and delete existing wire and cable definitions.
- Add new wire and cable definitions.
- Import and export wire and cable libraries.

Access

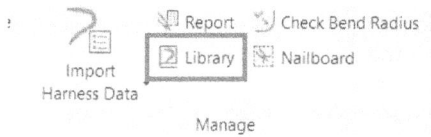

Ribbon: Cable & Harness tab>Manage panel

Keyboard Shortcut: L

Cable and Harness Library File Location

The Cable and Harness Library file contains all the cable and wire data that you use to create cables and wires in a harness assembly. By default, the file is named *Cable&HarnessDefaultLibrary.iwl* and is located in the Cable & Harness folder in the Design Data folder where you installed the software. You can change this location in the File Locations tab in the Harness Settings dialog box, in the File tab in the Application Options dialog box, or in the project file.

In the following figure, the active harness assembly is configured to use a specific library file instead of the library file located in the project's Design Data location. For greater versatility and ease of change, instead of calling out a specific library file for each and every harness assembly, you should have the harness assemblies use the option to have the design data location specify the library file.

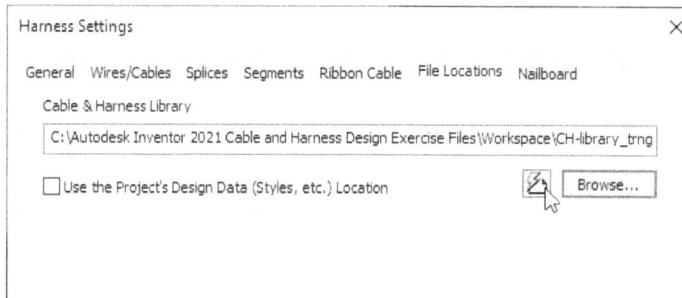

Typically, one library file is created and stored on a server for all harness assemblies to use. If the library file is accessed by multiple users, you must place it in a shared location. You can set a different library file and location for each harness assembly, but one central library file is recommended.

Only one person can open the library at one time to add, edit, or remove wires. All others attempting to access the library are notified that the library is being edited and that it cannot be accessed. When someone has it open, the library is read-only, so you can still insert any wire listed in the wire library into the harness assembly. However, if the wire library cannot be found, the default library wire is used. The default library wire cannot be modified.

Each time the library is opened, the system determines whether changes were made to the library data that require an update. Some changes are immediately available in the active harness assembly, and other changes are not. If an update is required, in the Manage tab, in the Update panel, click Update.

Example of the Cable and Harness Library

The following example shows the default list of object types in the Cable and Harness Library, and some of the categories and wire definitions within the wire object type. The list of available wires to select and use when adding a wire to a harness assembly is based on the wires that are listed in the library.

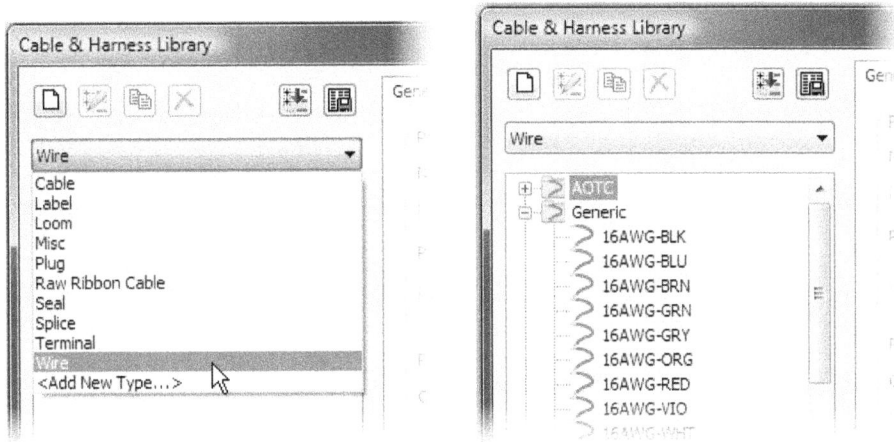

Adding a New Library Type

If your designs require multiple different types of custom virtual parts to be added to wires, cables, segments, or pins, you might want to organize your virtual parts in the library in custom library types. To organize your virtual parts in this manner, you need to know how to create a new library type in the cable and harness library.

In the following figure, the default library types available for a segment's virtual parts are limited to the types of Misc and Loom.

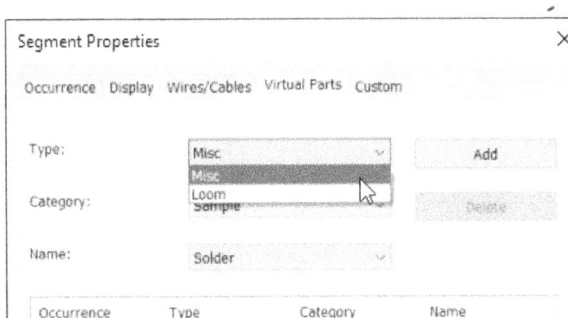

Cable and Harness Library: Add New Type

You add a new type to the Cable and Harness Library by selecting Add New Type in the list of types in the Cable & Harness Library dialog box. After you select to add a new type, you enter the name for the new type. When you add a new library type, the definitions in that library type are available for use only as virtual parts for wires, cables, segments, and pins.

After you enter the name for a custom type, you cannot rename or delete the custom type from the library object list using the Cable & Harness Library dialog box. To remove the custom type, you can either copy a backup version of the library file over the working library file, or edit the library file in a separate text editor application. If you edit the file in a text editor, scroll to the bottom of the file and delete the text between <USERDEFINEVPS> and </USERDEFINEVPS>.

> The list of library types is loaded into memory and does not refresh until Autodesk® Inventor® starts. So if you edited the library file, the list does not change until you exit and then start the Autodesk Inventor application again.

Procedure: Adding a New Library Type

The following steps give an overview of adding a new library type to the Cable and Harness Library file.

1.   Activate a harness assembly.

2.   Start the Cable & Harness Library tool.

3.   In the Cable & Harness Library dialog box, list of types, select Add New Type.

4.   In the new Library Type dialog box, enter the name of the new library type.

Adding Library Definitions

While the default Cable and Harness Library contains a large number of defined objects, if your designs require different wires, cables, or other objects, you can add a library definition to a library type.

The following figure shows a view of the many cables that are available in the default Cable and Harness Library.

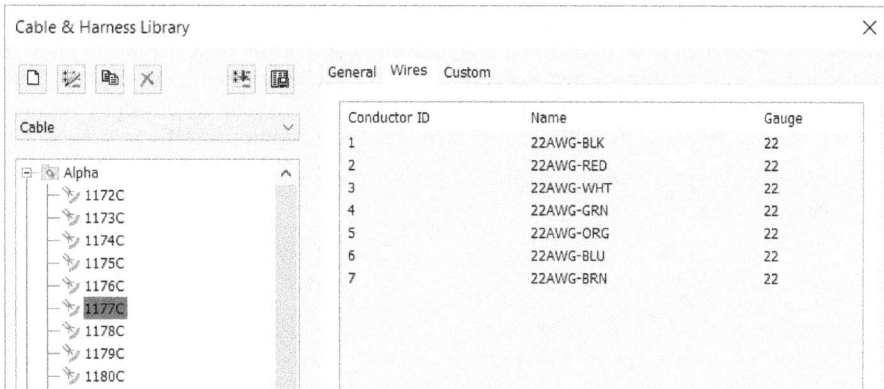

Description of Adding Library Definitions

When you add a new library definition to the Cable and Harness Library, the new library definition is added to the active library type. You add a library definition by selecting and copying an existing library entry, or by clicking the New option in the Cable & Harness Library dialog box. The category in which the new entry is created within the library type depends on the category name you select from the Category list, or the name you enter in the Category list.

The options for creating a new entry, editing a selected entry, copying a selected entry, or deleting a selected entry are available as buttons in the Cable & Harness Library dialog box. You can also access the delete, copy, and edit options in the shortcut menu after right-clicking an entry in the list.

The options in the dialog box are:

1. Use to begin defining a new entry from scratch in the active category.

2. Click to begin editing the entry that is selected in the list.

3. Use to create a new entry in the active category by copying the entry that is selected in the list.

4. Click to delete the entry that is selected in the list.

Library Entry Properties

After you click to create a new entry or edit an existing one, the fields and options for defining the properties of the item become active for editing in the General and Custom tabs. While the exact options in the General tab vary based on the type of entry you are editing, the primary and common properties in the tab are in the Properties and Physical areas. Like adding custom iProperties to a part or assembly, you can add multiple types of custom information to a library object in the Custom tab. If you are editing an entry for the Cable object type, you have additional settings in the Wires tab.

In the following figure, the General and Custom tabs are shown for a custom wire that is being added to the library.

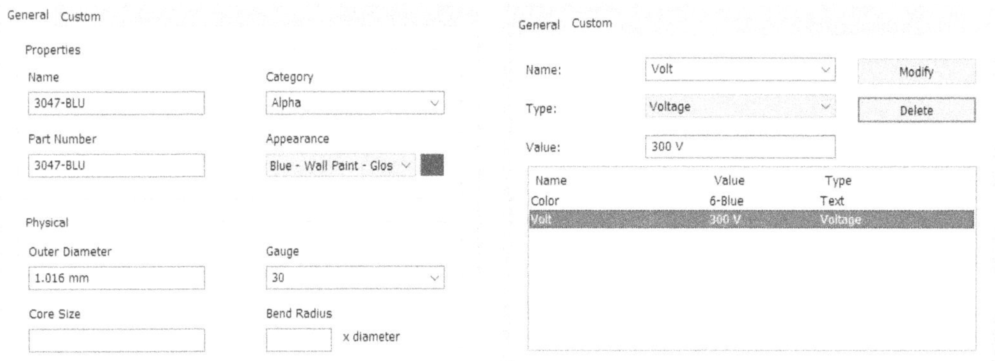

Creating a New Category

When you are adding new entries to a library type, you can further organize the list by organizing the categories into different sub-categories. If the category for the new item already exists, you assign the category it goes into by selecting the category name from the Category list. If the category doesn't exist, enter the new category name into the Category field. When you save the library item you are creating or editing, the new category is created. The item is also listed below that category.

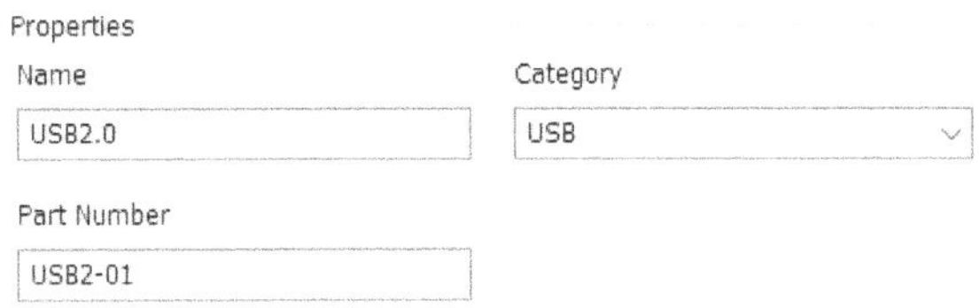

In the following figure, the default list of cable categories is shown on the left, and the list with a custom category and new cable is shown on the right.

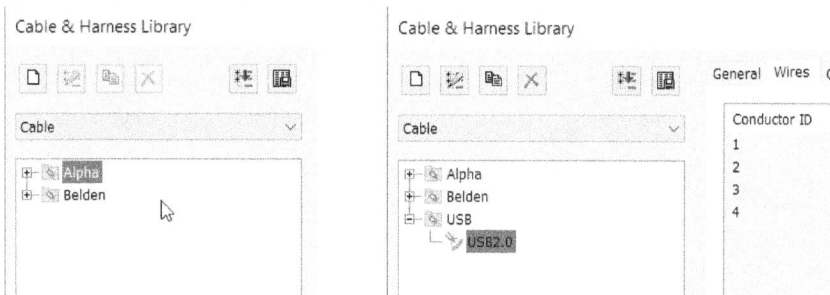

> When you delete the last entry in a category, the category is automatically removed from the list for that library type.

Procedure: Adding Library Definitions

The following figure shows an overview of adding a library definition to any library type.

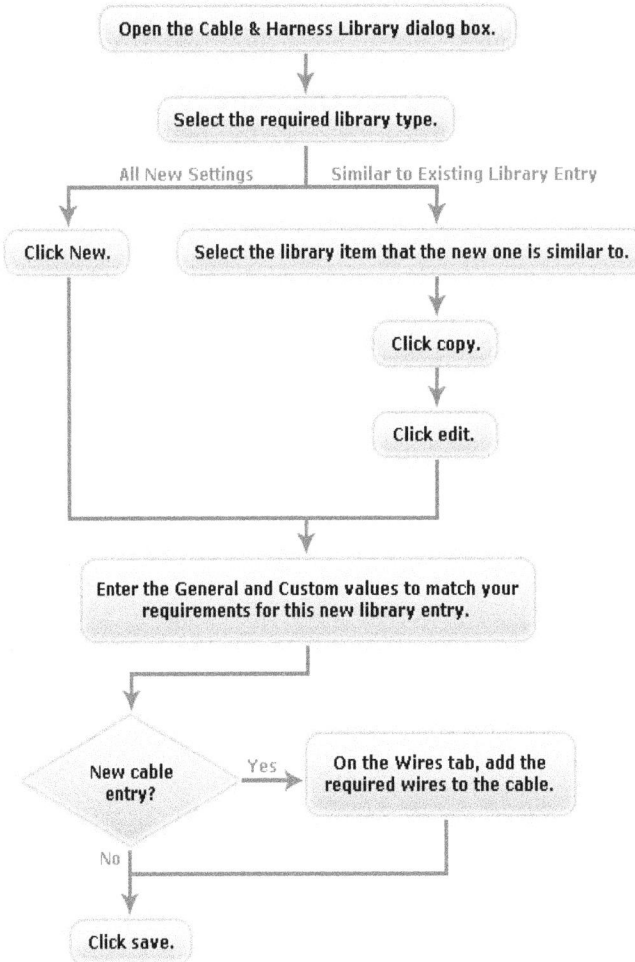

Exporting and Importing Library Objects

You can spend a significant amount of time configuring objects like custom wires and cables within a cable and harness library. To reuse your custom object configurations in other cable and harness libraries, you are required to export the library objects and then import them into a different cable and harness library.

Export and Import Library Objects

You export and import library object definitions from within the Cable & Harness Library dialog box. The objects you export or import depend on which library object type is currently selected in the harness object type list.

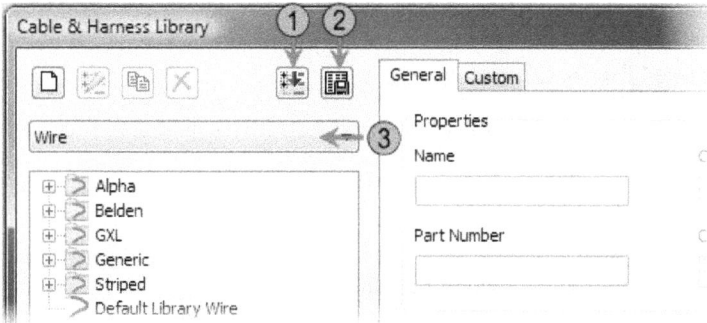

1. Use to import objects into the current object type from an external CSV file.

2. Use to export all of the objects for the current object type.

3. The current object type that objects will be exported from or imported to.

After you click to export or import library data, a dialog box opens for that task and object type. Within the dialog box, you specify the file that has the data to import, or you specify the file to export to. You also specify the configuration file that indicates the format of the data being exported or imported.

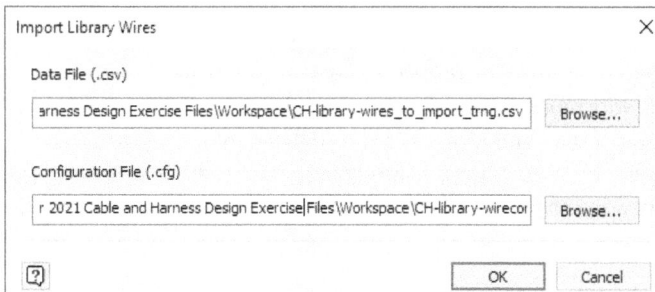

Procedure: Exporting Library Objects

The following steps give an overview of exporting library objects to a neutral CSV file.

1. In a separate application, configure the CFG file to use when importing and exporting library data.
2. Activate the harness assembly for in-place editing.
3. Open the Cable & Harness Library dialog box.
4. In the Cable & Harness Library dialog box, click Export Library Objects.
5. Specify the file location and name for the exported CSV content.
6. Select the CFG file to set the export information and format.

Procedure: Importing Library Objects

The following steps give an overview of importing library objects from a neutral CSV file.

1. In a separate application, configure the CFG file to use when importing and exporting library data.
2. If required, in a separate application, edit the CSV file that contains the library data so that it matches your requirements prior to importing that data.
3. Activate the harness assembly for in-place editing.
4. Open the Cable & Harness Library dialog box.
5. In the Cable & Harness Library dialog box, click Import Library Objects.
6. Specify the CSV data file to import and the CFG file that specifies that data's format.

General Guidelines When Importing

When you import a library of cable or wire objects, the system uses the following guidelines:

- Imported cable and wire definitions always overwrite or update existing library cable and wire definitions.
- New cables and wires are always added to the Cable and Harness library.
- New, previously undefined cable and wire properties are always added.
- Existing library cable and wire property values can be changed.
- Properties of existing library cables and wires cannot be deleted through importing.
- Properties of existing cables and wires can be overridden with a blank value by using two consecutive commas. Only one comma is required if the entry is the last one in the row.

Data File (CSV) Format

Data files are a critical part of exporting and importing cable and harness library objects. To import the right data into your library, you must understand the format and organization of data for a CSV data file.

Data File Description and Configuration

The file that you import and export library objects to and from is a neutral ASCII text file with a CSV file extension. Within this text file, the properties and settings for each object are positioned on separate rows with the data in a row separated by commas. The actual properties and settings for an object depend on the type of object. For data files that you are going to use for importing, you can edit the file and add comments to the data file by preceding the text with two forward slashes (//).

When you import or export data, the order of the properties and settings must exactly match the configuration file. The specified units must also be appropriate for the data type specified for the given property name.

The following example shows a comparison of the data file format and a portion of data for a wire data file and a cable data file. In the wire data file, each wire and its properties are listed on a separate line. In the cable data file, each wire within a cable is listed on a single line. The entire cable definition is the collection of all the rows of data with the same cable name. In this example, there are two cables shown. One cable has two wires within it, and the other cable has three wires within it.

Wire File Example:

//Wire Name,Color Style,Outer Diameter,Category,Part Number,Gauge

24AWG-BLK,black,0.024,Generic,24AWG_BLK,24

24AWG-BRN,brown,0.024,Generic,24AWG_BRN,24

24AWG-RED,red,0.024,Generic,24AWG_RED,24

24AWG-YEL,yellow,0.024,Generic,24AWG_YEL,24

24AWG-ORG,orange,0.024,Generic,24AWG_ORG,24

Cable File Example:

//Cable Name,Category,Part Number,Outer Diameter,Conductor ID,Wire Name

1172C,Alpha,1172C,0.16,1,22AWG-BLK

1172C,Alpha,1172C,0.16,2,22AWG-RED

1173C,Alpha,1173C,0.17,1,22AWG-BLK

1173C,Alpha,1173C,0.17,2,22AWG-RED

1173C,Alpha,1173C,0.17,3,22AWG-WHT

You can open and edit the data files directly in the Report Generator dialog box or in another program such as Notepad or Microsoft Excel.

In the following figure, the Report Generator is being used to review and edit the content of a wire data file.

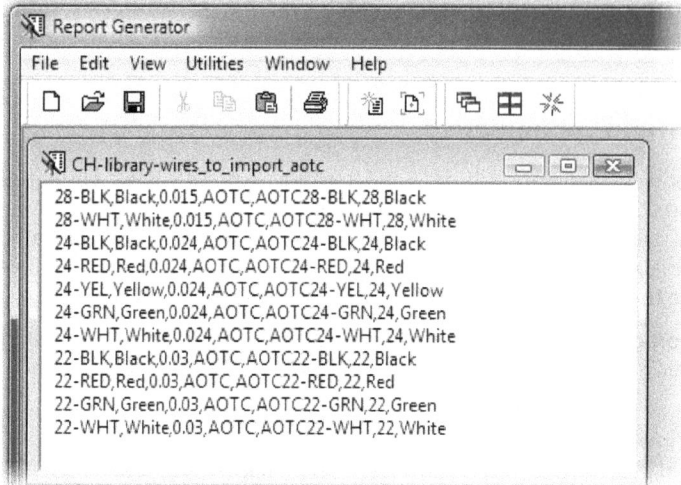

28-BLK,Black,0.015,AOTC,AOTC28-BLK,28,Black
28-WHT,White,0.015,AOTC,AOTC28-WHT,28,White
24-BLK,Black,0.024,AOTC,AOTC24-BLK,24,Black
24-RED,Red,0.024,AOTC,AOTC24-RED,24,Red
24-YEL,Yellow,0.024,AOTC,AOTC24-YEL,24,Yellow
24-GRN,Green,0.024,AOTC,AOTC24-GRN,24,Green
24-WHT,White,0.024,AOTC,AOTC24-WHT,24,White
22-BLK,Black,0.03,AOTC,AOTC22-BLK,22,Black
22-RED,Red,0.03,AOTC,AOTC22-RED,22,Red
22-GRN,Green,0.03,AOTC,AOTC22-GRN,22,Green
22-WHT,White,0.03,AOTC,AOTC22-WHT,22,White

Exercise: Create Library Definitions

In this exercise, you will review the settings in a cable and harness library, assign a harness assembly to use a custom library, and create additional library definitions by importing them, copying them, and creating them from scratch.

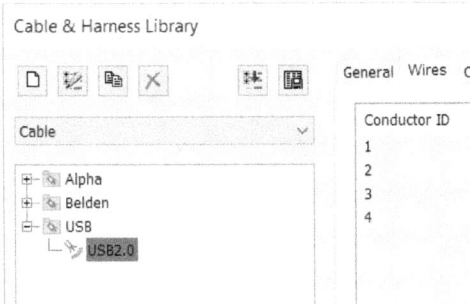

The completed exercise

1. Open *Control Module-10.iam*.

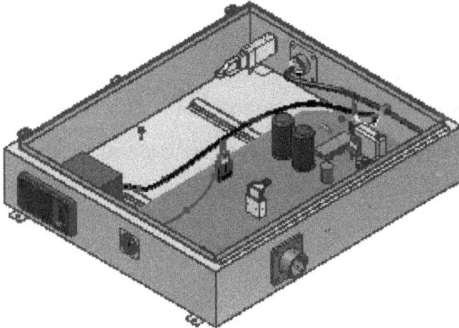

2. In the Browser, double-click on the PatchCable harness assembly.

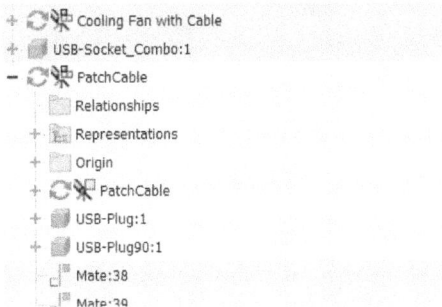

3. To review what is defined in the cable and harness library:

   ▪ In the Cable & Harness tab, in the Manage panel, click Library.
   ▪ In the Cable & Harness Library dialog box, for the Wire library type, review the categories and listed definitions.
   ▪ Click Close.

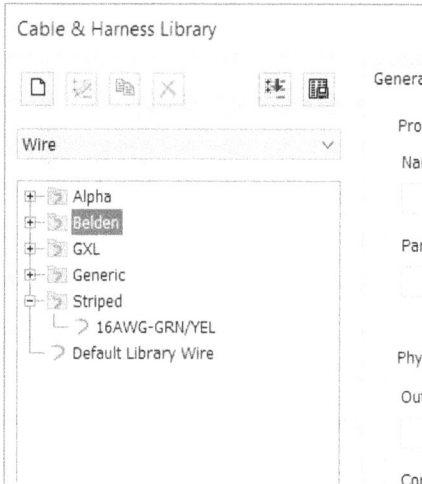

4. To begin setting a custom library file to this harness assembly:

   ▪ In the Browser, right-click on the PatchCable harness assembly and click Harness Settings.
   ▪ In the Harness Settings dialog box, in the File Locations tab, clear the Use the Project's Design Data Location check box.

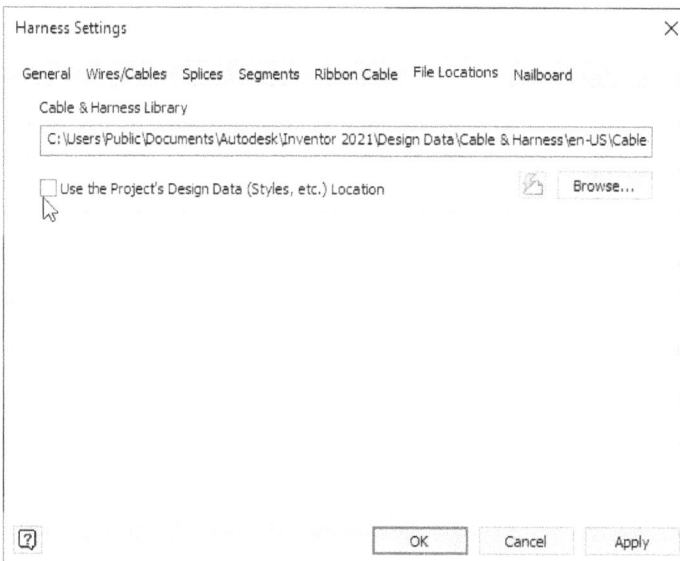

5. To select a different library file:

- Click Browse.
- In the Select Cable & Harness Library File dialog box, select and open *CH- library_trng.iwl*.
- In the File Locations tab, click Update.
- Click OK.

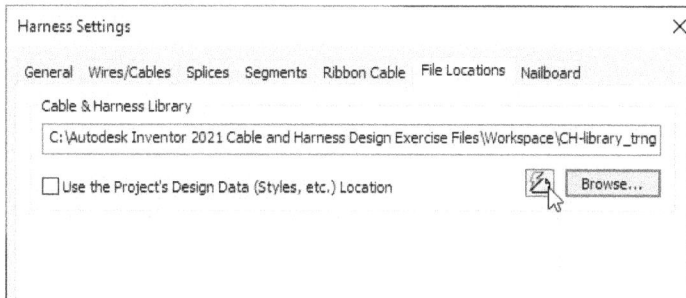

6. To review what is defined in the custom cable and harness library:

- In the Cable & Harness tab, in the Manage panel, click Library.
- In the Cable & Harness Library dialog box, for the Wire library type, review the categories and listed definitions.

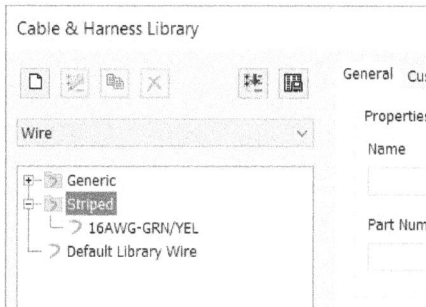

7. To begin importing wires that are defined in a comma-delimited file, in the Cable & Harness Library dialog box, click Import Library Objects.

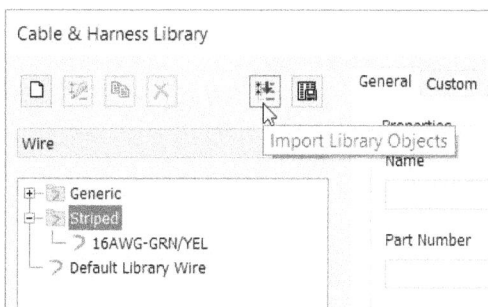

8. In the Import Library Wires dialog box:
   - In the Data File area, browse to and open *CH-library-wires_to_import_trng.csv*.
   - In the Configuration File area, browse to and open *CH-library-wireconfigfile_trng.cfg*.
   - Click OK.

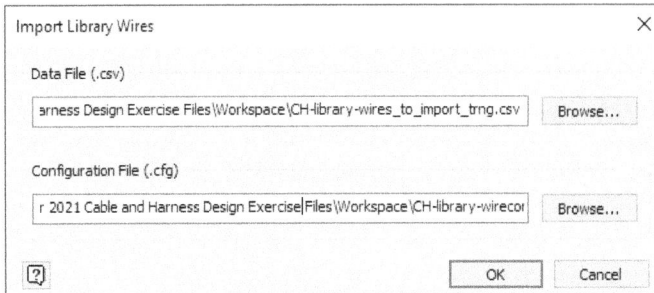

9. In the Import Library Wires message dialog box, click Close.

10. Review the new category and wires that were just imported.

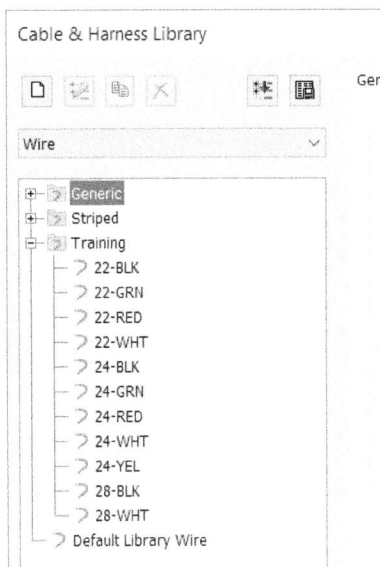

11. In the wire list, right-click on 28-BLK and click Copy.

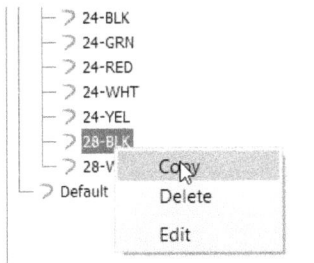

12. To begin modifying the name and properties of the copied wire definition, right-click on 28-BLK Copy and click Edit.

13. In the General tab, Properties area:

- For Name, enter **28-GRN**.
- For Part Number, enter **TRNG28-GRN**.
- In the Appearance list, select Green.

14. Click Save.

15. To begin creating a new cable in its own category, in the list of library types, select Cable.

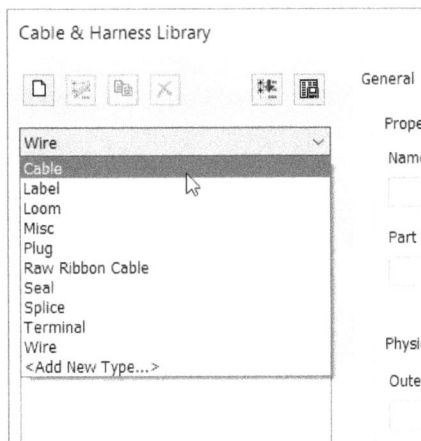

16. Click New.

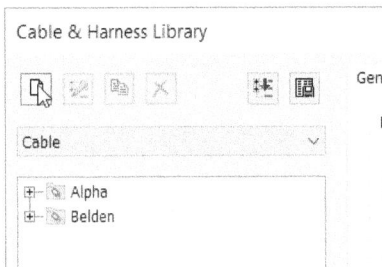

17. In the General tab, in the Properties area:
- For Name, enter **USB2.0.**
- For Category, enter **USB**.
- For Part Number, enter **USB2-01**.

18. In the General tab, in the Outer Diameter and Bend Radius areas, click the Calculate from Wires check boxes.

19. In the Wires tab, click Add.

20. In the Add Wires dialog box, expand the list for the Training wire category.

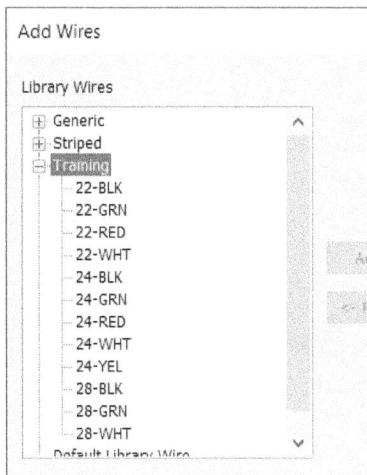

Add Wires

Library Wires

- Generic
- Striped
- Training
  - 22-BLK
  - 22-GRN
  - 22-RED
  - 22-WHT
  - 24-BLK
  - 24-GRN
  - 24-RED
  - 24-WHT
  - 24-YEL
  - 28-BLK
  - 28-GRN
  - 28-WHT
- Default Library Wire

21. Select and then click Add to add the wires in the order shown. Click OK.

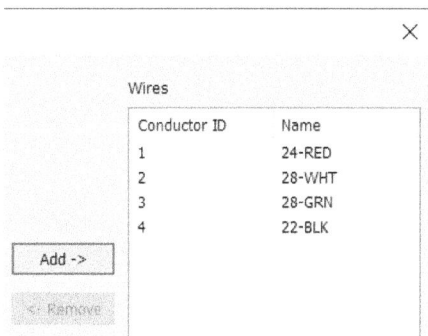

Wires

Conductor ID	Name
1	24-RED
2	28-WHT
3	28-GRN
4	22-BLK

Add ->

<- Remove

22. Click Save.

23. Review the new category and cable that you just added to the list of cables.

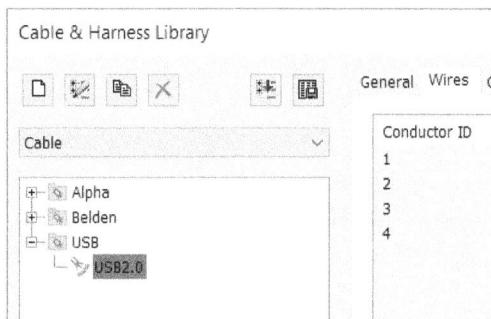

Cable & Harness Library

General   Wires   C

Cable

Conductor ID
1
2
3
4

- Alpha
- Belden
- USB
  - USB2.0

24. Click Close.

25. Close all files without saving changes.

Lesson: Configuration Files for Reports, Imports, and Exports

This lesson describes the editing of configuration files that are used for the generation of reports and for the importing and exporting of library data.

Understanding the format of configuration files and how to edit them is important when you are creating the configuration files so that they can be used by you or others.

In the following figure, the contents of the two types of configuration files are shown. The sample report configuration file is shown first and has been opened in the text editor. You can compare its format to the library configuration file that is shown second.

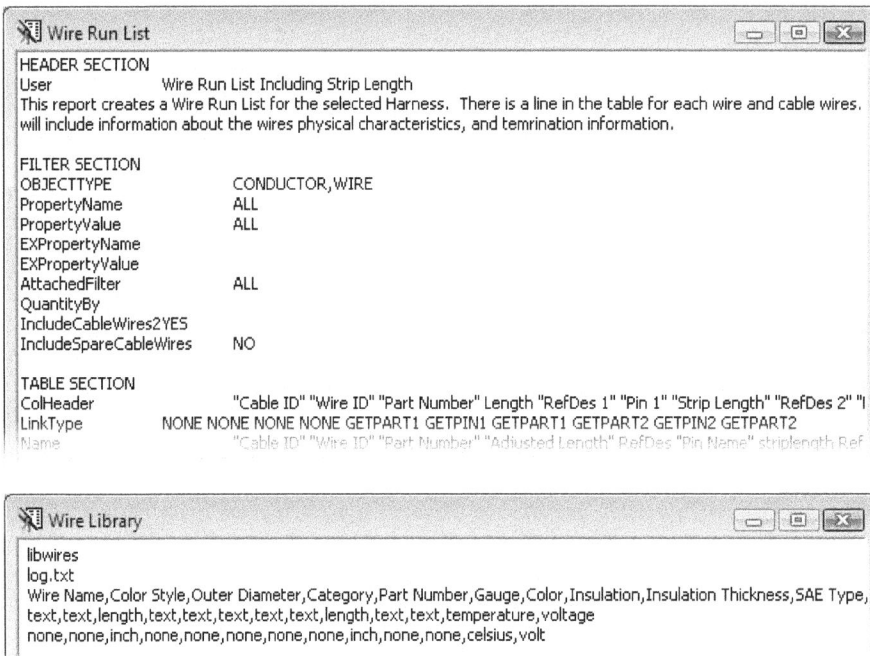

```
Wire Run List                                                        □ ▣ ✕

HEADER SECTION
User          Wire Run List Including Strip Length
This report creates a Wire Run List for the selected Harness.  There is a line in the table for each wire and cable wires.
will include information about the wires physical characteristics, and temrination information.

FILTER SECTION
OBJECTTYPE              CONDUCTOR,WIRE
PropertyName            ALL
PropertyValue           ALL
EXPropertyName
EXPropertyValue
AttachedFilter          ALL
QuantityBy
IncludeCableWires2YES
IncludeSpareCableWires  NO

TABLE SECTION
ColHeader               "Cable ID" "Wire ID" "Part Number" Length "RefDes 1" "Pin 1" "Strip Length" "RefDes 2" "I
LinkType        NONE NONE NONE NONE GETPART1 GETPIN1 GETPART1 GETPART2 GETPIN2 GETPART2
Name            "Cable ID" "Wire ID" "Part Number" "Adjusted Length" RefDes "Pin Name" striplength Ref
```

```
Wire Library                                                         □ ▣ ✕

libwires
log.txt
Wire Name,Color Style,Outer Diameter,Category,Part Number,Gauge,Color,Insulation,Insulation Thickness,SAE Type,
text,text,length,text,text,text,text,text,length,text,text,temperature,voltage
none,none,inch,none,none,none,none,none,inch,none,none,celsius,volt
```

Objectives

After completing this lesson, you will be able to:

- Describe the types and functions of configuration files.
- Edit the settings and options in a report configuration file.
- State the function of link types and identify the name values that can be set in the Table tab of the configuration editor.
- Define a configuration file to import or export library data.

About Configuration Files

During the process of creating reports for a harness design or exporting cable and harness library objects, you select a configuration file. To effectively create configuration files, you need to first understand the types and functions of configuration files and where you edit them.

Definition of Configuration Files

There are two completely different uses for configuration files. You can use a configuration file to generate an external report, or you can use configuration files to import and export cable and harness library objects. Both report and library configuration files are ASCII text files with a CFG file extension. Although these files have the same file extension, their formatting, the methods for editing them, and their location of use are quite different.

Configuration File	Description
Report CFG File	Used as a template to specify what data to extract from the active harness assembly and to specify how the data is written to a new external report file.
Import CFG File	Used as a template when importing data from a CSV data file into the cable and harness library. Describes the input properties, data types, and units of the data being imported.
Export CFG File	Used as a template to specify which cable and harness library properties for the active library type should be exported to a new external CSV data file.

As a standard practice, you should store library import and export configuration files in the same folder as your cable and harness library. You should store report configuration files in a central server location so multiple people on the design team can access and use them to generate reports for their designs.

Configuration File Edits

When you create or edit a library import or export configuration file, you can use the Report Generator or a text editor application like Notepad or Microsoft Excel. You use the Report Generator to create or edit a report configuration file.

The Report Generator enables you to open and edit files with the capabilities of a basic text editor. When you need to create or edit a report configuration file, you use the Edit a Configuration File tool in the Report Generator. This tool opens the file in a dialog box consisting of multiple tabs that assist and guide you in editing the file.

In the following figure, the same report configuration file is open in the Report Generator, Notepad, and the dialog box for the Report Generator's Edit a Configuration File option.

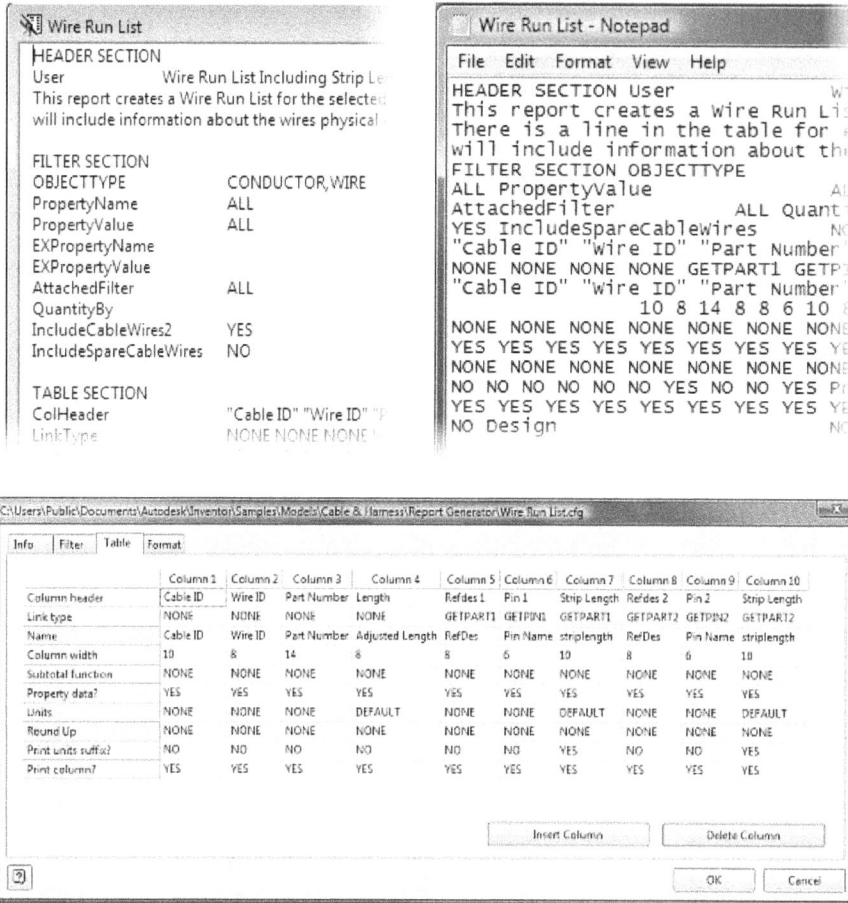

Wire Run List

HEADER SECTION
User   Wire Run List Including Strip Le
This report creates a Wire Run List for the selecte
will include information about the wires physical

FILTER SECTION
OBJECTTYPE   CONDUCTOR,WIRE
PropertyName   ALL
PropertyValue   ALL
EXPropertyName
EXPropertyValue
AttachedFilter   ALL
QuantityBy
IncludeCableWires2   YES
IncludeSpareCableWires NO

TABLE SECTION
ColHeader   "Cable ID" "Wire ID" "
LinkType   NONE NONE NONE

Wire Run List - Notepad

File Edit Format View Help

HEADER SECTION User   Wi
This report creates a Wire Run Li
There is a line in the table for
will include information about the
FILTER SECTION OBJECTTYPE
ALL PropertyValue   AL
AttachedFilter   ALL Quant
YES IncludeSpareCableWires   N
"Cable ID" "Wire ID" "Part Number"
NONE NONE NONE NONE GETPART1 GETP
"Cable ID" "Wire ID" "Part Number
                    10 8 14 8 8 6 10 8
NONE NONE NONE NONE NONE NONE NON
YES YES YES YES YES YES YES YES Y
NONE NONE NONE NONE NONE NONE NON
NO NO NO NO NO NO YES NO NO YES P
YES YES YES YES YES YES YES YES Y
NO Design   N

C:\Users\Public\Documents\Autodesk\Inventor\Samples\Models\Cable & Harness\Report Generator\Wire Run List.cfg

Info Filter Table Format

	Column 1	Column 2	Column 3	Column 4	Column 5	Column 6	Column 7	Column 8	Column 9	Column 10
Column header	Cable ID	Wire ID	Part Number	Length	Refdes 1	Pin 1	Strip Length	Refdes 2	Pin 2	Strip Length
Link type	NONE	NONE	NONE	NONE	GETPART1	GETPIN1	GETPART1	GETPART2	GETPIN2	GETPART12
Name	Cable ID	Wire ID	Part Number	Adjusted Length	RefDes	Pin Name	striplength	RefDes	Pin Name	striplength
Column width	10	8	14	8	8	6	10	8	6	10
Subtotal function	NONE	NONE	NONE	NONE	NONE	NONE	NONE	NONE	NONE	NONE
Property data?	YES	YES	YES	YES	YES	YES	YES	YES	YES	YES
Units	NONE	NONE	NONE	DEFAULT	NONE	NONE	DEFAULT	NONE	NONE	DEFAULT
Round Up	NONE	NONE	NONE	NONE	NONE	NONE	NONE	NONE	NONE	NONE
Print units suffix?	NO	NO	NO	NO	NO	NO	YES	NO	NO	YES
Print column?	YES	YES	YES	YES	YES	YES	YES	YES	YES	YES

Insert Column   Delete Column

OK   Cancel

Access

Ribbon: Nailboard tab>Manage panel

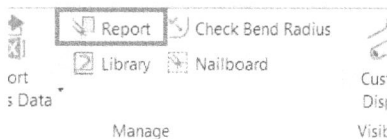

Ribbon: Cable and Harness tab>Manage panel

Example of a Configuration File

You generate different report types, such as wire run lists, bills of material, and connector tables, for a harness assembly so you can use the report information in other applications such as those used for procurement. You can also add the report information to a drawing to complete the documentation of the design. The format and content of the report are based on the report configuration file.

In the following figure, the *PartsList.cfg* file is shown open in the Report Generator editor. This report was used to generate a parts list of the harness design of the power supply. The report results are shown behind the editor dialog box.

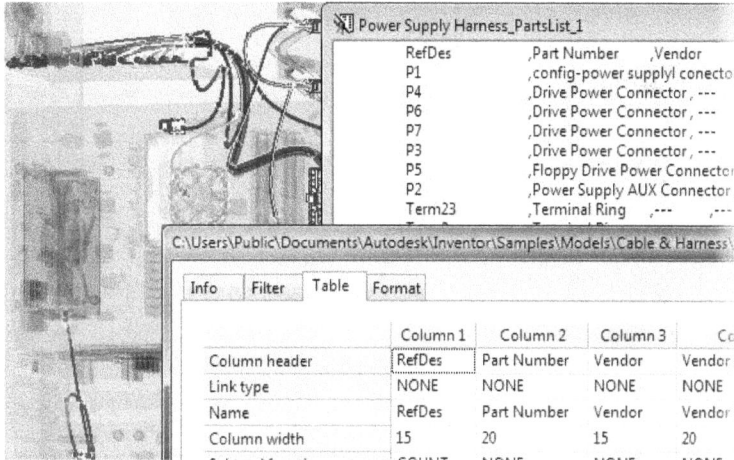

Editing a Report Configuration File

Report configuration files determine which information should be exported from a harness assembly and how the information should be reported. To create a report with the data you require and in the format you want, you need to understand the settings and options in a report configuration file, and how to edit a report configuration file.

In the following figure, two report files of the same harness assembly are shown. The reports were created using two different report configuration files that reported some of the same information.

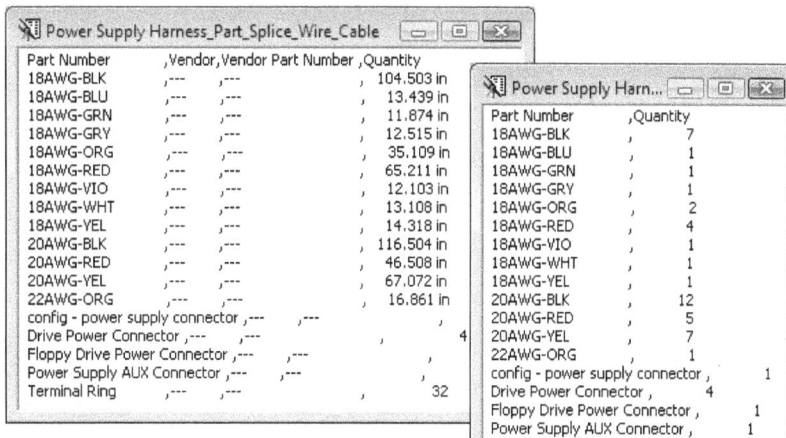

Sample Files

The easiest way to create a report is to use one of the sample configuration files. If the sample files do not meet your requirements, you can save a sample file with a new name and then modify and organize the report configuration file to include the information that you require. Starting from an existing sample file also helps reduce the time to create the configuration file and errors.

The default location for the sample files for generating reports is within the folder where Autodesk Inventor is installed, usually in the \Samples\Models\Cable & Harness\Report Generator subfolder. You might have to download the Autodesk Inventor Samples data sets from *http://www.autodesk.com/inventor-samples*.

The following are sample report configuration files and their output:

Report Configuration File	Description
Parts List Report (*PartsList.cfg*)	This report lists each electrical part in the design with its RefDes and vendor information.
Wire Run List (*Wire Run List.cfg*)	This report creates a wire run list for the selected harness. There is a line in the table for each wire and cable wire in the harness assembly. Each row includes information about the wire's physical characteristics and termination information.
Connector Table (*Connector.cfg*)	Creates a table for each connector and splice in a harness. The table has a line for each pin in the design and information about the wires attached to that pin.
Segment Table (*Segment Table.cfg*)	This report creates a table with information about the physical characteristics of each harness segment in a harness assembly.

> Only use the sample CFG files from the Report Generator sample folder. Do not use CFG files from the Wire Library directory because they have a different format and do not work for reports.

Edit a Report Configuration File

You use the Edit a Configuration (.cfg) File tool in the Report Generator to modify an existing configuration file or to create a new one. The Edit a Configuration File tool is located in the Report Generator located in the Utilities menu and in the main toolbar.

After you click to start the Edit a Configuration File tool, you select a file to edit. A configuration editor dialog box displays consisting of four tabs to make the task of editing the configuration file simple and efficient.

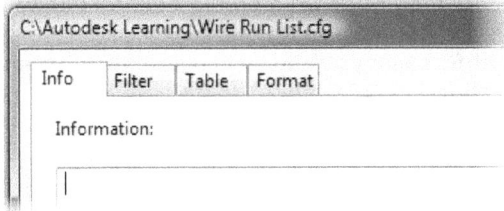

C:\Autodesk Learning\Wire Run List.cfg

| Info | Filter | Table | Format |

Information:

Configuration Editor: Info Tab

In the Info tab, you view and set the information to display as the file header. The file header often provides a brief description of the report. You can also include information such as the name of the project, the name of the model, or the date.

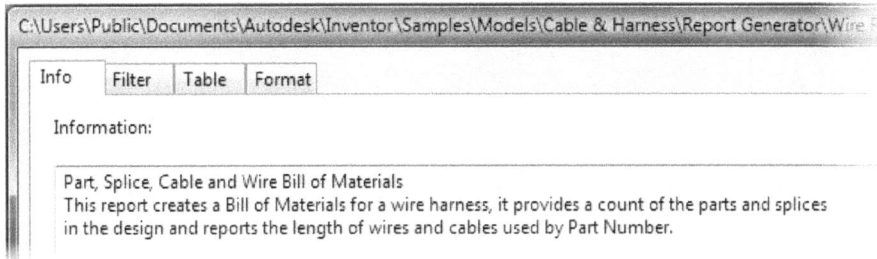

C:\Users\Public\Documents\Autodesk\Inventor\Samples\Models\Cable & Harness\Report Generator\Wire R

| Info | Filter | Table | Format |

Information:

Part, Splice, Cable and Wire Bill of Materials
This report creates a Bill of Materials for a wire harness, it provides a count of the parts and splices
in the design and reports the length of wires and cables used by Part Number.

Configuration Editor: Filter Tab

You specify the harness objects you want to include in the report by selecting the check box for that object in the Select Objects to Report area. You might select one, some, or all objects. The objects you select here determine what is included in the report, as well as the values that are available in the Table tab, Link Type row.

If you include cables in your report, you can also include spare (unterminated) cable wires by selecting the Include Spare Cable Wires check box in the Cable Wires area. By default, spare cable wires are not included.

In the Object Filters area, the Property Names, Property Values, and Exclusion Property work together to indicate items to include or exclude from the report. All are dependent on the properties you set on the harness object when it is created or edited.

- To include all property names or values, select All.
- To restrict reports to objects with a specific property name, clear the All selection and specify the property name or value.
- To omit an object with a specific property name and value, enter the property name to exclude from the report. You can also enter a value, but you must enter a property name first. This setting is most often used when All is selected.

Valid exclusion properties include any property defined for a harness object in the active harness. The exclusion Value is optional. If you choose to enter a Value, you must first enter the Name.

The Quantity by Property Name field enables you to set a property value to group like objects for quantity calculations. The calculation provides a total length or part count total. Valid properties include any property name used in the Table tab. This setting is also dependent on certain settings in the Table tab. For example, to get a total length for a wire, you must set the Quantity by Property Name to Part Number in the Filter tab. In the Table tab, include a Length or Adjusted Length column and add a Quantity column.

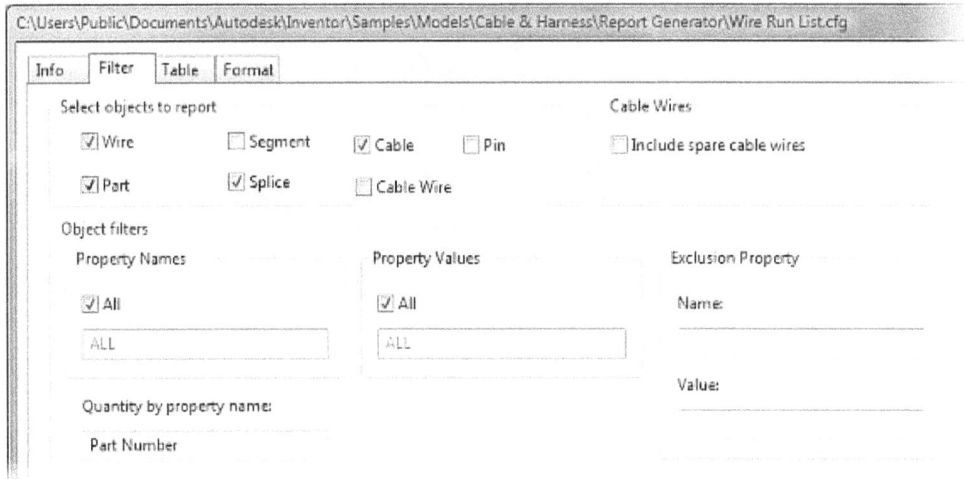

C:\Users\Public\Documents\Autodesk\Inventor\Samples\Models\Cable & Harness\Report Generator\Wire Run List.cfg

| Info | Filter | Table | Format |

Select objects to report   Cable Wires

☑ Wire   ☐ Segment   ☑ Cable   ☐ Pin   ☐ Include spare cable wires

☑ Part   ☑ Splice   ☐ Cable Wire

Object filters

Property Names   Property Values   Exclusion Property

☑ All   ☑ All   Name:

ALL   ALL

Value:

Quantity by property name:

Part Number

Configuration Editor: Table Tab

In the Table tab, you specify which properties to include in the report. Each column in the table represents one column in the report.

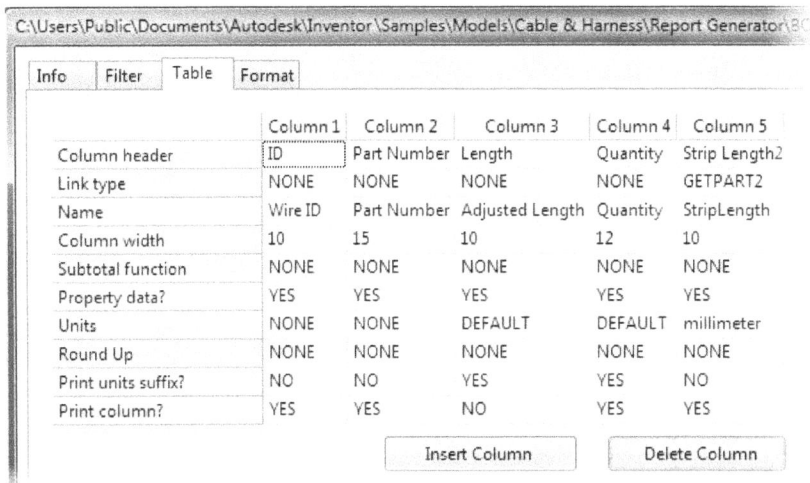

C:\Users\Public\Documents\Autodesk\Inventor \Samples\Models\Cable & Harness\Report Generator\BC

| Info | Filter | Table | Format |

	Column 1	Column 2	Column 3	Column 4	Column 5
Column header	ID	Part Number	Length	Quantity	Strip Length2
Link type	NONE	NONE	NONE	NONE	GETPART2
Name	Wire ID	Part Number	Adjusted Length	Quantity	StripLength
Column width	10	15	10	12	10
Subtotal function	NONE	NONE	NONE	NONE	NONE
Property data?	YES	YES	YES	YES	YES
Units	NONE	NONE	DEFAULT	DEFAULT	millimeter
Round Up	NONE	NONE	NONE	NONE	NONE
Print units suffix?	NO	NO	YES	YES	NO
Print column?	YES	YES	NO	YES	YES

Insert Column   Delete Column

The following table describes the rows in the Table tab.

Row	Description
Column Header	Sets the text for column headings. Enter any string.
Link Type	Link types obtain information about an object type other than the object type on which you are running the report. For example, if you are running a report on wires (as selected in the Filter tab) and you need to find the name of the pin to which the wire is attached, you select GetPin1 in the Link Type row. The choices listed depend on the objects that you selected in the Filter tab.
Name	Specifies the name of the property on which you report in the column. Name is typically set to a predefined property such as Color Style, Gauge, or Adjusted Length, but it can also be a user-defined custom property, such as Vendor or Strip Length, or a keyword, such as Quantity. Keywords enable functions in the Report Generator.
Column Width	Sets the width of the column in the report output.
Subtotal Function	Indicates whether to sum or count all the values in the column. The result is placed below the last row of the column.
Property Data?	Determines whether the data displayed in this column is a harness property. A NO value means that the property is a constant or special keyword.
Units	Selects the units to use for the column. DEFAULT uses the units set in the harness assembly.
Round Up	Selects the rounding value used for wire and segment lengths. Values depend on the Units setting.
Print Units Suffix?	Indicates whether to print a unit suffix after each value in the column. For example, if units are inches, then "in" is printed in the report.
Print Column?	Determines whether to print this column in the report.

Configuration Editor: Format Tab

In the Format tab, you set the options that define the report output. The formatting options include:

- Setting whether a single report file is generated or if multiple files should be generated.
- Setting how the data should be sorted.
- Specifying if and what type of placeholder should be included for blank or repeated values.
- Selecting what additional information should be written to the report.

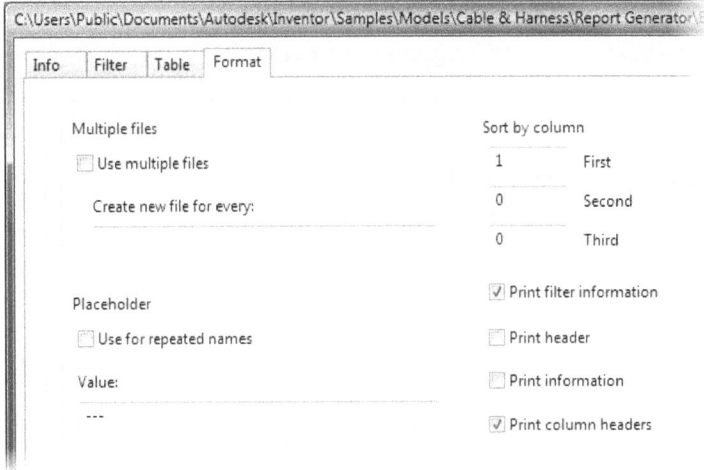

You can use a single report configuration file to generate multiple report files using the options in the Multiple Files area. By selecting the option Use Multiple Files and entering a property name, a report file is generated every time the value for that property name is unique. For example, if you use the connector.cfg sample file and enter the property RefDes, a report file is generated for each electrical connector that has a unique reference designator value.

The use of placeholders help to keep columns in the report aligned and uncluttered. The text or character string you specify to use as a placeholder is always used for blank values. You can select to use the placeholder when same value is used consecutively in a single column of a multiple line report.

> When you create reports that are to be placed as tables on a drawing sheet with the nailboard drawing, disable the options Print Filter Information, Print Header, and Print Information as they affect the parsing of the data when the table is created.

Process: Editing a Report Configuration File

The following steps give an overview of creating a new report configuration file by editing an existing report configuration file.

1. With a harness assembly or nailboard drawing view active, in the panel bar, click Report.

2. In the Report Generator, click Edit a Configuration (.cfg) File.

3. In the Open dialog box, navigate to and select an existing report configuration file.

4. In the configuration editor, modify the settings and options on each tab to match your requirements for the report.

5. Click OK and then in the Save As dialog box, enter a new unique file name.

Link Types and Name Values

When you are editing a report configuration file, in the Table tab of the configuration editor, there are some unique values and options that you can set for the rows Link Type and Name. To set these values so that they return the information you require to understand the options and capabilities.

Info	Filter	Table	Format			
		Column 1	Column 2	Column 3	Column 4	Column 5
Column header		Part Number	Length	Vendor	Vendor Part Number	Quanity
Link type		NONE	NONE	NONE	NONE	NONE
Name		Part Number	Adjusted Length	Vendor	Vendor Part Number	Quanity
Column width		20	10	15	20	12
Subtotal function		NONE	NONE	NONE	NONE	NONE
Property data?		YES	YES	YES	YES	YES

Link Types

After harness objects such as parts, wires, cables, and segments are placed into a harness assembly, they have a relationship to one another. For example, a harness segment contains a wire, the wire is connected to a pin, the pin is on a part, and so on. To traverse through the hierarchy of these relationships, you use link types. These relationships can be traversed through the hierarchy of the harness objects to view the connectivity, as well as the object definition and occurrence level properties placed on the objects.

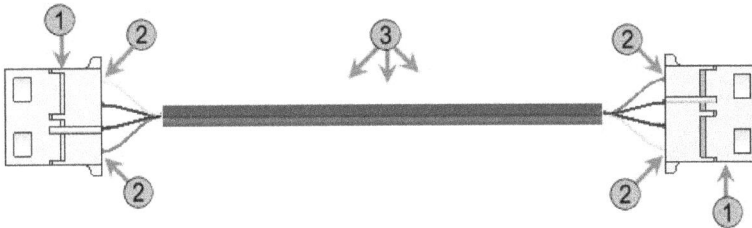

1. Part

2. Pins

3. Wire, cable, wire cable, or segment

A good example of the need for link types is for a wire run list where the main items in your report are wires and cables, but you also need the information on the related parts and pins. Link types such as GETPIN1, GETPIN2, GETPART1, GETPART2 enable you to get information on harness objects on both ends of the wire.

When you are configuring a report configuration file, the types of listed links depend on the objects that you select in the Filter tab. If a single harness object is selected in the Filter tab, then all link types available for that object display in the Link Type list. Link types are not supported when more than one object is being filtered unless you have selected a pair of objects that shares the same link types, such as those wires and cable wires or parts and splices. If you have multiple objects selected with different link types, then the only Link Type option is None.

The following figures show the relationship of link type options based on the objects to report.

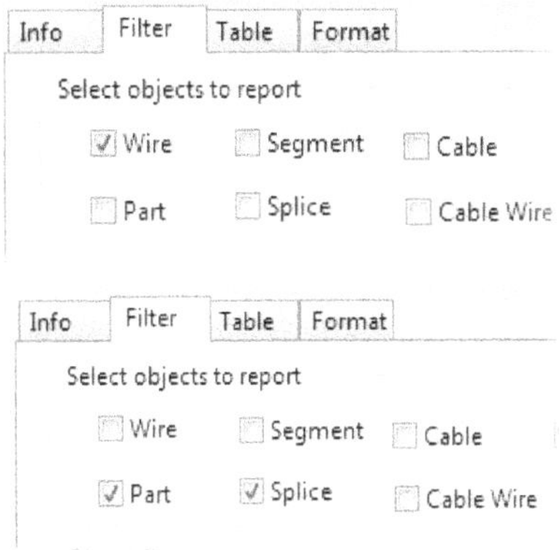

Selected objects to report

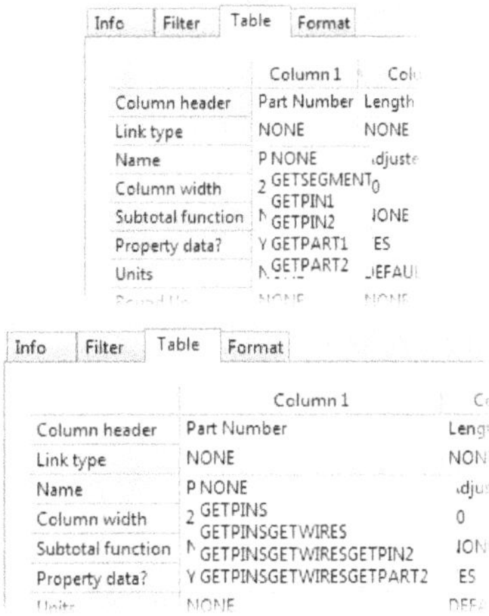

Link type options

Name Values

The Name row provides the most flexibility for the values you can enter. In this row, you can enter:

- Predefined keywords
- Constants
- Object property names

Predefined keywords are words or operations that initiate a function in the Report Generator. A constant is a static value that you enter and can be a text string or numeric value. Object property names are unique names for the properties that store information about that object. Part Number, Length, and Wire ID are some examples of the many possible properties. The object properties are values that are internal to the object and are automatically set to custom user-defined properties.

The following are special keywords that initiate a function in the Report Generator.

Keyword	Description
Quantity	Calculates the total quantity. For parts, it calculates the total count. For wires, cables, and segments, it calculates the total length based on the Length or Adjusted Length properties. To calculate the total length, include a column with the property Length or Adjusted Length.
Count Rows	Adds an incremental row number to each row of data in the report.

The following are mathematical operations that initiate a function in the Report Generator.

Operation	Description
ColumnNumber* ColumnNumber	Enter the numbers of the columns to multiply the values of those specified column numbers. For example, to multiply column 4 and column 5, you enter in the Name field 4*5.
ColumnNumber+ ColumnNumber	Enter the numbers of the columns to add the values of those specified column numbers. For example, to add column 4 and column 5, you enter in the Name field 4+5.

Defining an Import/Export Configuration File

Library configuration files are crucial for successful export and import of cable and harness library objects. For you to be successful in importing or exporting the library objects, you need to know how to create and define a library configuration file.

Import and Export Configuration Files

The library configuration (CFG) file describes the format of the CSV data file. This includes the input parameters, their associated data types, and the corresponding units. The configuration file is a space- or tab-delimited text file that describes the input parameter, and the associated data types and corresponding units. The configuration file consists of five rows of information with some rows having multiple delimited values. The data that is entered per line varies depending on the type of library object you are exporting or importing.

The configuration file must be configured in the following order and with the following information:

Row	Information	Description
1	Library Object	Type of object contained in the input file. For wire occurrences, the object is libwires. Object types are not case-sensitive. For cable occurrences, the object is libcables.
2	Log File Name and Location	The output log file path and name; for example, C:\WireListImport\wirelist_log.txt. If no path is listed, the log file is created in the same directory as the CSV file.
3	Property Names	The order, data type, and units of the input parameters. For wires, there must be a Wire ID, Wire Name, REFDES1, Pin1, REFDES2, and Pin2. For cables, there must be a Cable Name, Outer Diameter (if blank, then Calculate from Wires is used), Wire Name, and Conductor ID. The parameters can be in any order, as long as the minimum required subset is present. List additional wire properties after the minimum required properties.

Row	Information	Description
4	Data Types for the Properties	The data type associated with the property name in the same column.
5	Units of Measure for the Properties	The unit of measure associated with the data type in the same column.

You can open and edit library configuration files in the Report Generator or in another application like Notepad or Microsoft Excel.

The following example shows a comparison of the configuration file format for wire library objects and for cable library objects.

Library Configuration File for Wires:

libwires

C:\WireListImport\WireList_Log.TXT

Wire ID,Wire Name,RefDes1,Pin1,RefDes2,Pin2,Class,Strip Length

text,text,text,text,text,text,text,length

none,none,none,none,none,none,none,inch

Library Configuration File for Cables:

libcables

C:\CableListImport\CableList_Log.TXT

Cable Name,Category,Part Number,Outer Diameter,Conductor ID,Wire Name

text,text,length,text,text,text

none,none,inch,none,none,none

The text in row 1 specifically identifies the type of library object that is going to be imported or exported. The following list identifies the text you enter for the different types of objects.

Library Object	Row 1 Text
Wires	libwires
Cables	libcables
Splices	libsplices
Seals	libseals
Terminals	libterminals
Plugs	libplugs
Label	liblabel
Looms	liblooms
Virtual Parts	libvirtualpart
Ribbon Cables	libribboncables

Access additional information in the Autodesk® Inventor® Help system on library configuration file format and sample files for each object type. To access the information, in the Autodesk Inventor Help, select Inventor Help Topics>Cable and Harness Help>Harness assemblies>Importing and exporting cable and harness library data>Cable and Harness Library import configuration file format.

Process: Defining an Import/Export Configuration File

The following steps give an overview of creating and defining a new library configuration file for importing or exporting library data.

1. Create a new file in a text editor like Report Generator or Notepad.

2. On line 1, enter the text associated to that library object.

3. On line 2, enter the path and name of the log file for recording the success and use of this library configuration file.

4. On line 3, enter the names of the input parameters. Add the delimiter between each parameter.

5. On line 4, specify the data type for each parameter listed on line 3. Add the delimiter between each data type value.

6. On line 5, enter the unit of measure for each data type listed on line 4. Add the delimiter between each unit of measure value.

7. Save the file with a CFG file extension.

Exercise: Modify a Report Configuration File

In this exercise, you will create a new report configuration file by editing an existing report configuration file.

Object Type:"CONDUCTOR,WIRE "
Object Filter:ALL:ALL

ID	,Part Number	,Quantity	,Strip Length2
1001	,3048-ORG	, 386.881 mm,6.000	
1002	,3048-WHT	, 385.750 mm,6.000	
1003	,3048-RED	, 385.241 mm,6.000	
1004	,3048-YEL	, 727.225 mm,6.000	
1005	,3047-BLK	, 384.371 mm,6.000	
1006	,3047-GRN	, 385.750 mm,6.000	
1007	,3047-BLU	, 386.881 mm,6.000	
Wire1	,---	, 200.148 mm,4.000	

The completed exercise

1.   Open *Cable-Harness Design.iam*.

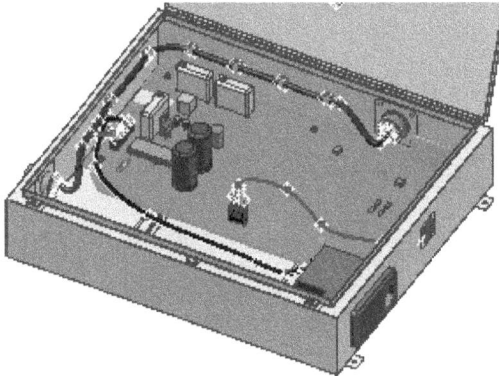

2.   In the Browser, double-click on Connector Harness to activate it for in-place editing.

3.   Click Report.

4.   To begin running a report to view the current results using a sample report configuration file, in the Report Generator, click Create Report.

5.   In the Create Reports dialog box, click Add File to List.

---

6. In the Open dialog box:

   - Select *Part_Splice_Wire_Cable_BOM.cfg*.
   - Click Open.

7. In the Create Reports dialog box, click OK. Review the data and columns of data that were added to the report.

```
Connector Harness_Part_Splice_Wire_Cable_BOM_1
Part Number    ,Vendor    ,Vendor Part Number    ,Quantity
---            ,---       ,---                    ,  200.149 mm
3047-BLK       ,Alpha     ,---                    ,  384.371 mm
3047-BLU       ,Alpha     ,---                    ,  386.881 mm
3047-GRN       ,Alpha     ,---                    ,  385.751 mm
3048-ORG       ,Alpha     ,---                    ,  386.881 mm
3048-RED       ,Alpha     ,---                    ,  385.242 mm
3048-WHT       ,Alpha     ,---                    ,  385.751 mm
3048-YEL       ,Alpha     ,---                    ,  727.226 mm
3605752        ,---       ,---                    ,        1
AOTC-3605752   ,AMP       ,---                    ,        1
LTP            ,Molex     ,---                    ,        1
```

8. To begin creating a revised report configuration file, in the Report Generator, click Edit a Configuration File.

9. In the Open dialog box, open *Part_Splice_Wire_Cable_BOM.cfg*.

10. In the Info tab, edit the text so it states: Cable Wire and Wire Bill of Materials. This report creates a Bill of Materials for a wire harness, it reports the length of wires and cable wires used by Part Number.

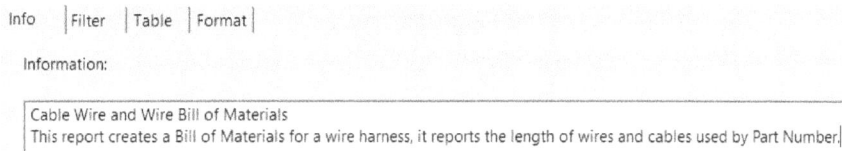

```
Info    │Filter │ Table │ Format │

Information:
_____

Cable Wire and Wire Bill of Materials
This report creates a Bill of Materials for a wire harness, it reports the length of wires and cables used by Part Number.
```

11. In the Filter tab, in the Select objects to report area, select and clear the check boxes so that only the Wire and Cable Wire check boxes are selected.

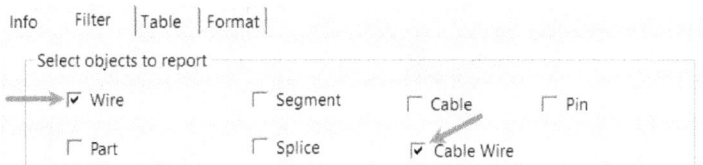

```
Info    Filter   │ Table │ Format │

 Select objects to report
   ☑ Wire          ☐ Segment      ☐ Cable        ☐ Pin

   ☐ Part          ☐ Splice       ☑ Cable Wire
```

12. To remove two columns of data, in the Table tab:

   - In the Table tab, click Delete Column.
   - In the Delete Column dialog box, enter **3**.
   - Click OK.

13. Repeat the previous step to delete column 3 again. The remaining table of columns displays as shown in the following figure.

	Column 1	Column 2	Column 3
Column header	Part Number	Length	Quantity
Link type	NONE	NONE	NONE
Name	Part Number	Adjusted Le	Quantity
Column width	20	10	12
Subtotal functio	NONE	NONE	NONE
Property data?	YES	YES	YES
Units	NONE	DEFAULT	DEFAULT
Round Up	NONE	NONE	NONE
Print units suffix	NO	YES	YES
Print column?	YES	NO	YES

14. To add a new Column 1:

- In the Table tab, click Insert Column.
- In the Insert Column dialog box, click OK.

	Column 1	Column 2	Colum
Column header	NONE	Part Number	Length
Link type	NONE	NONE	NONE
Name	NONE	Part Number	Adjusted L
Column width	10	20	10
Subtotal functio	NONE	NONE	NONE

15. To configure the settings for Column 1:

- In the Column Header field, enter **ID**.
- In the Name field, enter **Wire ID**.

	Column 1	Column 2	Colum
Column header	ID ⟵	Part Number	Length
Link type	NONE	NONE	NONE
Name ⟶	Wire ID	Part Number	Adjusted L
Column width	10	20	10
Subtotal functio	NONE	NONE	NONE
Property data?	YES	YES	YES
Units	NONE	NONE	DEFAULT
Round Up	NONE	NONE	NONE

16. To add a new column to the right of the last column:
    - In the Table tab, click Insert Column.
    - In the Insert Column dialog box, enter **5**.
    - Click OK.

mn 1	Column 2	Column 3	Column 4	Column 5
	Part Numb	Length	Quantity	NONE
E	NONE	NONE	NONE	NONE
ID	Part Numb	Adjusted Le	Quantity	NONE
	20	10	12	10
E	NONE	NONE	NONE	NONE
	YES	YES	YES	YES
E	NONE	DEFAULT	DEFAULT	DEFAULT
E	NONE	NONE	NONE	NONE
	NO	YES	YES	NO
	YES	NO	YES	YES

17. To configure the settings for Column 5:
    - In the Column Header field, enter **Strip Length2**.
    - In the Link Type drop-down list, select GETPART2.
    - In the Name field, enter **StripLength**.
    - In the Units drop-down list, select millimeter.
    - Note- If you are unable to modify values, continue the exercise until the configuration file is saved and then edit it to make the changes.

olumn 3	Column 4	Column 5	
ngth	Quantity	Strip Length2	⬅
NE	NONE	GETPART2	⬅
justed Le	Quantity	StripLength	⬅
	12	10	
NE	NONE	NONE	
S	YES	YES	
AULT	DEFAULT	millimeter	⬅
NE	NONE	NONE	
S	YES	NO	
	YES	YES	

18. In the Column Width field for Column 2, enter **15**.

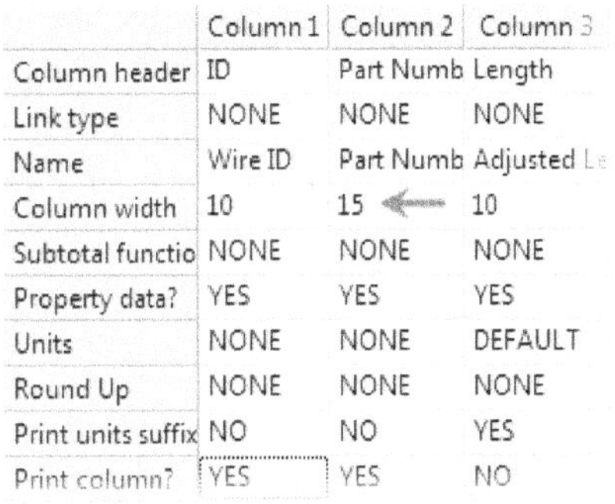

	Column 1	Column 2	Column 3
Column header	ID	Part Numb	Length
Link type	NONE	NONE	NONE
Name	Wire ID	Part Numb	Adjusted Le
Column width	10	15 ◄───	10
Subtotal functio	NONE	NONE	NONE
Property data?	YES	YES	YES
Units	NONE	NONE	DEFAULT
Round Up	NONE	NONE	NONE
Print units suffix	NO	NO	YES
Print column?	YES	YES	NO

19. In the Format tab, select the Print filter information check box to add information to the top of the report.

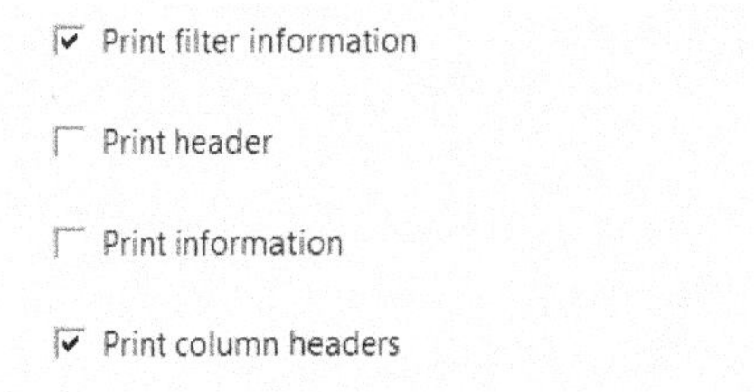

☑ Print filter information

☐ Print header

☐ Print information

☑ Print column headers

20. To save these changes as a new report configuration file:
- In the configuration editor dialog box, click OK.
- In the Save As dialog box, enter **BOM for Wires-Cable Wires.cfg**.
- Click Save.

21. Follow the earlier steps for creating a report to create a report using the report configuration file *BOM for Wires-Cable Wires.cfg*. The report displays as shown in the following figure.

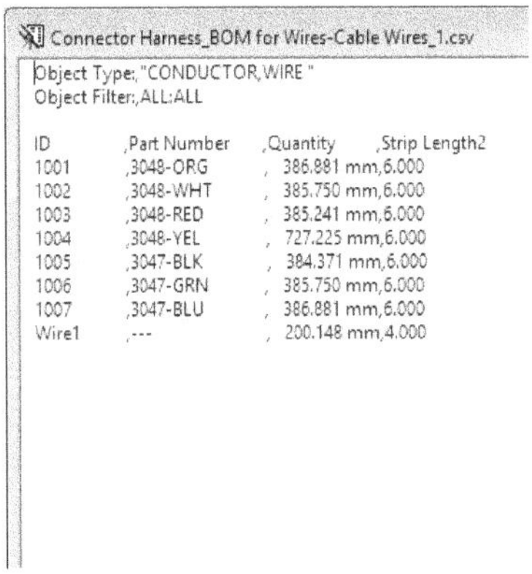

```
Connector Harness_BOM for Wires-Cable Wires_1.csv
Object Type:,"CONDUCTOR,WIRE "
Object Filter:,ALL:ALL

ID        ,Part Number   ,Quantity      ,Strip Length2
1001      ,3048-ORG      ,  386.881 mm,6.000
1002      ,3048-WHT      ,  385.750 mm,6.000
1003      ,3048-RED      ,  385.241 mm,6.000
1004      ,3048-YEL      ,  727.225 mm,6.000
1005      ,3047-BLK      ,  384.371 mm,6.000
1006      ,3047-GRN      ,  385.750 mm,6.000
1007      ,3047-BLU      ,  386.881 mm,6.000
Wire1     ,---           ,  200.148 mm,4.000
```

22. In the Report Generator, click File menu>Exit.

23. Close all files without saving changes.

Exercise: Create a Library Configuration File

In this exercise, you will create a new library configuration file and then use it to export and import library objects.

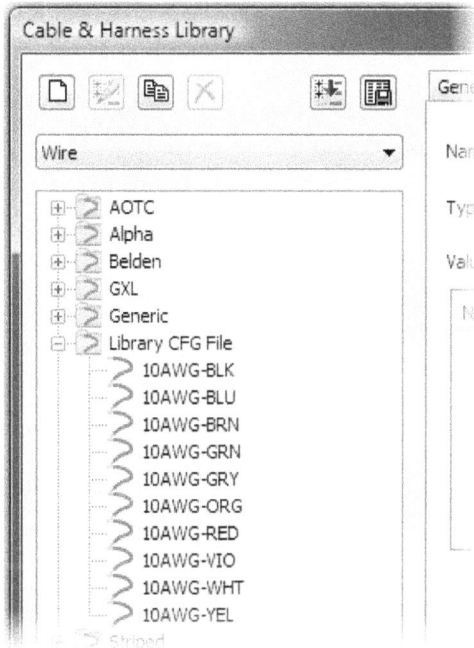

The completed exercise

Create a Library Configuration File and Export Library Objects

In this section of the exercise, you will create a new library configuration file and use it to export the wire objects from the cable and harness library.

1. Open *Cable-Harness Design.iam*.

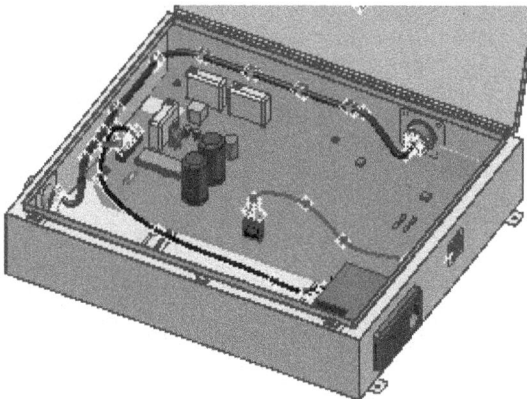

2. In the Browser, double-click on Connector Harness to activate it for in-place editing.

3. Click Report.

4. To begin creating a new library configuration file, in the Report Generator, click File menu> New.

5. In the new document, enter the text shown in the following figure:

libwires

C:\Autodesk Inventor 2021 Cable and Harness Design Exercise Files\Workspace\libwires.log

Wire Name,Color Style,Outer Diameter,Category,Gauge

text,text,length,text,text

none,none,inch,none,none

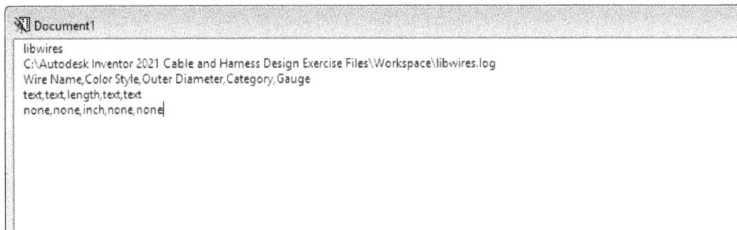

6. In the Report Generator:
   - Click Save.
   - In the Save As dialog box, navigate to the Workspace folder where the exercise files are installed.
   - Enter **Wire Library.cfg**.
   - Click Save.

7. Close the Report Generator.

8. In the Manage panel, click Library.

9. To begin exporting library objects:
   - Ensure that Wire is selected in the library type list.
   - Click Export Library Objects.

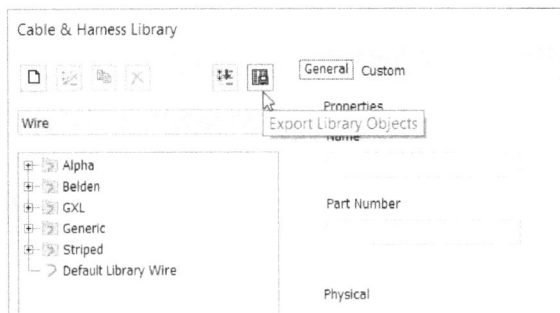

10. In the Export Library Wires dialog box:
    - For Data File, enter a file name of Default Wires.csv to be saved in the Workspace folder.
    - Under Configuration File, click Browse and select *Wire Library.cfg*.
    - Click Open.
    - In the Export Library Wires dialog box, click OK.

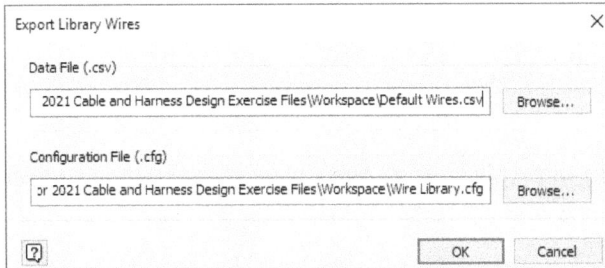

```
Export Library Wires                                    ✕

Data File (.csv)

2021 Cable and Harness Design Exercise Files\Workspace\Default Wires.csv    Browse...

Configuration File (.cfg)

or 2021 Cable and Harness Design Exercise Files\Workspace\Wire Library.cfg   Browse...

[?]                                       OK          Cancel
```

11. In the Export Library Wires message box, click Close.

    Note: There should be 0 errors and warnings.

12. In the Cable & Harness Library dialog box, click Close.

Import Library Content Using the Library Configuration File

In this section of the exercise, you will modify the exported library data file and then import that modified data back into the cable and harness library using the previously created library configuration file.

1. Click Report.

2. In the Report Generator, open *Default Wires.csv*.

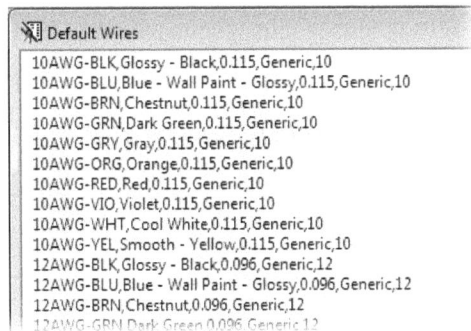

```
Default Wires
10AWG-BLK,Glossy - Black,0.115,Generic,10
10AWG-BLU,Blue - Wall Paint - Glossy,0.115,Generic,10
10AWG-BRN,Chestnut,0.115,Generic,10
10AWG-GRN,Dark Green,0.115,Generic,10
10AWG-GRY,Gray,0.115,Generic,10
10AWG-ORG,Orange,0.115,Generic,10
10AWG-RED,Red,0.115,Generic,10
10AWG-VIO,Violet,0.115,Generic,10
10AWG-WHT,Cool White,0.115,Generic,10
10AWG-YEL,Smooth - Yellow,0.115,Generic,10
12AWG-BLK,Glossy - Black,0.096,Generic,12
12AWG-BLU,Blue - Wall Paint - Glossy,0.096,Generic,12
12AWG-BRN,Chestnut,0.096,Generic,12
12AWG-GRN,Dark Green,0.096,Generic,12
```

3. Select and delete all lines of text below the line that starts with 10AWG-YEL.

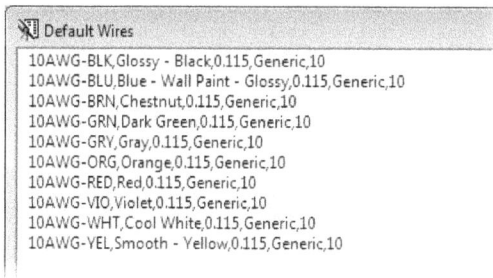

```
Default Wires
10AWG-BLK,Glossy - Black,0.115,Generic,10
10AWG-BLU,Blue - Wall Paint - Glossy,0.115,Generic,10
10AWG-BRN,Chestnut,0.115,Generic,10
10AWG-GRN,Dark Green,0.115,Generic,10
10AWG-GRY,Gray,0.115,Generic,10
10AWG-ORG,Orange,0.115,Generic,10
10AWG-RED,Red,0.115,Generic,10
10AWG-VIO,Violet,0.115,Generic,10
10AWG-WHT,Cool White,0.115,Generic,10
10AWG-YEL,Smooth - Yellow,0.115,Generic,10
```

4. To begin assigning the wires to have a new category property, in Report Generator, click Edit menu> Replace.

5. In the Replace dialog box:

   - For Find What, enter **Generic**.
   - For Replace With, enter **Library CFG File**.
   - Click Replace All.
   - Close the Replace dialog box. The file displays as shown in the following figure.

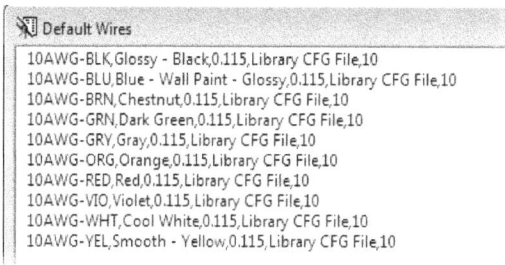

```
Default Wires
10AWG-BLK,Glossy - Black,0.115,Library CFG File,10
10AWG-BLU,Blue - Wall Paint - Glossy,0.115,Library CFG File,10
10AWG-BRN,Chestnut,0.115,Library CFG File,10
10AWG-GRN,Dark Green,0.115,Library CFG File,10
10AWG-GRY,Gray,0.115,Library CFG File,10
10AWG-ORG,Orange,0.115,Library CFG File,10
10AWG-RED,Red,0.115,Library CFG File,10
10AWG-VIO,Violet,0.115,Library CFG File,10
10AWG-WHT,Cool White,0.115,Library CFG File,10
10AWG-YEL,Smooth - Yellow,0.115,Library CFG File,10
```

6. Click File menu>Save As.

7. In the Save As dialog box, enter **Common Wires.csv**. Click Save.

8. Close the Report Generator.

9. Click Library.

10. In the Cable & Harness dialog box, click Import Library Objects.

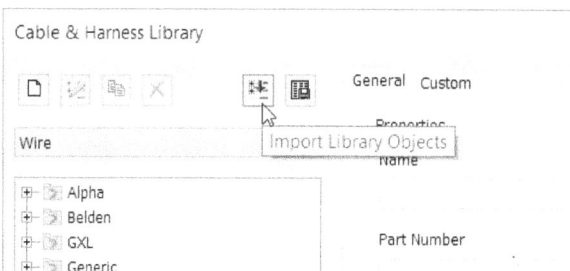

11. To import the modified list of wires using the previously created library configuration file, in the Import Library Wires dialog box:

- For Data File, click Browse and select *Common Wires.csv*.
- For Configuration File, click Browse and select *Wire Library.cfg*.
- Click OK.

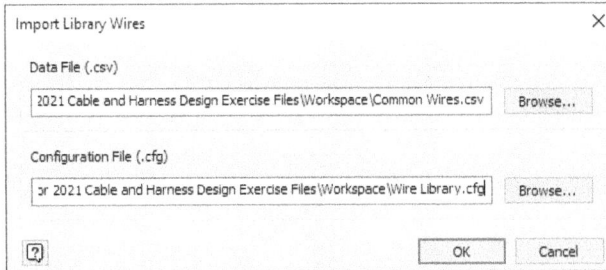

12. In the Import Library Wires message box, click Close.

Note: There should be 0 errors and warnings.

13. Review the new category and list of wires.

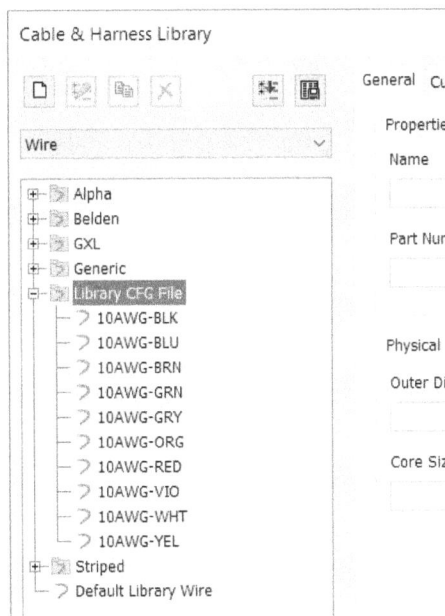

14. In the Cable & Harness Library dialog box, click Close.

15. Close all files without saving changes.

Chapter Summary

In this chapter, you learned how to add and edit library definitions and manage the cable and harness library file. You also learned how to create and edit the configuration files used for generating reports and for importing and exporting wire library data.

Having completed this chapter, you can:

- Add and edit library definitions and manage the cable and harness library file.
- Create and edit the configuration files used for generating reports and the import and export of library data.

Autodesk

Create, Author, and Publish Electrical Content

In this chapter, you learn how to create, author, and publish electrical parts and connectors to a custom Content Center library so that they can be easily and quickly reused by you or other members of your design team.

Objectives

After completing this chapter, you will be able to:

- Create, author, and publish electrical parts and connectors to a custom Content Center library.
- Manage the libraries that are included in the Content Center, as well as your own libraries of cable and harness components.
- Author and publish your own cable and harness content.
- Manage the properties and settings of published cable and harness content.

Lesson: Defining Electrical Parts and Connectors

This lesson describes the attributes of electrical parts, how to add pins to electrical parts, and how to modify pin and part properties.

Electrical parts are connectors to which you can attach wires. These parts are standard Autodesk® Inventor® parts that have special cable and harness work points, called pins, added to represent wire connection points. After defining them, you can author the parts and then publish them as electrical content to the Content Center for reuse.

The following figure shows a completed electrical component.

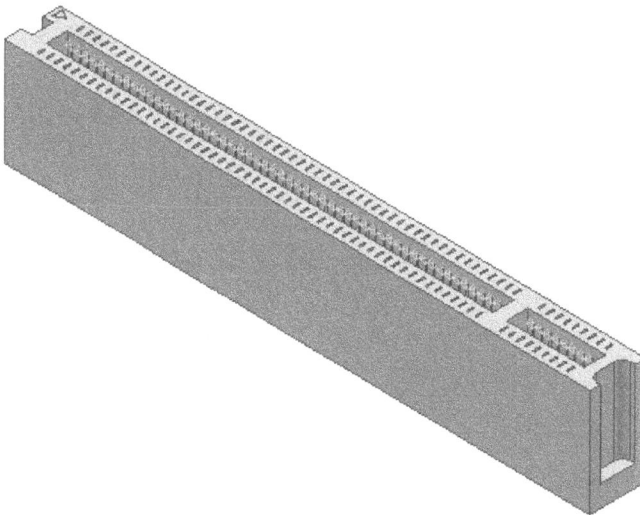

Objectives

After completing this lesson, you will be able to:

- Describe the characteristics of electrical parts.
- Explain the process for creating an electrical part.
- Add a pin to an electrical part and configure the pin properties.
- Add and edit a rectangular array of pins on an electrical part.

About Electrical Parts

Electrical parts are standard Autodesk Inventor parts or iParts that have extended properties and one or more defined connection points, known as pins. Electrical parts include any parts to which you connect wires, such as connectors, terminal strips, PLC input/output terminal blocks, power supplies, switches, and indicator lamps.

In the following figure, electrical parts have been assembled on a computer motherboard in preparation for creating a harness assembly.

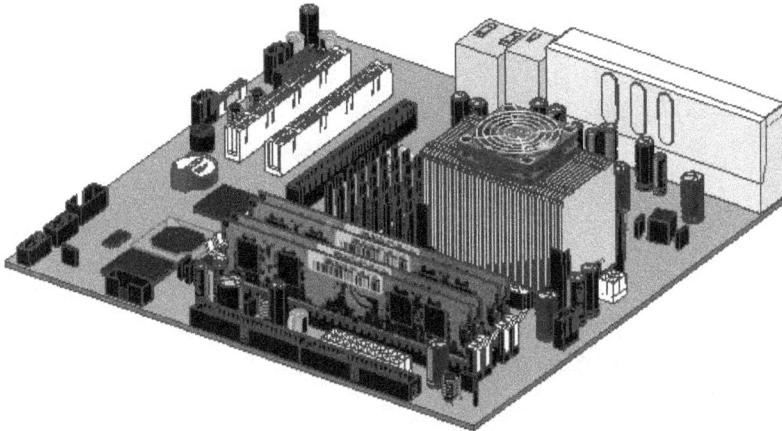

Electrical Parts Defined

Electrical parts are the only harness components that are not created in the context of a harness assembly. Instead, you create electrical parts by editing normal Autodesk Inventor parts. When you edit the parts, you add special work points, called pins, and supply required properties. You can also add custom properties. After you define the electrical part, you place it in an assembly.

The part can be fully modeled or be created as a simple representation, as long as geometry exists to designate the pins. For example, the part could be a simple plane with work points representing the pins. The pins are the attachment points for the wires in the harness assembly.

When published to the Content Center, electrical parts are referred to as connectors. In order to author a part as a connector, you must add one or more pins and harness properties to a part.

RefDes Defined

Specific properties must be added to a part to provide a complete electrical definition. The part name and part number are set automatically based on the part file name and the Autodesk Inventor part number. You can also set a placeholder for the reference designator (RefDes) property.

The reference designator, or RefDes, is a unique identifier that maps the part to the schematic design. You typically add a placeholder identifier, such as U?, in the part environment and then add a specific identifier for each occurrence of the part in the context of the assembly. For example, if you place three occurrences of a certain RS232 connector in an assembly, each occurrence must have a unique identifier, such as U1, U2, or U3.

Anatomy of an Electrical Part

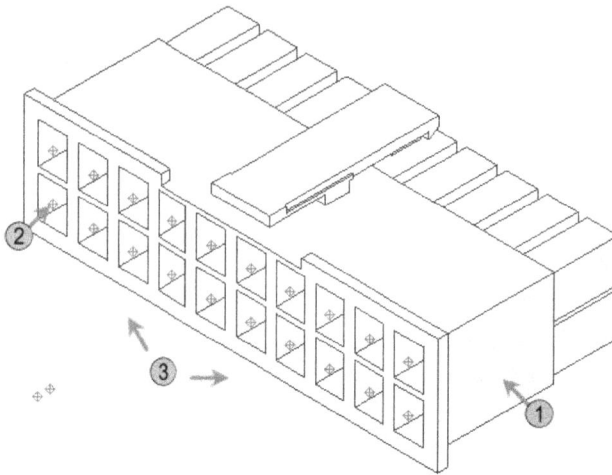

[1] Create a standard Autodesk Inventor part file representing the electrical component or use an existing part file.

[2] Add a pin definition to the part assigning a unique name.

[3] Add a group of pins in a rectangular pattern if required.

Example of Electrical Parts

In the following figure, a variety of electrical components are shown. Each component that you use can be modeled as a part file, authored, and published to the Content Center for use in your cable and harness designs.

Creating an Electrical Part

You create your electrical parts from existing part models or design them for a specific job. When the part is complete, you add connection locations and harness properties to the part in order to prepare it for use in a harness assembly.

Electrical Part Creation

The first requirement for creating an electrical part is to complete an Autodesk Inventor part file that represents the component you need. You have the option of creating this component with complete detail or using a simplified representation of the component.

After the part file is complete, you use the Harness Part Features panel to populate the part file with pins and harness properties. A minimum of one pin or pin group is required prior to authoring a connector.

Authoring the connector adds cable-and-harness-specific data to your part file so that you can include it in a harness assembly.

To optimize the use of your custom cable and harness parts, you publish the authored connector to a custom library in the Content Center.

The following figure demonstrates your options when creating electrical components. You can create an IDE male connector that exactly replicates the part (1), or a simple rectangular box that represents the bounding box of the part (2).

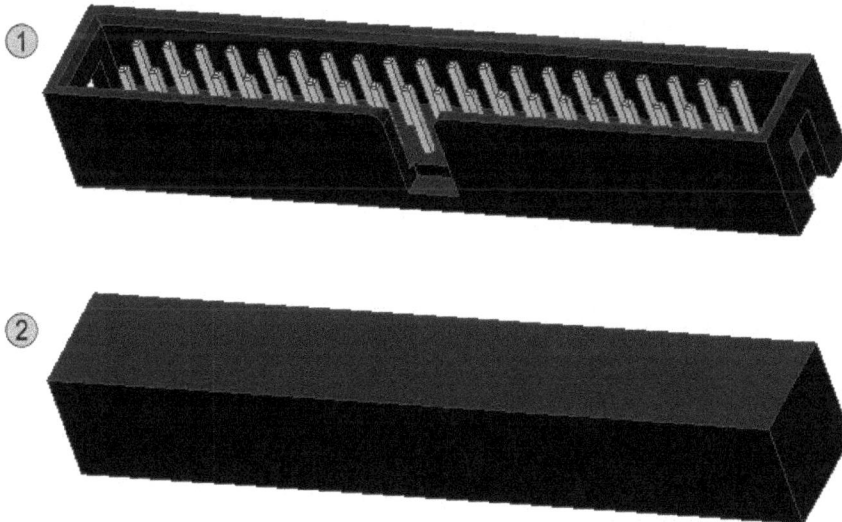

Process: Creating an Electrical Part

The following steps give an overview of creating and defining an electrical part.

1.   Create a new part file that represents your electrical component, or open an existing part file.

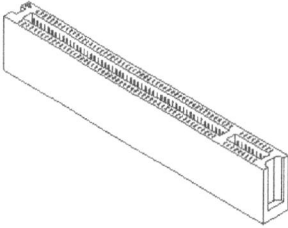

2.   Click Properties to display the Part Properties dialog box.

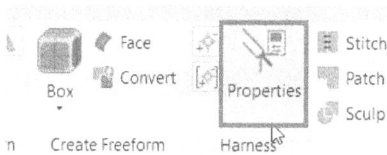

3.   Set the optional harness properties related to the part from both the General and Custom tabs.

4.   Add one or more pins or pin groups and set their properties.

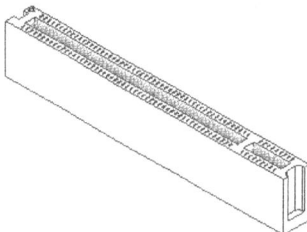

5. Author the connector.

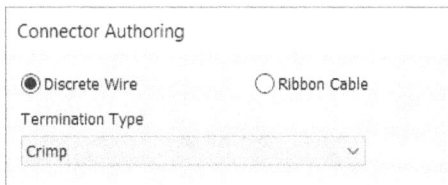

Adding a Pin to an Electrical Part

You use the tools in the Harness panel to add pins and harness properties to your part. A connector can have one or more pins that can be placed individually or as a group.

In the following figure, a part is shown before adding pins (left) and after adding pins (right).

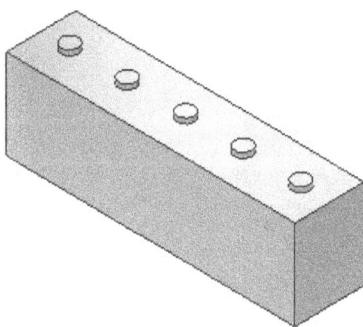

Part before pins are added   Part after pins are added

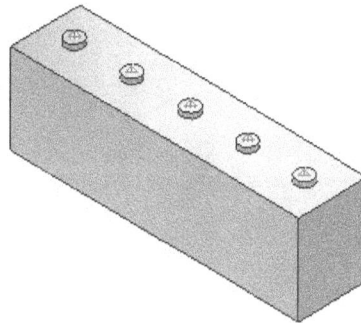

Placing a Pin

Valid geometry for pin selections includes both associative and nonassociative points. The points that you select determine whether the pins are updated when you modify the geometry to which they are associated.

To specify a nonassociative point, place an arbitrary point on any face of the part. Nonassociative points are not updated if the geometry changes.

Associative Point Geometry Selection Options

To specify an associative point that is updated as you modify the geometry, select one of the following:

- Existing work points.
- Center points on any circular component such as a face, a hole, or cylindrical cuts or arc edges.
- Existing sketch points.
- Model vertices.

Pin Properties

All cable and harness components contain properties. Some properties, such as pin number or part number, are required to uniquely identify a component and are applied automatically.

You can add custom properties to any component with additional information such as vendor, vendor part name, amperage rating, or temperature rating. You can extract custom properties when you create a report. You can place custom properties on either the part or the pins. You typically place properties such as vendor or electrical ratings on the part rather than on the pins.

Custom properties that are unique to a given pin can be placed at the pin level. When you place a pin, you specify a unique name for it. By default, the pin name is a sequential number starting with 1.

Pins in the Browser

In the following figure, on the left, the pins are shown in the browser. On the right, the part displays with the pins.

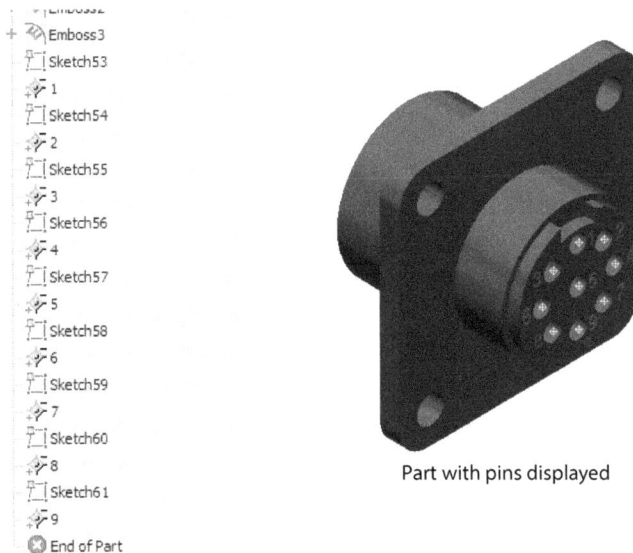

Part with pins displayed

Browser with pin definitions

Access

Ribbon: 3D Model tab>Harness panel

Keyboard Shortcut: P

Note: If the Harness panel is not available you will have to add it to the display.

Procedure: Adding a Pin to an Electrical Part

1. With a part file open, start the Place Pin tool.

2. Select an associative or nonassociative point for the pin location.

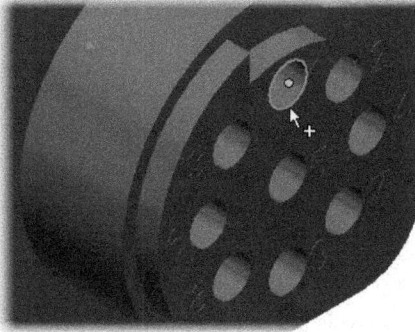

3. Enter the pin identifier in the Place Pin input box. Select the check box, or press ENTER to place the pin.

4. Continue adding individual pins or press ESC to cancel the Place Pin command.

Note that each pin identifier within the selected part is unique. The pin identifier that you specify is also the name of the work point listed in the Browser.

Adding a Group to an Electrical Part

You use the tools in the Harness panel to add a group of pins to your part. A connector can have one or more sets of pins that are placed as a group.

In the following figure, on the left, you can use Place Pin Group to create all 20 pins at the same time, matching the rectangular configuration of the part. On the right, each pin must be placed individually because the Place Pin Group tool does not function in a circular pattern, only in a rectangular pattern.

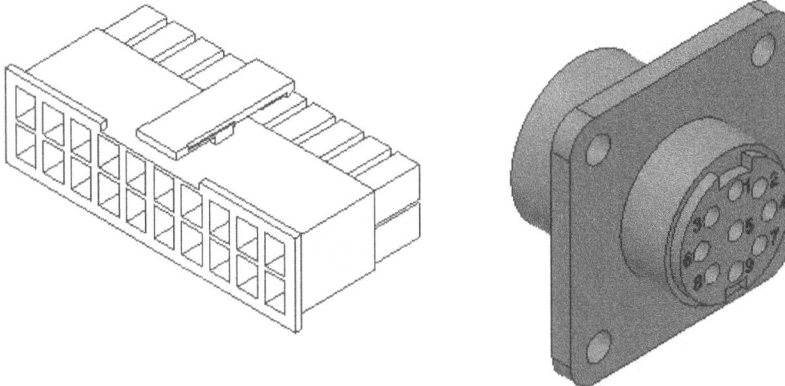

Place Pin Group Description

A pin group is a series of pins placed at the same time in a rectangular pattern. The pins created are not associative to the part geometry that they match.

Placing a pin group is ideal for ribbon cable connections and other connectors that are available in specific sizes, and with the pins located in a rectangular pattern.

Access

Ribbon: 3D Model tab>Harness panel

Place Pin Group Dialog Box

The following options are available in the Place Pin Group dialog box.

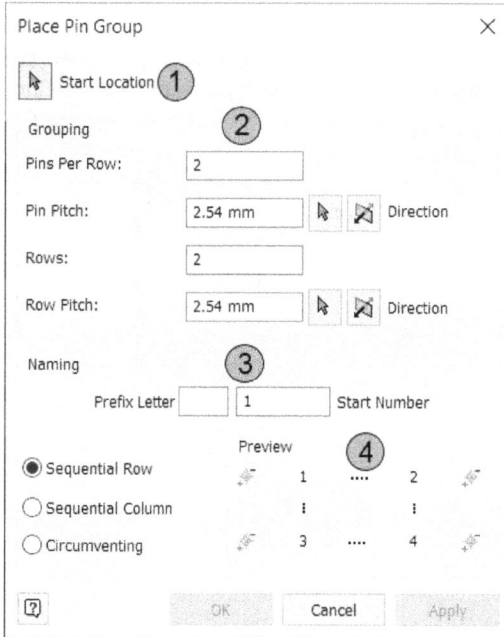

①   Start Location - Select the location for the first pin of the group.

②   Grouping area

- Pins Per Row - Designate the number of pins in each row of the group.
- Pin Pitch - Set the distance between pins in a row. You can include formulas as required. Use direction to select a linear edge that determines the direction of the pattern from the start location. Use the Flip button to reverse the direction.
- Rows - Designate the number of rows for the pin group.
- Row Pitch - Set the distance between rows in the group. When there is only one row, this area is not usable.

③   Naming area

- Prefix Letter - This optional selection sets a single letter as the prefix for the pin name.
- Start Number - Designates the first number to use for the pins in the group.
- Sequential Row - When selected, increases pin number by row.
- Sequential Column - When selected, increases pin number by column.
- Circumventing - This option is available only for two rows. The first row sequences from left to right and the second row from right to left.

④   Preview - Displays a preview of the pin arrangement and names based on your settings.

Procedure: Adding a Group of Pins to an Electrical Part

Follow these steps to add a group of pins to an electrical part.

1. With a part file open, start the Place Pin Group tool.

2. Select an associative or nonassociative point for the start pin location.

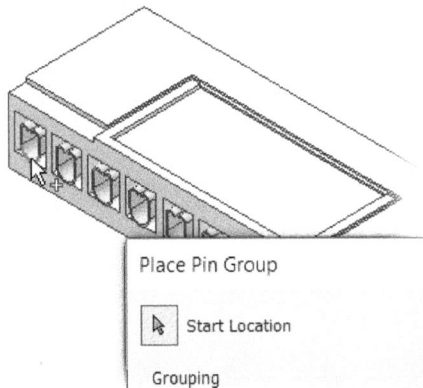

3. In the Grouping area, enter the number of pins per row, the pin pitch, and the number of rows. Use the Select option to select a linear edge, and the Direction option to flip directions if required. If you are creating two or more rows you will need to complete the required information for row pitch as well.

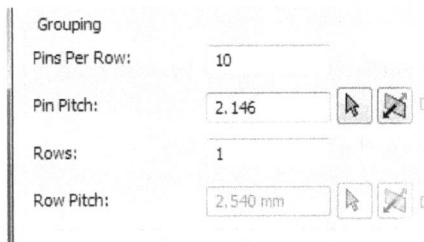

4. In the Naming area, enter the optional prefix letter and the start number. Select the sequence option and view the preview to verify your inputs are correct.

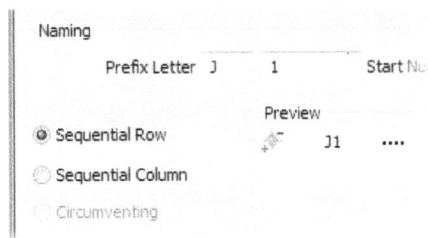

5. Click OK to create the pin group and exit the Place Pin Group tool.

Pin Group Editing Options

The following editing options are available in the shortcut menu when right-clicking on a pin group member in the Browser or in the drawing.

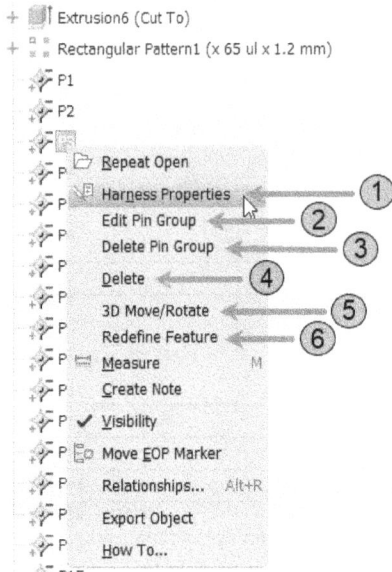

① **Harness Properties** - Modify the properties of the selected member including Pin Name and custom properties.

② **Edit Pin Group** - Returns you to the Edit Pin Group dialog box. You can change the start location, pin pitch, select a new linear edge, and flip direction.

③ **Delete Pin Group** - Deletes the pin group of the selected member.

④ **Delete** - Deletes the selected pin member.

⑤ **3D Move/Rotate** - Relocate the selected member using the 3D Move / Rotate mini-toolbar.

⑥ **Redefine Feature** - Use to relocate the selected group member to a new location.

Exercise: Define an Electrical Part

In this exercise, you will add single pins and pin groups to a part file and edit the pins.

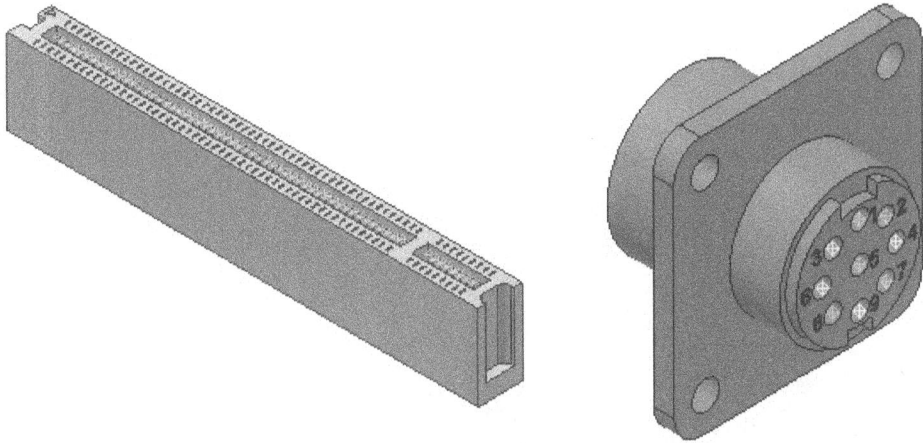

The completed exercise

Define Pins in an Electrical Part

In this portion of the exercise, you will define pins in an electrical part.

1. Open *Connector.ipt.*

2. In the 3D Model tab, in the Harness panel, click Place Pin. If the Harness panel is not displayed, toggle on its display using the Show Panels drop-down list at the right of the Ribbon.

   - On the part, select the cylindrical edge of the hole labeled 1.
   - In the Place Pin input box, select the check box to accept 1 as the pin name and place the pin.

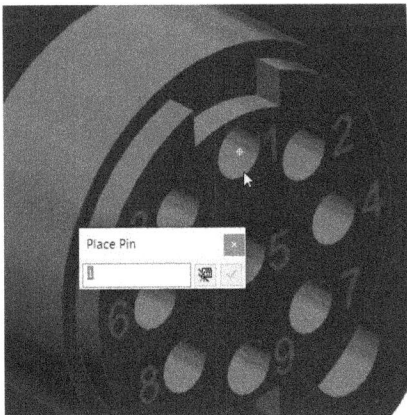

3. Note that the work point representing the pin is added to the part and to the Browser. In addition to the pin, a sketch is added to the browser. The sketch defines the location of the pin work point.

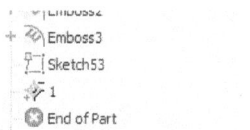

4. Continue to define pins 2 through 9, making sure the default name matches the labeled hole that you select. When all nine pins are defined, press ESC to exit the Pin command.

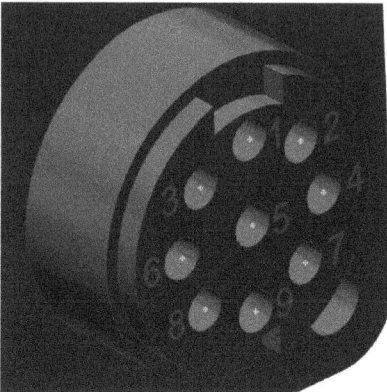

5. The electrical part is now prepared for authoring as a connector to be used in a harness assembly.

6. Close all files without saving changes.

Define and Edit Pin Groups in an Electrical Part

In this portion of the exercise, you will define and edit pin groups in an electrical part.

1. Open *PCI Slot.ipt*.

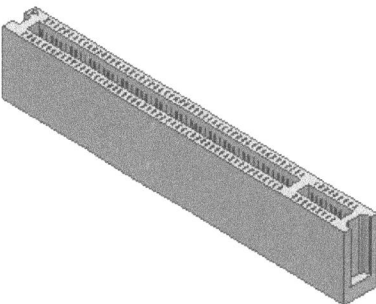

2. In the 3D Model tab, in the Harness panel, click Place Pin Group. For Start Location, select the first pin as shown in the following figure.

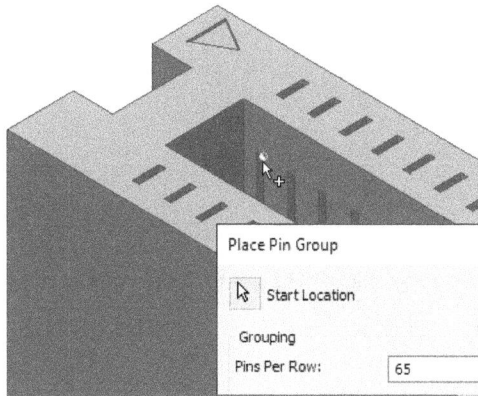

3. In the Grouping area:

- For Pins Per Row, enter **65**.
- For Pin Pitch, enter **1.2 mm**.
- For Rows, enter **1**.

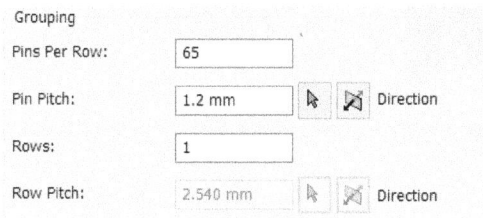

4. In the Grouping area, click Select to define the direction.

- Select the front top edge of the part.
- Click Direction to flip the arrow if required to match the following figure.

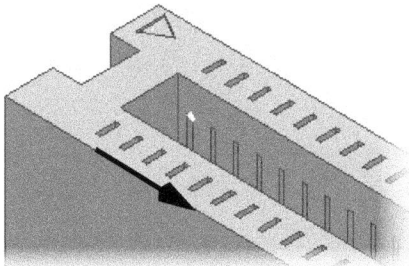

5. In the Naming area:

   ▪ For Prefix Letter, enter **P**.
   ▪ For Start Number, enter **1**.
   ▪ Ensure that Sequential Row is selected.

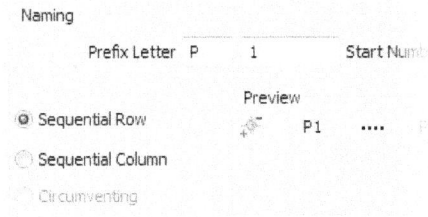

6. In the Place Pin Group dialog box, click OK to create the pin group and exit the tool.

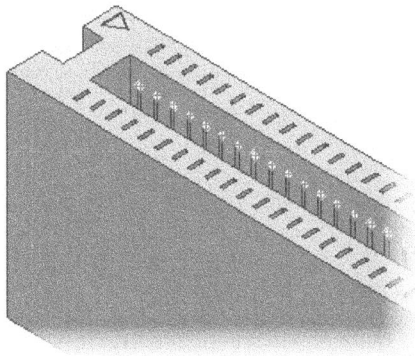

7. The part is shown transparently to identify that two of the pins are located within the part and are not required.

8. Right-click on each of the unnecessary pins and click Delete. It might be easier to select the pins in the Browser. You will delete pin numbers 55 and 56.

Note: When selecting pins in the Browser, press CTRL to select multiple pins for deletion at the same time.

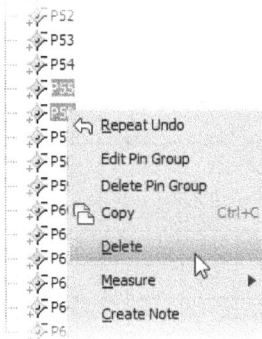

9. The electrical part is now prepared for authoring as a connector to be used in a harness assembly. Close all files without saving changes.

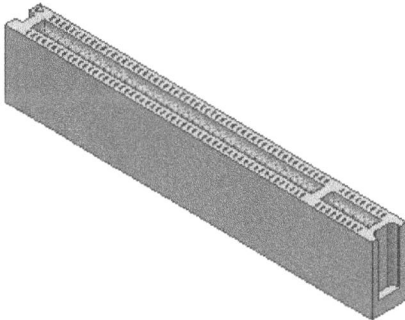

Lesson: Managing Libraries

This lesson describes the use and configuration of the Content Center Libraries.

By understanding how to use and configure the Content Center, not only do you benefit from reusing the industry standard-based wires, cables, plugs, and connections, you also benefit from the Content Center by using it to manage and access all of your company-specific cable and harness library content.

In the following figure, a custom connector that was published to a custom Content Center library is in the process of being added to a design.

Objectives

After completing this lesson, you will be able to:

- Describe the purpose and functionalities of the Content Center.
- Explain the difference between a Desktop install and an Autodesk Vault Server based install.
- Add a custom library to the Content Center.
- Configure the path for saving and accessing Content Center files.
- Transfer a custom library between Autodesk Vault Server and Autodesk Inventor Desktop Content.

About the Content Center

To benefit from the use and creation of Content Center data, you must first understand the purpose and functionalities of the Content Center.

The following figure shows just a few of the many possible parts that are available in the Content Center for use in your designs.

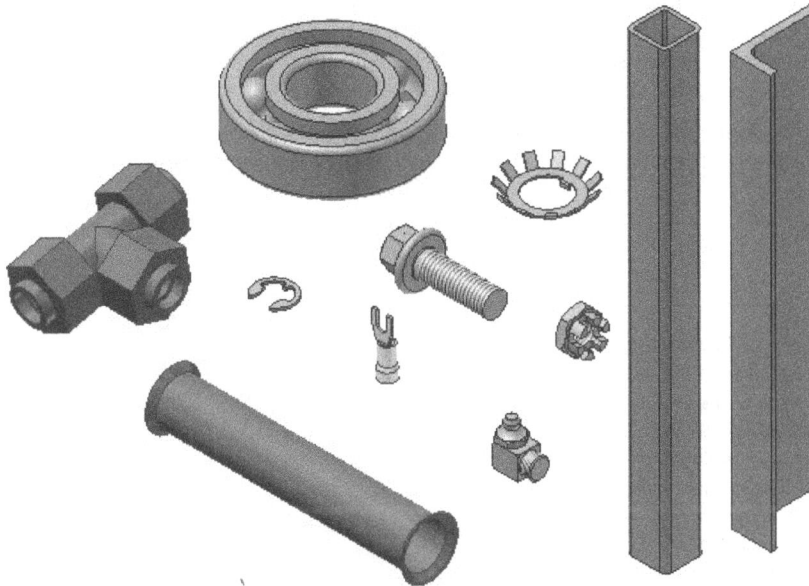

Definition of the Content Center

The Content Center is a central storage location for library data consisting of features and parts that you can select and insert into your part or assembly designs. The data in the Content Center is stored in different library databases. The location of the library database files depend on your work environment.

When you install the Content Center, you have the option of selecting one or more libraries that contain parts based on common industry standards. Along with these supplied industry-standard libraries, you can create your own custom libraries and publish your own parts or features to those libraries. By publishing your library content to custom Content Center libraries, everyone has access to the same published version of the data. Not only does reusing Content Center published data help you create a design more efficiently, it also helps establish consistency between designs and among designers.

The parts that you select and use from a common industry library are either fully defined by an industry standard, or defined by a standard along with the values you enter. In addition to directly selecting and inserting data from the Content Center, some of the tools that you use also reference and use data from the Content Center. For example, when you use the Bolted Connection Generator to add a bolted connection to your assembly, the bolts, washers, and nuts that you select are based on the content in the Content Center.

Content Center Access Options

The installation of the Content Center library content depends on your work environment. The two different ways that Content Center content libraries can be installed and accessed are:

- Autodesk Inventor Desktop Content
- Autodesk® Vault Server

In a Desktop Content installation the Content Center libraries are individual files that are stored and accessed on your computer. When using Desktop Content, you are not required to install additional software or services to access and use Content Center content. In a Vault Server installation the Content Center libraries are stored and accessible only through Vault Server.

In the following figure, the content libraries are shown listed in Autodesk Vault Server and as individual Desktop Content library files. The list of the Desktop Content library files is being viewed in Windows Explorer.

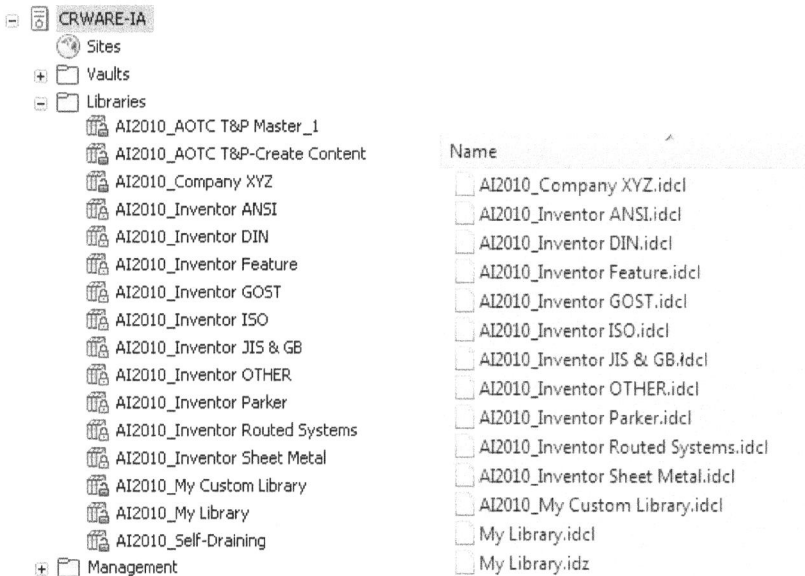

Autodesk Vault Server Libraries   Autodesk Inventor Desktop Content Libraries

If you are a stand-alone user or work using a laptop computer that might not always have access to the Autodesk Vault Server and your custom libraries, you will want to install using Desktop Content. If you are working as a member of a work group where multiple people access the same custom library content, then you will want to use Vault Server.

For More Information

Additional information on the options and settings for installing and configuring Content Center libraries is available in the Autodesk® Inventor® Help system. In the Help system, visit the topic Inventor Help Topics>Assembly Component Generators>Content Center>About Configuration of Content Center Libraries.

Structure and Contents of a Library

The Content Center library has three related aspects. The first aspect is the categories of library data. The second aspect is the families of parts or features within the category. The third aspect is the family members within the part family or feature family.

1. Categories within a library establish an organization to the content. Categories also define which parameters are optional or required in any subcategory, part family, or feature family. The categories display in a hierarchy structure similar to that of the folders in Windows Explorer. With logical names and a logical grouping of categories, it is easy to navigate through the available categories to the intended content.

2. A part family or feature family is the overall master model or template for the specific content. This master model is used to create the required variations of that part or feature. With the parametric model geometry, the family defines and stores parameter and image data.

3. Each of the defined variations for a part or feature family is referred to as a family member. The variations could be things like length, diameter, material, or part number.

Model geometry does not exist in the Content Center for every possible variation. Instead, only one set of model geometry is defined for a family, and the variations are based on the parameter values of the family members. The model geometry for the family member is added to your part or created as a part file when you require it. This enables you to have efficient storage and selection of library content.

Thus when you define or use Content Center content, you follow the order of creating or selecting a category, then a family, and then the family member. It is the family member that is ultimately added to your part or assembly design.

In the following figure, the Category View pane on the left shows some of the defined organizational categories for Cable & Harness type parts. By selecting the Discrete Wire category, the preview on the right lists and shows the families of parts defined within that category. By selecting the Connector_C120 part family, all of the defined members for that part family list in the lower right table.

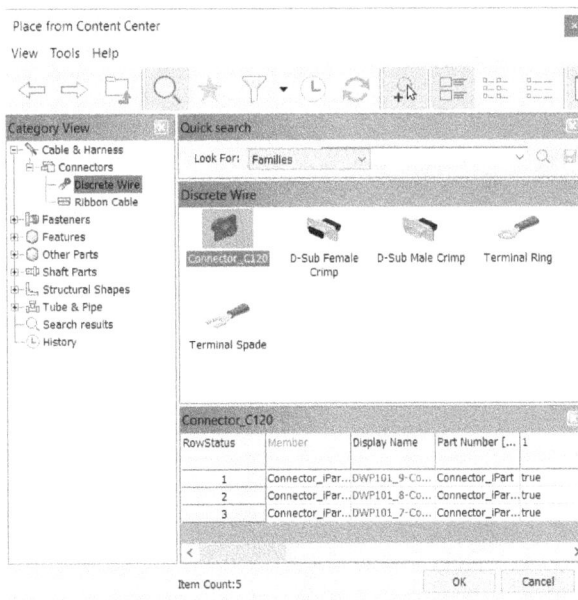

Content Center Roles

When you work with Content Center data, you either work with it as a consumer or as an editor. As a consumer, you access the libraries and use the stored parts or features within your design. As an editor, you can define the categories within a library and the required parameters for the categories, publish parts or features to the library categories, or define the published part or feature iterations that a consumer can select to reuse.

- **Content Center consumer** - When you reuse content from the Content Center to include it in your designs.
- **Content Center editor** - When you add parts or features to a library either one at a time or in a batch; when you add family members to a family; or, when you edit the parameters and properties of families or family members.

Example of Content Center Libraries and Content

As part of the Content Center, multiple libraries of preexisting content are available, which are based on industry standards. By accessing this Content Center content, you save yourself significant time researching possible sizes and modeling geometry to represent it in your design.

In the following figure, multiple categories of part content are listed in the Place from Content Center dialog box. In this case, a Slotted Regular Hex Head sheet metal screw has been selected for reuse. All the different defined variations for this part are listed in the family preview pane. By clicking OK, this part is created and ready for you to use.

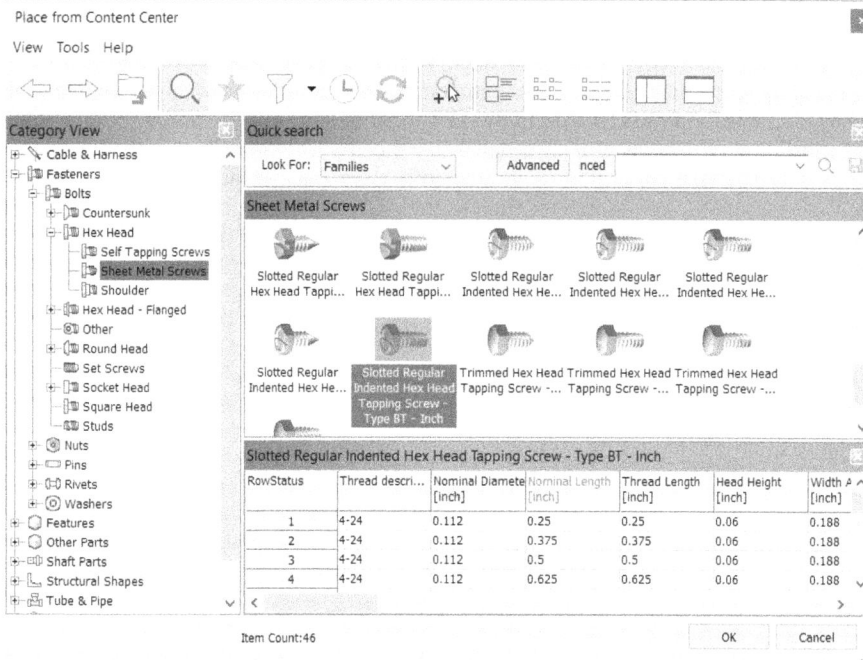

Installation Options

You have the option of configuring how you want Content Center to access libraries and what libraries are available for use. To configure the Content Center library access to match your design environment, you are required to know where the configuration settings are located and where to configure the available desktop content libraries per project.

Application Options for Content Center

You configure Content Center to access its libraries from either Autodesk Inventor Desktop Content or Autodesk Vault Server by selecting that option in the Application Options dialog box, Content Center tab, Access Options area. When the option Inventor Desktop Content is selected, you can specify the folder location where the content libraries reside. When the Autodesk Vault Server is selected, the list of available libraries and where you access them depends on the server you log into at a later time.

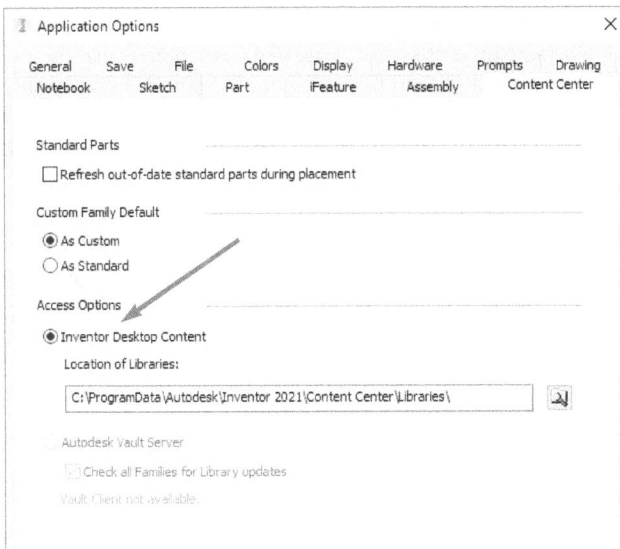

When you are configured to use Autodesk Vault Server, the access and use of library content is accomplished after logging in to Vault Server. The importing or creation of libraries occurs in the Autodesk Data Management Server Console (ADMS Console). The console is a separate application that you start by clicking ADMS Console on the desktop or from the Windows programs list. The console is also where user accounts, access permissions, and user groups are created and managed. Before a library can be used or you can modify the contents of a library, the library must exist in the Autodesk Data Management Server, and you must be setup as a user with correct permissions.

This lesson focuses its information on the use of Autodesk Inventor Desktop Content.

Configure Libraries per Project

To consume or publish content to a library, your active project file must be configured to access the content in that library. Of all the libraries that might be available in Autodesk Inventor Desktop Content or Autodesk Vault Server, you can limit which libraries list in Content Center. You specify which libraries are available on the basis of the active project file. If you have different project files, each project file can be configured to access different libraries. You specify which libraries are available in a project file in the Configure Libraries dialog box.

You access the Configure Libraries dialog box from the Projects dialog box by selecting the project file, and then clicking Configure Content Center Libraries.

When configured to use Desktop Content, the libraries that are available for use in the active project file have their In Use check box selected in the configure Libraries dialog box. Only the content that is defined in the selected libraries is available for reuse within your designs. Libraries that have an access of read/write are the only libraries that can have content published to them, or property and parameter values changed. To remove a library from being used, clear the check box in the row for that library and save the changes to the project file.

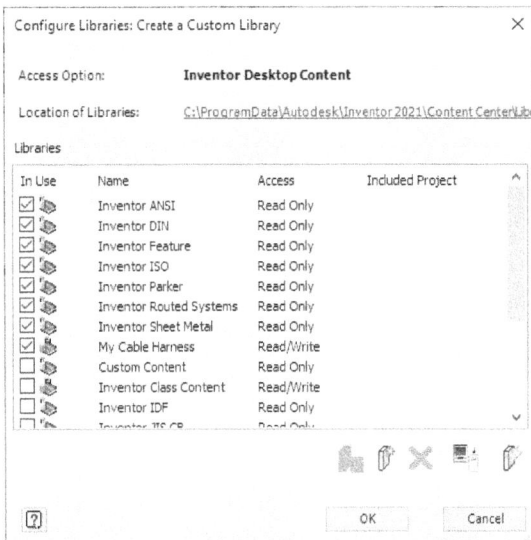

Select only the libraries that have the content you require for a project. That way only the content you require is listed in the Content Center and locating content is easier.

You can change the display name for a library. In the Configure Libraries dialog box, right-click on the library. Click Library Properties. Then in the Library Properties dialog box, enter a new name.

Adding a Custom Library

When Autodesk Inventor is configured to use Desktop Content libraries and you want to use the custom libraries, you can create a custom read/write library in the Configure Libraries dialog box. After you have included a custom library, you can copy component families and standard parts to the library in order to customize them to your specifications. You also can create your own standard parts and then publish them to your custom library for reuse.

In the following figure, the Content Center Editor dialog box displays showing the custom library My C-H Library and the custom components that have been published to the library.

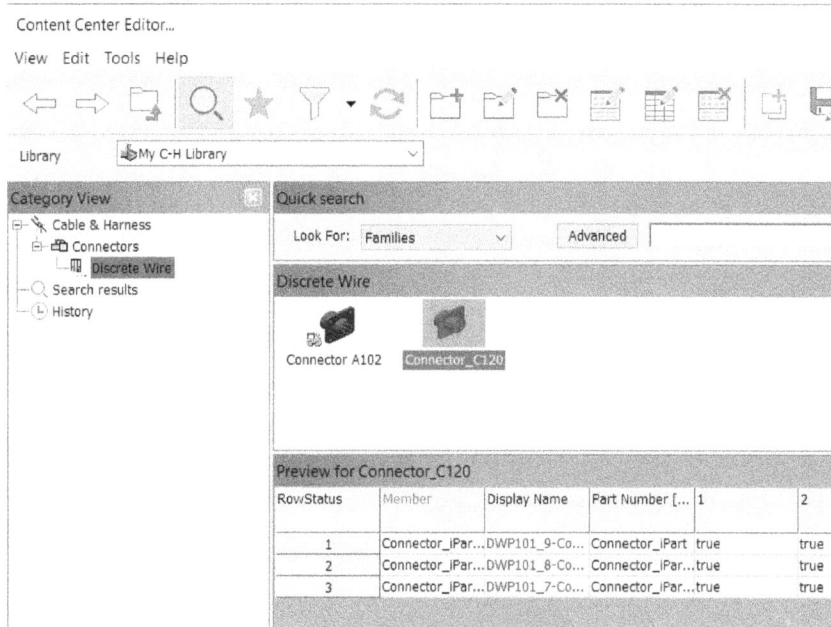

Purpose and Benefits of a Custom Library

The following list identifies the main purposes and benefits of creating custom libraries:

- Placing your custom components in the Content Center for reuse.
- Copying existing content from standard libraries, and modifying its properties to match your specific requirements.
- Increasing performance by decreasing the footprint of Content Center libraries. You copy just the component families that you will use from standard libraries to your custom library, and then detach the standard libraries that are loaded.

Custom Library Access

You initiate the creation of a custom desktop content library from within the Configure Libraries dialog box. After clicking the Create Library button in the Configure Libraries dialog box, the Create Library dialog box displays. Within the Create Library dialog box, you enter the display name for the new custom library and the name for the library database file. The display name is used as the library identifier in the Content Center.The new file is saved in the Desktop Content location.

In the following figure, the Create Library option in the Configure Libraries dialog box is used to create a new custom desktop content library. Note the existing custom library in the list is the My_Custom_Library, and also note the difference in the glyph between read only libraries and read/write libraries.

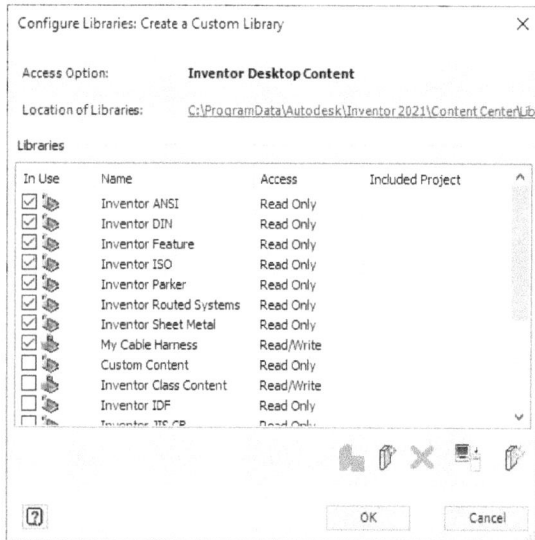

In the following figure, the Create Library dialog box is shown with a new custom library being created.

Procedure: Adding a Custom Library

The following steps give an overview of creating a custom desktop content read/write library.

1. In the Get Started tab, in the Launch panel, click Projects.

2. In the Projects dialog box, verify that the required project file is selected and then click Configure Content Center Libraries.

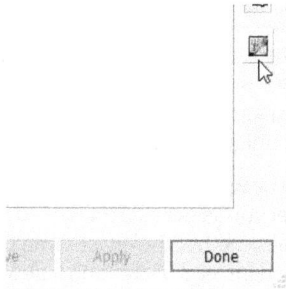

3. In the Configure Libraries dialog box, click Create Library.

4. In the Create Library dialog box, enter the display name and file name. Click OK.

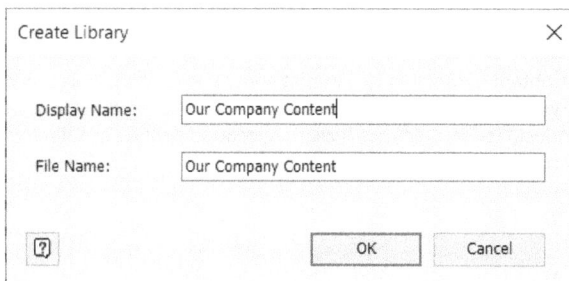

5. Close the dialog boxes and save the changes to the project file.

Configuring the Content Center File Path

When you use parts from the Content Center that are fully defined by an industry standard, those files are created and saved in a file location configured in your Autodesk Inventor software. To save the files to your preferred location, you are required to configure the path for Content Center files.

Purpose of the File Path

Content Center parts that are fully defined by an industry standard are true library parts. They are true library parts because they do not require any editing. For these parts, you do not enter any unique values, you only select a part based on set sizes or properties. Because you use them only as library parts, these parts are created and saved in a library path. For easier management and performance, the library path location for these Content Center parts is a unique and independent setting.

The path that you have set for the Content Center files also becomes a search location any time you place or open additional parts from the Content Center. After you select what you need in the Content Center, the Content Center searches the path location to see whether the exact same part already exists as a file. If one is found in the path, then that file is used instead of creating a new file. By doing this, the performance for accessing and using content is better and more efficient. To minimize the amount of time to search the path for an exact match, each part from the Content Center is created in a subfolder to the defined path. The name of the folder is a key because it identifies the part family.

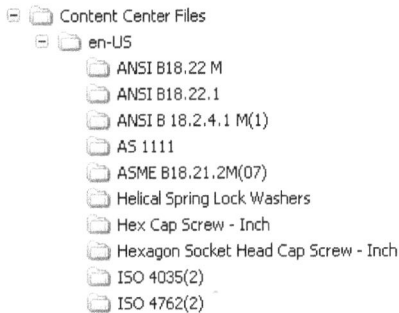

> You cannot modify a Content Center library part that you are using if it is in a library path. To have it not reside in a library path, you can either save the part to a location outside of the path, or activate a different project file that does not have that location defined as a library path.

Content Center Files Location

The path for the automatic saving and referencing of Content Center files is based on the current settings in the Application Options dialog box and the active project file.

You specify the default path for Content Center files on an Autodesk Inventor installation in the Application Options dialog box, in the File tab, in the Default Content Center Files field.

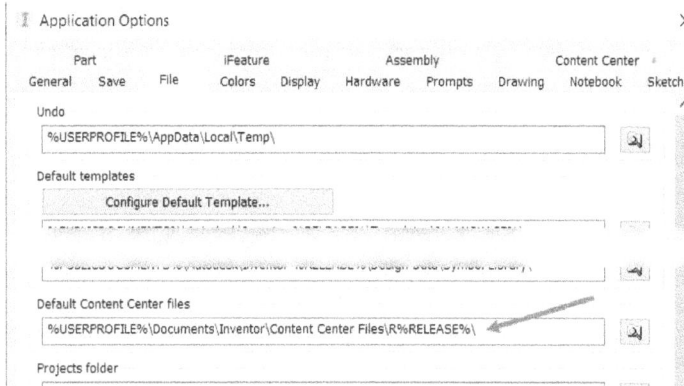

To use the default path specified in Application Options, the Content Center Files path under Folder Options in the active project file must be set to [Default] as shown in the following figure. If you want the active project file to use a different path other than the default, you can enter or select a different path. To return the Content Center Files to [Default] after specifying a different path, you can right-click on Content Center Files and click Use Default Folder.

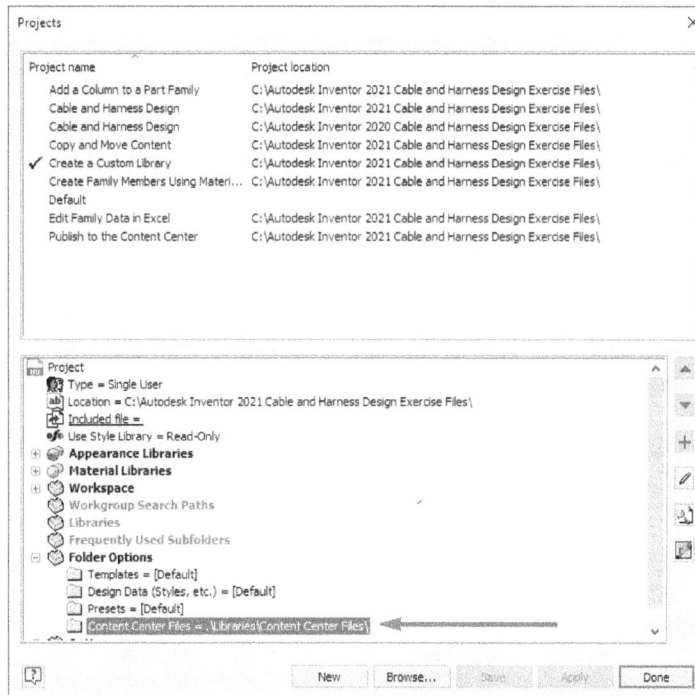

Process: Configuring the Default Content Center Files Path

The following steps give an overview of setting the default Content Center files path and having the active project use that default path.

1. In the Application Options dialog box, in the File tab, in the Default Content Center Files field, enter the required file path.

2. In the Projects dialog box, Folder Options, verify that the path for the Content Center Files option is set to [Default]. If it is not, right-click on Content Center Files and then click Use Default Folder.

Guidelines for Configuring the Content Center Files Path

Follow these guidelines when configuring the path for your Content Center files.

- Configure the default path to the required location instead of changing each path file. By doing this you have one set of Content Center files that all projects can reference.
- When working in a group environment, change the default path in each team member's Autodesk Inventor installation to point to a shared server location. The content files are then available for everyone, even when opening an assembly file created by a team member that contains references to Content Center parts.

Transferring Library Content

Depending on your work environment, you might have custom libraries configured in one library configuration and you want them available in another. To have a custom library configured for one type of installation and make it available in another installation type, you need to transfer a custom library between Autodesk Inventor Desktop Content and Autodesk Vault Server.

Transfer of Libraries

If your computer has a previous release of Autodesk Data Management Server with custom libraries defined and you install Autodesk Inventor to use Desktop Content, the first time you run Autodesk Inventor, you are given the option to transfer the legacy libraries to the Desktop Content location. If you do not transfer the libraries at that time, you can manually transfer the libraries at a later time.

You can manually transfer custom content library from Autodesk Vault Server to Autodesk Inventor Desktop Content or vice versa. You transfer custom content libraries when you want to:

- Move from using ADMS to using Desktop Content.
- Move from Desktop Content to using Autodesk Vault Server.
- Make Autodesk Vault Server content available to you when in a stand-alone mode.
- Make a custom library created in Desktop Content available in Autodesk Vault Server.

Accessing the Library Transfer Guide

You transfer a custom Content Center library from Autodesk Vault Server to Autodesk Inventor Desktop Content or vice versa in the Library Transfer Guide dialog box. You access the Library Transfer Guide option in the Configure Libraries dialog box. You display the Configure Libraries dialog box by selecting the project file to edit in the Projects dialog box and then clicking Configure Content Center Libraries. The following figure shows the access location for Configure Content Center Libraries in the Projects dialog box and Library Transfer Guide in the Configure Libraries dialog box.

Read Only
Read/Write
Read/Write

OK   Cancel

Library Transfer Guide...

Configure Content Center Libraries   Library Transfer Guide

Apply   Done

Process: Transferring Library Content

The following steps give an overview of transferring a custom content library.

1. In the Projects dialog box, select the project file to configure.

2. In the Project dialog box, click Configure Content Center Libraries.

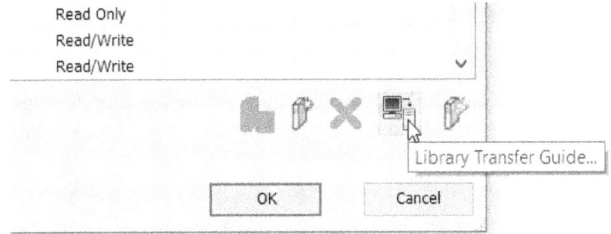

3. In the Configure Libraries dialog box, click Library Transfer Guide.

4. Select if you want to transfer custom libraries from Autodesk Vault Server to Autodesk Inventor Desktop Content or from Inventor Desktop Content to Autodesk Vault Server.

5. Specify the server, database, username, and password to log into Autodesk Vault Server.

6. Select the libraries to transfer.

7. If transferring the library to Desktop Content and the library is identified as needing migration, select and update the transferred library.

Exercise: Create a Custom Library

In this exercise, you will create a new Desktop Content library for custom cable and harness components, and you will configure your project file to use the new custom library.

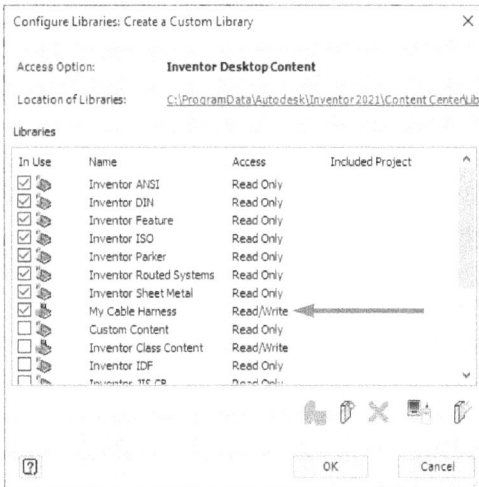

1. Start the Autodesk Inventor software but do not open any files. Close any open files.

2. In the Get Started tab, in the Launch panel, click Projects.

3. To add this exercise's project file to the Autodesk Inventor software:
    - In the Projects dialog box, click Browse.
    - In the Choose Project File dialog box, navigate to the directory with the exercise files and open *Create a Custom Library.ipj*.

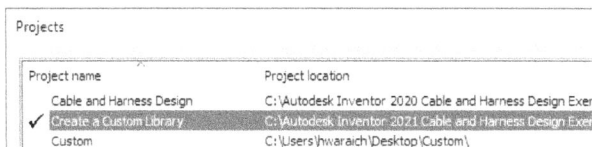

4. To create a new read/write library, in the Projects dialog box, click Configure Content Center Libraries.

5. In the Configure Libraries dialog box, click Create Library.

6. In the Create Library dialog box, for Display Name, enter **My Cable Harness** and click OK.

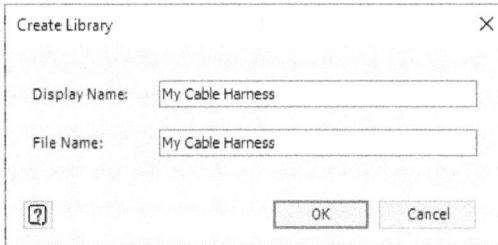

7. Verify that the custom Read/Write library is In Use.

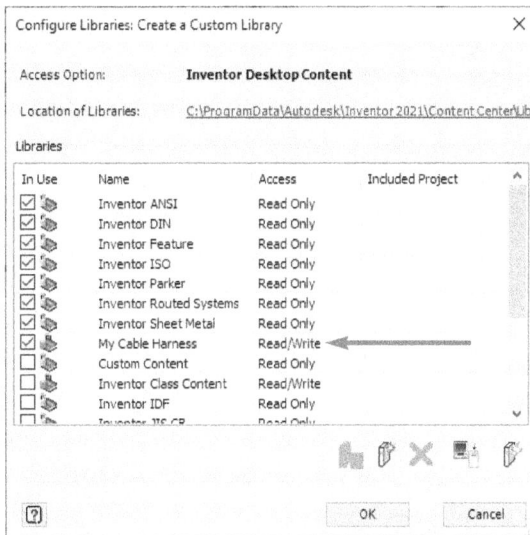

8. Click OK.

9. In the Projects dialog box, click Save. Click Done.

Lesson: Creating Library Content

This lesson describes how to author and publish your own cable and harness content.

Autodesk Inventor has multiple industry standards, and substantial part content within those standards that you can load and use in your designs. However, you probably require only certain parts and sizes within those standards. For those parts that you require, you might also require specific values for their properties such as their part numbers or stock numbers. In addition, you might have custom cable and harness components that you have developed specific to your applications. By understanding how to access and include these components in your library data, and modify the values and properties of library content, you can access and use Content Center data more efficiently in your designs.

The following figure demonstrates electrical parts that have been published to a custom library in the Content Center.

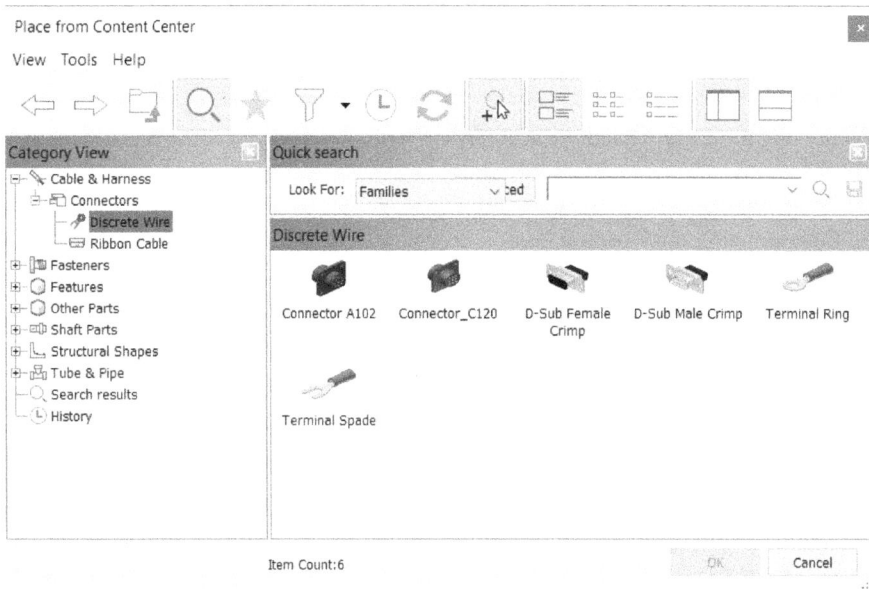

Objectives

After completing this lesson, you will be able to:

- Describe how to create custom content.
- Author electrical connectors to add specific cable and harness data.
- Publish electrical parts and connectors to a custom Content Center library.

Creating Custom Content

The supplied content libraries contain a limited number of components for cable and harness design. You can supplement the standard libraries by adding connectors and other components to one or more custom libraries. In addition to new connectors, you can add components that you use in your cable and harness designs such as cases, power supplies, boards, and other specialized components.

The following figure shows some sample content that you can create and add to the Content Center libraries.

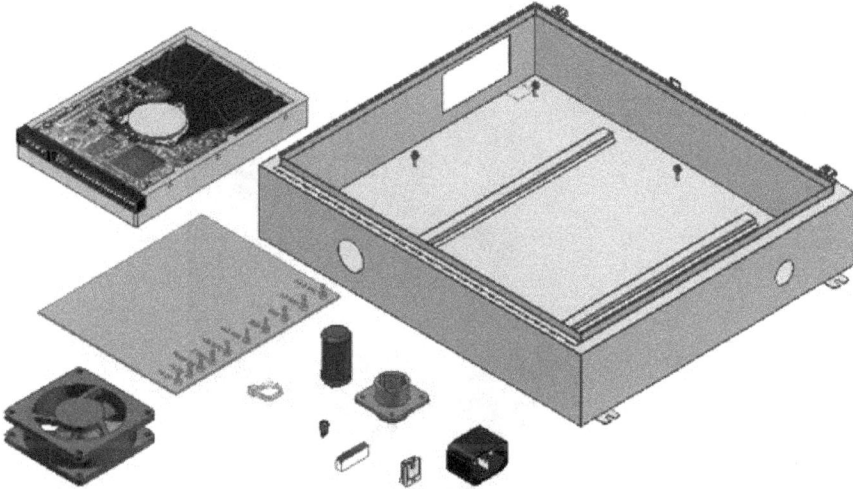

Process: Creating Custom Cable and Harness Content

The following steps outline the process for creating cable and harness content.

1. Create the component as a standard Autodesk Inventor part. If you have several variations (sizes) of the component, create an iPart.

2. Use the Harness Part Features tools to add pins and property information to the part.

3. Save the part file. The part is unchanged except that the pin and property information is now stored in the part file.

4. As an option, you can publish the part to a custom library for easy access and consistency of use for all designers. The publishing guide adds extra family and category information and stores the part definition in a library.

Authoring Electrical Connectors

The authoring process adds specific data to the connector in order to use it for cable and harness design. You can author iPart factory parts and publish the iPart variations to a custom library in the Content Center. The harness-specific information added in the authoring process is applied to all variations of the published fitting. The authoring process is the same for both standard parts and iParts.

In the following figure, an authored connector is shown with the browser demonstrating the included pin information.

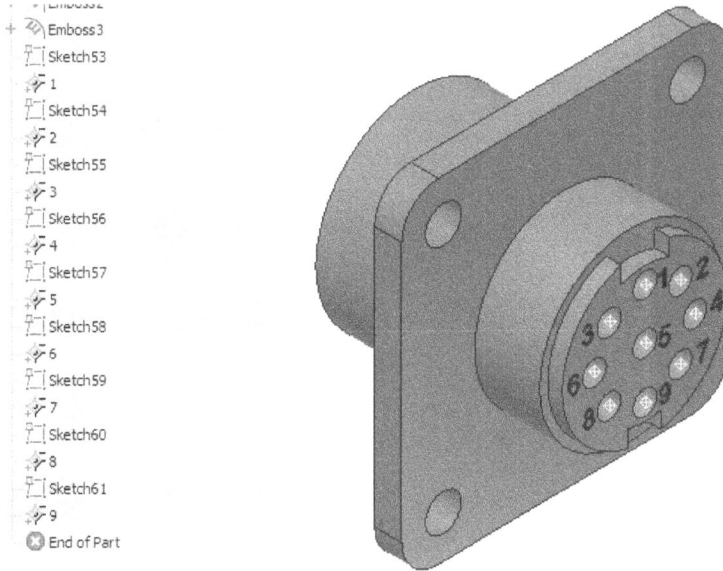

Access

Ribbon: Manage tab>Author panel> Component drop-down

Connector Authoring Dialog Box

When you author a part using the Connector Authoring dialog box, you must select either Discrete Wire or Ribbon Cable. In order to connect to a ribbon cable in the assembly, a connector must be authored as Ribbon Cable.

① Specify that the connector uses individual wires or cable wires.

② Specify that the connector uses ribbon cable.

③ Specify the type of connector to author.

- Insulation Displacement - Use for ribbon cable connectors and terminal connectors.
- Crimp - Use for terminal connectors only.

④ Specify how the conductors fit with the connector pins:

- Selection Arrow - Select geometry to specify the direction.
- Direction Arrow - Select to specify a single direction in either direction.
- Both Direction Arrow - Select to specify termination in both directions. This option is valid only with the Insulation Displacement option termination type.

⑤ Use the optional embedded length to specify an accurate wire length. This option produces a custom property.

- Direction 1 - Sets the embedded length for a single direction.
- Direction 2 - Sets the embedded length for a second direction when using an outward direction set to both.

6. The Start Pin and Pin Orientation options apply to ribbon cable only.

   - Start Pin - Select a specific pin on the connector to connect the ribbon cable to.
   - Pin Orientation - Use part geometry to specify the orientation of the ribbon cable in regard to the connector. Use the Flip button to reverse the direction.

7. Use for iParts only. Map the RefDes property to a column in the iPart.

Procedure: Authoring a Connector

The following steps give an overview of authoring an electrical connector for use in a cable and harness assembly.

1. Start the Connector authoring tool.

2. Select Discrete Wire or Ribbon Cable and the Termination Type.

3. Click the selection tool and select part geometry to indicate direction. Click a direction arrow to orient the direction.

4. Specify other optional parameters as required for your application such as Embedded Length.

5. Click OK to author the connector. Click OK in the Authoring Result dialog box to accept the successful result. You can use your connector in an assembly or publish the part to your custom library in the Content Center.

Publishing Electrical Parts and Connectors

When you have finished authoring a part, you can publish the part to a custom read/write Content Center library. To publish parts as content to a library, you need to know which tools to use and the procedure for publishing a part.

In the following figure, a power supply connector, which has been published to the Content Center, is placed into an assembly.

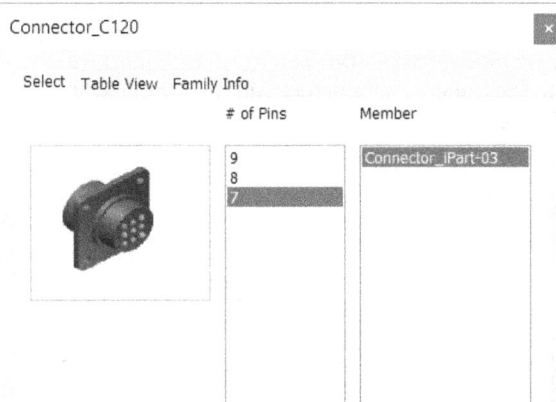

Publishing Parts

When publishing parts, you either publish multiple parts in a batch or publish one part at a time. You use the Batch Publish tool to publish multiple parts at one time. You use the Publish Part tool to publish a single part. To access the Publish Part tool, the part you want to publish must be open. You can also publish from within the Content Center Editor. When a part file is open, the option initiates the publishing of a single part. When an assembly file is open or no files are open, the option initiates batch publishing.

Access

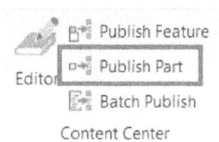	Ribbon: Manage tab>Content Center panel
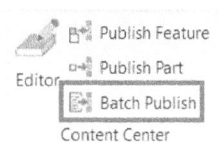	Ribbon: Manage tab>Content Center panel
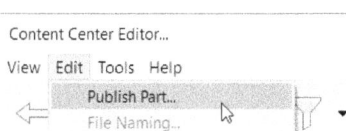	Content Center Editor menu: Edit>Publish Part (Publishes a single part if a part is open, batch publishes if the editor is opened with no Inventor files open.)

Options When Publishing a Part

After you start the process for publishing a single part, you specify multiple items in multiple pages of the Publish Guide dialog box. First, select the library to publish the part to and the language to publish it in. The next task is to select the library category the part should be published in. Based on the selected library category, you then map the defined parameters in the category to parameters in the part. After mapping the parameters, identify the category parameters that are the key columns of data. The next task is to enter the naming and industry standard information for this new part family. The last task is to specify the image to use for the part family thumbnail image, the default image or an alternate BMP or JPG file.

Discrete Wire and Ribbon Cable library categories list RefDes as the only category property. When prompted to map the family column to the category parameters, you can specify which parameter in the template should be used for the RefDes value.

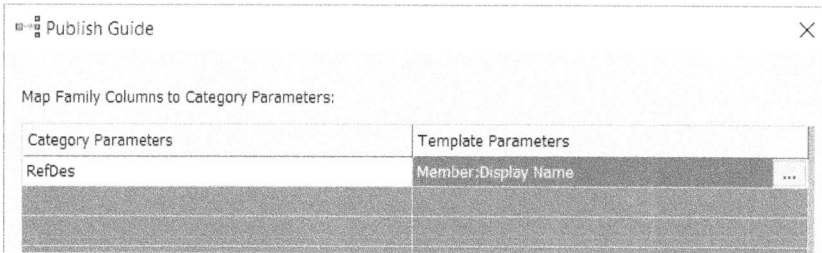

During the placement of a part, you are required to differentiate the family member to insert into your design. To help select the family member you want to include in your design, you identify category parameter columns as key columns. You can then select values within these key columns during the placement of a part family member. Along with identifying the columns of values you want to select from, at this publishing step, you also specify the order in which the columns appear. Their order of selection and thus importance are based on the order they are listed in the Key Columns list as shown in the following figure.

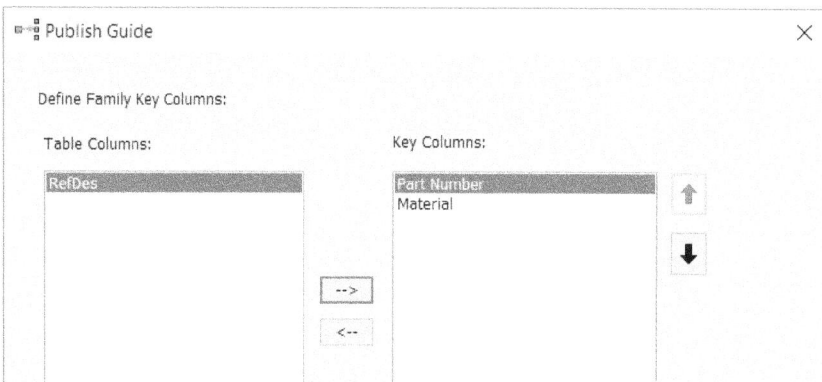

The name you enter in the Family Name field sets the Content Center part family name. This name must be unique from all the other part family names in that category. By entering a description and selecting standard information, you help identify information about the part.

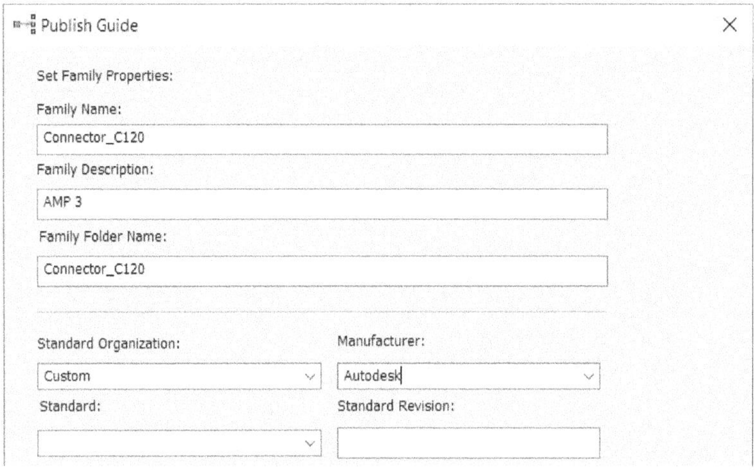

After publishing the part family, you can change the family name values, standard settings, parameter mapping, and thumbnail image by using the Family Properties option in the Content Center Editor. You also can add columns to the part family and map those added column values to the part's parameters.

Key Category Parameter Fields

The category parameter fields you specify for a part family are the fields of values you have to select from when you select to place in your assembly design. When placing a part and the Select tab is active, the order the fields are shown left to right is based on the key field list order you have set. After publishing a part family, you can change the order and columns of parameters that are key fields. You can also change the key fields after publishing in the Content Center Editor.

Category parameters can be configured to contain a set value for each family member or allow for a range of values. By default they are configured to have a set value.

Key fields display in red text when viewed in the table view during placement or in the Content Center Editor. When viewing a part family in table view that contains many defined members, it can be difficult or time-consuming to locate the exact configuration you require. This is one reason why you identify key columns of properties.

The following figure shows the Family Table dialog box with the key fields identified.

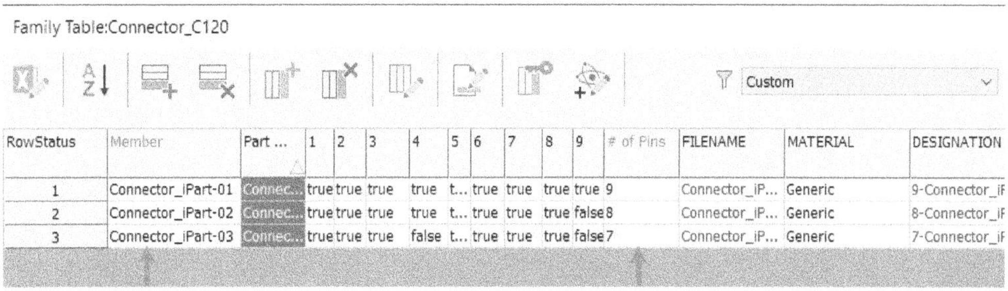

By defining key fields of category properties, you can identify the family member you want to include in your assembly design in a quick and efficient manner. In the Select tab, the left-to-right order of properties in the dialog box for placement of a Content Center part is based on the identification and order of the key fields.

In the following figure, the category parameter column # of Pins is the first key field, followed by Member. If nonrequired parameters are listed, selection of all the different possibilities is simple because the values listed in the subsequent columns to the right are dependent on what was selected for placement in the column to its left. In the following example, there are three # of Pins values defined that have a specific Member name assigned.

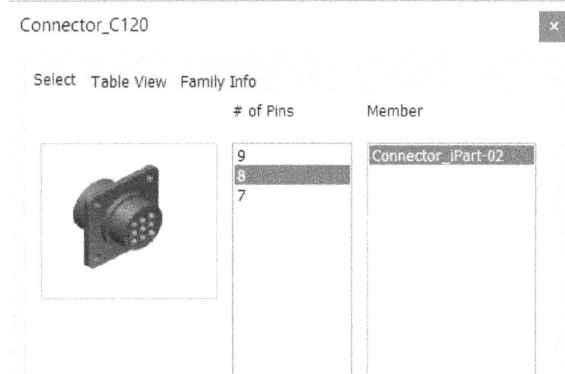

Procedure: Publishing Electrical Parts

The following steps give an overview of publishing an electrical connector to a library.

1. Start the Publish Part tool.

2. Specify the library and language.

3. The category is automatically selected for you based on the type that you specified in the authoring tool.

4. If required, assign the template parameter to populate the value for the RefDes category parameter.

5. Select the key columns. The selected key columns are the variations that display when you select the part from the Content Center. Typically, these are mapped automatically based on the information you provided when you created the iPart factory.

6. Specify the family properties. The information helps you find the part in the Content Center when you apply filters or use the search tool.

7. Accept the default thumbnail image or specify another.

Guidelines for Publishing Part Content

Follow these guidelines when publishing part content to a Content Center library.

- Export part parameters that you want to map to category parameters prior to publishing the part.
- Parameters that you mark as key fields appear in the dialog box for value selection when you are placing a published part.
- When setting the key fields, select the category parameters that help you identify the unique differences between the family members that you require in your assemblies.
- Set the order of the key fields based on the importance of the parameter values, or based on which values help categorize the differences among family members.

Exercise: Author an Electrical Part

In this exercise, you will use the Connector Authoring tool to add harness-specific information to a standard Autodesk Inventor part and to an iPart.

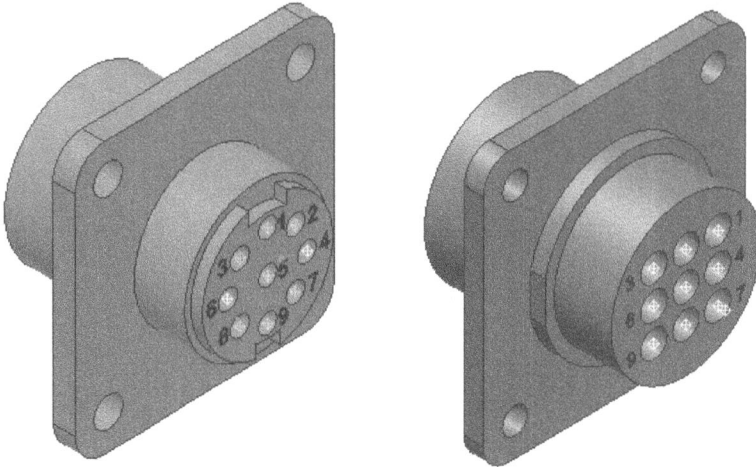

The completed exercise

Author a Standard Connector

In this portion of the exercise, you use the Connector Authoring tool to add harness-specific information to a standard Autodesk Inventor part.

1.   Open *Connector_Pins.ipt*.

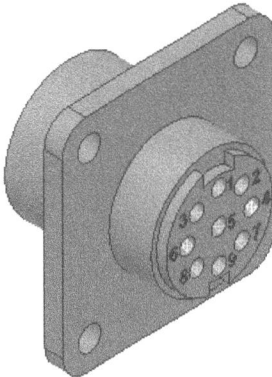

2. In the Manage tab, in the Author panel, open the Component drop-down list and click Connector.

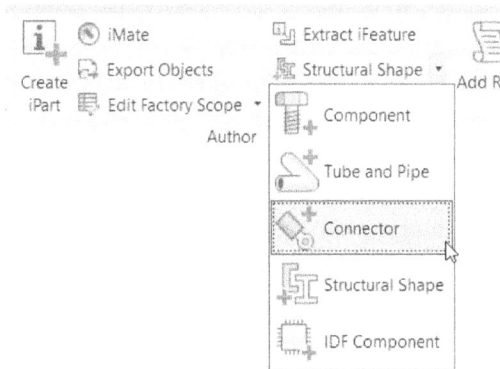

3. In the Connector Authoring dialog box, select Discrete Wire. For Termination Type, select Insulation Displacement.

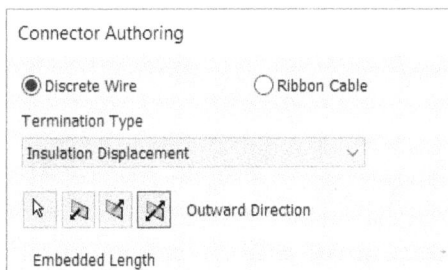

4. To designate outward direction:

- On the part, click the edge of the hole labeled 5.
- Click the outward direction button so that the arrow points away from the connector.

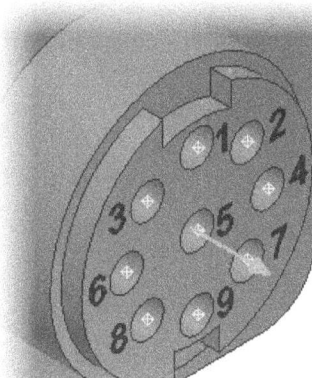

5. Click OK to author the part.

6. Click OK to close the Authoring Result dialog box.

7. Close all files without saving changes.

Note: In normal operation, you save the part after authoring it.

Author an iPart Connector

In this portion of the exercise, you add harness- specific information to an iPart for publishing to the Content Center.

1. Open *Connector_iPart.ipt*.

2. Expand the Table node in the Browser.

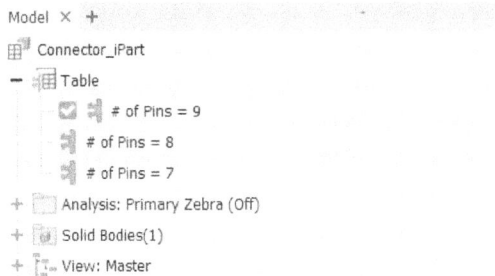

Note: If the keys are not displayed, right-click on the Table node. Click List by Keys.

3. In the Browser, right-click on Table and click Edit Table. Note the data in the iPart Author dialog box. The Number of Pins value is the primary key for the iPart.

iPart Author

Parameters Properties Suppression iFeatures IMates Work Features Threads Other

Connector _iPart.ipt
Extrusion1
   x: d0 [1.282 in]
   x: d1 [0.094 in]
   x: d2 [0 deg]
Fillet1
Hole1
Extrusion2
Extrusion3
Extrusion4
Extrusion5

Name

	Member	Part Number	1	2	3	4	5	6	7	8	9		# of Pins
1	Connector_iPart-01	Connector_iPart	Include	Include	Include	Include	Include	Include	Include	Include	Include		9
2	Connector_iPart-02	Connector_iPart-02	Include	Include	Include	Include	Include	Include	Include	Include	Exclude		8
3	Connector_iPart-03	Connector_iPart-03	Include	Include	Include	Exclude	Include	Include	Include	Include	Exclude		7

4. Click Cancel to close the iPart Author dialog box.

5. To begin to author a connector, in the Manage tab, in the Author panel, click Connector.

6. In the Connector Authoring dialog box, click Discrete Wire. For Termination Type, select Insulation Displacement.

Connector Authoring   ✕

● Discrete Wire   ○ Ribbon Cable

Termination Type

Insulation Displacement   ⌄

Outward Direction

7. To designate outward direction:
   - In the Connector Authoring dialog box, click the Select button.
   - On the part, click near the hole 5.
   - Click the outward direction button so that the arrow points away from the connector.

8. Click OK to author the part.

9. Click OK to close the Authoring Result dialog box.

10. Close all files without saving changes.

    Note: In normal operation, you save the part after authoring it.

Exercise: Publish to the Content Center

In this exercise, you will publish an authored connector to the Content Center.

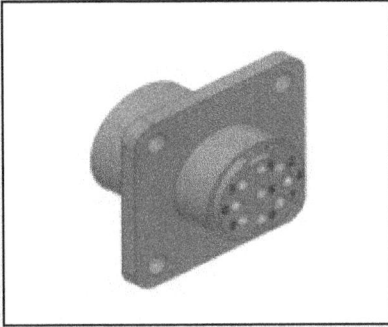

The completed exercise

Note: To complete this exercise, you must first have the custom library available and configured for use. If you completed the exercise Create a Custom Library in the lesson Managing Libraries, you can skip the exercise steps in the Setup and Load Library task up until step 8, where you set the project file for this exercise.

Setup and Load Library

In this section of the exercise, you will copy a custom Desktop Content library to the correct folder location so the project file you set active can use the custom library.

1. Start the Autodesk Inventor software but do not open any files. Close any open files.

2. In the Get Started tab, in the Launch panel, click Projects.

3. In the Projects dialog box, click Configure Content Center Libraries.

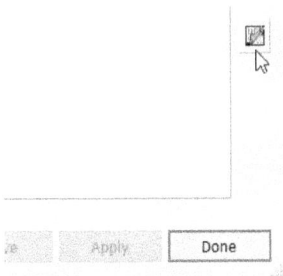

4. In the Configure Libraries dialog box, click the hyperlink text for Location of Libraries to open a Windows Explorer window viewing that folder.

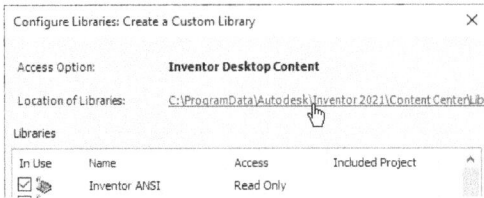

5. Open another session of Windows Explorer.

- Navigate to the install directory of the class files.
- Click to open the Libraries folder in the exercise directory.

6. Copy *My Cable and Harness.idcl* from the Library folder to the window opened by the hyperlink in a previous step.

7. Close the Windows Explorer windows and exit the Configure Libraries dialog box.

8. To add this exercise's project file to the Autodesk Inventor software:

- In the Projects dialog box, click Browse.
- In the Choose Project File dialog box, navigate to the directory with the exercise files and open *Publish to the Content Center.ipj*.

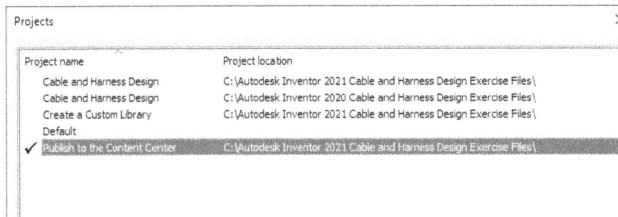

9. In the Projects dialog box, click Configure Content Center Libraries.

10. In the Configure Libraries dialog box, review the list of libraries that are set to be in use when this project file is active.

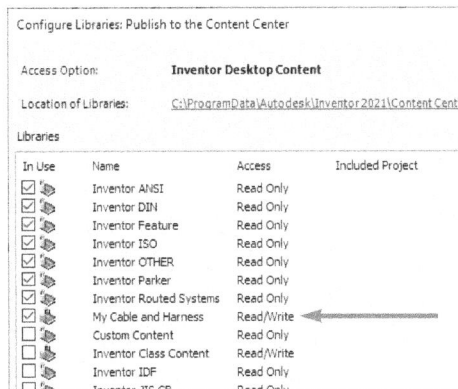

11. Close the Configure Libraries dialog box and the Projects dialog box.

Publish the Connector

In this portion of the exercise, you will publish an authored connector to the Content Center.

1. Open *Connector_Pins_Author.ipt*.

2. In the Manage tab, in the Content Center panel, click Publish Part. The Publish Guide dialog box opens. All of the remaining steps take place in the Publish Guide dialog box.

3. For Select Library to Publish to, verify that the library My Cable and Harness is selected.

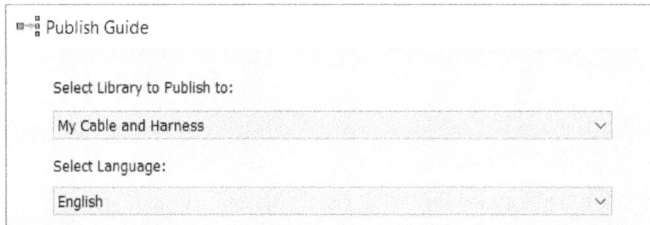

4. Click Next. For Select Category to Publish to, verify that Discrete Wire is selected.

5. Click Next. For Map Family Columns to Category Parameters, the required mappings were already defined during the authoring process.

6. Click Next. For Define Family Key Columns, under Table Columns, select Part Number. Click the arrow button (-->) to add the selected column as a Key Column.

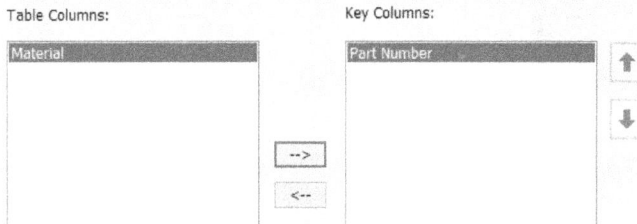

7. Click Next. For Set Family Properties, enter the following information:
   - For Family Name, enter **Connector A102**.
   - For Standard Organization, ensure Custom is selected.
   - For Manufacturer, enter **Autodesk**.

Set Family Properties:

Family Name:

Connector A102 ←

Family Description:

AMP 3

Family Folder Name:

Connector A102

Standard Organization: Manufacturer:

Custom ←   ▼   Autodesk ←

Standard: Standard Rev

8. Click Next. For Set Family Thumbnail Image, review the thumbnail image.

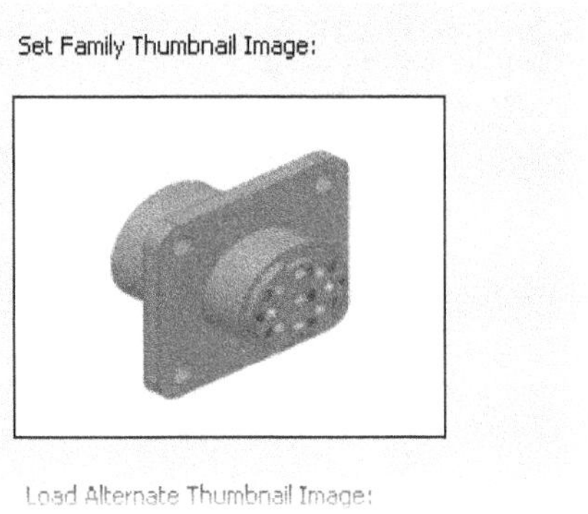

Set Family Thumbnail Image:

Load Alternate Thumbnail Image:

9. Click Publish. Click OK to close the message that confirms the part was successfully published to the library.

10. Close all files without saving changes.

Lesson: Managing Library Content

This lesson describes the management and editing of settings for your published cable and harness content.

You need to understand how published Content Center parts have their document setting values and file property values set in order to ensure that your published content has the document settings you require and the property values that reflect your company requirements. When a change is required, you need to know how to edit a published part family using the Content Center Editor.

Objectives

After completing this lesson, you will be able to:

- State the purpose of the Content Center Editor and how to access it.
- Copy content from an industry library to a custom Content Center library.
- Explain the document setting values of published Content Center parts.
- Add and edit the columns of values for a library part family so that they map to an Autodesk Inventor property.
- Add a property to a published part to set its browser display name.
- Edit Content Center family member data in Microsoft Excel.
- Use Material Guide to create new families and new members in Content Center.

Content Center Editor

The Content Center Editor is the entry point for managing and modifying published library content. Prior to learning specific content management tasks, you need to know where to access the Content Center Editor and its purpose.

You use the Content Center Editor to complete a number of tasks associated with populating and defining the properties of content in your custom library. Tasks you can accomplish in a custom read/write library include:

- Copying content from an industry library to the custom library.
- Copying the category structure of an industry library so you can publish custom content to the same structure but in a different library.
- Creating new category structures to identify where content can be published.
- Creating and defining all the family member variations of a part.
- Defining a file naming scheme for part family content.

Access

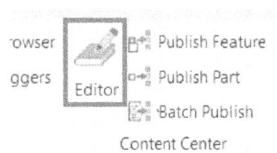

Ribbon: Manage tab>Content Center panel

Ribbon (with no files open): Tools tab>Content Center panel

Content Center Editor User Interface

The user interface and interaction in the Content Center Editor is similar to the user interface for Place From Content Center. The Content Center Editor has a number of tools available for creating and modifying categories and content. You access the various tools in the Content Center Editor by selecting a category or part family and clicking that tool name from the toolbar, shortcut menu, or Edit menu. You can select a category in the Category View pane or the Family Collection pane. You select a part family or feature family in the Family Collection pane.

One unique area to the Content Center Editor is the Library View list. Based on what you have selected in the list, either all of the components from all the available libraries will display or only the content in a single library will display. By selecting a specific library, you can easily review what content exists in that library and select the content you want to modify or copy.

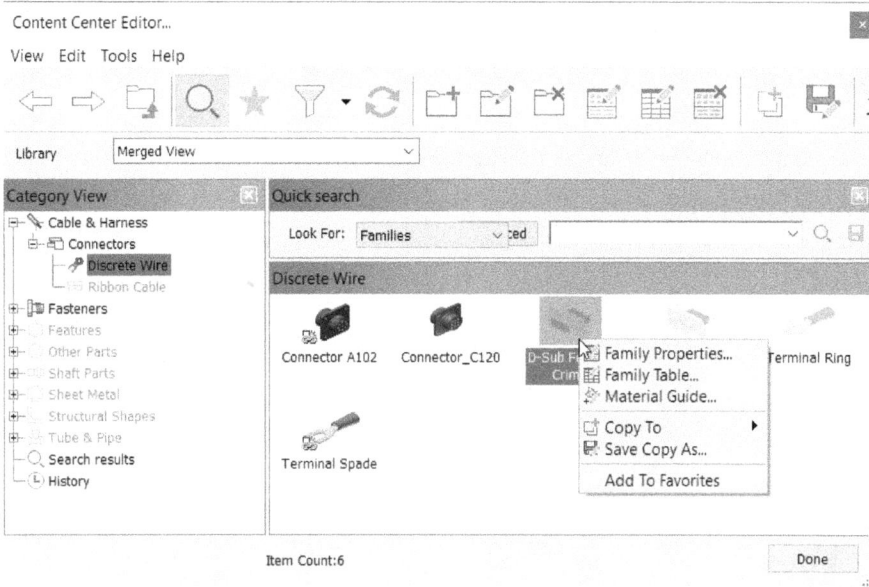

Access Family Table

You access the table of properties for a part family from within the Content Center Editor. After selecting the part family, you can select Family Table in the shortcut menu, toolbar, or Edit menu.

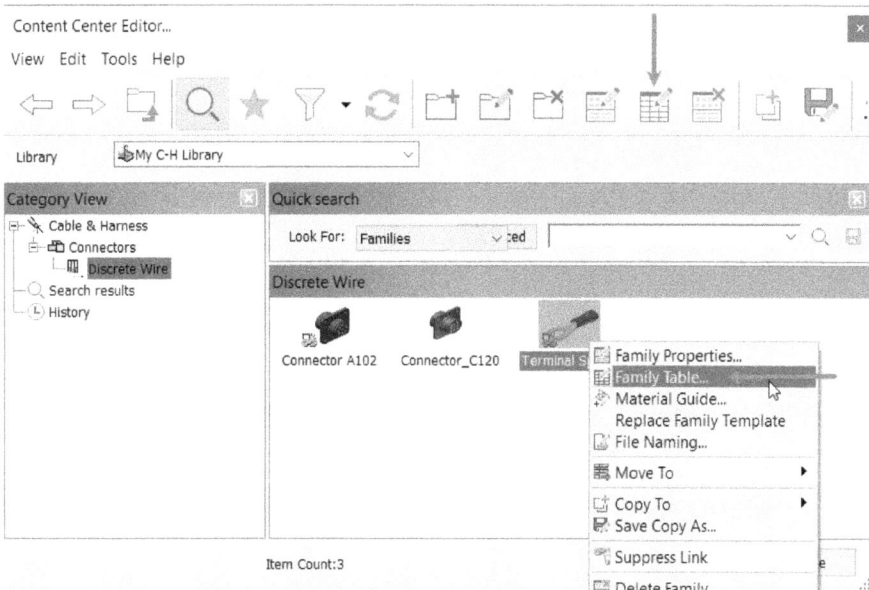

In the Family Table dialog box, you add part family members, add or remove property columns, select key columns, or change the properties for a family member.

Family Table:Terminal Spade

RowStatus	Member	Part Number [Pr...	Ring_S [in]	Ring_W [in]	Ring_C [in]	Ring_ID [in]
1	#6 Terminal Spade 22 - 18 AWG	#6 Terminal Spa...	0.146	0.316	0.303	0.062
2	#8 Terminal Spade 22 - 18 AWG	#8 Terminal Spa...	0.173	0.316	0.303	0.062
3	#10 Terminal Spade 22 - 18 AWG	#10 Terminal Sp...	0.198	0.316	0.303	0.062
4	#6 Terminal Spade 16 - 14 AWG	#6 Terminal Spa...	0.146	0.362	0.269	0.081
5	#8 Terminal Spade 16 - 14 AWG	#8 Terminal Spa...	0.173	0.362	0.269	0.081
6	#10 Terminal Spade 16 - 14 AWG	#10 Terminal Sp...	0.198	0.362	0.269	0.081
7	#6 Terminal Spade 12 - 10 AWG	#6 Terminal Spa...	0.146	0.375	0.301	0.128
8	#8 Terminal Spade 12 - 10 AWG	#8 Terminal Spa...	0.173	0.375	0.301	0.128
9	#10 Terminal Spade 12 - 10 AWG	#10 Terminal Sp...	0.198	0.375	0.301	0.128

Copying Content to a Custom Library

You copy existing content to a custom library in order to modify its properties to match your specific requirements, reduce the number of parts available in the Content Center, and to share the copied components with all designers.

In the following figure, on the left, a merged library view shows all of the available categories of content with the Discrete Wire category actively selected. The left view shows the Terminal Spade component family before it is being copied to the read/write library My_Custom_Library. After copying the component family and setting the library view to display only the content in My_Custom_Library, the content in the custom library displays as shown on the right.

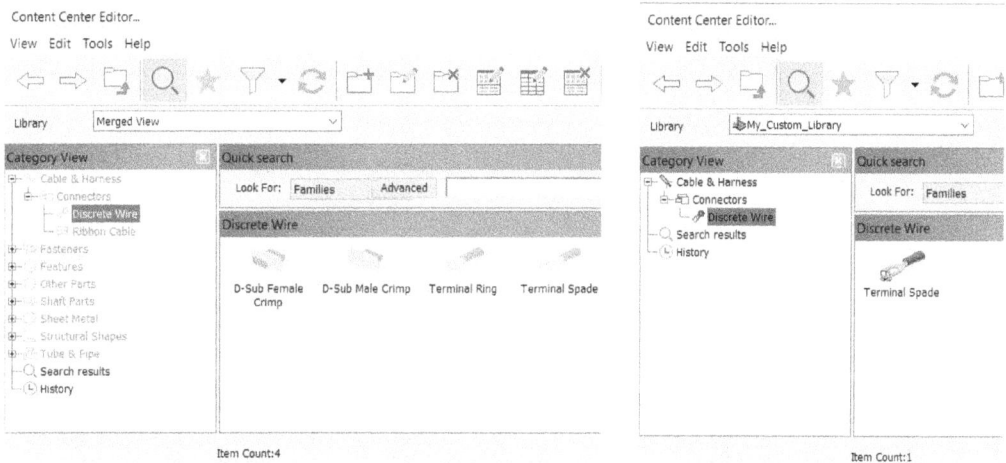

Merged View and Before Copying

Single Library View and After Copying

Copy To>Custom Library

You use the Copy To shortcut menu option to copy a single family, set of families, or a category from one library to a different read/write library. Access the Copy To option after you select the category or part family to copy. The available read/write libraries that you can copy the content to are then listed in the cascading menu from Copy To.

Procedure: Copying Content to a Custom Library

The following steps give an overview of copying a component family to a custom library.

1. Display the Content Center Editor.

2. In the Content Center Editor, right-click on the category or family you want to copy.

3. Click Copy To and select the custom library to copy to.

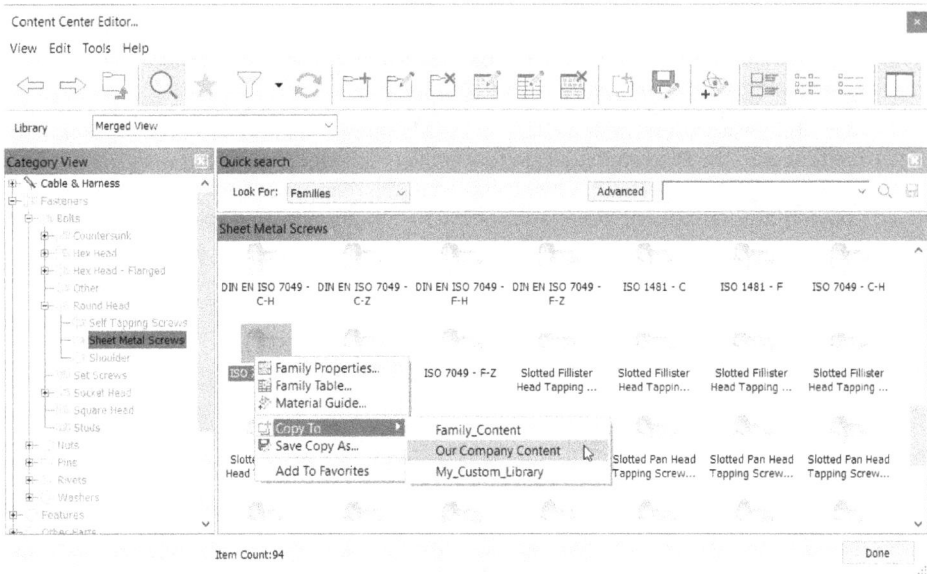

Stop Copying

When you select to copy content from one library to another, the amount of time it takes to copy depends on the amount of content selected to copy. You can stop the copying of content during the copy process by clicking Stop in the Copy To dialog box. When you click Stop, the copy process stops with just the content copied to that point in the target library. The content that was copied is complete and can be used within your digital prototypes.

In the following figure, the Fasteners category for Autodesk Inventor ISO library is selected to copy the entire category and its content to the custom library Family_Content.

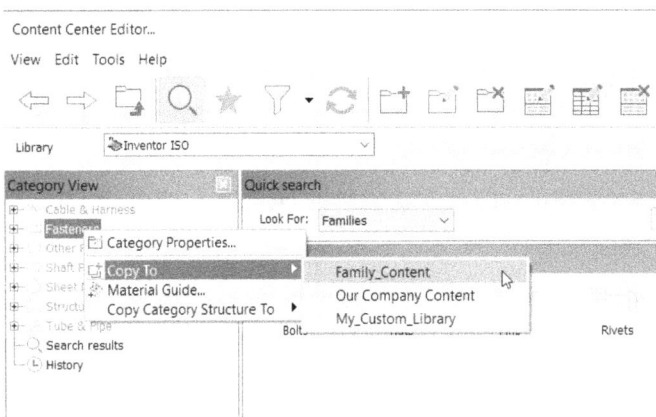

Clicking Stop after the copying process has already started, only the content that completed the copy process, before the stop option starts, is listed in the custom library.

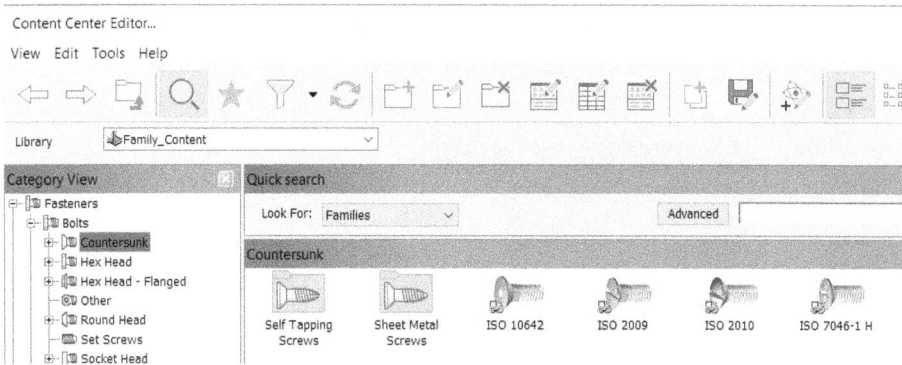

Suppress Link

Linked family content is created when you copy library content using Copy To or Save Copy As with the link option. For linked content, when the library is updated the copied family updates to be in sync with any changes made in the parent family. By suppressing the link, you keep the copied content from synchronizing with the parent when the libraries are updated. You can unsuppress the suppressed link at any time to enable the copied family to synchronize with the parent.

You access the Suppress Link and Unsuppress Link options in the shortcut menu after right-clicking on the content family in the Content Center Editor dialog box.

The following figure shows an example of the same content family with the different variations of its icon to illustrate the states of the family in a custom library.

Independent   Linked   Suppressed Linked
Content   Content   Content

Move Content

When you are configuring multiple custom read/write content libraries, if you have content in one library that should be in a different library, you can move a single family, set of families, or a category of families from one library to another. All aspects of the content is moved from one library to the other, including category and family properties and links to parent content.

To move content from one read/write library to another, you use the Move To shortcut menu option. You access Move To by right-clicking one or more selected families or categories in the Content Center Editor dialog box.

Exercise: Copy and Move Content

In this exercise, you will manage family content by copying content to a custom read/write library and move content from one read/write library to another.

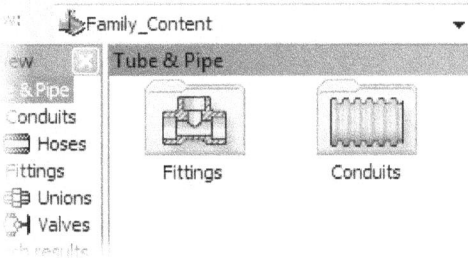

The completed exercise

Setup and Load Library

In this section of the exercise, you will set up the Autodesk Inventor software so that you can complete the exercise steps of moving and copying library content. You will load a custom library, set a project file as current, and create a new custom library.

1. Start the Autodesk Inventor software but do not open any files. Close any open files.

2. In the Get Started tab, in the Launch panel, click Projects.

3. In the Projects dialog box, click Configure Content Center Libraries.

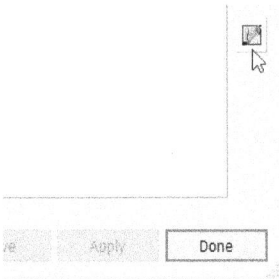

4. In the Configure Libraries dialog box:
   - Click the hyperlink text for Location of Libraries to open that folder.
   - Click Cancel.

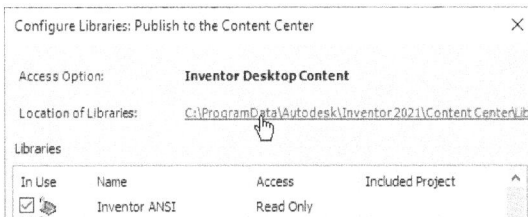

5. Open another session of Windows Explorer.

- Navigate to the install directory of the class files.
- Click to open the Libraries folder in the class files directory.

6. Copy *My_Custom_LIbrary.idcl* from the Library folder to the window opened by the hyperlink in a previous step.

7. Close the Window Explorer windows and exit the Configure Libraries dialog box.

8. To add this exercise's project file to the Autodesk Inventor software:

- In the Projects dialog box, click Browse.
- In the Choose Project File dialog box, navigate to the directory with the class files and open *Copy and Move Content.ipj*.

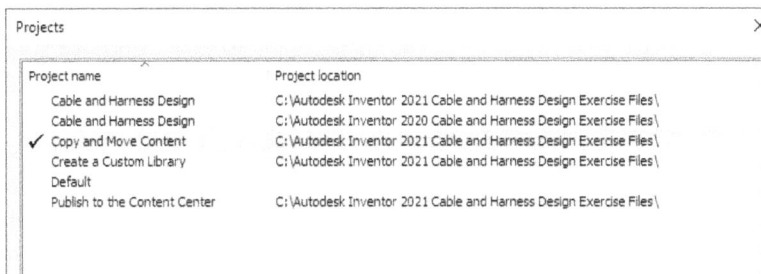

Projects	✕

Project name	Project location
Cable and Harness Design	C:\Autodesk Inventor 2021 Cable and Harness Design Exercise Files\
Cable and Harness Design	C:\Autodesk Inventor 2020 Cable and Harness Design Exercise Files\
✓ Copy and Move Content	C:\Autodesk Inventor 2021 Cable and Harness Design Exercise Files\
Create a Custom Library	C:\Autodesk Inventor 2021 Cable and Harness Design Exercise Files\
Default	
Publish to the Content Center	C:\Autodesk Inventor 2021 Cable and Harness Design Exercise Files\

9. In the Projects dialog box, click Configure Content Center Libraries.

10. In the Configure Libraries dialog box, review the list of libraries that are set to be in use when this project file is active.

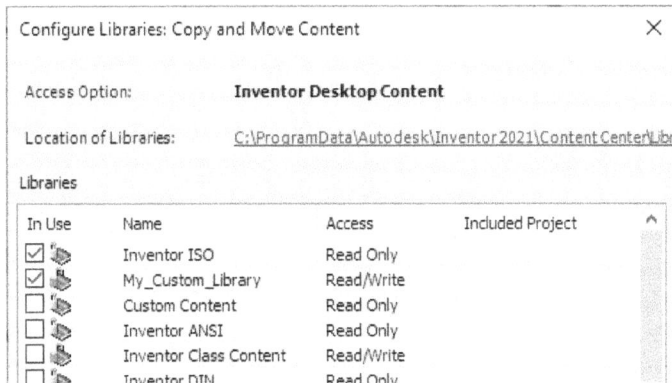

Configure Libraries: Copy and Move Content	✕

Access Option: **Inventor Desktop Content**

Location of Libraries: C:\ProgramData\Autodesk\Inventor 2021\Content Center\Libr

Libraries

In Use		Name	Access	Included Project	^
☑		Inventor ISO	Read Only		
☑		My_Custom_Library	Read/Write		
☐		Custom Content	Read Only		
☐		Inventor ANSI	Read Only		
☐		Inventor Class Content	Read/Write		
☐		Inventor DIN	Read Only		

Copy and Move Content

In this section of the exercise, you create a new custom library and then move and copy content from a different custom library into the newly created custom library.

1. To begin creating a new read/write library, in the Configure Libraries dialog box, click Create Library.

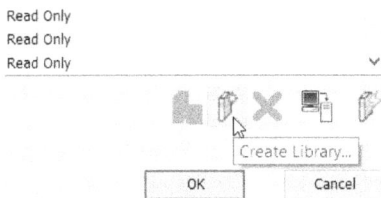

2. In the Create Library dialog box, for Display Name, enter **Family_Content**. Click OK.

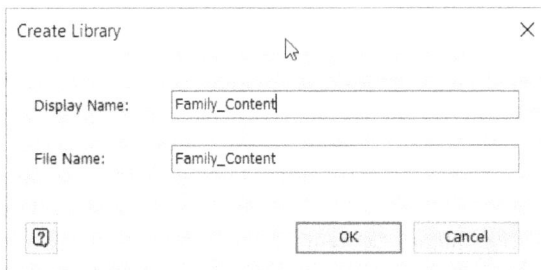

3. In the Configure Libraries dialog box:

    - Review the list of libraries that are in use within this project.
    - Click OK.

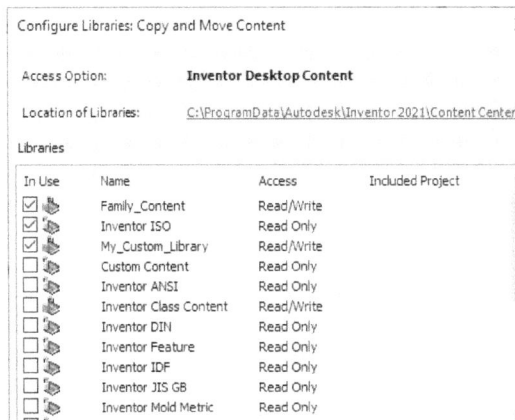

4. In the Projects dialog box, click Save. Click Done.

5. To access the Content Center editor, in the Tools tab, in the Content Center panel, click Editor.

---

6. To specify the source library, in the Content Center Editor dialog box, in the Library View list, select My_Custom_Library.

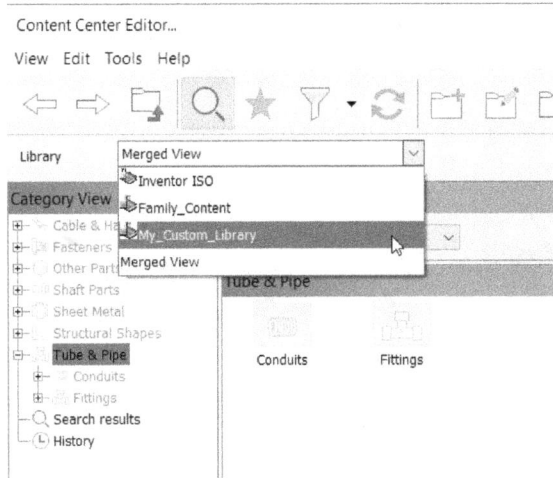

7. To move a category of data from this library to another library:

- In the Category pane, select Tube and Pipe.
- In the Tube & Pipe pane, right-click on Fittings. Click Move To>Family_Content.

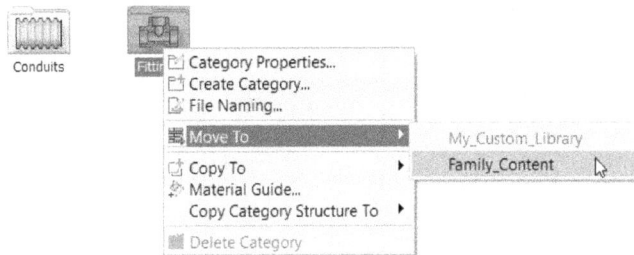

8. In the Library View list, select Family_Content. Note the Fittings category.

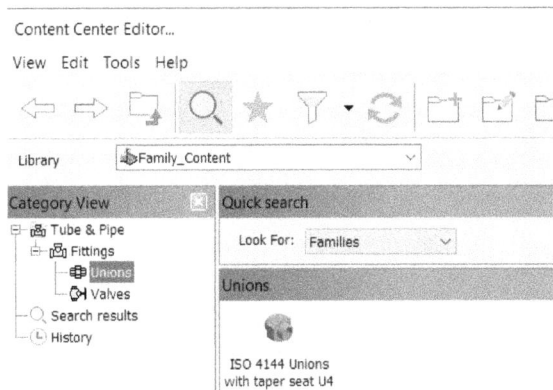

9. In the Library View list, select My_Custom_Library.

10. To copy content from one library to another:
    - In the Category pane, select Tube and Pipe.
    - In the Tube & Pipe pane, right-click on Conduits. Click Copy To>Family_Content.

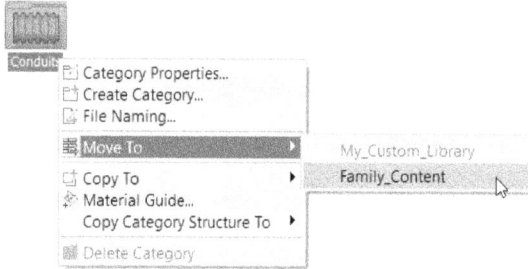

11. Set the Library View to Family_Content. Review the listed content in the library.

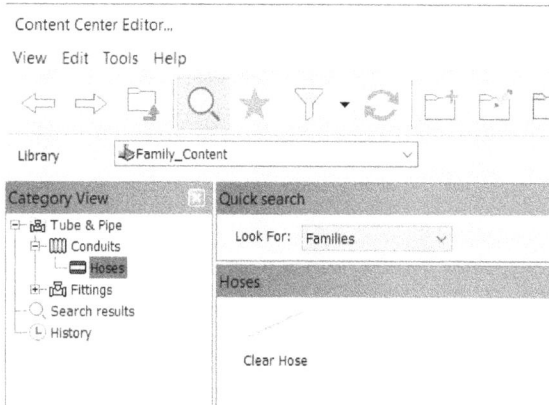

12. Close the Content Center Editor.

    Note: To restore your system, navigate to the folder that contains your Content Center libraries, and delete *My_Custom_LIbrary.idcl* and *Family_Content.idcl*.

Document Settings for Published Parts

Parts published to the Content Center not only contain the 3D geometry for the parts, the published parts also contain information that describes, identifies, and defines the parts. Some of that published information includes the values for the parts' document settings. To ensure that your published content has the document settings you require, you need to understand how published Content Center parts have their document setting values set.

BOM Document Settings

When you publish a custom part to a Content Center library, the template that is created contains the same document settings as the part file that was used as the basis of the publication. While some properties for the part family like Name and Description can be modified in the Content Center Editor, other properties are set within the template at the time the part was published to the Content Center.

Bill of material document setting values are some of the document properties that are set in the template only during the time of publication. The bill of material values that are set in the document settings include the values for:

- Default BOM Structure
- Base Quantity
- Base Unit

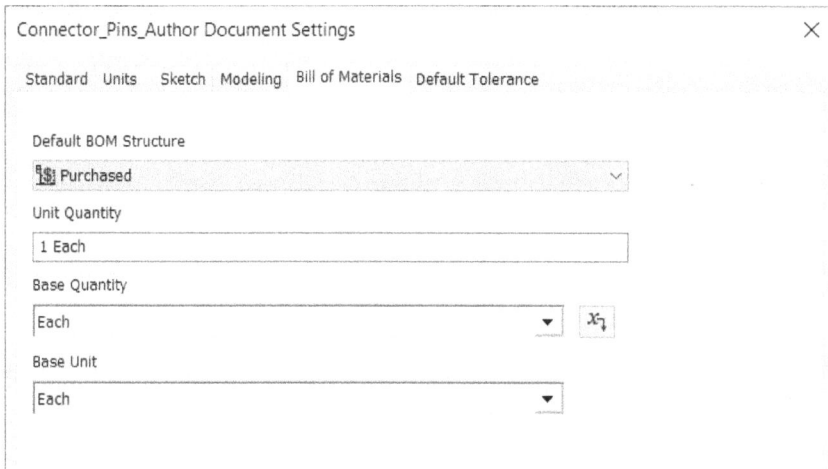

Replace Family Template Option

You can change the document settings for parts already published to the Content Center by replacing the family template with a modified part.

The Replace Family Template option is a shortcut menu option available in the Content Center Editor. To access this option, you right-click on the family part after selecting the corresponding read/write library in the Library View list.

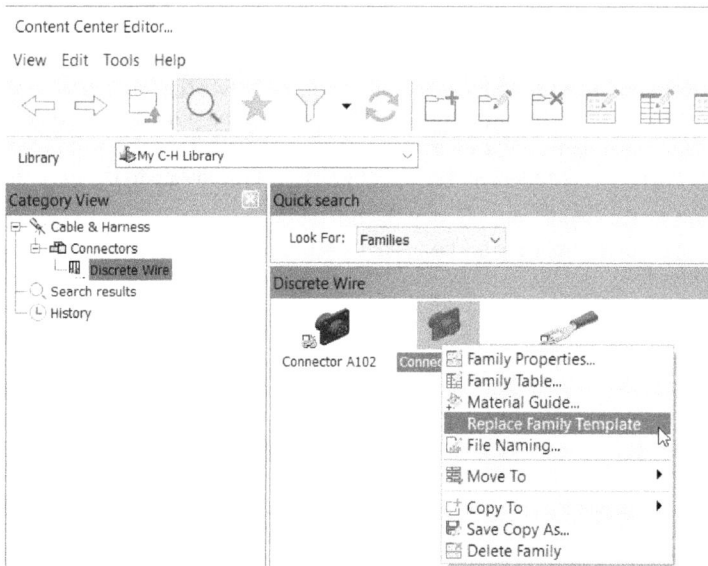

To obtain a version of the library part that you can modify and use to republish, use Open from Content Center from the application menu and save the part to a folder not located within the library path. With the part saved outside the library path, you can make and save your required changes. After saving the changes, you select the modified part after selecting the Replace Family Template shortcut menu option.

> Changes made to the part family template in the Content Center do not automatically update library parts that are being referenced in assemblies. To have the assemblies reference a part that contains the new document values, the library part saved on your computer or the server must be overwritten by a new version of the part. Use Refresh Standard Components from the Content Center panel in the Manage tab to overwrite existing standard part files with new versions in the Content Center.

Adding and Editing Family Column Values

A key aspect of any part is the additional information available about that part. For Autodesk Inventor files, this additional part information is stored in the file's property fields.

The individual library family members can have unique property information for different iterations of the part, the file property values for a library part must be written at the time that the part is instanced into an assembly. To have these property values automatically reflect your company requirements, you must add and edit the columns of values for a library part family so that they map to an Autodesk Inventor property.

In the following figure, the project properties for this library part are automatically entered based on the values for that content family member, as assigned in the Content Center Editor. With the value set correctly for the family member, every time the part is added to an assembly by any user, the correct values are automatically entered. These values can then be listed in the parts list or exported for use by other applications.

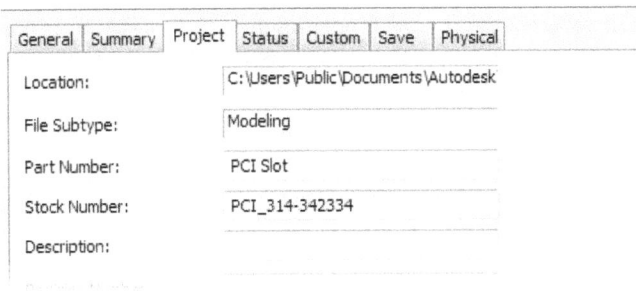

General	Summary	Project	Status	Custom	Save	Physical

Location:	C:\Users\Public\Documents\Autodesk
File Subtype:	Modeling
Part Number:	PCI Slot
Stock Number:	PCI_314-342334
Description:	

Access to Add or Edit Columns

In the Family Table dialog box, you can add columns by right-clicking the row for the column headers and then selecting Add Column, or by clicking Add Column in the toolbar. By clicking a column header before selecting Add Column, the new column is added directly after the selected column.

To open the Column Properties dialog box to edit the properties of an existing column, you can double-click on the column header, right-click on the column header, and then click Column Properties. You can also select the column header and click Column Properties in the toolbar.

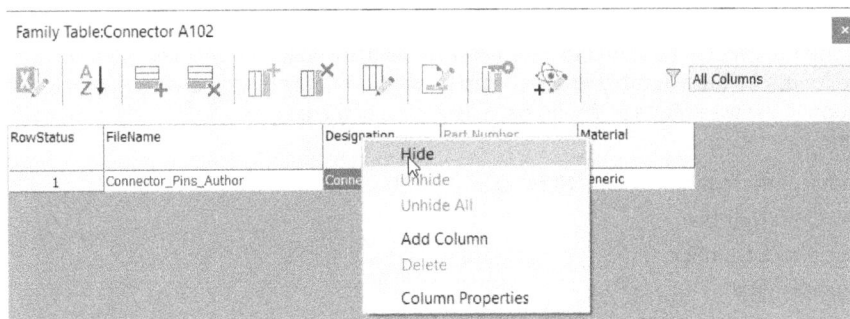

Family Table:Connector A102

RowStatus	FileName	Designation	Part Number	Material
1	Connector_Pins_Author	Conne		eneric

Hide
Unhide
Unhide All
Add Column
Delete
Column Properties

Column Properties

Select Add Column or Column Properties to open the Column Properties dialog box, enabling you to enter properties for the column and column fields.

When you are adding a new column, the Column Name field is an empty editable field. After the column has been created, this field is a read-only field. Within the Column Properties dialog box, you set values for the type of data being stored in the cells of that column. You also set units if applicable for the data type, the heading caption for the column, an expression that can reference values from other columns, and mapping for the property value to a predefined or custom file property.

Depending on the data types of the columns, an expression can be a mathematical formula that calculates a new value, or it can concatenate values into a single string. To reference the value in a different column, you can enter the column name in all capitals encased in brackets ({ }), or by clicking the Browse button to the right of the expression field and selecting the column name from the list. If you are entering the column name manually, remember to enter the column name and not the column caption.

When you add or change an expression in the Column Properties dialog box, all of the cells in that column are automatically edited to have the same value or expression. You can also enter values and expressions directly into the individual cells.

Column Properties

Column Name:

Co_StockNo

Data Type:

String

Column Caption:

Company Stock Number

Units:

☑ Expression

◉ Expression Column   ○ Custom Column

XYZ-315_{DESIGNATION}   [...]

Map To Inventor Property:

Project.Stock Number

By mapping the value of a column to a file property field, the value for that family member is then available for use by the assembly where the part is instanced. For example, it can be included as information in the assembly's BOM and parts list. Some of the property fields include but are not limited to:

- Summary Information.Revision Number
- Project.Part Number
- Project.Stock Number
- Project.Material
- Project.Size Description

If you want to map a column value to a file property and an appropriate property does not currently exist, you select Custom from the list and then enter a new custom property name. This property is then automatically added to the part template as a custom property.

Parameters with a Range

Parameter values can be set by the individual family member, or you can configure the family members to allow for an entered value. You configure a parameter to accept a range of values by selecting the Expression option of Custom Column and then specifying the range criteria. When you specify a family table column to accept a range of values, when the part is being placed in an assembly, you have a value field to enter a value.

In the following figure, because the custom part was configured with a range of values for the Length table column parameter, a value must be entered during placement of the part.

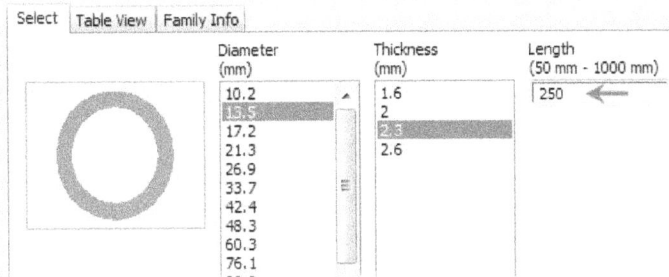

To configure a table column family to be a range of values, right-click on the column label and click Column Properties. In the Column Properties dialog box, select the Expression check box and then click Custom Column. Click the More button to open the Specify Range dialog box. In the Specify Range dialog box, specify the required criteria for the value.

In the following figure, the Length column is set to a default value of 250. The value must be greater than 50 but not more than 1000.

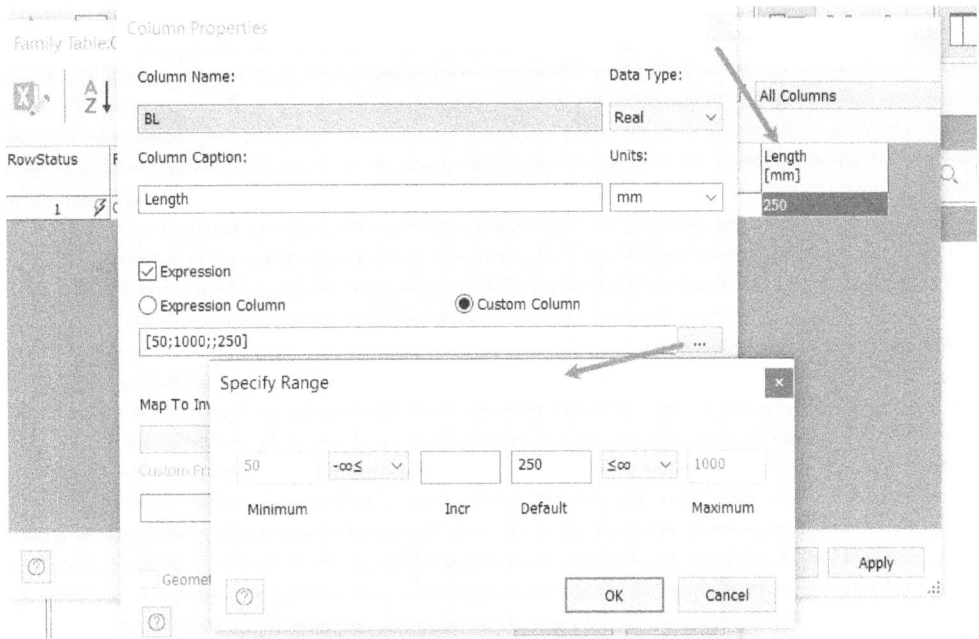

Process: Adding and Editing Column Values

The following figure shows an overview of adding and editing column values for a library part family.

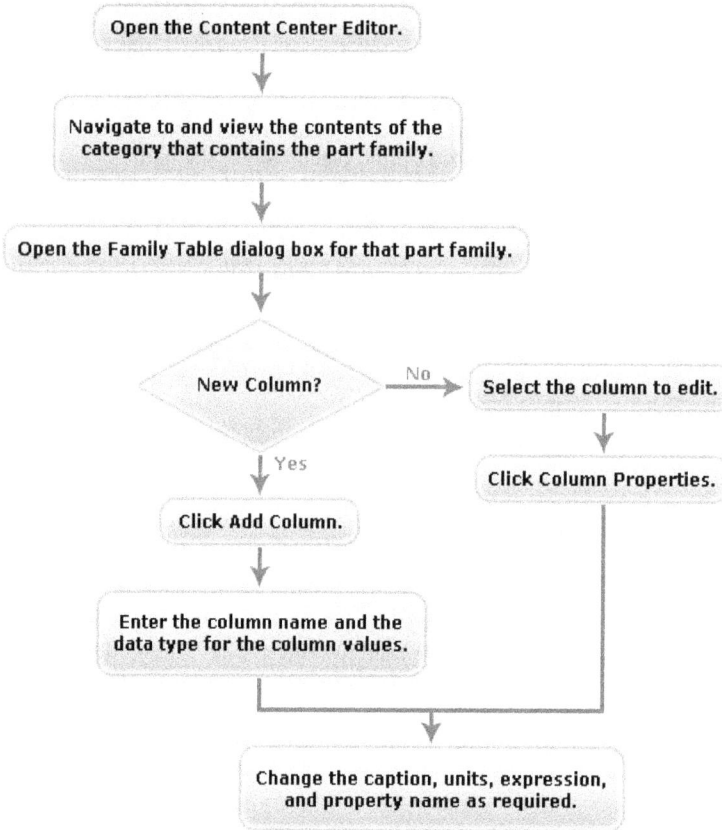

```
        Open the Content Center Editor.
                     |
                     v
      Navigate to and view the contents of the
       category that contains the part family.
                     |
                     v
   Open the Family Table dialog box for that part family.
                     |
                     v
              New Column?  --No-->  Select the column to edit.
                     |                       |
                    Yes                      v
                     |              Click Column Properties.
                     v                       |
            Click Add Column.                |
                     |                       |
                     v                       |
         Enter the column name and the       |
        data type for the column values.     |
                     |                       |
                     +-----------+-----------+
                                 |
                                 v
                  Change the caption, units, expression,
                       and property name as required.
```

Adding a Custom Display Name

After you publish a part to the Content Center, you can edit the table in the Content Center Editor. You can edit values, add or delete members, or add additional columns and map their values to Autodesk Inventor iProperties.

One typical change is to customize the Browser display name for parts generated from the family. When you place a fitting from the Content Center, the name displayed in the Browser is a concatenation of the family name and the designation. To use another display name, you can either edit the values or expression for the Designation column, or create a new column in the Content Center table and map the new column to Autodesk Inventor Display Name property.

In the following figure, two different members from the same Content Center library family have been added to the design. The browser names were automatically set based on the configuration in the Content Center. The primary difference between these two occurrences is the number of pins they are configured for as identified by the browser name and number of visible pin connections.

Procedure: Adding a Custom Display Name

You can edit a published part to add additional columns and map those columns to Autodesk Inventor properties. The following steps outline how to add a custom display name for library parts.

1. Start the Content Center Editor.

2. Display the family table for the member you want to edit.

3. Add a new column.

4. In the Column Properties dialog box, enter values for Column Name (no spaces) and Column Caption.

5. Select the Expression check box. For Expression, enter an expression using fixed text and selected parameters. To add a parameter to the expression, click the Browse button to the right of the Expression box.

6. In Map to Inventor Properties, select Member.Display Name.

7. Apply the Family Table changes and then exit the Content Center Editor.

The following figure shows sections of the Family Table and the Column Properties dialog boxes. The Column Properties dialog box is showing the configuration of the custom column Display Name. The results of this column configuration can be seen in the Family Table dialog box. Note that the Display Name column is a concatenation of a fixed string and the contents of the Designation column.

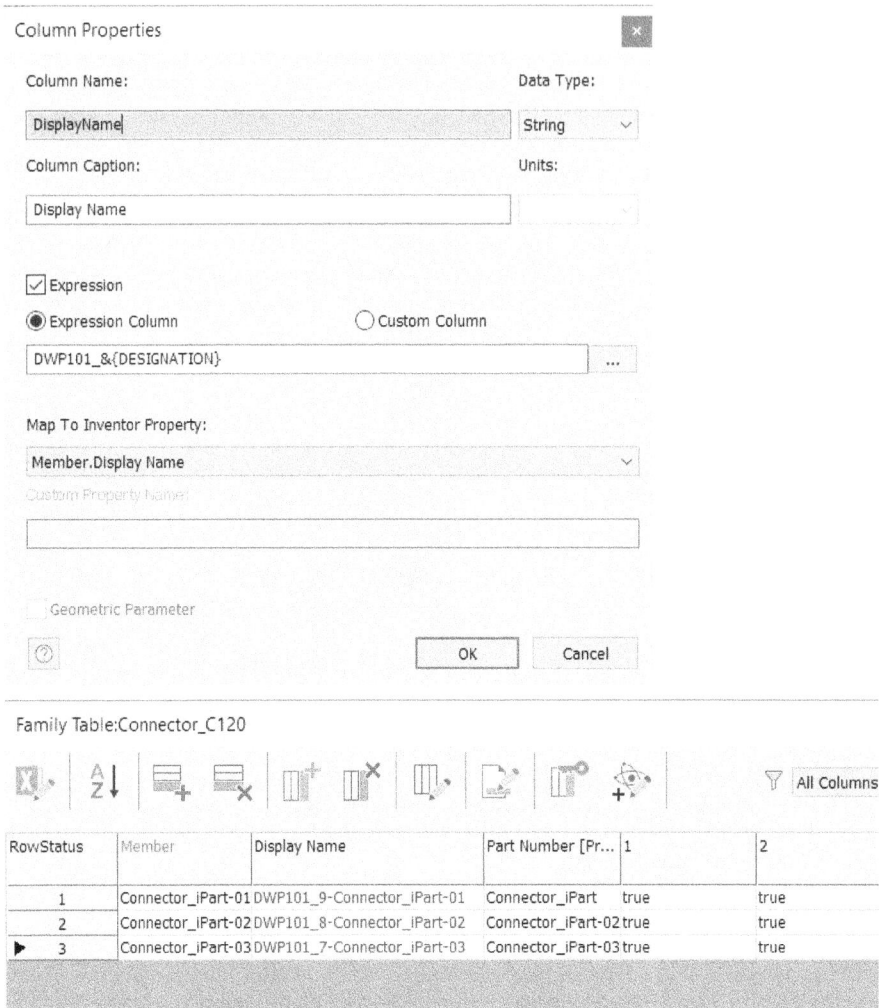

Column Properties   [×]

Column Name: Data Type:

DisplayName   String   ∨

Column Caption: Units:

Display Name

☑ Expression

● Expression Column   ○ Custom Column

DWP101_&{DESIGNATION}   ...

Map To Inventor Property:

Member.Display Name   ∨

Custom Property Name:

☐ Geometric Parameter

⊘   [OK]   [Cancel]

Family Table:Connector_C120

RowStatus	Member	Display Name	Part Number [Pr...	1	2
1	Connector_iPart-01	DWP101_9-Connector_iPart-01	Connector_iPart	true	true
2	Connector_iPart-02	DWP101_8-Connector_iPart-02	Connector_iPart-02	true	true
▶ 3	Connector_iPart-03	DWP101_7-Connector_iPart-03	Connector_iPart-03	true	true

Exercise: Add a Column to a Part Family

In this exercise, you will add a custom property column to a part family and assign its value to the Part Name file property field.

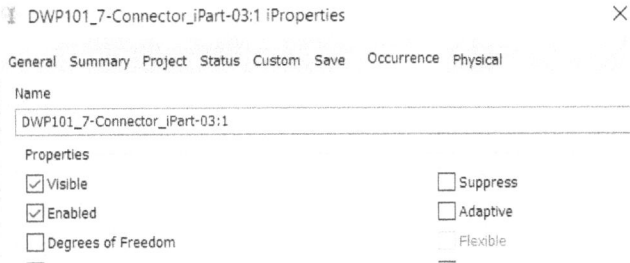

The completed exercise

Setup and Load Library

In this section of the exercise, you will copy a custom Desktop Content library to the correct folder location so the project file you will set active can use the custom library.

1. Start the Autodesk Inventor software but do not open any files. Close any open files.

2. In the Get Started tab, in the Launch panel, click Projects.

3. In the Projects dialog box, click Configure Content Center Libraries.

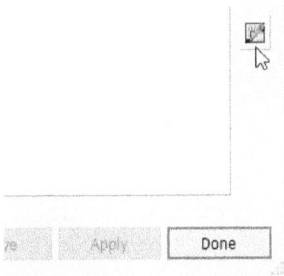

4. In the Configure Libraries dialog box, click the hyperlink text for Location of Libraries to open a Windows Explorer window viewing that folder.

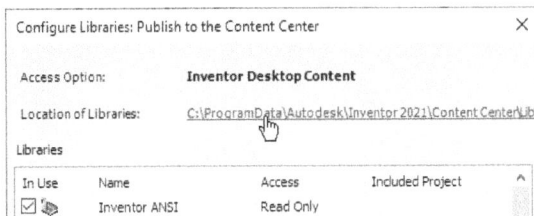

5. Open another session of Windows Explorer.
   - Navigate to the install directory of the exercise files.
   - Click to open the Libraries folder in the exercise directory.

6. Copy *My C-H Library.idcl* from the Library folder to the window opened by the hyperlink in a previous step.

7. Close the Windows Explorer windows and exit the Configure Libraries dialog box.

8. To add this exercise's project file to the Autodesk Inventor software:
   - In the Projects dialog box, click Browse.
   - In the Choose Project File dialog box, navigate to the directory with the class files and open *Add a Column to a Part Family.ipj*.

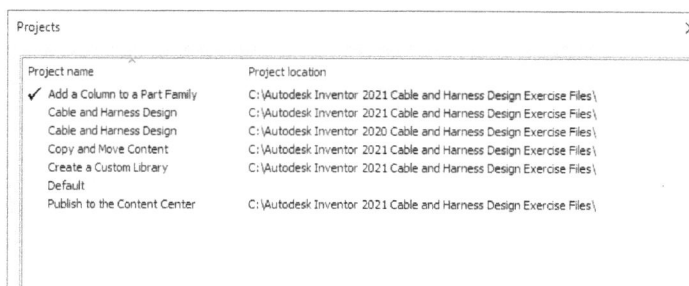

9. In the Projects dialog box, click Configure Content Center Libraries.

10. In the Configure Libraries dialog box, review the list of libraries that are set to be in use when this project file is active. Enable the My C-H Library if not already set.

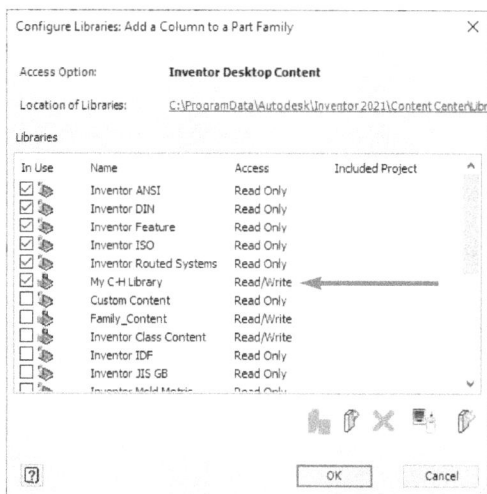

11. Close the Configure Libraries dialog box and save and close the Projects dialog box.

Add a Column to a Part Family

In this section of the exercise, you will add and configure a custom column to a Content Center library part and place an occurrence of that part into an assembly to review its use.

1. Start a new assembly file.

2. In the Manage tab, in the Content Center panel, click Editor.

3. To access the family table information for Connector_C120:

- In the Library View list, select My C-H Library.
- In the Category View pane, under Cable & Harness, under Connectors, click Discrete Wire.
- In the family pane for Discrete Wire, right-click on Connector_C120 and click Family Table.

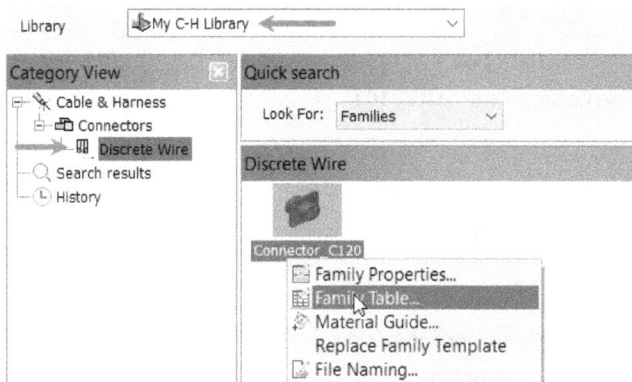

4. To begin adding a new custom column after the Member column:

- Click the Member column header.
- Right-click on the heading and click Add Column.

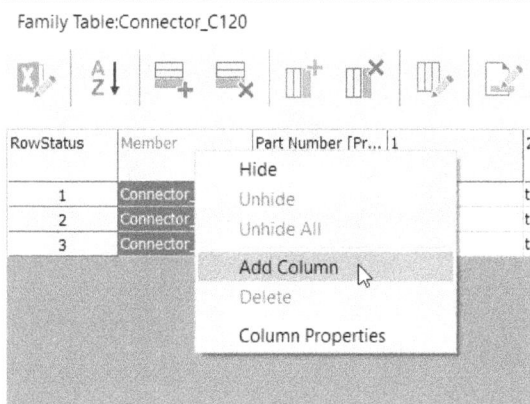

5. In the Column Properties dialog box:
   - For Column Name, enter **DisplayName**.
   - For Column Caption, enter **Display Name**.

Column Properties			×
Column Name:		Data Type:	
DisplayName		String ⌄	
Column Caption:		Units:	
Display Name|			

6. To begin setting the values in the column:
   - Select the Expression check box.
   - Under Expression Column, enter **DWP101_**.

☑ Expression

◉ Expression Column   ○ Custom (

DWP101_|

Man To Inventor Property:

7. To have the current value in another column display in the expression:
   - Click the Browse button to the right of the expression field.
   - In the Parameter Name column, double-click on DESIGNATION.

...	̰d	
Parameter Name	Parameter Descri...	
Member	Member	
PARTNUMBER	Part Number [Pro...	
1	1	
2	2	
3	3	
4	4	
5	5	
6	6	
7	7	
8	8	
9	9	
# of Pins	# of Pins	
FILENAME	FILENAME	
MATERIAL	MATERIAL	
DESIGNATION	DESIGNATION	

8. In the Map to Inventor Property list, select Member.Display Name.

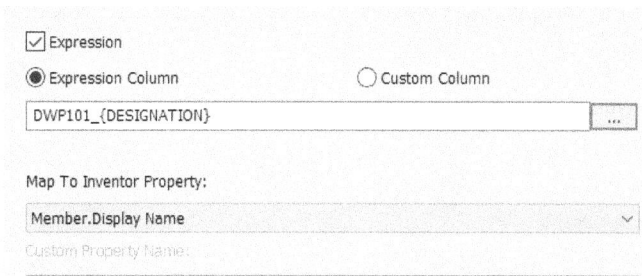

☑ Expression
⦿ Expression Column   ◯ Custom Column

DWP101_{DESIGNATION}   [...]

Map To Inventor Property:

Member.Display Name   ⌄

Custom Property Name:

9. Click OK. The Family Table dialog box now displays the custom column.

Family Table:Connector_C120

RowStatus	Member	Display Name	Part Number [Pr...	1	2
1	Connector_iPart-01	DWP101_9-Connector_iPart-01	Connector_iPart	true	true
2	Connector_iPart-02	DWP101_8-Connector_iPart-02	Connector_iPart-02	true	true
▶ 3	Connector_iPart-03	DWP101_7-Connector_iPart-03	Connector_iPart-03	true	true

10. To complete the change:

- In the Family Table dialog box, click OK to close the dialog box and write the information to the Content Center for this part family.
- Click OK when informed the information was published successfully.
- Click Done to close the Content Center Editor.

11. To begin adding a connector to the assembly:

- In the Assemble tab, in the Component panel, open the Place drop-down list, and click Place from Content Center.
- In the Category View list, under Cable & Harness, under Connectors, click Discrete Wire.
- In the family pane, double-click on Connector_C120.

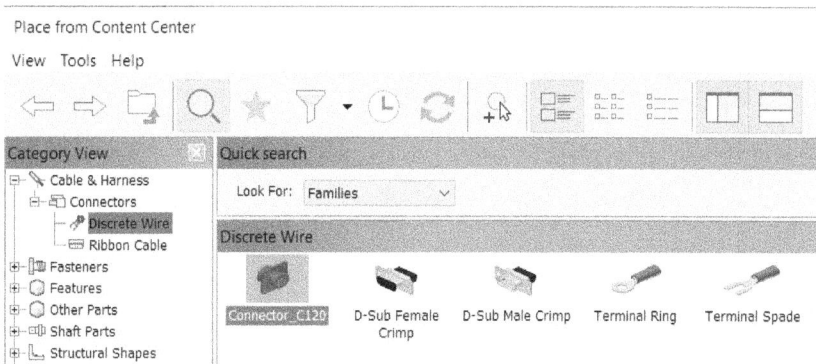

Place from Content Center

View Tools Help

Category View
- Cable & Harness
  - Connectors
    - **Discrete Wire**
    - Ribbon Cable
- Fasteners
- Features
- Other Parts
- Shaft Parts
- Structural Shapes

Quick search

Look For: Families ⌄

Discrete Wire

Connector_C120   D-Sub Female Crimp   D-Sub Male Crimp   Terminal Ring   Terminal Spade

12. To add an instance of the connector:

- In the part family dialog box, # of Pins list, select 7. Select "As Custom" at the bottom and click OK.

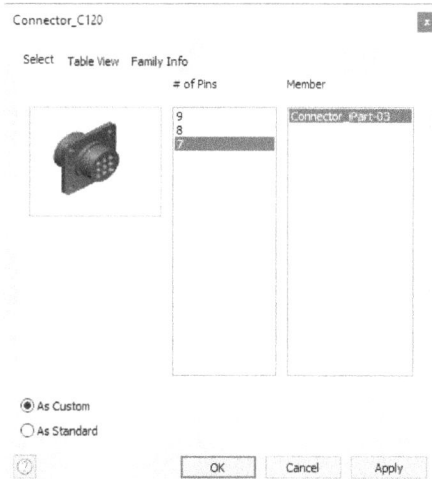

- In Save As Window, click Save.

13. To place an instance of the part in the graphics window, right click and select Place Grounded at the origin. Press ESC. Rotate the connector as required to view the connection points.

14. In the Browser or graphics window, right-click on the Connector and click iProperties.

15. To observe the results of the added column:
    - In the iProperties dialog box, in the Occurrence tab, review the Part Name value for the placed instance of the connector.
    - Review the displayed part file name in the Browser.
    - Note that both names match the added column from the part family.
    - Click Close.

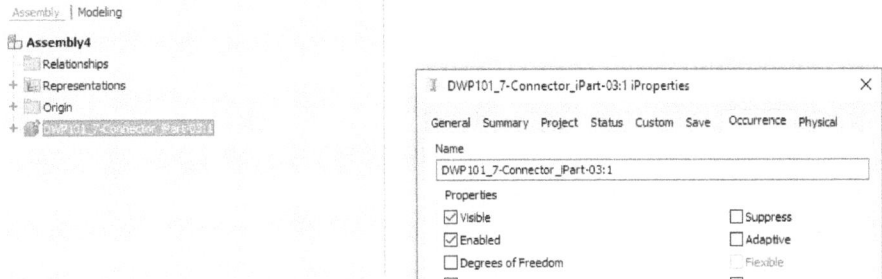

16. Close all files without saving changes.

Editing Family Table Data in Excel

If you are modifying a lot of data for a family of content in Content Center, you might find some of the edits you need to make are quicker to make in Microsoft Excel. To make changes to the data in a family table, you need to know the process for sending the data to Microsoft Excel and having the changes you make in Excel written back to the Family Table in Content Center.

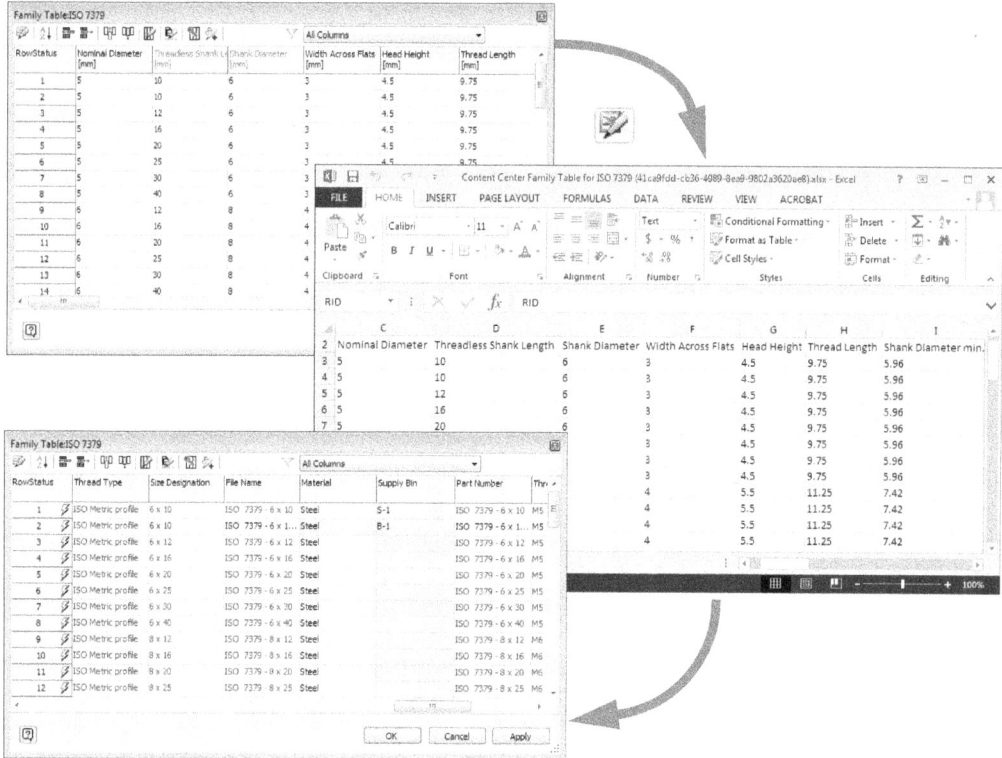

Edit in Microsoft Excel

When you edit the contents of a family table in Microsoft Excel, you extend your options and capabilities for editing the properties of members within the selected family. You can use tools in Microsoft Excel to add rows and columns, rearrange rows and columns, change cell values, quickly fill cell values, and find and replace values. You can use macros that you create in your template spreadsheet to make common or more complex changes.

Keep the following points in mind as you edit the values and properties of family members in Microsoft Excel.

- Do not edit or delete hidden row 1 or hidden columns A and B.
- You can add columns in the spreadsheet. Do not add entirely blank rows or columns in the table area because that will remove a column from the table when going back to the Family Table dialog box.

- Duplicate column names have a suffix number added to keep the names unique.
- You can add rows and enter values for new family members.
- You can delete rows and columns of values. Key columns and columns used in expressions do not get deleted from the table.
- To use a common spreadsheet template whenever you edit family table data in Microsoft Excel, create a template file with the name CC Family Edit Template.xlt (.xltx, or .xltm) in the correct location. Locations: (for Windows XP) %INSTALLDIR%\Autodesk\Inventor <VERSION>\Design Data, or (for Windows Vista and Windows 7) %PUBLICDOCUMENTS%\Autodesk\Inventor <VERSION>\Design Data.

Access

To open the contents of a family table so you can edit its member properties in Microsoft Excel, you must first display the Family Table dialog box for that content family. From within the Family Table dialog box, you click Edit Via Spreadsheet.

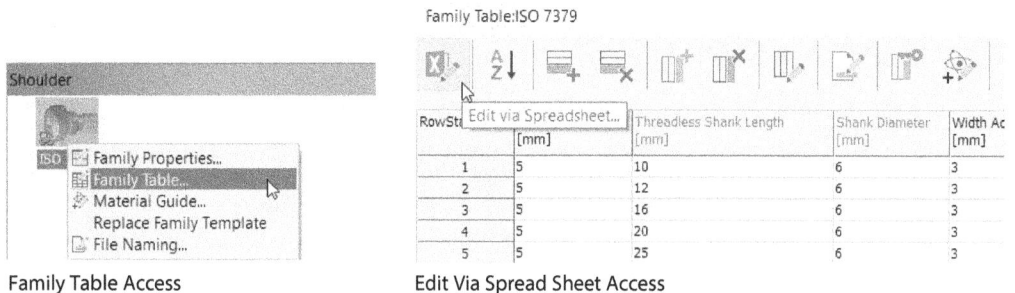

Family Table:ISO 7379

RowSt	Edit via Spreadsheet...	Threadless Shank Length [mm]	Shank Diameter [mm]	Width Ac [mm]
1	5	10	6	3
2	5	12	6	3
3	5	16	6	3
4	5	20	6	3
5	5	25	6	3

Shoulder

ISO Family Properties...
Family Table...
Material Guide...
Replace Family Template
File Naming...

Family Table Access

Edit Via Spread Sheet Access

Process: Editing Family Table Data in Excel

The following steps give an overview of editing family table data in Microsoft Excel.

1. In the Content Center Editor, select to open the Family Table for the family of content you want to edit.

2. In the Family Table dialog box, click Edit via Spreadsheet.

3. In Microsoft Excel make the changes you require.

4. Save your changes and then close Microsoft Excel to have the changes written back to the Family Table dialog box.

Exercise: Edit Family Data in Excel

In this exercise, you will create a read/write library and copy data to it. You will then edit the data using Excel.

File Name	Material	Supply Bin	Part Number
ISO 7379 - 6 x 10	Steel	S-1	ISO 7379 - 6
ISO 7379 - 6 x 10-B	Steel	B-1	ISO 7379 - 6
ISO 7379 - 6 x 12	Steel		ISO 7379 - 6
ISO 7379 - 6 x 16	Steel		ISO 7379 - 6
ISO 7379 - 6 x 20	Steel		ISO 7379 - 6
ISO 7379 - 6 x 25	Steel		ISO 7379 - 6
ISO 7379 - 6 x 30	Steel		ISO 7379 - 6

The completed exercise

Create a Read/Write Library

In this section of the exercise, you will create a read/write library table.

1. Start the Autodesk Inventor software but do not open any files. Close any open files.

2. In the Get Started tab, in the Launch panel, click Projects.

3. To add this exercise's project file to the Autodesk Inventor software:

    -   In the Projects dialog box, click Browse.
    -   In the Choose Project File dialog box, navigate to the directory with the class files and open *Edit Family Data in Excel.ipj*.

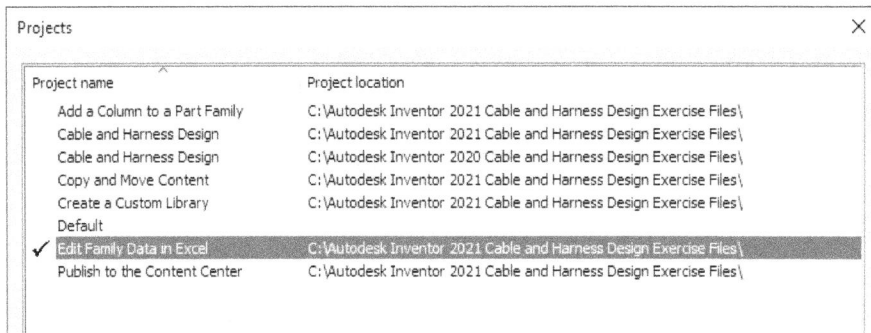

4. To begin to create a new read/write library:

- In the Projects dialog box, click Configure Content Center Libraries.
- In the Configure Libraries: Default dialog box, click Create Library.

5. In the Create Library dialog box, for Display Name, enter **Custom_Fastener**. Click OK.

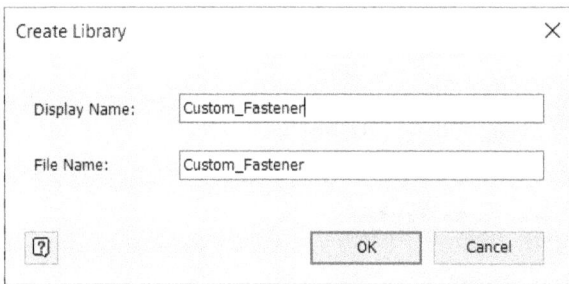

6. Verify that the custom Read/Write library is In Use. Click OK.

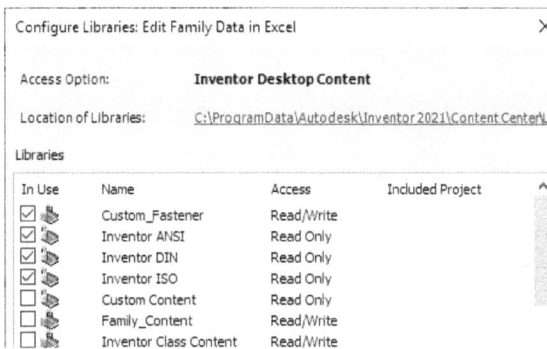

7. In the Projects dialog box, click Save. Click Done.

Edit Family Data in Excel

In the section of the exercise, you will edit a custom read/write table in Excel and review the changes in the family table.

1. To start the Content Center Editor:
   - In the Tools tab, in the Content Center panel, click Editor.

2. To locate a family:
   - In the Content Center editor dialog box, in Category View, expand Fasteners.
   - Expand Bolts.
   - Expand Socket Head.
   - Select Shoulder.

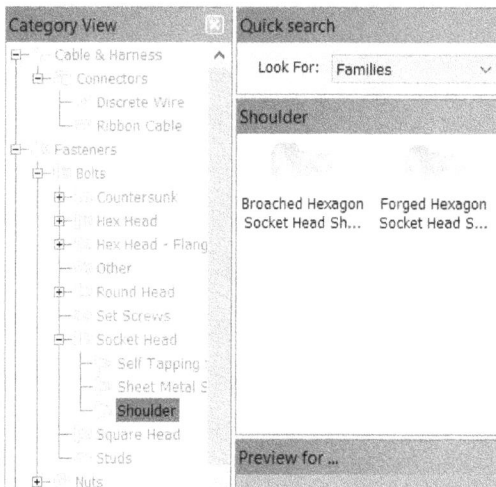

3. To copy a family:
   - In the Shoulder pane, right-click on ISO 7379.
   - Click Copy To>Custom_Fastener.

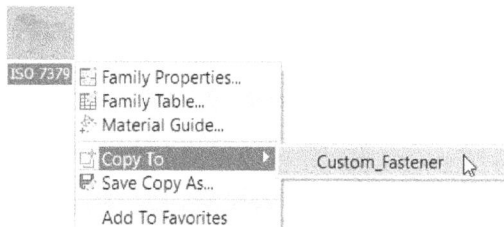

4. Change the Library View to Custom_Fastener.

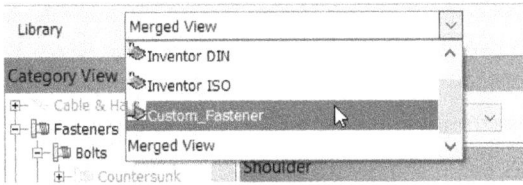

5. To begin to edit the family table:

- In the Shoulder pane, right-click on ISO 7379.
- Click Family Table.

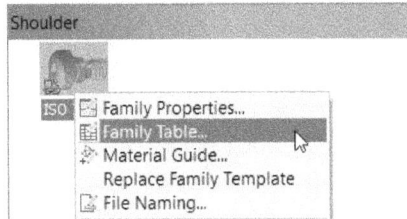

6. To edit the table in Microsoft Excel, in the Family Table:ISO 7379 table, click Edit via Spreadsheet.

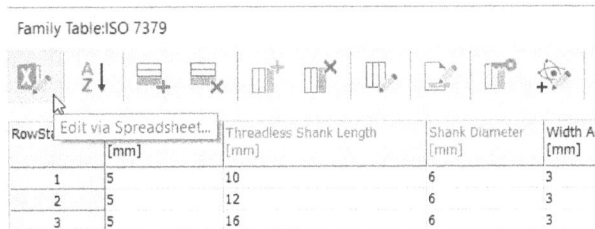

7. To begin to add a row:

- Right-click on row 3.
- Click Copy.

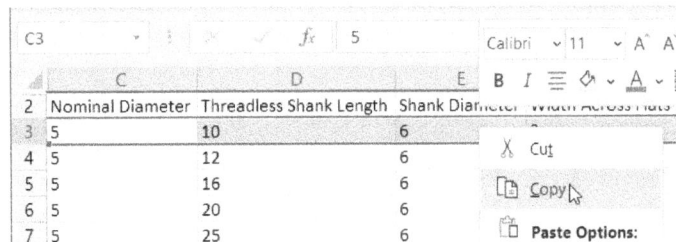

8. To insert the copied row:

  - Right-click on row 3.
  - Click Insert Copied Cells.
  - The row is inserted and highlighted.

3	5			10		6	3	4.5
4	✕ Cut					6	3	4.5
5						6	3	4.5
6	⬚ Copy					6	3	4.5
7	⬚ **Paste Options:**					6	3	4.5
8						6	3	4.5
9	⬚ ⬚ ⬚ ⬚ ⬚ ⬚					6	3	4.5
10						8	4	5.5
11	Paste Special...	>				8	4	5.5
12	Insert Copied Cells					8	4	5.5
13						8	4	5.5
14	Delete					8	4	5.5

9. To Edit the new row:

  - Use the slider bar to display columns AI through AK for row 4.
  - For the File Name and Part Number columns in row 4, edit each cell to add the suffix **-B** to the values.

AI	AJ	AK
File Name	Material	Part Number
ISO 7379 - 6 x 10	Steel	ISO 7379 - 6 x 10
ISO 7379 - 6 x 10-B	Steel	ISO 7379 - 6 x 10-B
ISO 7379 - 6 x 12	Steel	ISO 7379 - 6 x 12
ISO 7379 - 6 x 16	Steel	ISO 7379 - 6 x 16

10. To add a column:

  - Right-click on column heading AJ.
  - Click Insert.

AI	AJ	AK	
File Name	Material	✕ Cut	read d
ISO 7379 - 6 x 10	Steel		5
ISO 7379 - 6 x 10-B	Steel	⬚ Copy	5
ISO 7379 - 6 x 12	Steel		5
ISO 7379 - 6 x 16	Steel	⬚ **Paste Options:**	5
ISO 7379 - 6 x 20	Steel		5
ISO 7379 - 6 x 25	Steel	⬚	5
ISO 7379 - 6 x 30	Steel		5
ISO 7379 - 6 x 40	Steel	Paste Special...	5
ISO 7379 - 8 x 12	Steel	Insert	5
ISO 7379 - 8 x 16	Steel	Delete	5
ISO 7379 - 8 x 20	Steel	Clear Contents	5

11. To enter values for the column:

- To enter a heading, click cell AJ2 and enter **Supply Bin**.
- For cell AJ3, enter **S-1**.
- For cell AJ4, enter **B-1**.

AI	AJ	AK	
Name	Supply Bin	Material	Part N
7379 - 6 x 10	S-1	Steel	ISO 7
7379 - 6 x 10-B	B-1	Steel	ISO 7
7379 - 6 x 12		Steel	ISO 7
7379 - 6 x 16		Steel	ISO 7
7379 - 6 x 20		Steel	ISO 7

12. To move the column:

- Right-click on column heading AJ and click Cut.
- Click heading AL.
- Right-click and click Insert Cut Cells.

	AJ	AK	AL	
	Material	Supply Bin	Part Number	
	Steel	S-1	ISO 7379 - 6 x 10	
-B	Steel	B-1	ISO 7379 - 6 x 10-B	
2	Steel		ISO 7379 - 6 x 12	
6	Steel		ISO 7379 - 6 x 16	
0	Steel		ISO 7379 - 6 x 20	

13. Save the spreadsheet, then Close.

14. In the Family Table dialog box of the Autodesk Inventor software, use the slider bar to display the new row and column. Note the yellow display of the new data.

le Name	Material	Supply Bin	Part Number
SO 7379 - 6 x 10	Steel	S-1	ISO 7379 - 6
SO 7379 - 6 x 10-B	Steel	B-1	ISO 7379 - 6
SO 7379 - 6 x 12	Steel		ISO 7379 - 6
SO 7379 - 6 x 16	Steel		ISO 7379 - 6
SO 7379 - 6 x 20	Steel		ISO 7379 - 6
SO 7379 - 6 x 25	Steel		ISO 7379 - 6
O 7379 - 6 x 30	Steel		ISO 7379 - 6

15. To change the material:

- Click the cell for row 2 under the Material column.
- Click the down arrow.
- Select Brass, Soft Yellow.

	Material	Supply Bin	Part Number
- 6 x 10	Steel	S-1	ISO 7379 - 6 x 10
- 6 x 10-B	Steel ▼	B-1	ISO 7379 - 6 x 10
- 6 x 12	Acetal Resin, White		12
- 6 x 16	Alloy Steel		16
	Aluminum-6061		
- 6 x 20	Aluminum-6061-AHC		20
- 6 x 25	Brass, Soft Yellow		25
	Bronze, Soft Tin		
- 6 x 30	Carbon Steel		30
	Cast Bronze		
- 6 x 40	Cast Copper		40
- 8 x 12	Cast Iron		

16. In the Family Table:ISO 7379 table, click Apply. In the Publish Result message box, click OK.

17. Close Family Table:ISO 7379.

18. Click Done in the Content Center Editor.

Creating New Families or Adding Members Using Material Guide

Parts are often available in different materials. The material you select for a part depends on how that part will be used in the assembly and how it is to perform. If that part is a library part, that part needs to be defined in the library for each material variation. To keep from spending a lot of time creating part variations in a library solely based on its material, you need to know how to use the Material Guide to create new families and new members in Content Center.

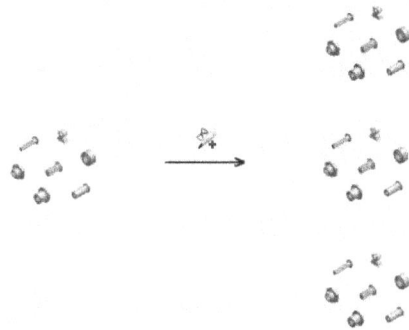

Material Guide

You use the Material Guide tool to create new family members that are copies of existing family members but have a different material. You can set the Material Guide to add the new family members to the existing family or you can set it to create a new family for each material and create the members within their respective material family. You can also use the Material Guide to remove family members from a family based on a specified material. When you use the Material Guide, you can add or remove family members based on material for selected members within a family or all members of selected families.

In the following figure, two new families were created from the ISO 7092 washer family. The new families were added to the library so washers that match this industry standard and made from this material can be easily added to the digital prototype of an assembly design. In this example, the new families were set to be linked to the parent family. This enables the copies to be updated if the parent family is edited.

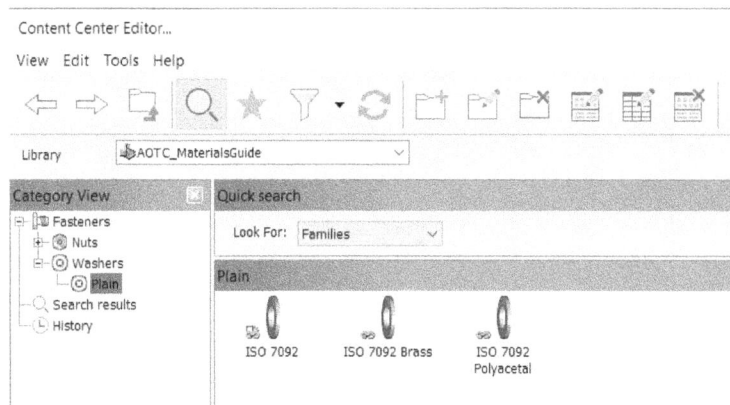

Access

You can access the Material Guide tool at two levels: family level or at the member level, and depends on where you want to use it. To access the tool, you must select one or more families or family members. To use the Material Guide at the family level, you access the tool on the menu bar in the Content Center Editor dialog box or the shortcut menu. To use the Material Guide at the member level, you access the tool on the menu bar in the Family Table dialog box or the shortcut menu.

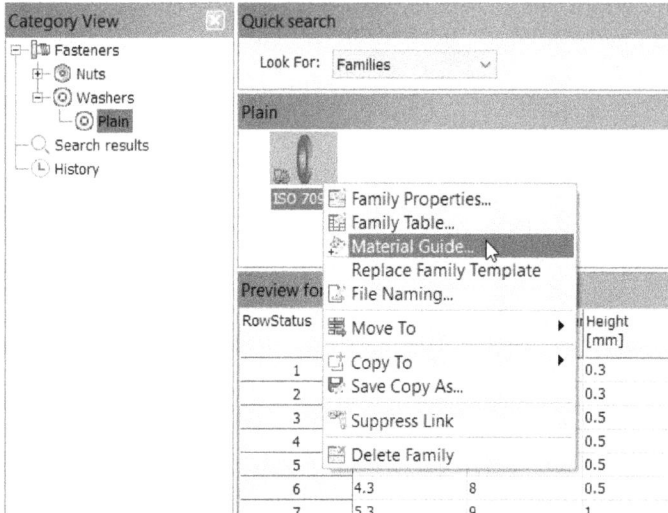

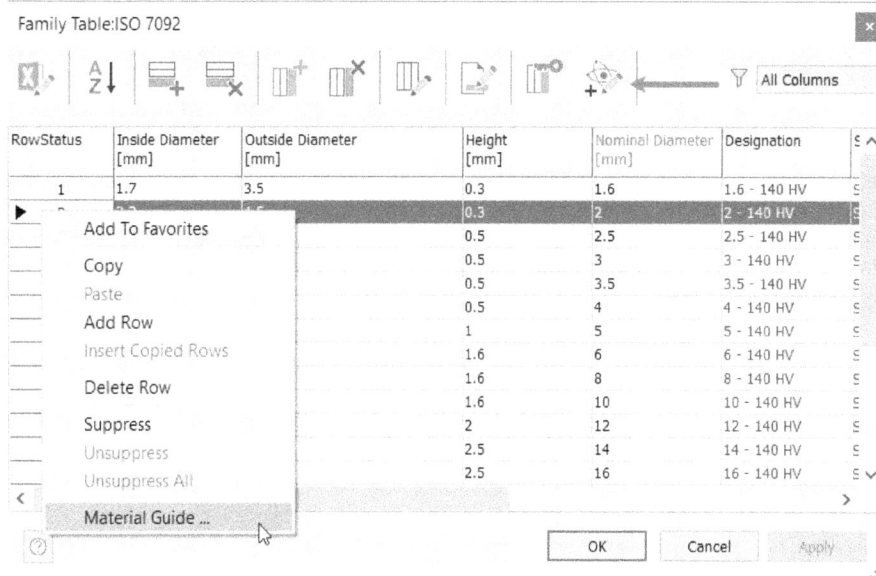

Material Guide Options

When you use the Material Guide, you interact with a series of pages in the dialog box. The options on some pages depend on if you selected to create new families for each material, if you are going to add members to the existing family, or if you are going to delete family members based on their material.

The first option you are presented with is to create new families for each material or add members to the existing family. If you select to create new families for each material, you specify if the new family is independent or if it should be linked to the parent family. You also select what read/write library the new families are created in.

The next thing you specify is what materials need to be added or deleted. The list of materials that you can select in the Material Guide dialog box is based on the materials in the Styles library.

If you want to use a shortened material name within the part, you enter a material alias for the material names you selected. Each material alias must be unique and the aliases you enter are saved in the computer registry.

To have each member and family remain unique, you specify to have the material name or material alias as a differentiator and have it added as a suffix or prefix. The differentiator is added to the file name when the library part is created. You can also select to have the differentiator added to the part number. If you selected to create new families for each material, the family name automatically has the differentiator added to it and you can select to add it to the family description. The Review button on this page displays the Review dialog box where you can review or customize the expressions used for naming the families, files, and part numbers.

Material Guide - Custom Expression

In the Review dialog box, you can review the naming values and expressions for the family names, file names, and part numbers for the individual members in that family. By selecting the Customize check box, you can enter a custom name or expression. This overrides the previously selected values for the prefix or suffix differentiator configuration. Clicking the more button to the right of the Expression field displays the list of parameter names defined in the library family that you can select to add to the equation.

In the following figure, the Customize check box has been selected and the expression for file names and part numbers for the ISO 7092 Brass family have been modified from their initial configuration. The family ISO 7092 Polyacetal is still configured to use the initial expression.

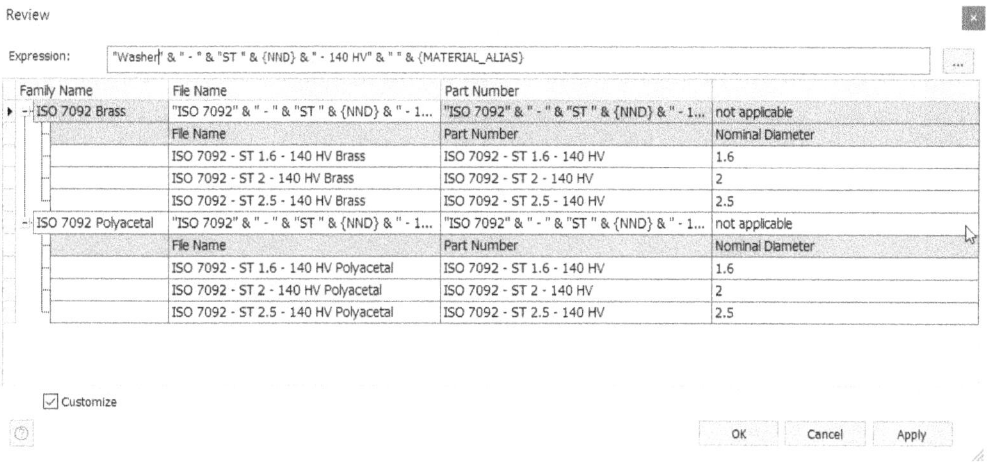

Review
[x]

Expression: "Washer" & " - " & "ST " & {NND} & " - 140 HV" & " " & {MATERIAL_ALIAS}
[...]

Family Name	File Name	Part Number	
ISO 7092 Brass	"ISO 7092" & " - " & "ST " & {NND} & " - 1...	"ISO 7092" & " - " & "ST " & {NND} & " - 1...	not applicable
	File Name	Part Number	Nominal Diameter
	ISO 7092 - ST 1.6 - 140 HV Brass	ISO 7092 - ST 1.6 - 140 HV	1.6
	ISO 7092 - ST 2 - 140 HV Brass	ISO 7092 - ST 2 - 140 HV	2
	ISO 7092 - ST 2.5 - 140 HV Brass	ISO 7092 - ST 2.5 - 140 HV	2.5
ISO 7092 Polyacetal	"ISO 7092" & " - " & "ST " & {NND} & " - 1...	"ISO 7092" & " - " & "ST " & {NND} & " - 1...	not applicable
	File Name	Part Number	Nominal Diameter
	ISO 7092 - ST 1.6 - 140 HV Polyacetal	ISO 7092 - ST 1.6 - 140 HV	1.6
	ISO 7092 - ST 2 - 140 HV Polyacetal	ISO 7092 - ST 2 - 140 HV	2
	ISO 7092 - ST 2.5 - 140 HV Polyacetal	ISO 7092 - ST 2.5 - 140 HV	2.5

☑ Customize

OK   Cancel   Apply

Process: Creating New Family Members Using Material Guide

The following figure gives an overview of creating a new family or family members using the Material Guide tool. There are two separate workflows shown in this diagram. The shared steps between the workflows in this process are shown in the middle where the two flow together.

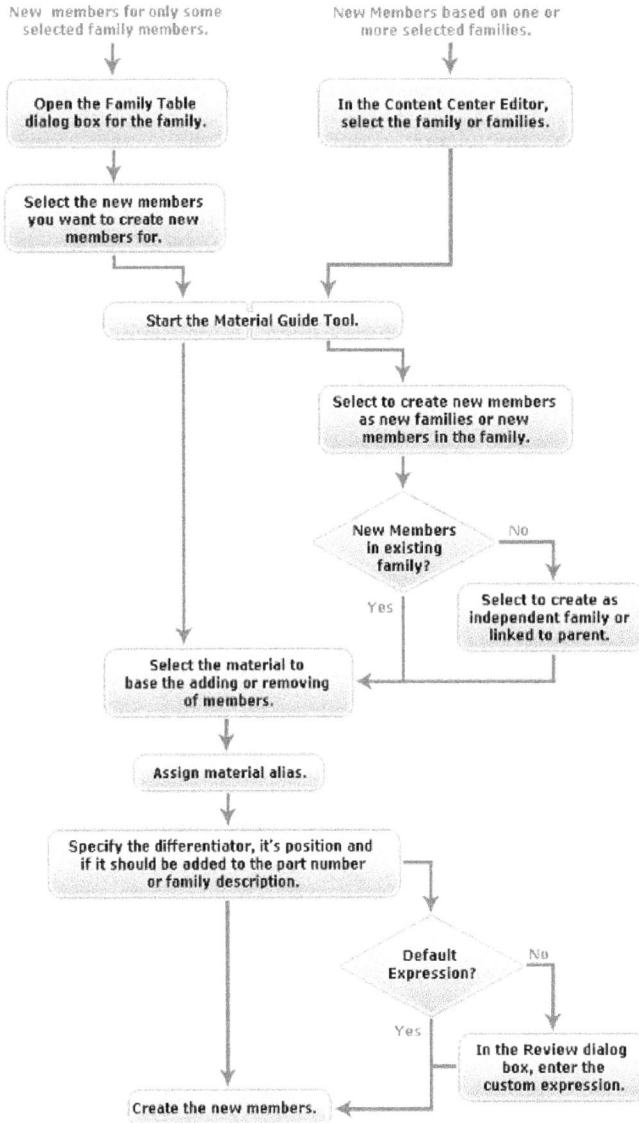

Exercise: Create Family Members Using Material Guide

In this exercise, you will create new family members in a read/write content library using the Material Guide.

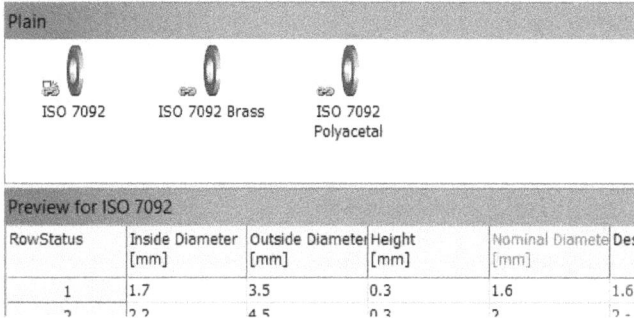

The completed exercise

Setup and Load Library

In this section of the exercise, you will set up the Autodesk Inventor software so you can complete the exercise steps of creating new library content by using the Material Guide. You will load a custom library and set a project file current.

1. Start the Autodesk Inventor software but do not open any files. Close any open files.

2. In the Get Started tab, on the Launch panel, click Projects.

3. In the Projects dialog box, click Configure Content Center Libraries.

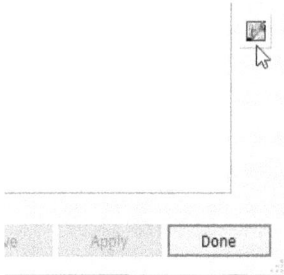

4. In the Configure Libraries dialog box:
    ■ Click the hyperlink text for Location of Libraries to open a Windows Explorer window viewing that folder.
    ■ Click Cancel.

5. Open another session of Windows Explorer.
    ■ Navigate to the install directory of the exercise files.
    ■ Click to open the Libraries folder in the exercise files directory.

6. Copy *AOTC_MaterialsGuide.idcl* from the Library folder to the window opened by the hyperlink in a previous step.

7. Close the Windows Explorer windows and exit the Configure Libraries dialog box.

8. To add this exercise's project file to the Autodesk Inventor software:
    ■ In the Projects dialog box, click Browse.
    ■ In the Choose Project File dialog box, navigate to the directory with the exercise files and open *Create Family Members Using Material Guide.ipj*.

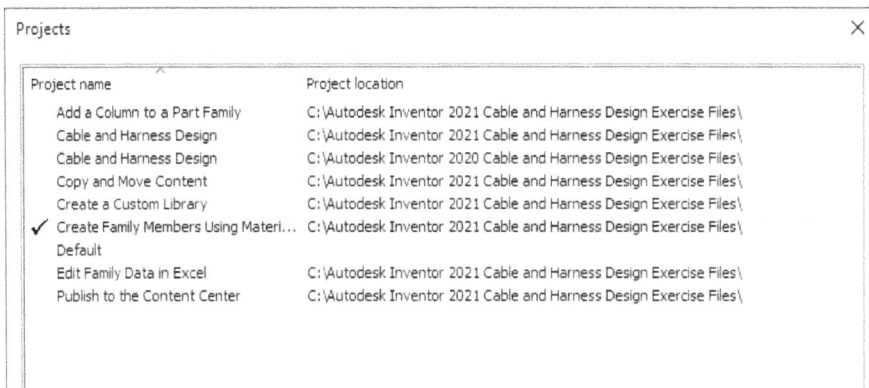

9. In the Projects dialog box, click Configure Content Center Libraries.

---

10. In the Configure Libraries dialog box, review the list of libraries that are set to be in use when this project file is active.

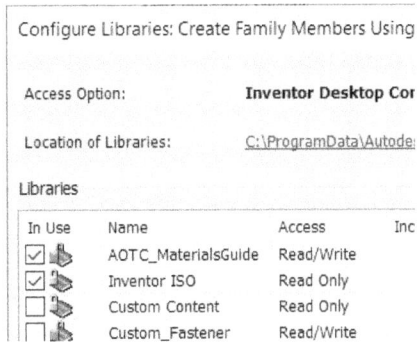

11. Close the Configure Libraries dialog box and the Projects dialog box.

Content Center Search for Part with a Material

In this section of the exercise, you search the Content Center to place a washer with a specific material and identify that the content needs to be added to the library.

1. Open *B1998-MaterialGuide.iam*.

2. In the Assemble tab, in the Component panel, click Place drop-down>Place from Content Center.

3. To begin searching the Content Center for a brass washer, in the Place from Content Center dialog box, in the toolbar, click Search.

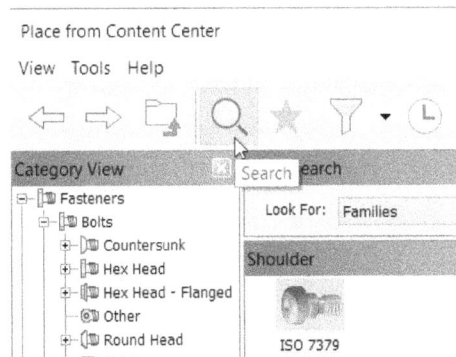

4. In the Quick search pane, click Advanced Search.

5. To set to only search through available washer content:
   - In the Advanced Search dialog box, click Categories.
   - In the Choose Categories dialog box, under Fasteners, under Washers, select the Plain check box.
   - Click OK.

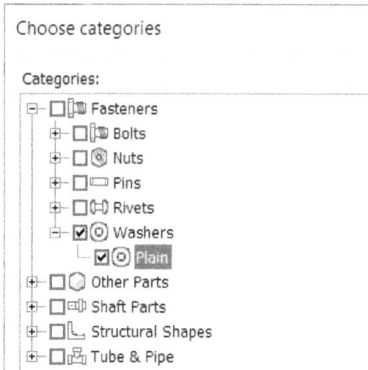

6. In the Advanced Search dialog box, under Define more criteria:
   - Set Parameter to Material.
   - Set Condition to Equal To.
   - In the Value field, select Brass, Soft Yellow.
   - Click Add to list.

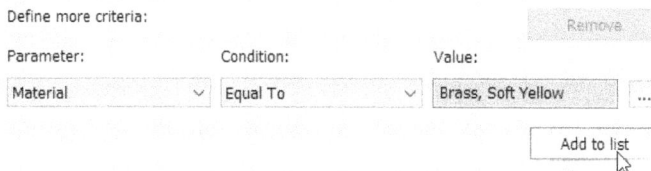

7. Click Search Now.

8. After the search results return No Components Found, click Cancel.

9. In the Place from Content Center dialog box, click Cancel.

Add Content Using Material Guide

In this section of the exercise, you add new family members to the Content Center with the exact same sizes as an existing part but with different materials.

1. In the Manage tab, in the Content Center panel > Editor.

2. In the Content Center Editor, ensure the Library View list is set to AOTC_MaterialsGuide.

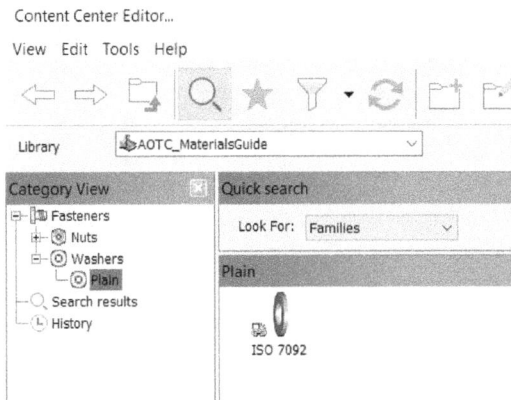

3. To review the members in the ISO 7092 content family:

   ▪ In the Category View list, under Fasteners, under Washers, click Plain.

   ▪ In the Plain pane, click ISO 7092.

   ▪ In the Preview pane, review the list of members in the table.

   Note: Toggle on the Preview pane if it is not on by clicking Family Preview in the toolbar.

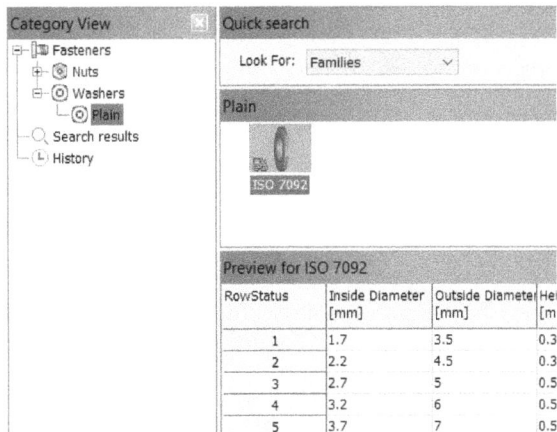

RowStatus	Inside Diameter [mm]	Outside Diameter [mm]	Hei [m
1	1.7	3.5	0.3
2	2.2	4.5	0.3
3	2.7	5	0.5
4	3.2	6	0.5
5	3.7	7	0.5

4. To create new families with the exact same member sizes as listed for ISO 7092 but with different materials, in the Plain pane, right-click ISO 7092 and click Material Guide.

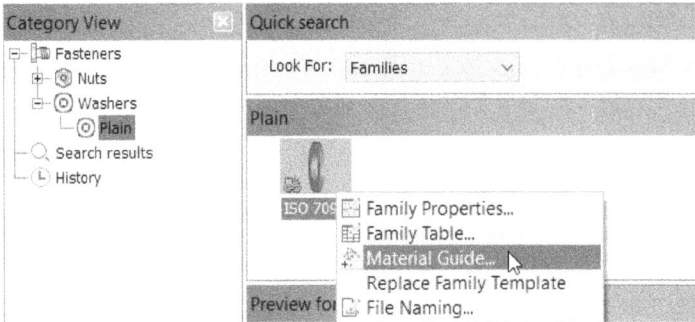

5. In the Material Guide dialog box:
   - On the first page, click Next.
   - Click Create new family for each material.
   - Click Link to parent family.
   - Click Next.

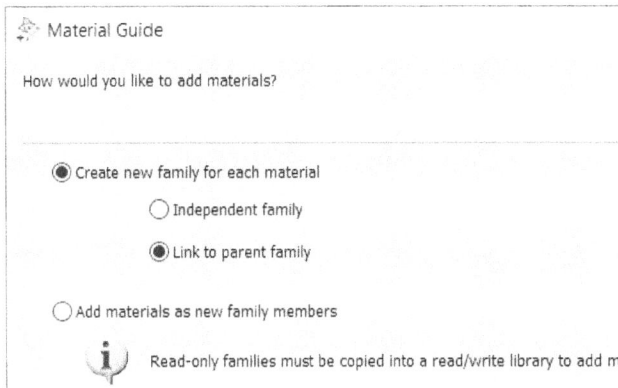

6. With the read/write library AOTC_MaterialsGuide displayed in the list, click Next.

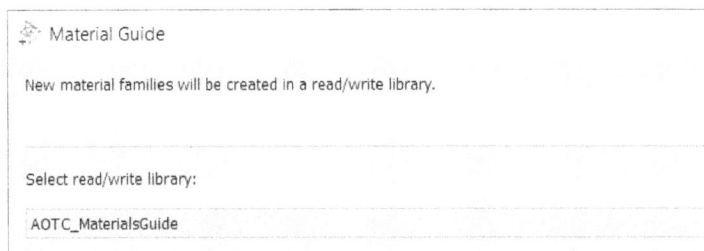

7. To specify Brass, Soft Yellow as a material to create a new family of washers:

    ■ In the Select Materials list, select Brass, Soft Yellow.

    ■ Click to move it to the Materials To Add list.

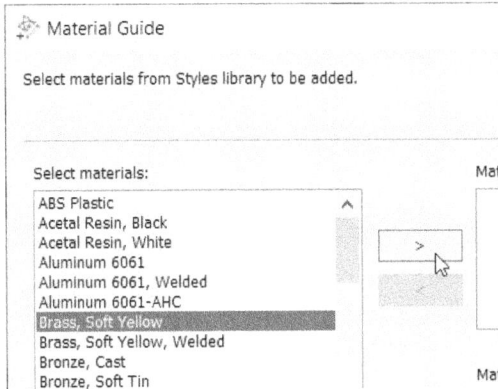

8. Follow the same process to add the material Acetal Resin, Black to the list and then click Next.

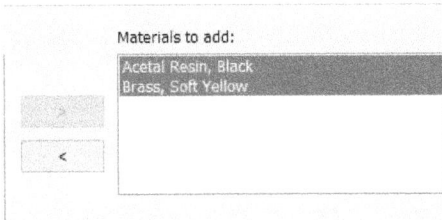

9. In the table for material aliases, enter the alias names as follows:

    ■ For Acetal Resin, Black, enter **Polyacetal**.

    ■ For Brass, Soft Yellow, enter **Brass**.

    ■ Click Next.

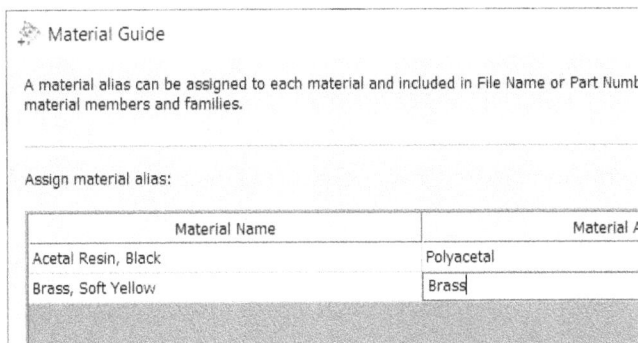

10. On the page for specifying the differentiation method:

- Click Material Alias and then click Suffix.
- Select the Family Description check box.

11. To review and further modify the file naming for the new content:

- Click Review.
- In the Review dialog box, select the Customize check box.
- Click the File Name cell for the ISO 7092 Brass family.

12. In the Expression field:
    - Delete the text "ISO 7092".
    - In its place enter **"Washer"**.
    - Click OK.

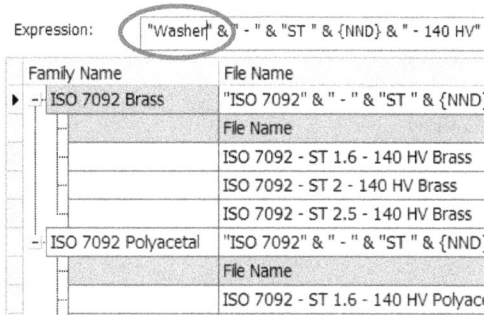

Expression: "Washer" & " - " & "ST " & {NND} & " - 140 HV"

Family Name	File Name
► ─ ISO 7092 Brass	"ISO 7092" & " - " & "ST " & {NND}
	File Name
	ISO 7092 - ST 1.6 - 140 HV Brass
	ISO 7092 - ST 2 - 140 HV Brass
	ISO 7092 - ST 2.5 - 140 HV Brass
─ ISO 7092 Polyacetal	"ISO 7092" & " - " & "ST " & {NND}
	File Name
	ISO 7092 - ST 1.6 - 140 HV Polyac

13. To complete the creation:
    - Click Next.
    - Click Start.
    - Click Finish.
    - If a message box opens, click Yes.

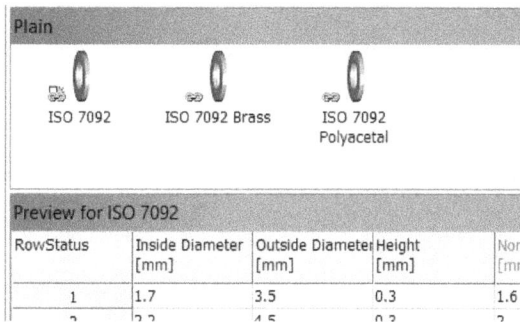

Plain

ISO 7092   ISO 7092 Brass   ISO 7092
                                      Polyacetal

Preview for ISO 7092

RowStatus	Inside Diameter [mm]	Outside Diameter [mm]	Height [mm]	Non [mr
1	1.7	3.5	0.3	1.6
2	2.2	4.5	0.3	2

14. In the Content Center Editor, click Done.

Place Material Guide Created Content

In this section of the exercise, you place a member from the family of content you just created using the Material Guide.

1. In the Assemble tab, in the Component panel, click Place From Content Center.

2. In the Quick Search pane, click Advanced Search and specify the search criteria as previously done.

   - Click Categories and specify the Plain washer category.
   - For Material, select Brass, Soft Yellow.

3. To locate the brass washers in the Content Center, in the Advanced Search dialog box:

   - Click Search Now.
   - In the Search Results list, select ISO 7092 Brass.
   - Click Move To Content Center.

4. To begin adding the washer to the assembly, in the Search Results pane, double-click on ISO 7092 Brass.

5. Place and constrain an instance of the washer, using a 4mm Nominal diameter, into the assembly:

6. Close the file, do not save changes.

Chapter Summary

In this chapter, you learned how to create, author, and publish electrical parts and connectors to a custom Content Center library so that they can be easily and quickly reused by you or other members of your design team.

Having completed this chapter, you can:

- Create, author, and publish electrical parts and connectors to a custom Content Center library.
- Manage the libraries that are included in the Content Center, as well as your own libraries of cable and harness components.
- Author and publish your own cable and harness content.
- Manage the properties and settings of published cable and harness content.